Studies in Comparative World History

Cross-cultural trade in world history

Cross-cultural trade in world history

PHILIP D. CURTIN

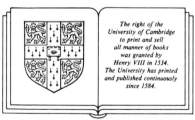

The right of the
University of Cambridge
to print and sell
all manner of books
was granted by
Henry VIII in 1534.
The University has printed
and published continuously
since 1584.

CAMBRIDGE UNIVERSITY PRESS

Cambridge

London   New York   New Rochelle
Melbourne   Sydney

Published by the Press Syndicate of the University of Cambridge
The Pitt Building, Trumpington Street, Cambridge CB2 1RP
32 East 57th Street, New York, NY 10022, USA
10 Stamford Road, Oakleigh, Melbourne 3166, Australia

© Cambridge University Press 1984

First published 1984
Reprinted 1985, 1986 (twice)

Printed in the United States of America

Library of Congress Cataloging in Publication Data
Curtin, Philip D.
Cross-cultural trade in world history.
(Studies in comparative world history)
Bibliography: p.
Includes index.
1. Commerce – History.   2. World history.   I. Title.
II. Series.
HF352.C87   1984   382'.09   83-23202
ISBN 0 521 26319 0 hard covers
ISBN 0 521 26931 8 paperback

Contents

Illustrations

Maps

Figure

Preface

Most historical writing fits into known categories of time, place, and subject matter. This study is somewhat unorthodox. First of all it lies in a no-man's-land between recognized disciplines in the social sciences where historical economic anthropology is as convenient a label as any. But of the three disciplines represented, its first commitment is to history. It also lies in the small but growing field of comparative world history – "comparative" because it abstracts particular phenomena having to do with cross-cultural trade and looks for similarities and differences; "world" because it tries to avoid a Western ethnocentric outlook, not because it will try to "cover" what went on everywhere; "history" because it is concerned with change over the very long run of time. It is also history because it asks the historians' question, How and why did human societies change through time? But it is also concerned with the kinds of change economists and anthropologists deal with. It therefore borrows from their conceptual toolbags.

Using this combination of attitudes about history and borrowing from other disciplines also exacts a price. This book is not about a number of other things that may be of equal or greater importance. First of all, it is not a history of world trade. It looks at aspects of commercial practice at several times and places between the agricultural and commercial revolutions. In so doing, it contains a thread of development over time, but it does not seek to "cover" all important traders or trade routes. The principle of selection is to find examples that illustrate the variety of cross-cultural trade – not those that were important for the quantity of goods carried, or those that had the greatest impact on other aspects of history. The overland trade routes across Asia, for example, or the overland trade between Russia and China are barely mentioned, not because they were insignificant, but because the evidence about these commercial practices is not so rich as other evidence about other times and places. Many cultures are therefore slighted, and many time periods are given less attention than they properly deserve. Another historian, even one asking these same questions, might well have made another choice of examples.

Another important aspect of history this book will *not* cover is the history of trade *within* major culture areas. The price paid for limiting its scope to *cross-cultural* trade is the omission of the immensely important rise of internal commerce in Song China a little after 1000 A.D., or the equivalent rise of commerce within Western Europe.[1]

A third price to be paid is a decided neglect of political history and the affairs of individual men and women. Nor is this study much concerned with the sequences of events so central to conventional historical writing.

The other side of that coin is a concern with patterns – sometimes repetitive patterns or regularities. Without seeking anything so formal or iron-clad as historical "law," it is nevertheless worth noting in what circumstances particular patterns of behavior are likely to recur. Looking for patterns implies abstraction. All historical writing is, indeed, an abstraction from the full body of knowable data about a particular time and place. I will be concerned here with only a narrow part of human affairs, that is, the way people exchanged goods with other people who had a different way of life.

I have tried for a non–Europe-centered view of the human past, though even that attempt involves an important problem. Every social scientist is caught in the web of his own culture and his own time. Even with a conscious effort to rise above our natural ethnocentrism, history has to be expressed in a Western language, using the social science concepts common to Western culture of our time. Just as inevitably, it is limited by the kind and extent of information now available, and this is changing constantly. Well over half of the most valuable authorities I consulted were published after the early 1970s, when the idea of writing this book first began to take shape.

The range of examples is also limited by linguistic constraints. I know only a few of the more common languages of Western Europe and North America. With a good reading knowledge of Russian or Armenian or Chinese, this study could have been considerably more authoritative in several areas. On the other hand, to have taken the time necessary to learn all relevant languages would have meant that it would never have been written at all.

---

[1] For alternate treatments that do some of this, see Fernand Braudel, *Civilization and Capitalism: 15th–18th Century. Volume II, The Wheels of Commerce* (New York, 1982); William H. McNeill, *The Pursuit of Power: Technology, Armed Force, and Society since A.D. 1000* (Chicago, 1982); Mark Elvin, *The Pattern of the Chinese Past* (Stanford, 1973); Tapan Raychaudhuri and Irfan Habib (eds.), *The Cambridge Economic History of India*, 2 vols. (Cambridge, 1982).

One final statement of intent. Both historical and social scientific knowledge have grown so much in recent decades that scholars have become more and more specialized. They therefore tend to write within the framework of a specialized subprofession, which implies a small but select audience. I have tried here to write from the conviction that it may well be possible to say something new to the historical and social scientific community, and yet have it be comprehensible and relevant to the educated public as well. Only they will know whether I have succeeded.

The many friends, colleagues, and students who have contributed to this book through discussion, suggestions, and conversation are far too numerous to mention. I should, however, recognize the yeoman service of the Inter-Library Loan Department of the Eisenhower Memorial Library of the Johns Hopkins University in Baltimore. I am also especially grateful to Patricia Romero Curtin, Richard Hellie, Allen Isaacman, Paul Lovejoy, William H. NcNeill, Anthony Reid, John F. Richards, William Rowe, and A. J. R. Russell-Wood, who were kind enough to read all or part of the manuscript and to give me detailed criticism. Needless to say, I alone am responsible for the result, especially in those instances where I persisted in error in spite of their good advice.

I am also grateful for financial support during the preparation of this work from the Carnegie Corporation of New York, through the Program in Comparative World History at the University of Wisconsin, and from the John Simon Guggenheim Memorial Foundation.

PHILIP D. CURTIN

1

Trade diasporas and cross-cultural trade

Trade and exchange across cultural lines have played a crucial role in human history, being perhaps the most important external stimuli to change, leaving aside the unmeasurable and less-benign influence of military conquest. External stimulation, in turn, has been the most important single source of change and development in art, science, and technology. Perhaps this goes without saying, since no human group could invent by itself more than a small part of its cultural and technical heritage. Take as simple an example as the manufacture of this book. The English language is derived from one of those that came into Western Europe with German immigrants, combined with elements of Latin, originally imposed by imperial conquerors from the south, plus other borrowings. The alphabet came from the Phoenicians. The page numbers are "Arabic," which actually means that the Europeans learned about them from the Arabs, who had borrowed them in turn from the Indians, who invented positional notation in the first place. A few years ago, a book like this would have been printed with movable type, which would have given it a possible Chinese heritage as well.

On the negative side, cross-cultural trade and communication pose special problems. People with a different way of life are strangers by definition; their ways seem unpredictable, and the unpredictable is probably dangerous as well. Communication itself is difficult. Even after an appropriate medium comes into existence, like a second language in common, understanding is hard to come by. Strangers may appear not to be hostile, but they are still not to be trusted in the same full sense that neighbors and kinfolk can be trusted. These problems in cross-cultural understanding in general have meant that cross-trade has almost always been carried out through special institutional arrangements to help guarantee the mutual security of the two sides.

Trade diasporas

The earliest phases of cross-cultural trade are lost beyond any possibility of historical reconstruction. Even the recent customs of people with the least-developed technologies, like the Stone Age hunting and gathering peoples whose way of life was relatively untouched by outsiders till a century or so ago – even these "primitive" ways are not necessarily a good guide to the distant past. But it is possible to imagine that the earliest cross-cultural trade took place during random encounters of hunting bands, or that it was mixed with phases of warfare. One can also imagine that the earliest trade between different communities took place at the border between them. Linguistic evidence suggests that this was the case in ancient Greece, and later on, Hermes was both the god of trade and the god of the boundary stones separating one city from another.[1] But this early phase of boundary markets ended for the Greek cities by the eighth century B.C. If similar institutions existed elsewhere in the ancient world, they disappeared with the earliest phases of urbanization. Early urban markets tended to appear near the heart of the city, not on the outskirts, presumably because the traders wanted to have the best possible access to potential customers.

Whatever the earliest forms of cross-cultural trade, the most common institutional form after the coming of city life was the trade settlement. Commercial specialists would remove themselves physically from their home community and go to live as aliens in another town, usually not a fringe town, but a town important in the life of the host community. There, the stranger merchants could settle down and learn the language, the customs, and the commercial ways of their hosts. They could then serve as cross-cultural brokers, helping and encouraging trade between the host society and people of their own origin who moved along the trade routes. At this stage, a distinction appeared between the merchants who moved and settled and those who continued to move back and forth. What might have begun as a single settlement soon became more complex. The merchants who might have begun with a single settlement abroad tended to set up a whole series of trade settlements in alien towns. The result was an interrelated net of commercial communities forming a trade network, or trade diaspora – a term that comes from the Greek word for scattering, as in the sowing of grain.[2]

---

[1] Norman O. Brown, *Hermes the Thief: The Evolution of a Myth*, 2nd ed. (New York, 1969), pp. 38–46; Jean-Christophe Agnew, "The Threshold of Exchange: Speculations on the Market," *Radical History Review*, 21:99–118 (1979), pp. 101–3.
[2] The term "trading diaspora" originated with the anthropologist Abner Cohen, who defined it as "a nation of socially interdependent, but spatially dispersed communities," in "Cultural Strategies in the Organization of Trading Diasporas," in Claude Meillassoux (ed.), *The Development of Indigenous Trade and Markets in West Africa* (London, 1971), p. 267. Other anthropologists tend to use "trade networks," with less attempt at such a precise definition. See Lloyd A. Fallers (ed.), *Immigrants and Associations* (The Hague, 1967); Karl A. Yambert, "Alien Traders and Ruling Elites: The Overseas Chinese in Southeast Asia and the Indians in East Africa," *Ethnic Groups*, 3:173–98 (1981).

Trade communities of merchants living among aliens in associated networks are to be found on every continent and back through time to the very beginning of urban life. They are, as we shall see, one of the most widespread of all human institutions over a very long run of time, yet limited to the long period of human history that began with the invention of agriculture and ended with the coming of the industrial age. Some of the best evidence of how they worked comes from Africa between the seventeenth century and the nineteenth, but other examples are as various and familiar as the chains of Phoenician and Greek trading towns that spread westward from the Levant or the Aegean coasts. Or, some two thousand years later, merchants from Cologne on the Rhine settled along the trade routes leading down the Rhine and then eastward along the coast of the North Sea and the Baltic, laying the foundations for what was to become the Hanseatic League of independent trading towns.

Some trade diasporas moved overland or followed inland water courses. Among the most familiar are the North American routes up the Great Lakes, pioneered by the French-Canadian *coureurs de bois*, whose pursuit of the fur trade among the Indians carried them to the Mississippi and beyond. Archaeological evidence suggests the probable existence of trade diasporas in the Middle East as early as 3500 B.C. By 2000 B.C., clay tablets covered with cuneiform inscriptions give detailed evidence about the commercial operations of an Assyrian trade settlement in Cappadocia in Asia Minor.

These networks were organized in many different ways, some so informally that the individual settlements were linked by little more than the solidarity of a common culture. Others, like the great European trading firms of the seventeenth and eighteenth centuries, were formally organized, chartered by European states, granted certain monopoly rights, empowered to govern as well as trade, and to use their own military and naval forces.

Life histories: trade diasporas over time

In the search for testable hypotheses about the way people have conducted cross-cultural trade through time, one immediately striking generalization is that trade diasporas tend to work themselves out of business. They began because cultural differences created a need for mediation, but centuries or even decades of mediation reduced cross-cultural differences and hence the need for cross-cultural brokers. Where at first, trade at a distance required a kinsman or at least a trusted fellow-countryman to act as agent, with time, a variety of other agents came to be available. In the longest run of time, Western commercial culture became the common culture of commerce throughout the world in an era of multinational corporations.

But, under the cover of this first and largest generalization, individual trade diasporas worked themselves out of business in quite different ways. Some withdrew to their cultural homeland, leaving people of their host society to carry on in their former role. This pattern was typical of the trade diasporas that sprang up in the European Middle Ages. Formal commercial settlements abroad tended to be withdrawn by the end of the sixteenth century. The Hanseatic League, for example, gave up its special trade enclave in London, called the "Steelyard." Calais, in northern France, was an English possession until the middle of that century. It had served as the principal point for the distribution of English raw wool to the Continent, but it then returned to French control. The English Company of Merchant Adventurers, the main outlet for English woolen cloth sold abroad, originally had its headquarters in Antwerp rather than in England, but Antwerp lost its special status in the 1550s, as English cloth began to be sold through a greater number of Continental cities. Indeed, the institutions of the "factory system," the semipublic establishment of separate premises for foreign merchants or factors, which had first evolved in medieval Flanders, began to disappear in Europe in the sixteenth century, just as it began to reappear as a common way of dealing with European trade with Asia and Africa.[3] Within Europe, international trade came to depend much more on local commission agents, rather than having each merchant house maintain agents of its own nationality in a foreign city. Tudor London, for example, had a large group of resident Italian merchants at the beginning of the century, but they gradually decreased in numbers even as Anglo-Italian trade increased. It was simply cheaper by this time to use the services of commission agents.[4]

Other trade diasporas, however, left a legacy in the form of cultural minorities in foreign lands, even though these minorities no longer devoted themselves to long-distance trade. The beginnings of Chinese settlement in Southeast Asia go back to trade diasporas that started to operate in the first centuries A.D., though they were later supplemented by contract laborers and other kinds of immigration. In the twentieth century, these overseas Chinese no longer ran a trade diaspora, though they kept much of their commercial tradition and still tend to dominate wholesale and retail trade. This is one of several instances where cultural minorities left over from a trade diaspora were able to use their original

[3] Kristof Glamann, "European Trade, 1500–1750," in Carlo M. Cipolla (ed.), *The Fontana Economic History of Europe*, 6 vols. (London, 1974), 2:514.

[4] M. E. Bratchel, "Italian Merchant Organization and Business Relationships in Early Tudor London," *Journal of European Economic History*, 7:5–32 (1978), pp. 6, 29.

commercial bent, and their community solidarity, to establish a partial monopoly over the commercial life of the host society.

Indian trading communities in Tanzania, Kenya, and Uganda had a similar experience. Their commercial importance dates only from the nineteenth century, but they dominated the retail trade of all three colonies till the coming of independence. Although the Indians in Uganda were largely driven out, those who remained in Tanzania, and especially in Kenya, have been able to move from retail trade into many other sectors of the economy, as the Chinese in Southeast Asia began to do a century or so earlier.

Merchants and their hosts

One of the most striking variables in the comparative study of trade diasporas is the wide range of possible relationships between the trade community and the host society. In some circumstances, rulers of the host society treated the traders as a pariah caste, to be exploited or robbed at will, whose presence was tolerated only because it was useful. With many local variations, this was often the situation of Jewish merchants in medieval Europe. Other merchants sought successfully to establish themselves as autonomous, self-governing communities, often by a self-conscious pacifism and neutrality toward all political struggles. The Jahaanke in seventeenth- and eighteenth-century West Africa are a successful example of such a policy. At the extreme end of this spectrum were the European trading-post empires in Asia from the sixteenth century through the eighteenth. They not only sought to have trade enclaves under their own military control; they also tried to use coercion to control Asian trade and to shift the terms of trade in their favor. Toward the end of the eighteenth century, they had used force so effectively that at least the British East India Company in India and the Dutch East India Company on Java had stopped being militarized trade diasporas and became true territorial empires that were to be the nucleus of the British *raj* in India and the Netherlands East Indies, respectively.

Whatever the balance of power between the traders and their hosts, the relationship was necessarily asymmetrical. The traders were specialists in a single kind of economic enterprise, whereas the host society was a *whole* society, with many occupations, class stratification, and political divisions between the rulers and the ruled.

The occupation of merchant was also somewhat special in the outlook of many societies. Professional traders were necessarily a minority in preindustrial societies, where the vast majority of the people were needed to work the land. Since they were not, in any very obvious way, a productive class, they tended to earn the suspicion of others who either

worked the land or carried out some other, apparently necessary function like political rule or intercession with the gods. Some such sentiment
as this may well lie behind the fact that commerce was often a low-
status occupation in societies as distant from one another as ancient
Greece and Tokugawa Japan. The unpopularity of merchants as a class
could easily be reinforced, if they were simultaneously people of great
wealth as well as low status. And merchants in long-distance trade had
obvious and unusual opportunities to make extraordinary profits at extraordinary risk.

If people tend to be suspicious of merchants, they are even more
suspicious of foreigners; yet some societies actually encouraged foreign
merchants. Where commerce was regarded as such an unpleasant occupation, it was seen as better left to foreigners; and this was a common
attitude in some circles in ancient Greece, even though the role of Greek
merchants through history has been extremely important. In much the
same way, the Christian Europeans of the Middle Ages preferred to
leave moneylending to the Jews. In any case, long-distance trade required *someone* to go abroad and become a foreigner. Envy and suspicion
of foreigners, as such, could easily reinforce the envy and suspicion of
merchants.

Norman O. Brown has worked out some of these relationships for
classical antiquity by tracing the myth of the god Hermes through its
various literary manifestations.[5] The earliest Hermes was god of the
boundary stones, but he gradually became the god of the merchants,
the professional boundary crossers. At the same time, he was not quite
as respectable as the other gods – a messenger, but also a trickster and
a thief, a marginal god for people who were marginal to Greek society.
Plato himself disliked trade, which, like other professions based on a
search for profit, was hardly compatible with a life of virtue, as he
understood it.

In the Christian Middle Ages, the theme recurs at the upper end of
the intellectual spectrum in Thomas Aquinas's suspicion that merchants
may well have a hard time attaining salvation because of the temptation
to sin inherent in their occupation. At the lower end, many merchants
carried a thief's thumb as a talisman; Saint Nicholas was the patron saint
of thieves and merchants alike.

Merchant settlements and their relations with one another

Relations between the individual nodes of a trade diaspora are a second
important variable, and the range of variation is extremely wide. Some-

[5] Brown, *Hermes the Thief*, esp. pp. 82–7. See also Agnew, "The Threshold of Exchange,"
pp. 100–5.

times the scattered settlements of the same culture had no formal ties of any kind. They were united only by the solidarity that could be built on the sentimental ties of a common religion, language, or distant kinship. At the other extreme were trade diasporas that were founded as political entities, with each node under central control. The Estado da India, the sixteenth-century Portuguese empire in Asia, is one example, where the Viceroy in Goa ruled over the subordinate bases like Mozambique in East Africa, Melaka near the present-day Singapore, and Macao in southern China.

To a degree, relations between nodes varied with relations between the host society and the merchants in a single node. That is, where the host society dominated, the merchants were unlikely to develop formal political relations with other merchant communities. At the same time, where the merchants controlled a settlement and its neighborhood, it was at least possible – indeed likely – that they could have political relationships of some sort with other, equivalent settlements.

But many other variations were also possible. Sentimental ties might be strong, even where political ties were weak. Greek trading settlements sometimes grew into independent city-states, though they looked with respect to the metropolis – literally the "mother city" – with which they might or might not have continued religious and political ties. In some cases, the parent could disappear from the system. This happened with the original Phoenician homeland of Levantine trading cities like Tyre and Sidon. They first fell to foreign conquest and were later assimilated into the greater Hellenistic world created by the successors of Alexander the Great after the fourth century B.C. This left the Phoenician colonies in the western Mediterranean on their own, though Carthage came in time to take the place of the original mother cities.

The Hanseatic League of northern German cities illustrates another kind of relationship between the points of a trade diaspora. That network began with merchants from Cologne, who spread outward in the twelfth and thirteenth centuries – first to Bremen and Hamburg to the west of the Jutland peninsula, then to Lübeck farther east, and a string of port towns along the south shore of the Baltic. The towns of the league reached a peak of wealth and influence in the fourteenth and early fifteenth centuries, when trade reached from London and Bruges in the west, north to Bergen in Norway, and east as far as Novgorod, deep inside Russia. In spite of the economic strength of the league, each settlement was independent of the rest. When, with the passage of time, Cologne dropped from the picture, Lübeck became the chief Hanse city, but it was not a capital in any effective political sense. The Hanse was a league of independent cities, never a sovereign state. It fought wars, but each war was fought by an alliance created for that occasion, with nothing more than informal pressure to force any city to participate.

At the opposite organizational extreme were the tightly controlled trade diasporas of the chartered European trading companies in eastern seas. Here the European metropolis was at once a political capital and the management center of a trading firm, in contrast to the thousands of independent Hanseatic firms operating out of dozens of independent cities.

The full range of possibilities along this spectrum was still more complex. Settlements along a trade diaspora were specialized cities or parts of cities. They therefore partook of the set of wider relationships governing cities in general. Urban theory recognizes that cities are not merely dense concentrations of people, though they are that too; they are also concentrations of people doing different things, and their urban character derives more from that variety of activity than it does from sheer numbers.[6]

At an early stage in human material life, hunting and gathering peoples had to spread out across the landscape in order to survive. Even with early agriculture, concentration in villages and hamlets was limited by peoples' need to get to the fields. More specialized functions, however, could be carried out almost anywhere, but they tended to be carried out at a central place. It may have begun with a temple to serve the gods, which would also attract crowds. Crowds would have drawn merchants and retail traders. The temple, the crowds, and the traders would all be a source of attraction for political rulers, courts, and tax gatherers. The order of appearance is not significant. The point is that specialized functions tended to cluster, forming urban settlements where many different things took place. Having these things take place was, in turn, essential to the continuing life of the whole society of which the cities formed a part. But a city was related to its hinterland in a one-sided way. It alone tended to perform the rarest and most specialized functions, whereas villages and smaller centers did fewer things – and much the same range of things, like tending herds or raising crops.

Even among cities, some were more multifunctional than others. Cities were therefore related to one another in much the same way each individual city was related to its own hinterland. Cities that did more things had an advantage over others that did fewer, just as the smaller cities had an advantage over the countryside. The most multifunctional cities, and they alone, performed some functions that were essential for the whole society. As a result, with or without the political framework

---

[6] Eric Lampard, "Historical Aspects of Urbanization," in P. M. Hauser and Leo F. Schnore (eds.), *The Study of Urbanization* (New York, 1965).

of the state, cities came to constitute an urban network arranged in a hierarchy of multifunctionality.

In this rudimentary form, the model is simple, but it has important implications for the changing relationships between cities through time, and these implications extend to relationships between settlements of a trade diaspora. The model suggests two theoretical hypotheses: first, that the functional dependency of the less multifunctional cities on the more multifunctional can be the basis for economic and political dependency as well; and second, that the more technically proficient a society, the greater its range of multifunctionality. Hence, the passage of time, which tends in human societies to bring with it a more complex technology, will also increase the potential dependence of the places low in the hierarchy on those higher up.

The use of the term "dependence" suggests a possible relationship to a body of recent theory and empirical research sometimes called dependency theory. It has been extensively developed by scholars like André Gunder Frank, Arghiri Emmanuel, and Immanuel Wallerstein, among others.[7] Scholars of the dependency school, however, are concerned mainly with relations between the developed, capitalist countries and the less-developed countries in recent centuries. As neo-Marxists, they have been concerned with relations between the "center" and the "periphery" of a world dominated by capitalism. My hypotheses about relations between cities are quite different. These relations are not governed by particular economic systems set in specific chronological eras. Nor are they always a dominant force in "making" historical change. They are only one influence on the course of history, among many. They are derived mainly from some of the geographical concepts known somewhat loosely as "central-place theory," or as location theory in economics.[8]

Relations of potential dependency among cities can cause two different kinds of conflict. One kind involves cities at different levels in the hierarchy of multifunctionality. The second has to do with rivalry between

[7] The literature of the dependency school is large and diverse. As a sample see Charles K. Wilber (ed.), *The Political Economy of Development and Underdevelopment*, 2nd ed. (New York, 1979); Arghiri Emmanuel, *Unequal Exchange: A Study of the Imperialism of Trade* (New York, 1972); Immanuel Wallerstein, *The Modern World-System*, multivol. (New York, 1974–).

[8] The theoretical groundwork began to be laid in the 1930s in Germany, notably in the work of Walter Christaller, translated as *Central Places in Southern Germany* (Englewood Cliffs, N.J., 1966), and of August Lösch, translated as *The Economics of Location* (New Haven, Conn., 1954). The pioneering application to historical analysis is the work of G. William Skinner, "Marketing and Social Structure in Rural China," *Journal of Asian Studies*, 24:3–43 (1964), followed by G. William Skinner (ed.), *The City in Late Imperial China* (Stanford, Calif., 1977). Historical application to trade and trade routes is found in Allen M. Howard, "The Relevance of Spatial Analysis for African Economic History: The Sierra Leone-Guinea System," *Journal of African History*, 17:365–88 (1975).

cities at the same level. These tensions can be conveniently illustrated from North American history in the eighteenth and nineteenth centuries. The highest point on the hierarchy of multifunctionality was London, and London continued to dominate in economic matters even after American independence. Lower down were the main ports of entry on the East Coast, which were both dependent on London and rivals of one another for influence over their common hinterland. Montreal had the special advantage of the Saint Lawrence valley as a natural water route to the Great Lakes. In response, New York built the Erie Canal; Baltimore built the Baltimore and Ohio Railroad; other port towns around to New Orleans responded in their own ways, or were simply left behind.

Sometimes these rivalries were dominant over the resentment of London they all shared – but sometimes not. In the events leading to the American Revolution, port towns from Charleston to Boston joined in opposing London with a solidarity based on their common status as colonial towns. Montreal, however, remained loyal, in part at least because of its special hold on the Saint Lawrence route and the fur trade of the West, though it also had a history of earlier rivalries with the cities to the south. Similar rivalries turn up later in time and farther into the interior. Frontier resentment of the metropolis was chronic in circumstances as diverse as the Whiskey Rebellion or rural, populist resentment against the banks, the railways, and "the East" in general. Other rivalries, like that between Chicago and New Orleans, had a place in the more complex patterns that went into the American Civil War, though in that case it was a minor theme.

This simple conflict model is useful to help point up recurring themes, but actuality was, as always, much more complex. Even as a model, it requires qualification, first of all because the hierarchy of multifunctionality is not the same in all spheres of life. With American independence, for example, London dropped out of the political hierarchy, but it remained at the top of the economic hierarchy for some decades. The hierarchy of religious functions was again different – and different for each different religion. Take the example of Islam, beginning with a small village in the Moroccan Atlas Mountains. The religious life of villagers was partly self-sufficient in that they could pray to God in their own way, but other religious needs had to be met elsewhere. Among the higher centers would be other villages inhabited by the *shorfa*, or descendants of Muhammad. These men were necessary, in the local version of Islam, for certain judicial and religious functions that only they could perform. Beyond the shorfa villages were local holy towns and pilgrimage centers, like Moulay Idris. Still further up the urban hierarchy was Fez, a Moroccan center of religious knowledge and education. At a greater distance, Cairo served as the intellectual center for

Muslim learning throughout North Africa, and beyond Cairo were the holy cities of Mecca and Madina, centers for the pilgrimage enjoined on every Muslim at least once in his lifetime. Obviously, a similar hierarchy can be identified for other religious communities, most clearly for Anglicans, Roman Catholics, and Mormons, but also present in a more amorphous form for Hindus, Buddhists, and Baptists.

Similar patterns in the several different realms of human affairs appear in the relationships between the nodes of a trade diaspora. Political dependence down the hierarchy is clear enough. Its formal structure embodied in an institution like the Estado da India ran from Lisbon to Goa, to Macao, to Timor, and a religious hierarchy ran parallel to it. In more informal relations, like those between Greek city-states, religious, economic, and political hierarchies could be quite distinct.

Cultural blends

People of a trade diaspora were not only members of an urban society; they were also members of a plural society, where two or more cultures existed side by side. In most instances, this was a source of stress – alongside the other tension between merchants and other occupations. With the passage of time, cultural differences in a single society would be expected to disappear. Indeed, this was part of the process by which a trade diaspora worked itself out of existence. But the actual course of cultural integration was extremely variable. Some trade diasporas tried very hard to protect the integrity of their original culture. In spite of their role as cross-cultural brokers, they developed intricate systems of social control to prevent their traveling merchants from "going native." One of the most elaborate systems of this kind was that of the Mizabi religious and trading community with its oasis base in southern Algeria. Though they traded for centuries with the towns of northern Algeria, they held firmly to their own peculiar version of Islam and their own Berber language.[9] (See Chapter 3.)

In other circumstances, men who went abroad to trade without wives from home ended by marrying abroad, which could speed the process of culture change. On eighteenth-century Java, for example, the intermarriage of Chinese merchants with local women led to the creation of a new mixed culture called *peranakan* – partly Javanese and partly Hokkienese from southern China – but the new, mixed culture then stabilized. By the nineteenth century, it had its own quarter in most Javanese towns, its own special status in Dutch colonial law, and its own occu-

[9] L. Vigourous, "L'émigration mozabite dans les villes du Tell algerien," *Travaux de l'institut de recherches sahariennes*, 3:87–102 (1945), pp. 95–7.

pational specialization in retail trade and petty commerce, though most of its cultural forms were drifting gradually toward the Javanese pattern.

Although some diaspora merchants sought only to protect their cultural integrity, others tried to convert their hosts. Their success was sometimes spectacular. Hindu merchants from India carried not only their religion but also a lot of Indian secular culture to Southeast Asia. Later on, Muslim Indians carried Islam throughout island Southeast Asia. Although the merchant settlers abroad usually went out in order to learn how to function as cross-cultural brokers, they might or might not have learned as much about the host culture as some people in the host society learned about theirs. Along the West African coast in the era of the slave trade, for example, few of the Europeans in the trade enclaves ever learned African languages. Instead, the local African merchants learned European languages, mainly creole Portuguese or English, though other aspects of the culture of commerce were as much African as European.

Alternate models of cross-cultural trade

The idea of a trade diaspora is comparatively new to economic anthropology or historical studies generally, at least under that name. Historians have written about trading-post empires for decades; institutions like the Hanseatic League or the Phoenician trade network in the Mediterranean were too important to be overlooked, but they were rarely associated explicitly with the special problems of cross-cultural trade.[10] Cross-cultural trade was, however, discussed in several other contexts.

One of the oldest is Herodotus's description of silent trade somewhere on the northern or western coast of Africa. Here, and in many similar descriptions by later travelers, traders from a distance are described as bringing their goods to an accustomed place of exchange in the countryside, away from towns or villages. They deposited the goods and went away. Local traders then appeared, deposited a quantity of their own goods and went away in their turn. When the first traders returned, they judged the value of the goods they found. If they thought an exchange was equitable, they took the new goods and left their own. If

---

[10] The exception is Africa, where a number of trade diasporas have been studied in some detail. See P. D. Curtin, *Economic Change in Precolonial Africa: Senegambia in the Era of the Slave Trade*, 2 vols. (Madison, Wis., 1975), 1:59–66, 68–76, 92–152; Richard Roberts, "Long Distance Trade and Production: Sinsani in the Nineteenth Century," *Journal of African History*, 21:169–88 (1980); Paul Lovejoy, *Caravans of Kola: The Hausa Kola Trade, 1700–1900* (Zaria, 1980); Robert W. Harms, *River of Wealth, River of Sorrow: The Central Zaire Basin in the Era of the Slave and Ivory Trade, 1500–1891* (New Haven, Conn., 1981); Stephen B. Baier, *An Economic History of Central Niger* (London, 1980).

not, they adjusted the quantity of their offering and went away again, to await a silent response from their trade partners.[11]

The account is interesting for its recognition of the special problems of cross-cultural trade, even more so for its ingenuity in showing how such trade might take place without brokers or spoken communication, indeed, without the trading partners' even seeing each other. It has been repeated with variations as having occurred in many different parts of the world, perhaps a clearer indication of the story's inherent fascination than of its accuracy. The empirical evidence for any of these accounts is extremely weak. Whoever wrote them down either heard about silent trade at second or third hand, or else the "silent" trade described was silent only in the kind of communication used in bargaining. In a loose sense a present-day auction is "silent" when the bidder accepts a price with a nonverbal indication. Many nonverbal signals are used in face-to-face bargaining in many cultures, but this is not the same as the no-contact, cross-cultural trade found in Herodotus's account. And Herodotus's model, taken full strength, is improbable on the face of it. To bargain with such elaborate avoidance, yet to assume that total strangers will act with honesty and good faith, calls for an unusual degree of cross-cultural understanding from both parties – and to believe it requires unusual credulity from the reader.[12]

Still another model of cross-cultural trade is the "port of trade" introduced in three separate articles by Robert B. Revere, Anne Chapman, and Rosemary Arnold in an important volume on early trade chiefly inspired by Karl Polanyi.[13] The port of trade in this sense is not simply a port where trade often took place. It was held to incorporate a whole set of institutional practices typical of cross-cultural trade in premodern societies. The port of trade was a town or small state, not necessarily on the seacoast. It was recognized as a neutral spot in the struggles of

[11] Herodotus, *Histories*, IV, 196. Other accounts of silent trade are discussed in P. J. Hamilton Grierson, *The Silent Trade: A Contribution to the Early History of Human Intercourse* (Edinburgh, 1903).

[12] For recent controversy about silent trade see Lars Sundstrom, *The Trade of Guinea* (Lund, 1965), esp. pp. 22–31; P. F. de Moraes Farias, "Silent Trade: Myth and Historical Evidence," *History in Africa*, 1:9–24 (1974); John A. Price, "On Silent Trade," and Schinichiro Kurmoto, "Silent Trade in Japan," both in George Dalton (ed.), *Research in Economic Anthropology*, 3:75–108 (1980).

[13] Karl Polanyi, Conrad M. Arensberg, and Harry W. Pearson, *Trade and Markets in Early Empires* (New York, 1957), pp. 38–63, 114–53, 117–87. The concept was later elaborated and given a more rigorous definition by A. Leeds, "The Port of Trade as an Ecological and Evolutionary Type," in *Proceedings of the 1961 Annual Meeting of the American Ethnological Society* (Seattle, 1961). Some of Polanyi's articles in this area are conveniently collected in George Dalton (ed.), *Primitive, Archaic and Modern Economies: Essays of Karl Polanyi* (New York, 1968). The literature on both sides of this argument is very large, but S. C. Humphreys, "History, Economics, and Anthropology: The Work of Karl Polanyi," *History and Theory*, 8:165–212 (1969), is a convenient summary.

larger states and kept that way intentionally. Long-distance trade, more-over, was closely controlled by the state and subordinated to state ends. The state established the terms of exchange, fixed prices, and maintained them over long periods of time. The institution of a price-fixing market was explicitly excluded. Prices were not allowed to fluctuate with the influence of supply and demand.

The port of trade was one element in a more extensive controversy between Polanyi and his school (sometimes called substantivists) and those who follow the main traditions of Western economic theory (the formalists). The substantivists hold that formal theory is mistaken in concentrating on the way people economize in allocating desirable goods and services. This emphasis leads to a value theory based on the play of supply and demand, exerted through the market bargaining of buyers and sellers. Substantivists prefer to regard price-fixing markets as a re-cent innovation in human experience, hardly important before the eigh-teenth century. For the past, they place more emphasis on the way the economic processes are "imbedded" in noneconomic institutions – and on the importance of nonmarket exchanges through reciprocity (mutual gift giving) and redistribution (where goods are passed to a central au-thority and then passed out again on the basis of social values). The formalists argue, in return, that the play of market forces is of over-whelming importance, even in setting the values attributed to gifts or other forms of exchange.

The controversy has not been especially enlightening. Some substan-tivists write as though formalists believe their theoretical models are reality, rather than a mere representation of *some aspects* of reality. Some formalists in turn write as though the substantivists deny any role at all to the play of market forces. In fact, the best social scientists on either side recognize that both market and other forms of exchange have a role to play. The problem is to measure the influence of each in specific situations.

Aspects of the controversy inevitably recur here and there in the chap-ters that follow. These and other theoretical possibilities, however, will have to be examined in the light of particular circumstances of individual trade diasporas, seen over the long run of time and on a worldwide basis. Before going back to the earliest evidence, however, it is useful to begin by examining African trade diasporas in recent centuries, where available evidence is comparatively detailed. Some observations from the recent past may then strike chords or suggest interpretations that may help us to understand the thinner evidence from the distant past.

2

Africa:
Incentives to trade, patterns of competition

Sub-Saharan Africa remained isolated from the main currents of world trade far longer than most of the rest of the Afro-Eurasian landmass. Even though Asian sailors reached much of the eastern coast by about 200 B.C., North Africans regularly crossed the Sahara by about 800 A.D., and European sailors reached the western coasts in the fifteenth century, much of the interior remained comparatively isolated until the eighteenth and nineteenth centuries – cut off by the aridity of the Sahara and its own patterns of disease environment. Tsetse flies and the trypanosomes they carried made pack animals useless through much of the African tropics, thus impeding long-distance trade. Other diseases, especially falciparum malaria and yellow fever, were so fatal to humans from other disease environments that Africa remained the continent least known to outsiders until the second half of the nineteenth century.

Textbooks and other summary treatments of African economic history sometimes illustrate the "penetration" of Africa with maps showing arrows leading from the coasts into the interior – from Egypt up the Nile valley, from the east coast into the highland lake region, from the Maghrib across the Sahara to the western Sudan, from the Atlantic coast into the Congo basin. Such maps are accurate enough to show the flow of foreign goods. Arrows in the opposite direction could also show how African goods and people moved along trade routes to the outside world. But intercontinental trade was only part of the whole. In Africa, as elsewhere in the world, local exchange was more important than long-distance trade. As a general proposition, the longer the distance, the more trade had to be confined to products of comparatively high value and low bulk, though bulkier goods could be carried farther as the technology of transportation improved over time.

Overemphasis on external trade can also lead to an overemphasis on external initiative. One of the myths of African history is the old view that commerce in Africa was largely pioneered by outsiders who penetrated a stagnant continent. In fact, trade beyond the village level began

15

on local, African initiative. Traders moved out along the trade routes, set up trade diasporas that crisscrossed the continent in patterns of increasing complexity. When the European "explorers" of the nineteenth century *did* travel from the coast into the interior, they did so with the help and guidance of established African merchants who were already in the business of long-distance trade.

Incentives to trade

The most obvious and ancient explanation of why some people take up commerce and others do not is the differing resource endowments. Where people lived in a homogeneous environment stretching over some distance, there was no obvious incentive to trade beyond the village level; nor was there much reason for specialization within the village where almost everyone was necessarily involved in food production. Where different environments lie side by side, specialization and trade become likely. One of the most dramatic and important dividing lines between diverse environments in any part of the world is the desert edge, the *sahel*, separating land where agriculture can be practiced from the arid steppe and desert where only pastoral nomadism is possible. Nomads are specialized producers from necessity, with meat and milk but little or no access to grain, or fiber to make cloth. A sedentary, farming household can produce for itself most of the goods it will consume. Nomads must move with their cattle, which makes it very hard for them to raise anything else. Although people can, in a pinch, live on animal products alone, most nomads prefer to trade with sedentary people for grain, cloth, and metals. The result through history has been a long struggle of competitive cooperation between sedentary societies and their nomadic neighbors. Relations across the desert fringe could be those of peaceful trade, or those of violence represented symbolically by the story of Cain and Abel, but goods normally pass across this ecological divide with greater intensity than they do in more homogeneous environments.

In Africa, the Sahara has a desert edge to the north and to the south. Across the southern sahel lies the great savanna belt. Still farther south is another ecological dividing line where the savanna meets the tropical forest. There, too, diverse environments made for exchange of products like the yams or palm oil of the forest for the shea-nut oil and peanuts that grew better in the savanna. In this case, however, the communities on both sides of the line were sedentary farmers; neither was as specialized as the nomadic pastoralists were; and early trade across the ecological frontier can be assumed to have been less than it was across the sahel.

Other ecological frontiers come from differences in altitude. In East Africa, linguistic evidence suggests that some of the earliest markets originated where Mount Kilimanjaro and Mount Kenya provide a rich and well-watered environment nearly surrounded by a comparatively arid and lightly populated plain.[1] Similar differences abound in the Ethiopian highlands and along the mountain chain that reaches south toward the Cape of Good Hope.

Salt, iron, and fish

Resources still more unevenly distributed across the landscape were also important inducements to early trade. Archaeological evidence shows that copper, iron, and certain kinds of shells entered trade at a very early date, though the record is necessarily silent as to who carried them and how. Much of the earliest trade is assumed to have been a relay trade, carried on by people who bought and resold without going far from home. Goods could move a long way in a series of short stages. The known sources of a natural product like salt could also serve as an attraction for many different groups for miles around. In many, perhaps most, recorded instances, however, it was the owners or specialist producers of the rare commodity who made it their business to move out along the trade routes in order to sell to strangers, founding a trade diaspora in the process, which later evolved to handle a greater variety of products. Several interior peoples in tropical Africa, both east and west, founded trade diasporas based initially on salt deposits but then moved on to become specialists in long-distance trade in a much greater variety of products. The Dendi of southern Niger, for example, began with salt but then spread their trade network so widely that by the nineteenth century, the Dendi language had become the dominant trade language over much of the present Republics of Togo and Benin.[2]

Sea salt was available along all the coasts of Africa, either by boiling seawater or allowing natural evaporation from specially constructed pools. Several coastal peoples in West Africa, who later became important traders, seem to have begun the commercial penetration of the hinterland in order to take advantage of their local salt monopoly. The Avikam and Alladian peoples of the southern Ivory Coast and the Ijo of the

---

[1] L. J. Wood and Christopher Ehret, "The Origins and Diffusions of the Market Institution in East Africa," *Journal of African Studies*, 5:1–17 (1978).

[2] Paul E. Lovejoy, *Caravans of Kola: The Hausa Kola Trade, 1700–1900* (Zaria, 1980), pp. 32–3; N. Levtzion, *Muslims and Chiefs in West Africa: A Study of Islam in the Middle Volta Basin in the Pre-Colonial Period* (London, 1968), pp. 173–4; Charles M. Good, "Salt, Trade, and Disease: Aspects of Development in Africa's Northern Great Lakes Region," *International Journal of African Historical Studies*, 5:543–86 (1972).

Niger delta are notable examples.[3] Where salt was especially scarce, as it was in the savanna country of West Africa, it was sometimes the interior people who created and operated trade routes for access to coastal supplies. Two such routes from the Mande heartland – one westward to the mouth of the Gambia, the other south through what is now Liberia – have left their imprint on the distribution of African peoples. A ribbon of Malinke-speaking people, whose homeland was southern Mali, are still found to the west along the line of the Gambia River, where their ancestors first went in search of sea salt. And the Vai of southern Liberia are thought to be a similar linguistic remnant of an old Malinke trade route to the Liberian coast, a remnant that was later cut off from the main body of Malinke-speaking people.[4]

In Africa, iron is far more widely distributed than salt, but specialized skills in iron production and smith's work lay behind several trade diasporas. Whether it did so or not depended on the way iron production fitted other social patterns. In West Africa generally, iron workers were often considered to be a group apart from the rest of society, one of a half-dozen or so special, occupational castes that could only marry among themselves. They were respected for their technical knowledge, but they were also feared; to work with iron called for dangerous interference with the gods – with those of the earth they dug for ore and those of the trees they killed to make charcoal. Like merchants in ancient Greece, such a dangerous occupation made smiths simultaneously feared and despised. In much of West Africa they were relegated to a subordinate position.

In Wasulu, however, a group of merchant-blacksmiths who came to be called Kooroko were able to turn this low social position to their own advantage. Wasulu was a region in present-day Mali near the frontiers with Guinea-Conakry and the Ivory Coast. It lay near the ecological boundary between the savanna and the forest. The rulers of the several small states that made up Wasulu regarded hunting, cattle keeping, and agriculture as the only occupations worthy of free people. They relegated minstrels, wood workers, leather workers, and blacksmiths to a separate and subordinate status. Merchants were not a separate caste, nor were they respected, but the ancestors of the Kooroko gained one advantage from their low status. They could circulate freely within Wasulu, as high-

---

[3] Marc Augé, "L'organisation du commerce pré-colonial en basse Côte d'Ivoire et ses effets sur l'organisation sociale des populations côtières," in Claude Meillassoux (ed.), *The Development of Indigenous Trade and Markets in West Africa* (London, 1971); E. J. Alagoa, "Long Distance Trade and States in the Niger Delta," *Journal of African History*, 3:319–29 (1970).
[4] Philip D. Curtin, *Economic Change in Precolonial Africa: Senegambia in the Era of the Slave Trade*, 2 vols. (Madison, Wis., 1975), 1:212–13; Adam Jones, "Who Were the Vai?" *Journal of African History*, 22:159–78 (1981).

status people could not. A noble away from home was a threat to the local nobility and ran the risk of death or enslavement.

The Kooroko emerged in the nineteenth century as an important trading group within a limited sphere. At first, they circulated mainly within Wasulu, selling their own ironware, pottery, and leather products. They then moved into the transit trade, buying kola nuts on the southern frontiers of Wasulu in return for the salt they had bought in the north. Their larger success came only in the twentieth century, when they moved out from Wasulu and began to settle as diaspora merchants in the larger towns of the French Sudan (now Mali), and especially in Bamako. In the colonial setting, they were no longer a cross-cultural trade diaspora so much as a skilled commercial community that was able to take advantage of trucks and telegrams to succeed in the fiercely competitive kola-nut trade from the producing zone in the forest to a broader market throughout savanna country.[5]

The Yao from the vicinity of Malawi in southeast Africa also founded an important trade on the basis of iron production. Before the sixteenth century, the Yao had been farmers with hunting as an important sideline. Then the Wachisi, a group of skilled iron workers, immigrated into Yao society and adopted Yao culture. They began to make iron tools and to sell them locally. Other Yao then began iron production combined with trading expeditions, taking over the occupational niche previously assigned to hunting. The sexual division of labor had made hunting possible by leaving much of the agricultural work to women. Other customs that allowed prolonged absence to hunting parties could be easily shifted to do the same for trading expeditions. Village chiefs who had once headed hunting parties now led trading parties. Old ways to secure protective medicine and ritual ablution, and to prevent adultery by the wives of the absent, were transferred to commercial travel. By the sixteenth century, the Yao had pioneered a trade route from their homeland west of Lake Malawi to the coast near Mozambique City and on to Kilwa, in Tanzania. As trade developed, iron decreased in importance, replaced by an exchange of ivory for sea salt and imported goods. Like the Kooroko, the Yao began to draw goods from the far interior into their operations, until they had become one segment of a much more complex commercial network between the Indian Ocean coast and the heart of southern Africa.[6]

---

[5] The principal authority on the Kooroko is Jean-Louis Amselle, *Les négociants de la savanne: histoire et organisation sociale des Kooroko (Mali)* (Paris, 1978); see esp. pp. 25–48, 101–71.

[6] Edward A. Alpers, *Ivory and Slaves in East Central Africa: Changing Patterns of International Trade to the Later Nineteenth Century* (London, 1975); Jan Vansina in Philip D. Curtin et al., *African History* (Boston, 1978), pp. 421–4. For similar institutions of a restricted relay trade see Igor Kopytoff, "Aghem Ethnogenesis and the Grassfields Ecumene," in Claude Tardits (ed.), *Contribution de la recherche ethnologique à l'histoire des civilisations du Cameroun*, 2 vols. (Paris, 1981), 2:371–81.

Fishermen on the seacoast or along rivers were drawn into trade for the same reason pastoral nomads were. They had a specialized product that could be exchanged for a better-balanced diet. They had boats they could use to take their own product to market or carry other goods for profit. On all the major rivers, cultures evolved early on that have been categorized as "aquatic." They differed a good deal from one another, just as pastoral nomadism had many variants, but the Bobangi of the middle Congo or Zaire can serve as an example of the type.[7]

The Bobangi came in time to dominate a 500-kilometer stretch of the river southward from the equator to Stanley Pool, or Pool Malebo. In the early eighteenth century, however, they were only one among several culture groups with similar aquatic cultures living along this stretch of the river. They kept permanent villages on high ground. Then, when the water level dropped with the dry season, they moved out to temporary villages, more convenient to the low-water fishing possibilities. They were therefore able to fish all year round, producing large quantities of surplus fish for sale in return for the manioc, yams, and other vegetable products of their agricultural neighbors. In one sense, they were semi-nomads using their boats as cattle nomads used pack oxen to move their tents.

When river trade on the Congo began to increase in the late eighteenth century, the Bobangi began to expand their trade area up and down the river, making alliances with similar aquatic people as they did so. The result was not a normal trade diaspora, stretching into alien territory – or, if so, only in the short run. The Bobangi assimilated the other peoples along this stretch of the river so that they all became Bobangi, distinguished politically and culturally from their nonaquatic neighbors who lived back from the river along the full length of the Bobangi river dominion.

This success came from technological superiority, not military power. Bobangi freight boats, about 10 meters long and capable of carrying up to 1.5 metric tons, won an easy victory in competition with head porterage, the only alternative for carrying goods. Their trade could therefore include bulky commodities like African-made iron and copper, manioc and fish, camwood, barkcloth, several kinds of palm mats, tobacco, palm oil, and palm wine. Intercontinental exports like ivory and slaves and intercontinental imports like Indian or European cloth were only a small part of the total by either quantity or value.

---

[7] The authoritative study of the Bobangi is Robert W. Harms, *River of Wealth, River of Sorrow: The Central Zaire Basin in the Era of the Slave and Ivory Trade, 1500–1891* (New Haven, Conn. 1981).

Camels, dates, and the trans-Sahara trade

The trans-Sahara trade was the first and most important outside contact for western sub-Saharan Africa, and its origins also help to illustrate some general patterns of early trade. Pictures of carts, engraved on stones in the Sahara, mark two probable routes across the western Sahara to the great northern bend of the Niger River, where Timbuktu was later to be a major desert port. The Niger brought year-round water well out into the semiarid steppe, and it made possible relatively efficient boat transportation either upstream toward Mali or downstream toward Nigeria. One desert route ran northwest toward Morocco, the other northeast toward Tunisia. Travel across the desert was thus possible as early as the first millennium B.C., but extensive and regular commerce probably came somewhat later. Roman North Africa had defense lines against Saharan invaders, but the Romans knew nothing of the western Sudan. Nor is there evidence of any considerable trade across the western Sahara in Roman times. The Romans knew the Nile valley, the Ethiopian highlands, and the East African coast as far south as Tanzania, but not the west.

The introduction of camels to the Sahara in the second to fifth centuries A.D. marked the real beginning of trans-Sahara trade. The most acceptable hypothesis about the introduction of camels suggests that the one-humped dromedary now used throughout the Saharan region was domesticated in southern Arabia. Its use spread first to Somalia and later north into Egypt in the first or second century B.C. Meanwhile, camel herding spread westward along the southern desert edge to the vicinity of Lake Chad and beyond. Camels then reached northwest Africa from the south, probably introduced by the Berber-speaking nomadic ancestors of the present-day Tuareg.

Camels are among the most efficient of all pack animals, more efficient in most circumstances than carts pulled along roads. Their ability to go for long periods without water made them essential for desert travel, but their superiority to other pack animals at this period meant that the Sahara not only ceased to be a barrier – it actually became a favored region of cheap transportation whenever nomadic raiders could be kept in check.[8]

Knowledge of the earliest stages of the trans-Saharan trade is lost beyond possible recovery. By the late eighth century, however, with the beginnings of Islamic civilization in North Africa, camel caravans were

---

[8] For camels generally see Richard W. Bulliet, *The Camel and the Wheel* (Cambridge, Mass., 1975), esp. pp. 7–27, 111–40. For calculations of transport efficiency in the western Sahara see Philip D. Curtin, *Senegambia*, 1:278–85.

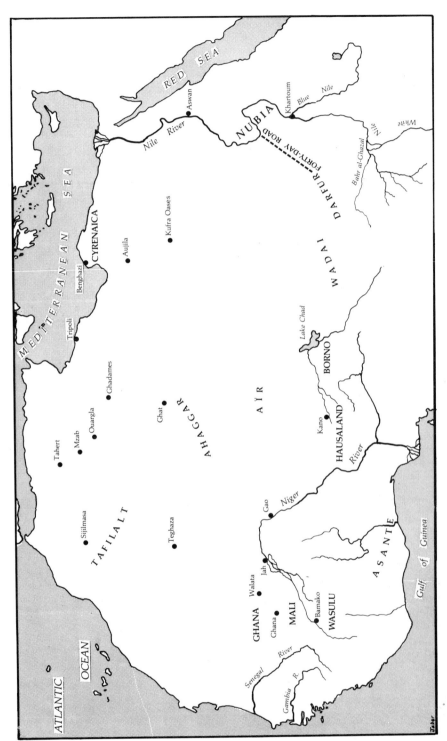

Map 2.1. Northern Africa

operating regularly across the desert. They can be presumed to have been operating somewhat earlier. By the fourth century, gold of sub-Saharan origin began to be imported into North Africa, and copper of presumed North African origin dated to about 400 A.D. turns up in the ruins of the substantial commercial town of Jenné-Jenno on the Niger River in Mali, well south of the Sahara. Little is known about early trade in the savanna country, which must have been extensive somewhat earlier, but the people who initiated the trans-Saharan trade and dominated the trade of the desert fringe in North Africa itself were oasis dwellers from a group of date-producing oases stretching from southern Morocco eastward through southern Algeria and Tunisia, and on to Tripolitania and the Fezzan of present-day southern Libya. Their trans-Saharan routes reached out to several different desert ports in the south: to the ancient empire of Ghana north of the Senegal and Niger, to the Niger bend, and from the southern Tunisia to the region of Lake Chad.[9]

These oases had a geographical environment especially well suited to the rise of long-distance trade based on camel caravans. Not only did they have the usual advantages of the desert edge, but they also had date palms (*Phoenix dactylifera*), one of the most productive of all trees. The palms had first been domesticated in ancient Mesopotamia, but they were already common in North Africa by pre-Roman times. Date palms require a very specialized environment, a hot, dry climate with temperatures around 30 degrees centigrade for several months of the year. They need irrigation water, not rain. Rainfall can actually damage the fruit at certain seasons. They also grow well in the sandy, alkaline soils characteristic of the North African desert edge. In optimum conditions, a single date palm can produce 40 to 80 kilograms of fruit a year. The sugar content is extremely high, which makes them a useful supplement to many possible diets, but not an adequate staple diet. Date producers are, in short, like cattle nomads or fisherfolk. They have a valuable product, but they can make the most of it only through trade.

Trade at a distance required transport, and this is where date-producing oases and surrounding camel nomads provided a natural setting for trade. Tafilalt in southeastern Morocco can serve as an example that became, over the centuries, one of the most important of all the desert ports looking across the Sahara toward the western Sudan. The water of the Ziz River, flowing down from the Atlas Mountains, is the basis for a ribbon oasis at first, broadening then into an irrigated plain about 20 kilometers by 15. Today, the oasis supports hundreds of thousands

---

[9] Tadusz Lewicki, "Traits d'histoire du commerce transsaharien: marchands et missionaires ibadites au Soudan occidental et central au cours des VIIIe–XIIe siècles," *Ethnografia Polska*, 8:291–311 (1964). Timothy F. Garrard. "Myth and Metrology: The Early Trans-Saharan Gold Trade," *Journal of African History*, 23:443–61 (1982).

of date palms, interplanted with small quantities of grain and vegetables. In the late nineteenth century, before the French conquest, the region supported a population estimated at about 100,000, implying a population density of more than 300 per square kilometer.

Natural rainfall was normally less than about 10 centimeters a year, far too little for agriculture but enough to provide pasturage for camels and even a few goats and sheep. The date-camel combination was the key, first for trade north to Fez, Meknes, and other cities in Morocco, and later for the trans-Sahara trade in gold, slaves, and tropical products. Though the trans-Sahara trade was an important reach to the south, it was only a sideline compared to the northern traffic in dates.[10]

In addition to these north–south exchanges, Tafilalt was in a position to participate in east–west trade as well. Camel caravans crossing the steppe south of the main range of the Atlas could reach similar oasis towns to the east. In southern Algeria, Ouargla along with Ghardaya and other oasis towns in the Mzab valley, had a similar environment and a similar early connection with dates and with the trans-Sahara trade. Still farther east, the Libyan oasis towns of Ghat, Ghadames, and Kufra were also date-producing bases for trade diasporas, reaching across the Sahara, but also passing goods on to Egypt from both Maghrib and the western Sudan.[11]

The same date-camel-trade complex recurs still farther east. The Nubian reaches of the Nile, from Aswan south to the vicinity of Khartoum, were a corridor for communication between Egypt and sub-Saharan Africa, but this was also a date-producing region, where sedentary farmers lived symbiotically with camel nomads on either side of the narrow belt of watered land. People from here were to play a major role in the final, nineteenth-century rise and decline of trade diasporas in this part of Africa (see Chapter 11).[12] Skipping across the Ethiopian highlands, the complex reappears in Somalia, where a ribbon oasis of the upper Juba River provided a base for the merchants who carried trade from highland Ethiopia to the Somali coast.[13]

[10] Ross E. Dunn, *Resistance in the Desert* (Madison, Wis., 1977); Dunn, "The Trade of Tafilalt: Commercial Change in Southeast Morocco on the Eve of the Protectorate," *International Journal of African Historical Studies*, 6:271–304 (1971), esp. 270–6.

[11] Donald C. Holsinger, "Migration, Commerce and Community: The Mīzābīs in Eighteenth- and Nineteenth-Century Algeria," *Journal of African History*, 21:61–74 (1980); Terrence Walz, *Trade Between Egypt and Bilad-as-Sudan, 1700–1820* (Cairo, 1978); Dennis D. Cordell, "Eastern Libya, Wadai, and the Sanusiya; A Tariqa and a Trade Route," *Journal of African History*, 18:21–36 (1977); Stephen Baier, *An Economic History of Central Niger* (New York, 1980), pp. 57–78.

[12] See William Y. Adams, *Nubia: Corridor to Africa* (Princeton, N.J., 1977).

[13] Mordechai Abir, "Caravan Trade and History in the Northern Parts of East Africa," *Paideuma*, 14:103–20 (1968); Abir, "Southern Ethiopia," in Richard Gray and David Birmingham (eds.), *Pre-Colonial African Trade: Essays on Trade in Central and Eastern Africa before 1900* (London, 1970).

From the desert to the forest

Evidence about commercial conditions south of the Sahara before about 1000 A.D. is extremely thin, but a schematic reconstruction is possible. The camel caravans that pioneered the trade met a natural barrier at the southern desert fringe. Their camels could not remain healthy much farther south in the comparatively humid savanna country that was the western Sudan. They themselves lacked immunities to the killing diseases of the more humid tropics. They therefore tended to stop at the sahel, at desert ports like Walata in the kingdom of Ghana, or on the northern bend of the Senegal or the Niger River.[14] In the first instance, they acted as cultural intermediaries for others who came from the north. Then, within a few centuries, if not decades, some of the sahelian people converted to Islam and had assimilated enough of the North African culture to fill the brokers' role themselves.

Some, at least, of the original Islamized cross-cultural brokers on the desert edge must have been Soninke-speaking people from the heartland of ancient Ghana, in the region between the Niger bend and the northward bend of the Senegal River. In any event, they moved south as traders and set up their own trade colonies, so that they in turn could act as cross-cultural brokers for their fellow countrymen who traveled south from the desert edge. In time, they adopted the language and some aspects of the culture of the people among whom they settled, but they kept Islam as their religion, and they continued to trace their ancestry back to the desert edge and to claim Soninke origin. In the twentieth century, their descendants have retained some of their ancient commercial traditions. The most common name for them is Wangara, though this sometimes means nothing more than a Muslim merchant. Many subdivisions of these diasporas have separate identities as Yarse, Maraka or Marka, Juula (Dyoula), or Jahaanke (Diakhanke).[15]

In the 1350s, Ibn Battuta, the North African traveler, left a detailed, eyewitness account of the desert crossing and his travels in the western Sudan. He crossed from Tafilalt to the desert port of Walata, where he

---

[14] See Michael Brett, "Ifriqiya as a Market for Saharan Trade from the Tenth to the Twelfth Century, A.D.," *Journal of African History*, 10:347–64 (1969).

[15] Paul E. Lovejoy, "The Role of the Wangara in the Economic Transformation of the Central Sudan in the Fifteenth and Sixteenth Centuries," *Journal of African History*, 19:341–68 (1978); Ivor Wilks, "Wangara, Akan, and the Portuguese in the Fifteenth and Sixteenth Centuries," *Journal of African History*, 23:333–50, 463–502 (1982); Said Hamdun and Noel King, *Ibn Battuta in Black Africa* (London, 1975), is a convenient translation of his travels in East and West Africa. Claude Meillassoux, *Trade and Markets in West Africa*, pp. 199–284; Curtin, *Senegambia*, 1:75–83; Richard Roberts, "Long Distance Trade and Production: Sinsani in the Nineteenth Century," *Journal of African History*, 21:169–88 (1980); Susan Keech McIntosh, "A Reconstruction of Wangara/Palolus, Island of Gold," *Journal of African History*, 22:145–58 (1981); Levtzion, *Muslims and Chiefs*.

found North African merchants resident and still active in the trans-Sahara trade. He later returned north with merchants from the Libyan oasis city of Ghadames. The desert edge was still the main breaking point between the trade of the North Africans and that of the Wangara, but North African merchants were resident as far south as the court of the kingdom of Mali in the upper Niger valley.[16] By this time, desert-edge merchants carried their trade as far south as they could go with their donkeys. In the southernmost savanna and in the tropical forest along the Gulf of Guinea, tsetse fly was too prevalent for these pack animals. Human head-loading or canoes on the rivers had to be used there, so that forest people tended to carry the trade of their own zone; but some savanna merchants, Muslim in religion, traveled as far as the Gulf of Guinea before Europeans appeared on that coast in the late fifteenth century.

Trade to the tropical African coasts

Sub-Saharan Africa had three distinct "coasts": that of the Sahara, that of the Indian Ocean, and that of the Atlantic. Alien merchants came to settle on all three, and Africans dealt with these visitors in quite different ways in the three regions. Regular contact began first in the east, about the first century B.C. or eight hundred years before regular contact across the Sahara. The coastal region from Somalia southward to Tanzania then became part of the commercial world of Indian Ocean shipping. By analogy to experience on the desert edge of the western Sudan, one might expect a breaking point between carriers to occur at the port towns on this coast, as it did between the trans-Saharan traders and the Soninke-Wangara of the sahel. That is, one might have expected coastal people to carry alien goods into the interior.

This did not happen in East Africa. Neither the Indian Ocean shippers, mainly Arabs and Persians, nor the old inhabitants of the coast carried trade to the hinterland. In Somalia, oasis people with a camel-date complex reached down to the coast – not the reverse. In the northern Swahili coast, now Kenya and Tanzania, no considerable or regular long-distance trade with the interior developed from either direction till the eighteenth century. When it did develop, the commerical pioneers came from the interior – Kamba from central Kenya, Nyamwezi from central Tanzania – not from the coast. Earlier trade was confined to coastal products like tortoise shells and some ivory from the immediate hinterland, plus utilitarian products like mangrove poles for house construction on the arid shores of the Persian Gulf. Even farther south, trade from the Zimbabwe

---

[16] Hamdun and King, *Ibn Battuta*, pp. 22–59.

goldfields to the port of Sofala was carried by Africans from the interior, not by seafaring Arabs before the sixteenth century. In all the considerable literature in Arabic describing the coast before the arrival of European mariners about 1500 A.D., there is not one account, even secondhand, by or about any foreigner or coastal merchant who ventured inland as far as Ibn Battuta had ventured south from the Sahara fringe to the capital of Mali.[17]

It is always possible that much more happened, and the record is now lost. But the most likely explanation lies with a transportation problem. Tsetse flies in the interior meant that goods had to be carried by head porterage, as they were carried in quantity during the eighteenth and nineteenth centuries. For earlier periods, we have to suppose that maritime traders were not interested or skilled in overland trade – even more, perhaps, that the products of the far interior could not be sold on the coast at a price high enough to cover the cost of transport and still show a profit – nor could the common products of Indian Ocean trade be sold competitively in the far interior. The one exceptional area may have been the route to the Zimbabwe goldfields, where Arabs were to be found inland as far as Sena by the early sixteenth century. It could have been profitable enough to lure them inland some years earlier. It was only after the Portuguese appearance off the coast after 1500 that a complex patten of penetration from the interior to the coast, and from the coast to the interior, came into existence.

In West Africa, trade between the coast and the interior began well before Europeans arrived there in the middle of the fifteenth century. Much of it, however, was based on coastal salt and reached only a short distance. Much was also relay trade, with segments usually only a few hundred kilometers and often confined to a single culture area. At times the individual relays were very short indeed, as in coastal Gabon, where, even in the nineteenth century, goods for export from only a few hundred kilometers in the interior still passed through as many as three tiers of relay traders.[18]

Part of the explanation is the forest itself, tsetse ridden, with transportation limited to porterage or boats. Forest conditions also favored stateless societies and microstates, though more elaborate political structures like Benin, Oyo, or Asante existed at least partly in the forest. To

[17] See G. S. P. Freeman-Grenville (ed.), *The East African Coast: Select Documents from the First to the Earlier Nineteenth Century* (Oxford, 1962), for a useful collection of source documents, including Ibn Battuta.

[18] Georges Dupré, "Le commerce entre sociétés lignagères: les Nzabi dans la traite à la fin du XIXᵉ siècle (Gabon-Congo)," *Cahiers d'études africaines*, 12:616–58; Jan Vansina in Philip D. Curtin et al., *African History*, pp. 421–4. For similar institutions of restricted relay trade see Igor Kopytoff, "Aghem ethnogenesis."

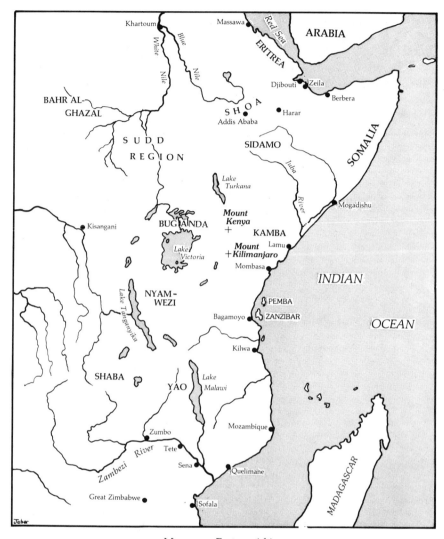

Map 2.2.   Eastern Africa

organize trade through a stateless area required elaborate cultural ad-
justments, often including complex manipulation of kinship and religious beliefs (see Chapter 3). In any event, relay trade with comparatively
short stages called for frequent exchange between different groups of
traders.

Transit markets

Markets where different groups of traders meet are sometimes called
transit markets. Their location can be dictated by physical geography,

by ethnic boundaries, or by political and power considerations. In the nineteenth-century Congo, for example, the reaches dominated by the Bobangi ended on the downstream side at Stanley Pool. Boats could go no farther; the river drops over impassable rapids for the next 350 kilometers to the deep water of the Congo estuary. In the eighteenth and nineteenth centuries, trade from the pool to the coast was mainly carried by coastal people, who specialized in the use of human porters, just as the Bobangi specialized in boat transport.[19] The upstream limit of Bobangi territory, however, depended on political and military, not physical, conditions. The Bobangi sought a monopoly for their own people over their own stretch of river, enforced by violence if necessary. Their upstream neighbors did the same. The result was a point of division at a disputatious and sometimes-violent transit market.[20]

On the lower Niger, there was no natural breaking point as spectacular as the Congo rapids, nor were the Niger boatmen as jealous of their rights as the Bobangi and their neighbors were. There were nevertheless transit markets at intervals: Aboh at the apex of the delta rivers, Asaba opposite the modern city of Onitsha, and another in the kingdom of Igala, just below the confluence of the Niger and the Benue rivers. There, in the nineteenth century, the market crowds sometimes numbered 6,000 people, and as many as 11,000 slaves are thought to have passed through in a single year. The spacing between these major markets varied from 120 to 160 kilometers. Each was governed and protected by the state where it was located, and each reach of the river between major markets tended to be dominated by a particular ethnic group – Ijo from the coast to Aboh, Aboh traders on north to Asaba, Igala traders above Asaba. But these lines were not fixed; Ijo could and occasionally did take their boats as far as Igala, and northerners sometimes came down to the delta. The Asaba people were not themselves long-distance traders, though they ran their markets and sold their surplus yams into the general trade.[21]

The role of the state in establishing transit markets could vary, from neutrality to an attempt to fix their location by administrative fiat. Even where physical conditions suggested a "natural" location for a transit

[19] Jan Vansina, *The Tio Kingdom of the Middle Congo 1880–1892* (London, 1973), esp. pp. 257–310; Phyllis M. Martin, *The External Trade of the Loango Coast, 1576–1870: The Effects of Changing Commercial Relations on the Vili Kingdom of Loango* (Oxford, 1972).

[20] Harms, *River of Wealth*, pp. 142–91.

[21] For the the trade of the lower Niger see Alagoa, "The Niger Delta states and their neighbors, to 1800," in J. F. A de Ajayi and Michael Crowder (eds.), *History of West Africa*, 2nd ed., 2 vols. (London, 1976), 1:331–72; G. I. Jones, *The Trading States of the Oil Rivers* (London, 1963); K. Onwuka Dike, *Trade and Politics in the Niger Delta, 1830–1885* (Oxford, 1956); Elizabeth Isichei, "Historical Change in an Ibo Polity: Asaba to 1885," *Journal of African History*, 10:421–38 (1969); David Northrup, *Trade Without Rulers: Pre-Colonial Economic Development in South-Eastern Nigeria* (Oxford, 1978).

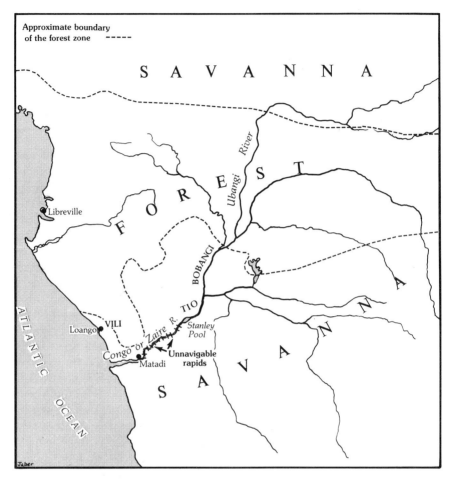

Map 2.3.   West central Africa and the lower Congo basin

market, state power could sometimes shift it one way or the other. The
policy of the kingdom of Asante (in present-day Ghana) toward transit
trade near its northern frontier is a case in point. The natural division
here would have been between the human porters of the forest zone
and donkey caravans of the savanna. With the rise of Asante in the
eighteenth century, the government set out first of all to control its own
internal trade and then to regulate that of foreign merchants. Especially
in the early nineteenth century, the ruler, or Asantehene, became concerned with cultural contamination from Islam – and many of the merchants from the north were Muslim. In the 1840s, he expelled all non-
Asante Muslims from his capital and decreed that only Asante subjects

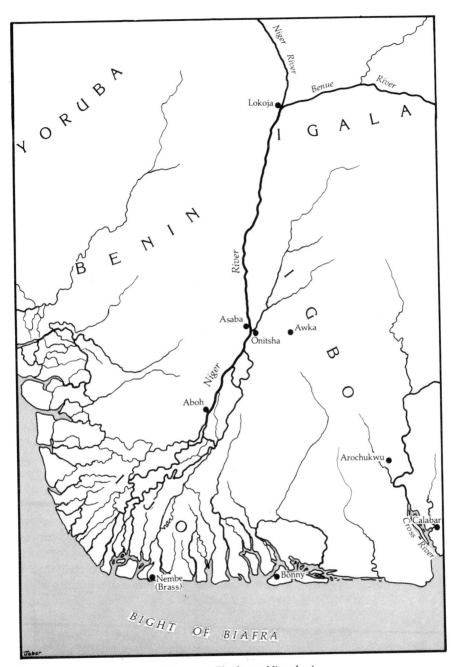

Map 2.4. The lower Niger basin

would be allowed to trade between Asante and the market town of Salaga, well to the north of the Asante culture area and north of the natural breaking point between donkey transport and head loading. During most of the nineteenth century, Asantehenes were able to enforce this decision, but when Asante power weakened in the late nineteenth century, the merchants began to use Kintampo, a good deal farther south, as their main transit market.[22]

Side-by-side competition

Most trade diasporas operated within a competitive economic order – not, perhaps, "free competition" and not without the use of force, but competition nonetheless. Individual firms usually competed with one another. The nodes or trade settlements of a diaspora competed with one another for power or influence within a particular network. A trade diaspora could also use the combined power of its participants to push the transit market forward, so as to control a longer stretch of a route shared with other traders. Finally, many trade diasporas carried goods in competition with traders along routes that were roughly parallel. The importance of these differing forms of competition changed through time, in response to underlying changes in technology, or to the play of political and military events.

Sometimes, competition between parallel routes could run as an important theme in regional history for as long as a thousand years. Perhaps the longest-lasting example in African history is the rivalry between the Senegal and Gambia Rivers in Senegambia, the region that takes their names. Both rivers rise in the Fuuta Jallon highlands in present-day Guinea-Conakry. Both flow north and then westward to reach the sea at Saint Louis for the Senegal and Banjul for the Gambia. Continuous navigation on the Senegal reaches some 350 kilometers inland from Saint Louis, while the Gambia is actually tidal to a point about 170 kilometers directly inland from Banjul. Both routes came into existence at least a thousand years ago, initially for the salt trade. The traders and groups of traders have changed many times over the centuries, and so have the products they exchanged, but the two parallel routes and their rivalry have several times changed the cultural and political geography of the

[22] Ivor Wilks, *Asante in the Nineteenth Century: The Structure and Evolution of a Political Order* (Cambridge, 1975), pp. 178–9; Wilks, "Asante Policy Toward the Hausa Trade in the Nineteenth Century," in Meillassoux, *Trade and Markets in West Africa*; Kwame Arhin, *West African Traders in Ghana in the Nineteenth and Twentieth Centuries* (London, 1979), esp. pp. 1–50; Levtzion, *Muslims and Chiefs*, pp. 27–9; Paul E. Lovejoy, "Polany's 'Ports of Trade'; Salaga and Kano in the Nineteenth Century," *Canadian Journal of African Studies*, 16:245–77 (1982); Paul E. Lovejoy, *Caravans of Kola*.

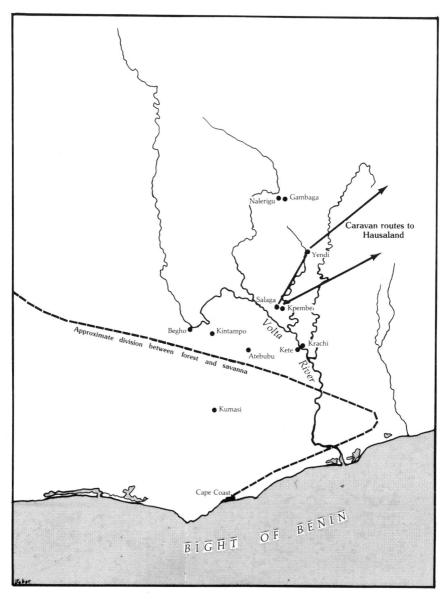

Map 2.5. Asante and its neighbors

region, helping to form, among other things, the British colony of Gambia and the independent republic that succeeded it.[23]

[23] For a detailed account of this competition, see Curtin, *Senegambia*, pp. 59–152.

East Africa: the evolution of trade networks

In another example, this time from eastern Africa, the theme of competing trade diasporas can be traced over nearly as long a time. A schematic narrative of successive stages can help to illuminate the conflict
and the ways it changed through time.

The prize in this case was the gold from the Zimbabwe goldfields. At
the first stage we know anything about, a Middle Eastern seaborne trade
diaspora reached down the east coast of Africa, leaving settlements of
merchants in a series of way stations. Romans and Persians and others
had participated in this trade, but, by the fifteenth century, it was mainly
in Arab hands. Long-distance Arab traders came as far as Kilwa in
Tanzania each season of favorable winds. Other Arab traders carried
the trade between Kilwa and Sofala in Mozambique. African traders,
presumably from the goldfields, brought gold and other merchandise
overland to Sofala; African authorities discouraged the coastal Arabs
from going inland on their own.[24] At this stage, then, the schematic
pattern of trade involved three segments: Arabia–Kilwa, Kilwa–Sofala,
and Sofala–goldfields. Two were run by merchants who were culturally
Arabian, one by merchants who were culturally African. There was
competition between firms, potential end-to-end competition centered
on the location of transit markets, and an implicit hierarchy of cities
involved in the trade, namely, the metropolitan cities in Arabia at the
top, Kilwa in second rank, perhaps Sofala at a third level, and the minor
ports between Kilwa and Somalia in fourth rank. Competitive tensions
between them would be expected, though the actual evidence is slight.

Then came a revolutionary change. In 1505, the Portuguese sailed into
the Indian Ocean with a fleet that was powerful by the standards of that
time on those waters. They seized Sofala, destroyed Kilwa, and set up
their own fortified trade enclave on the island of Mozambique. For nearly
400 years, they were to control the southern end of the maritime route
between Sofala and Arabia, but rarely the northern end, though in 1593
they began work on Fort Jesus at Mombasa in present-day Kenya in an
effort to do so. Again schematically, the Arab–Portuguese conflict during
these centuries was a long-played-out contest to win as much as possible
of the coastal trade route, and neither side won it all.

The second part of the Portuguese program was to seize control of
trade from the coast to the goldfields – perhaps of the goldfields themselves. To this end, they established a fortified base at Quelimane near
the mouth of the Zambezi, as anchor for a series of fortified trading

---

[24] Duarte Barbosa, *The Book of Duarte Barbosa*, 2 vols. Edited from original composed about
1518 by Mansel Longworth Dames (London, 1908), pp. 6–14.

posts farther up the river: Sena, about 160 kilometers; Tete at 250 kilometers; finally, in the eighteenth century, Zumbo, nearly 800 kilometers from the coast.

For all their military display, the Portuguese never succeeded in buying as much gold as the Arabs had done, but they completely rearranged the hierarchy of cities – first by detaching the southern towns from their former Arabian metropolis, and second by creating a new hierarchy that began in Lisbon, with Goa as a very important second rank in immediate political and economic command, then Mozambique, and lower down, the government posts on the Zambezi. The whole operation was theoretically centralized and controlled from the top, but in practice individual commanders intervened on their own in the affairs of neighboring African states. Private Portuguese subjects were also permitted to fortify private trading posts. Though these posts, called *prazos*, were created with government permission, the government found them hard to control. The initial form of the Portuguese operation was nevertheless that of a fortified trade diaspora or trading-post empire, seeking to control trade but not to administer territory.

Then, over the seventeenth century and on into the nineteenth, the structure changed. The government posts kept the essentials of a trading-post empire, but the prazos did not. Many of the original *prazeros* had been Portuguese from Portugal, but many of their successors were Goanese from India, Afro-Portuguese, or simply Africans who chose to accept a Portuguese identity. The prazos became cross-cultural communities, gradually more African than European, and the prazeros did a variety of different things in their position of nearly independent African rulers, including the operation of trading posts. Some bought gold and ivory for export in return for cotton textiles and other Indian products, which they then sold in their neighborhood. Others bought slaves and set themselves up as cotton planters and textile manufacturers. Still others sent out trade caravans manned by prazo slaves under a slave-administrator who traded on the prazo's account. An individual prazo might do several of these at the same time.[25]

By the late eighteenth century, the prazo economy was in decline. Commerce was less important than it had been, though individual prazeros continued as great landlords with control over hundreds or thousands of servile dependents. Their cotton textiles, however, could not compete easily with those from India; their slave caravan leaders could not compete easily with African traders. The central-place hierarchy had

[25] M. D. D. Newitt, *Portuguese Settlements on the Zambezi* (New York, 1973); Allen F. Isaacman, *Mozambique: The Africanization of a European Institution; The Zambezi Prazos, 1750–1902* (Madison, Wis., 1972).

also been modified with time. Lisbon still had the last word politically, but Goa was the effective economic capital. Its merchants supplied the capital for the African operations, and Goa greatly overshadowed the smaller posts, even Mozambique City.[26]

During these same centuries from the sixteenth to the eighteenth, rival traders began to compete along parallel routes from the goldfields to the wider world of Indian Ocean trade. The Yao traders from west of Lake Malawi began to reach the coast around Kilwa in the late sixteenth century (see map 2.2). By the seventeenth century, they were the main carriers of ivory from the far interior, not for sale simply to European ships, but also to Arabs who had reentered East African trade. By the eighteenth century, the Arabs from Oman had recaptured Fort Jesus in Mombasa and had become the most important shippers along the East African coast. The result was a Yao–Oman axis parallel to the Zambezi–Goa axis. And the two were similiar in other ways as well. Just as the dominant central place for military and political purposes was Lisbon for the Portuguese, it was Oman for the Arabs. Just as the dominant central place for banking and capital was Goa for the Portuguese, for the Arabs it was the mainly Muslim trade community of Gujarat in northwest India, and especially the city of Surat.[27] Neither of these competing trade diasporas was any longer simply an African phenomenon; both were attached to metropolises in India and hence to the amazingly complex world of the Indian Ocean economy in that century.

This attachment to the commercial world of the Indian Ocean meant that East Africa began to feel, however indirectly, the revolutionary economic impact of the industrializing world of Europe and North America. A new pace of economic change became evident over the period from about 1780 to 1820. Here, and elsewhere in Africa, the sheer quantities of goods entering trade, and especially those exported overseas, increased manyfold. The first and most important influence was a rapidly rising price for ivory, as the distant demand from industrializing Europe joined the older trade to India alone. One result was that two new trade diasporas from the interior began to reach the coast opposite Zanzibar. They may have existed earlier, but they now became important enough to enter the historical record. One, pioneered by the Kamba of south-central Kenya, reached the coast near Mombasa. Ultimately, it also reached further into the interior along the present line of the Uganda railway. The Nyamwezi from central Tanzania pioneered a second dias-

---

[26] Isaacman, *Mozambique*, pp. 82–4; Alpers, *Ivory and Slaves*, pp. 85–94.
[27] Alpers, *Ivory and Slaves*, pp. 70–208.

pora from their homeland to Bagamoyo on the coast. In time, it also reached inland across Lake Tanganyika into what is now eastern Zaire.[28]

By the early nineteenth century, a new demand for slaves also began to be felt. It was a derived demand, based partly on European demand for sugar, which European managers produced offshore in the Mascarene Islands, or far away in Brazil. There was also a derived demand for slaves to work new clove plantations on the islands of Zanzibar and Pemba, and other agricultural enterprises on the African mainland. These new currents brought enormous increases in the slave trade, which had been comparatively unimportant in East Africa up to this time. The Yao in particular responded by buying large numbers of slaves in the vicinity of Lake Malawi and selling them on the coast near Kilwa, but the two new northern routes of the Nyamwezi and Kamba also played a part.

The new flow of trade brought competition for all the existing trade networks in eastern Africa. Afro-Arabs and other Swahili-speaking people from the East African coast began to outfit their own caravans for the interior, using capital supplied by Indian bankers who had recently migrated to the coastal cities. And the cities themselves fell ever more closely under the political control of Oman. These new caravans from the coast were not so much a replacement of those from the interior as a supplement, competing along the same routes. It was simply the entry of new firms – and to some degree of new technology, since the coastal caravans were far better armed than caravans had been in the past. Along with the new entrants came a new level of violence. The coastal caravan leaders sometimes raided for slaves, rather than simply buying those offered on the market. They also furnished arms to African political authorities with the intention that they, in turn, would use them to kill elephants and capture slaves. This new phase was, in short, the beginning of a transition ultimately traceable to the start of industrialization in Europe, and one that was to end with the European conquest of most of Africa by the end of the century.

[28] Andrew Roberts, "Nyamwezi Trade," and John Lamphear, "The Kamba and the Northern Mrima Coast," both in Gray and Birmingham (eds.), *Pre-Colonial African Trade*, pp. 39–102.

3

Africa:
Traders and trade communities

At first glance, there is no apparent reason why traders living in an alien society must necessarily live separately from their hosts, but physical segregation of this kind was almost universal. In part, this separation was necessary simply to preserve the cultural integrity of the trade community. Without barriers of some kind, the traders from abroad would likely disappear through assimilation into the host society within a generation or so; their capacity to act as cross-cultural brokers would then come to an end. Diaspora merchants needed contact with their hosts, but they also needed to keep their distance and enough of their original culture to serve as brokers for the traveling merchants from the original homeland. The host society also had reason to keep alien merchants at a distance. They were, after all, normally considered to be unpleasant people on the double qualification of being both merchants and foreigners – however profitable it might be to have them around when needed. The interests of the hosts and the strangers alike suggest that a slightly distant contact was the most desirable relationship between the two communities.

For northern Africa, this kind of physical and social separation went back to the dawn of historical knowledge, as we will see in the next chapter. At the beginning of the eighth century, the division of the Mediterranean basin between a Christian north and a Muslim south reinforced the traders' need for security. The result was the factory system, which provided for the physical segregation of aliens on either shore of the sea in special residences with attached warehouses, variously called *fundaco* or *funduq* or *feitoria*.

With the growth of trade across the Sahara in these same centuries, a somewhat different pattern developed along the desert edge south of the Sahara. Sub-Saharan variants of the factory system were common, but it was also common to allow, or to force, foreign merchants to live in a separate town of their own. The result was a widespread occurrence of double towns – one for merchants of all origins, the other for the political and military leadership and their followers. The two towns were sometimes close together, but they could be as far as 10 kilometers apart. The capital of ancient Ghana was a double town on this model even before the year 1000. So too was Gao, the principal trading city on the Niger bend.

Another possibility was to have a merchants' town, an ethnically distinct, professionally specialized urban center without a nearby or equivalent political capital. Jah (or Dia) on the Niger not far above the bend appears to have been a town of this sort when Ibn Battuta visited there in the fourteenth century. In later centuries, autonomous merchants' towns were to be extremely common, especially in the westernmost western Sudan, where the various groups of Soninke-Wangara merchants practiced their trade. Some of these settlements were little more than a large village or a small, walled town, but with autonomous jurisdiction over its own affairs. Autonomy might originate from simple usurpation in circumstances where royal officials found it hard to exercise day-by-day authority in any case. Or it could originate as a formal grant by the local political authorities. By the early eighteenth century in Senegambia, for example, there were literally hundreds of such towns and villages, sometimes called a merchants' town (*juulakunda* in Malinke), more often *morikunda*, or Muslim town, which was much the same thing in a society where Muslim was synonymous with trader.[1]

Separation was all the easier because many West African societies had an ancient tradition in political thought that dichotomized the spheres of religion and commerce, on one hand, as against political and military functions on the other. The two were not quite equal, though the merchant-clerics stood higher than merchants have done in many societies. Even in power relationships, their religious prestige could threaten supernatural sanctions, balancing to some degree the physical power of the state and the military. Some merchant groups of Soninke extraction, the Jahaanke in particular, underlined their political neutrality through forthright pacifism, preferring where necessary to flee rather than fight. Others sought only neutrality for their caravans and autonomy for their towns. Richard Jobson, one of the earliest English visitors to the Gambia, reported of the mercantile clerics on the lower river:

They have free recourse through all places, so that howsoever the King and Countries are at warres and up in armes, the one against the other, yet still the Marybucke [*marabout* or learned Muslim] is a privileged person, and many follow his trade or course of travelling, without any let or interruption of either side.[2]

[1] Philip D. Curtin, *Economic Change in Precolonial Africa: Senegambia in the Era of the Slave Trade*, 2 vols. (Madison, Wis., 1975), 1:66–83, 106.
[2] Jobson, *The Golden Trade, or a Discovery of the River Gambia* (London, 1932), p. 106. First published 1623.

In some regions, double towns were interspersed with other centers where foreign merchants were simply assigned a quarter or ward, often called by the Hausa word, *zongo*, not only in the Hausa-speaking region of northern Nigeria and vicinity, but also along trade routes that reached out from there. Along the kola-nut route southeast to the Volta River basin of present-day Ghana, many of the zongos founded in the nineteenth century still survive as ethnic islands, even where their old autonomy and commercial dominance are gone. The zongo in Kumasi, former capital of Asante, for example, had a population larger than 60,000 at the time of Ghanian independence, still Muslim in religion and Hausa speaking – and, incidentally, a much larger population than the usual zongos of the nineteenth century.[3] Sometimes the commercial half of a double town had separate wards for each visiting nationality. Salaga, at its mid-nineteenth-century peak of prosperity, had separate wards for each different group of merchants from the north: for Yarse from the Mossi kingdoms, for Juula from the northwest, for Ligby and Hausa from the northeast.[4]

These double or multiple towns came into existence in several different ways. The town of Parakou in the northern Benin Republic, for example, was founded by Muslim merchants who passed that way en route to the kola region (see map 2.5). The local political authority recognized the usefulness of the town and then located his own capital nearby. The process could also be reversed, with the political center coming first. At Gambaga, a bit farther west, the first town was the seat of the *na*, or ruler, of Mamprussi. The court attracted merchants, but then, as they became numerous, the na decided to move to a new capital at Nalerigu (literally, the town of the na) 4 or 5 kilometers to the east.[5]

Relations between the political authorities and the commercial community could vary greatly. Where the merchants in West Africa found it fairly easy to gain autonomy, in the Ethiopian highlands enforced settlement in merchants' villages was a device for royal control. In the nineteenth century, the highlands were dominated by a number of Christian princes, whereas most of the foreign merchants who traveled into the highlands were Muslim, either from the oases of Somalia, the

---

[3] Ivor Wilks, "Asante Policy toward Hausa Trade in the 19th Century," in Claude Meillassoux (ed.), *The Development of Indigenous Trade and Markets in West Africa* (London, 1971), pp. 124–39. For anthropological studies of present-day zongos see Abner Cohen, *Customs and Politics in Urban Africa: A Study of Hausa Migrants in Yoruba Towns* (Berkeley, 1969), and Enid Schildkraut, *People of the Zongo: The Transformation of Ethnic Identities in Ghana* (Cambridge, 1978).

[4] Paul E. Lovejoy, *Caravans of Kila: The Hausa Kola Trade 1700–1900* (Zaria, 1980), pp. 18–23; Nehemia Levtzion, *Muslims and Chiefs in West Africa: A Study of Islam in the Middle Volta Basin in the Pre-Colonial Period* (London, 1968), pp. 28–29.

[5] Levtzion, *Muslims and Chiefs*, pp. 174–5; 103–7.

coast of Eritrea, or from Muslim kingdoms of the highlands itself, like the ancient commercial city-state of Harrar. Foreign merchants were forced to settle in separate merchants' villages, called *mandar*. The kingdom of Shoa, later core of an Ethiopian empire, tried to enforce strict control from its capital at Addis Ababa. It required each ethnic group to live in its own separate mandar – one for Tigrinyans from the north highlands, another for people from coastal Djibouti, still another for the Harari from the eastern highlands. Shoan authorities also tried to prevent Muslim merchants from passing through Shoa to the markets farther south and otherwise manipulated trade to suit their political interests. Other rulers did the same, sometimes for political and sometimes for economic ends, like that of favoring local merchants over strangers.[6]

Protection costs, coercion, and the state

Relationships between the diaspora merchants and the state were both competitive and complementary. Governments usually knew that trade helped the local economy. They also needed revenue, and merchants were an obvious class of taxable people without strong links to powerful local elites, even when they were not actually foreigners. Merchants needed protection for themselves and their goods, and they were often willing to pay for it. The ancient West African dichotomy between the political-military and religious-commercial sphere is more than an artifact of local West African culture. It also represents a broader difference between force-using enterprises and more peaceful forms of profit seeking – in stark terms, the difference between plunder and trade.

Frederick Lane has pointed up some economic functions of protection and "protection" payments in an important series of articles. They were based on the experience of the medieval Mediterranean, but their relevance is much wider.[7] Lane argued that one of the fundamental costs of any productive enterprise is the cost of protection from violent seizure or damage. In recent Western experience, the state is expected to provide "law and order." It is therefore easy for historians to overlook this item of cost, since it is paid for in our society by generalized taxes. Only insurance costs or night watchmen's wages would normally appear as

---

[6] Mordechai Abir, *Ethiopia: The Era of the Princes* (London, 1968) pp. 60 ff.; Abir, "Caravan Trade and History in the Northern Parts of East Africa," *Paideuma*, 14:103–20 (1968), and "Southern Ethiopia," in Richard Gray and David Birmingham, *Pre-Colonial African Trade: Essays on Trade in Central and Eastern Africa before 1900* (London, 1970), esp. p. 124.

[7] These were originally published in various learned journals, but are now available in Frederick C. Lane, *Venice and History* (Baltimore, 1966). They are "Economic Consequences of Organized Violence," "Force and Enterprise in the Creation of Oceanic Commerce," and "The Economic Meaning of War and Protection."

a protection cost. In other societies, however, protection costs appear in many different forms. Long-distance overland traders could either arm their caravans or else pay off local rulers with a variety of tolls and tariffs for protection on the road. "Protection" payments to potential bandits for not attacking caravans served the same function economically. Indeed, from an economic point of view, it made little difference whether protection costs yielded their return as a passive shield against enemies or an aggressive force to plunder others. One of the options open to merchants who controlled their own military forces was exactly that: to plunder rather than trade, or to do both by turns.

In either case, some form of protection payment – some form of implied or actual coercion – was a normal cost of doing business. Some firms, and some societies, for that matter, were more efficient at it than others were. One of Lane's important contributions was the concept of a "protection rent." By extension from the concept of an economic rent (a payment for possession of land that was better placed or more fertile than what was otherwise available) a firm or a society with lower protection costs than its competition would enjoy higher profits. The difference between these higher profits and those of the competition was a protection rent.[8]

In nineteenth-century West Africa, it is possible to see how some of these underlying principles worked in practice. Traders competed against one another, but the coercion-using political authorities were also in competition for the passage of traders, both for the sake of the economic activity they encouraged and for their protection payments to the state. Where states were small, a ruler who tried to charge more protection money than his neighbors ran the risk of driving trade away altogether. Alternate routes were often available. When parallel routes were in competition, as with the Gambia and Senegal routes to the West African interior, political authorities as well as traders had a stake in making a route commercially viable and keeping it that way. These strategic interests could involve very complex maneuvers lasting over decades, if not centuries.[9]

Actual relationships between traders and the state could vary enormously. Victor Azarya recently published a comparative analysis of three neighboring West African states in the nineteenth century – all three associated with trade along the axis of the upper Niger River and with its overland feeder routes farther south. These three were the caliphate of Hamdallahi in the region of Maasina, the new empire created by

[8] Lane, "Economic Meaning of War and Protection," pp. 388–9.
[9] See Curtin, *Senegambia*, 1:83–91, for a narrative analysis of some of these possibilities.

Samori Ture between the 1860s and the 1890s, and the older state of Kong.[10]

All three lay within the area of the ancient Soninke-Wangara trade network and its offshoots. All three were associated with the broad movements of Muslim religious reform that dominated so much of West African political life during the precolonial nineteenth century. All three were newly founded in that or the previous century, and in all three Muslims ruled over a population that was still incompletely Muslim, if not outright pagan. But there the similarity ended.

In Maasina, centered on the internal delta of the Niger River southwest of the bend, a Pulo (pl. Fulbe) cleric founded a religious reformist state in 1818. Although his immediate circle were very serious Muslim reformers, their broader following came from the pastoral Fulbe who were very numerous in the middle valley of the Niger River. They had the same disdain for commercial pursuits as their kinsmen, the nobility of Wasulu. Unlike commercial Muslim leadership, according to Azarya,

The Fulbe were deeply committed to their own ethnic-culture code of behavior (the *pulaaku*) which despised entrepreneurial activities undertaken for profit, which they considered dangerous and fundamentally immoral.[11]

The new state built its capital away from the Niger valley, the main artery of trade. Although the new oligarchy objected to commerce on moral grounds, it made no effort to persecute traders or to collect inordinate protection payments. Traders were, at the very least, Muslim in a world where a probable majority of the population was not. For the leaders of Maasina, religious and political goals were foremost; economic considerations of any kind had a low priority.

Kong, the neighboring state to the south had a different origin and a strikingly different set of relations between the merchants and the state. The town of Kong had originally been a non-Muslim, Senufo village, where Muslim Juula traders came to settle. In the early eighteenth century, one of them, Seku Wattara, revolted and set up an independent state dominated by the Muslim traders. It expanded gradually to the north and south till it reached north nearly to Jenne on the Niger and south into what is now the central Ivory Coast. As the state developed, the Juula founders lost some of their power to a warrior class, drawn from men who were mainly of non-Juula origin and had little of the ancient commercial tradition in their own culture.

For the merchants of Kong, the problem of "protection" can be laid out in somewhat schematic terms. The original founders sought to use

[10] Victor Azarya, "Traders and the Center in Massina, Kong, and Samori's State," *International Journal of African Historical Studies*, 13:420–56 (1980).
[11] V. Azarya, "Traders and the Center," p. 431.

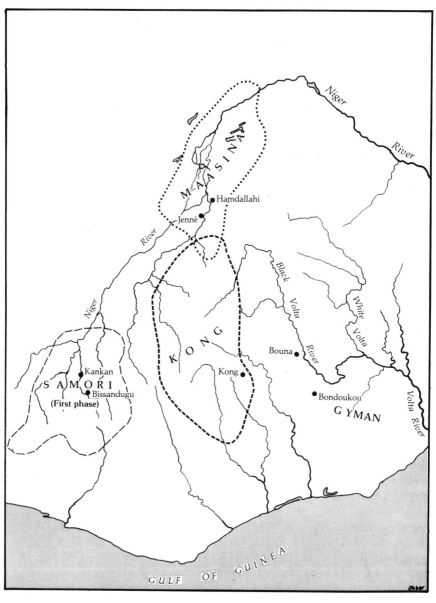

Map 3.1.   Three kingdoms of the Niger and Volta basins in the early nineteenth century

the state to protect trade directly. But they lost part of their early control over the state to the very group whose function it was to do the protecting. The commercial and military elites nevertheless cooperated with one another. Both were Muslim, but not reforming Muslims who laid great stress on religion, as the Maasina leadership was to do. They were not interested in religious reform so much as the gains to be had from control over trade. They tended, therefore, to concentrate military force on protecting trade routes and posting garrisons to key points. In effect, they created a reasonably close parallel to the kind of overland trading-post empire being developed in this same period in North America by the French *coureurs de bois* or the Hudson's Bay Company.

Samori Ture's empire was created farther west and later in time, and its origins have much in common with those of Kong. Yves Person, Samori's biographer, calls the rise of this new state "Juula revolution," as indeed it was.[12] But the *juula*, the Malinke word for merchant as well as the name of the ethnic group that ruled Kong, never dominated here to the extent they dominated Kong. Though he had a juula background and drew on juula support, Samori found the professional interests of the juula too narrow to help create a feeling of solidarity within the large state he wanted to conquer and then to rule. He therefore shifted to other alternatives. At one time, he followed the model of a Muslim reformist state like Maasina. At another, he tried to appeal to the possible feelings of ethnic solidarity among the large Malinke ethnic group.[13] As a soldier first and foremost, he had something in common with the military in Kong. When he later posed as a religious leader, he had something in common with the clerical oligarchy of Maasina; but his policies were never antimerchant. When he could, he favored merchants, though he built his capital of Bissandugu away from the main trade routes, and he took away the autonomous status of important merchant towns like Kankan. And Samori was not the only military leader to favor the commercial community. The kingdoms of Bouna, Bondoukou, and Gyman between Kong and the Akan goldfields were all founded by military conquerors who nevertheless favored juula merchants over other subjects.[14]

---

[12] Y. Person, *Samori: une revolution dyula*, 3 vols. (Dakar, 1968–75).

[13] Azarya, "Traders and the Center," pp. 437–42, 448–9.

[14] This set of class relations can appear anomalous in neo-Marxist economic anthropology. See Jean-Louis Boutillier, "La cité marchande de Bouna dans l'ensemble économique Ouest-Africain pré-colonial," in C. Meillassoux (ed.), *Trade and Markets in West Africa*; Emmanuel Terray, "Long-Distance Exchange and the Formation of the State: The Case of the Abron Kingdom of Gyaman," *Economy and Society*, 3:315–45 (1974).

From blood brotherhood to treaty

Merchants of a trade diaspora were linked to one another by several kinds of mutual solidarity: common profession, religion, language, and so on. At times, they also needed a way to create new bonds of solidarity where none had existed in the past, especially solidarity between the diaspora traders and members of the host society. In any event, *some* institutions were required to establish conditions of peace and friendship so that commercial transactions could take place. Today, the status of aliens is governed by law or bilateral treaty, and the terms and conditions are spelled out. In earlier times, the same end might be reached by elaborate mutual gift giving, through artificial kinship ties, or the exchange of hostages. The range of possibilities is wide, but two examples can illustrate some of those that occurred in African stateless societies.

One group of stateless traders were the Nzabi and their neighbors, living inland from the sparsely settled coast of Gabon and the Congolese Republic.[15] In the late nineteenth century, they may have numbered about 50,000 people, or a few less. The political pattern of the region was one of stateless societies or microstates, with many different ethnic groups participating in trade. The problem here was to overcome the ethnic diversity so as to pass traders and goods through to the coast. Two important institutions for doing this had developed by the end of the nineteenth century. One was fictitious kinship. Most ethnic groups of this region had similar kinship systems. They were organized by lineages, and these small lineage groups were considered in turn to belong to larger units that can be called clans. Each of these clans had a particular animal as its symbol or totem. By using the improbable assumption that clans with the same totemic animal, though belonging to different ethnic groups, were, in fact, kinfolk, it was possible to endow the whole region with a single kinship system, no matter how divided it was otherwise. Once this initial mental leap was widely accepted, a traveler from any part of the region would have fictive kin almost everywhere, and he could make claims on them *as* kin.

A second and related institution was the concept of partnership or comradeship between buyers and sellers. Where many societies regarded those who bought or sold goods from one another as natural antagonists, these societies did not. Instead, they saw a special kind of amicable relationship called *mukangu* or *mutete*. Not only was each partner expected to deal fairly with the other by giving correct value for

---

[15] This account is based on the research of Georges Dupré, "Le commerce entre sociétés lignagères: les Nzabi dans la traite à la fin du XIXe siècle (Gabon-Congo)," *Cahiers d'etudes africaines*, 12:616–58 (1972).

goods received, but each was supposed to repay the other by giving even greater value at some future time.[16] It seems obvious that this kind of overgenerosity would not have been possible indefinitely in practice, and equally obvious that as an ideal, it would go far to ease the natural tensions between buyers and sellers.

Occupational solidarity among merchants was common in precolonial Africa, as in many other societies. Though commercial competition was a fact of life, merchants were conscious of ill-feelings of others toward their occupation, and this drew them together. In Senegambia, for example, occupational solidarity was considerably stronger than ethnic solidarity.[17] On Richard Jobson's visit to the Gambia in 1620, a local merchant appealed to Jobson's own sense of fellow feeling for other merchants. As Jobson put it:

In our time of trading together, if it were his owne goods he bartered for, he would tell us, this is for my self, and you must deale better with me, than either with the Kings of the Country or any others, because I am as you are, a Julietto [juula], which signifies a Merchant, that goes from place to place, neither do I, as the Kings of our Country do which is to eate, and drinke, and lye still at home among their women, but I seeke abroad as you doe.[18]

In the densely settled Igbo country of present-day southeastern Nigeria, another and different way of dealing with the problems of trade in a stateless society had evolved by the nineteenth century. Unlike the ethnically fragmented society along the coast of Gabon and in the northern Congo Republic, the Igbo were a large culture group of several million people, speaking a set of mutually intelligible dialects. For the most part, they had no permanent political chiefs or states in the usual sense of the term. The largest political unit was a village group, and the normal source of authority was even smaller, namely, the members of a particular lineage in any individual village. Within the general area of the Igbo language, however, a number of linguistic and cultural subgroups were self-conscious of their identity, even though it had no single institutional representative.

One of these Igbo subgroups was the Aro, whose home country was at the southeast fringe of Igboland. The Aro were distinguished by their own variant of the Igbo language, by a special and separate network of kinship ties, and by their religious prestige, which centered on their important oracle, Ibinukpabi. It was located near the main Aro town, Arochukwu, but people from all of Ibgoland visited and respected it (see map 2.4). The Aro were also important traders, with commercial

---

[16] Dupré, "Les Nzabi."
[17] See P. D. Curtin, *Senegambia*, 1:89–91.
[18] Jobson, *Golden Trades*, p. 125.

settlements throughout the rest of Igbo-speaking territory and eastward through Ibibio country toward the Cameroon highlands.[19]

The Aro population as a whole was thus divided between those who had settled abroad and those who stayed in the original Aro territory. By the late eighteenth century, the scattered Aro settlements abroad were a clear majority of all the Aro people – nearly a hundred separate settlements in non-Aro territory. Both these settlers abroad and the home-based Aro moved as traders along a network that linked the various settlements to the homeland, to major markets, and to points of transfer to other trade networks.

Moving about in a stateless society required special adaptations, not least of which was the existence of the scattered Aro settlements that acted as hosts to other Aro, with a variety of landlord and brokerage services. The oracle's religious prestige gave the Aro special status as "God men," respected by other Igbo. Individual Aro traders also entered into artificial kinship ties with non-Aro, who became blood brothers and were thus able to act as hosts in villages where no Aro resided permanently.

The Aro who moved about protected themselves by traveling in substantial groups. These trading troops usually came from a single village and were united by genuine kinship ties. The nucleus of such a troop was often a group of male kinsmen, perhaps thirty or forty in all. With associated slaves, carriers, and hangers-on, the total might rise to 100 or 200 people. But it was not a closed group; nonkinsmen could join, often non-Aro as well, if they paid the appropriate fees. But no brief description can do justice to the great variety and flexibility within the Aro trade network. Some villages, for example, specialized in particular routes, where they maintained their net of blood brotherhood and trade partners for years on end. Other caravan troops had a semipermanent existence, reconstructed year after year by the same group of kinsmen.

In spite of the fact that no permanent authority had enough powers of coercion to protect trade, the system worked with surprisingly little coercion on the part of the Aro on their own behalf. It was held together, fundamentally, by the mutual self-interest of the Aro traders and the sedentary agricultural communities that recognized the benefits they themselves drew from the existence of external commerce. That was true of the Nzabi and related trade systems as well, but with a difference in the Aro case that came from the special religious prestige of the "God

[19] This account is based on F. Ifeoma Ekejiuba, "The Aro Trade System in the Nineteenth Century," *Ikenga*, 1:11–26, 2:10–21 (1972); G. I. Jones, *The Trading States of the Oil Rivers* (London, 1963); David Northrup, *Trade Without Rulers: Pre-Colonial Economic Development in South-Eastern Nigeria* (Oxford, 1978); Ukwu I. Ukwu, "The Development of Trade and Marketing in Iboland," *Journal of the Historical Society of Nigeria*, 3:647–62 (1967).

men." Though they traveled widely through non-Aro territory, they traveled very little beyond the sphere of the oracle's region of respected authority within Igboland.

The exclusive and comprehensive functions of religion

Religion sometimes appears as the exclusive possession of the body of believers, who are either uninterested in spreading the word or actually try to guard their secret. Other religions seek to spread their truth to all mankind. Both the exclusive and the proselytizing forms of religion have played important roles in the history of trade diasporas. The Aro are one example. The Aro wanted others to respect their oracle and their religious prestige, but not to the extent of coming under the cloak of sanctity and becoming "God men" in their own right.

Islam, on the other hand, was a universal religion whose believers were supposed to act under God's command to spread the word to all people. And the community of Islam often brought commercial advantages to its members. Most Muslim trade centers in West Africa, like the Hausa *Zongos* in the tropical forest or the mercantile-clerical towns of Senegambia, were open to any and all Muslim traders. In the earliest phases of the trans-Sahara trade, the Soninke merchants of the desert edge no doubt saw commercial as well as spiritual advantages in adopting the religious faith of the desert traders. And this pattern of Islam spreading first to a local commercial class and only afterward to society at large can be found historically on the frontiers of Islam from Senegal to the Philippines.

But all versions of Islam were not necessarily proselytizing. At times, Islam could serve as an exclusive possession of a particular ethnic or commercial group, helping to further its sense of internal solidarity and to preserve the purity of the ethnic identity. The oasis towns of the southern Maghrib had a version of Islam that tended in this direction. At the time of their pioneering activity in the trans-Sahara trade, they had adopted the Kharajite version of Islam, a sect that had split off from both the major branches (*sunni* and *shi'a*) in the early years of the Muslim conquest of the Middle East. In its earliest version, it represented elements of a puritanical and nomadic reaction to the luxury of the newly conquered sedentary empire. In recent centuries, the Ibadi community was effectively confined to a series of date-producing oases in the Mzab Valley of southern Algeria. These oasis cities are remnants of the once-powerful Ibadite state that had dominated the desert fringe in southeastern Algeria, southern Tunisia, and western Libya. Over time, pressure from successive sunni governments in the north drove them to seek refuge, first to the relatively well-watered oasis of Ouargla, then, after about 1000 A.D. to the less hospitable Mzab Valley, where they founded the five cities that have been their home ever since.

No longer important in the trans-Sahara trade, they turned to the north to sell their dates and to enter more generally into various branches of the retail trade of the major cities. The pattern is typical of that followed by many aging trade diasporas. After cross-cultural brokerage was no longer required – and that had clearly happened by the nineteenth century – a network of associated trade communities could be turned to new purposes. As a tight ethnic community of traders with an exclusive religion, and with settlers strategically placed in the major towns, the Ibadi from the Mzab were in a position to monopolize at least some aspects of retail trade.[20]

Well before the end of the eighteenth century, the Mizabi trade diaspora began to take new shape in the cities of northern Algeria. Deprived of their previous control over large numbers of camels, the cities of the Mzab no longer traded extensively to the south. Instead, they became a transit market for trans-Saharan goods and a source of dates for export northward. The dey of Algiers recognized them as a separate and alien trade community, with autonomous control of their own affairs under their own leader or *amin*, though they were only one among a number of communities with equivalent privileges, including black Africans and European Christians, among others. The dey's officials bargained separately with each alien commercial group, and the terms usually included a payment for value received. The Mizabi privileges included a monopoly over flour milling, baking, and the provision of public baths, along with somewhat less extensive privileges in the retail meat trade.[21] After the French began their conquest of Algeria in 1830, they recognized and maintained the privileges, with changes in detail. The fossilized remnant of the ancient Mizabi trade migration was thus able to last beyond the middle of the twentieth century.

With the passage of time, however, the economic and social reality of the Mizabi migration began to change. What had once been an economically viable commercial enterprise turned into a form of labor migration. By the early twentieth century, the date groves could no longer support the population of the five cities of the Mzab oases. Young men were then forced to seek work in the north, with more than a third of

---

[20] For the Mzab in general see Donald C. Holsinger, "Migration, Commerce and Community: the Mīzābīs in Eighteenth- and Nineteenth-Century Algeria," *Journal of African History*, 21:61–74 (1980), and L. Vigourous, "L'émigration mozabite dans les villes du Tell algerien," *Travaux de l'institut de recherches sahariennes*, 3:87–102 (1945).

[21] Venture de Paradis, "Alger au xviiie siècle," *Revue africaine*, 39:266–314 (1895), p. 267; René Lespès, "Quelques documents sur la corporation des Mozabites d'Alger dans les premiers temps de la conquêt," *Revue africaine*, 66:197–218 (1925), pp. 198–202.

the male population absent at any moment. Mizabi society could not survive without emigrants' remittances.

The mechanisms that had once functioned to preserve the integrity of the Mizabi community in an alien, though Muslim, society became all the more rigid. Political control in the Mzab rested with the Ibadite clerical leadership, in effect a form of theocracy limited by French over-rule. Clerical councils prescribed rules for conduct in the Mzab itself and for the temporary emigrants to the north. Though migration was nec-essary, only a few young males from each family were allowed to be absent at the same time. Marriage was encouraged before emigration, but Mizabi women had to remain behind; and marriage contracts typi-cally required periodic home leave. Men could marry outside the Mizabi community, but women could not. The migrants were also governed by restraints designed to preserve the purity of their Berber language and the separate identity of the Ibadi faith within Islam. They often lived above their shops and mixed with the rest of the population as little as possible. Similar exclusiveness governed visitors to the Mzab cities, where non-Ibadi were allowed within the walls only during daylight hours. Some cities excluded strangers even from the suburbs. Mizabi society both at home and abroad was governed by a puritanical code of conduct that proscribed not only drinking, but also smoking, music, dancing, levity in general, and any kind of conspicuous consumption. Puritanism may not have been developed for the sake of trade, but puritanical patterns of consumption surely helped to keep the Mizabi of the diaspora competitive with other retail traders.[22]

Other Islamic institutions also helped diaspora traders in other places. One of the most ubiquitous features of African Islam was the *sufi* or mystical religious order. It could take many forms, but the members of a particular religious order generally followed the teachings of a found-ing holy man who had discovered a way to experience a closer sense of union with God. The generic name for such orders was the Arabic word for way or path, *tariqa* (pl. *turuq*). They were not sects; they did not claim a unique value for their own practices. They were therefore much less exclusive than the Ibadi of the Mzab. Each recognized the possibility that others might also have a valid route to true religious experience. All were therefore at least theoretically within the mainstream of sunni or orthodox Islam.

These orders played a wide variety of different roles in commerce. One of the most telling examples in nineteenth-century Africa was the Sanusiyya, a newly founded order that helped to organize trade in east-ern Libya and actually founded a new trade route across the Sahara. On

[22] Vigourous, "L'émigration mozabite," esp. pp. 95–7.

a scale of age to youth among trade diasporas, this was one of the last, but it continued a pattern represented by the Mzabi, the ancient and fossilized network that was one of the first to reach across the Sahara.

The founder of the new order was Muhammed ibn 'Ali al-Sanusi, born in Algeria toward the end of the eighteenth century, later educated in Egypt and the holy cities of Arabia. In 1837, he founded the new tariqa, and began to preach his message and to establish new religious centers in the oases of eastern Libya. The Sanusiyya revolutionized the political as well as the religious order of the region. The previous political order had been a kinship-based stateless society, in which patrilineages were in chronic warfare over rights to pasturage and wells, or the control of key oases. In this desert world of camel nomads, people were nominally Muslim, but the society had slipped from the usual pattern of literacy in Arabic and hence had lost close contact with the broader world of Islam.

The Sanusiyya mode of reform began with a religious center at a convenient oasis. The nucleus was a *zawiya* or lodge, often fortified with a mosque attached, a library, and residences surrounded by the zawiya's cultivated fields. The central zawiya in turn inspired the faithful to imitate it elsewhere with private funds derived through the kinship structure. The central lodge was thus the property of the order alone. Other lodges often belonged to the lineages, but the head of the order appointed a sheikh or religious teacher to be responsible for the management of each. The order, in short, became a new source of authority cutting across the jumble of kin ties.[23]

The political structure was oasis centered, based economically on date production and exchange for the nearby nomads' meat and milk, or for grain brought in from the northern coastal fringe of Cyrenaica. This trading pattern was already ancient, but the Sanusi lodges were natural centers, which merchant members of the order could use for safe storage of goods in transit. Thus the Sanusiyya first of all intensified existing commercial movements. It then went on to reestablish certain trade routes that had not been used in the recent past. From the 1850s, one of these ran from Benghazi on the Mediterranean south through the oases of Kufra, Jalu, and Aujila to Wadai, south of the Sahara – jointly sponsored by the Sanusi control over the oases and the sultan of Wadai at the southern terminus (see map 2.1). By the early twentieth century, the value of through traffic along this route was estimated at 200,000 pounds sterling – to the considerable profit of the Sanusi order as well as the people of Wadai and Kordofan, south of the desert, who now

---

[23] See E. E. Evans-Prichard, *The Sanusi of Cyrenaica* (Oxford, 1949), esp. pp. 63–89; C. C. Adams, "The Sanusis," *Muslim World*, 36:21–45 (1946), esp. pp. 31–5.

gained a commercial window to the greater world of the Mediterranean. Though this route was new, it was only one among several Saharan trade routes operated under the protection of the Sanusiyya in the nine-teenth century. Another from Tripoli through the Fezzan to Zinder (now in Niger) and on to northern Nigeria carried goods of even greater value.[24]

Landlords, brokers, and caravan leaders

Long-distance trade is rarely carried out by a single individual or a single firm. Too many specialized functions are involved. From producer to consumer, goods pass through the hands of freight agents, transporters, wholesalers, and many more. Trade diasporas in the past also performed a variety of functions, though two or more might in fact be carried out by a single individual or group. A broker might arrange transactions between other merchants, but also on occasion act as a merchant on his own account. A ship's captain might be the ship's owner as well, might act as agent for those who own the cargo, or might own some of the cargo for sale on *his* account. The possible permutations are endless, but in African trade diasporas *some* functions did tend to be carried out by different people. The most consistent distinction was between those who stayed put at a particular node in the trade network and those who moved back and forth in charge of the merchandise. Those who stayed tended to be informal cross-cultural brokers. They were often landlords as well as formal commercial brokers in the sense of arranging the terms of specific transactions. Traveling merchants were at a disadvantage in these matters for the very fact that they had to move. If they wanted to broaden their business, it was more common for them to transport goods for other owners as well as their own.

Sometimes the stayers and movers had different social origins, though they shared a common culture. Paul Lovejoy's research on the Hausa trade diaspora to the kola groves of central Ghana illuminates some of the variety of possibilities. There, the people who went to settle in the *zongos* scattered through non-Hausa territory were drawn from a wide variety of social strata in Hausaland – nearly a sample of Hausa society as a whole – whereas the movers along the routes were far more narrowly recruited. They tended, for example, to belong to particular *asali* in Hausaland. The Hausa institution of asali itself needs some explaining. An asali is neither a kinship group nor a subdivision of Hausa culture

[24] Dennis D. Cordell, "Eastern Libya, Wadai, and the Sanūsiya: A Tariqa and a Trade Route," *Journal of African History*, 18:21–36 (1977); Stephen Baier, *An Economic History of Central Niger* (Oxford, 1980), pp. 57–78.

(in the sense that the Aro are a subdivision of the Igbo) nor a people with a common geographical origin – yet it has aspects of all three, in rising order of importance. To belong to a recognized asali implies endogamy, but the prime meaning of the term was a common, usually distant place of origin.[25]

Asali in Hausaland are not necessarily commercial, but three commercially oriented asali came to dominate movement along the trade routes to and from the kola groves of the Volta basin. These three asali had become Hausa by assimilating Hausa culture, but all three traced their origin to the desert edge farther north, underlining once again the importance of the sahel in the origin of African commercial undertakings. Their very names are indicative. One was called Kambarin Beriberi; the name in Hausa means "Borno merchants," and they were in fact originally from Borno. A second group was called Tokarawa, a collective term used to describe people of servile origin who had immigrated from the desert-edge society of the Tuareg directly to the north. The third, the Agalawa, were also servile Tuareg to begin with, but their name meant "people of the south," probably because they lived at the southern end of the Tuareg commercial network. Their home villages were initially part of the Tuareg trade diaspora that led south from the desert into Hausaland. The significant point is that all three were offshoots of trade diasporas *into* Hausaland. After a time as settlers, at a distant node in one trade diaspora, all joined a new trade diaspora *out of* Hausaland. Their advantage over other Hausa who might have responded to the same opportunity was that they had family experience in long-distance trade.

This pattern of a trade diaspora moving or reestablishing itself at a new base is not uncommon. We have already seen examples of the Hanseatic League shifting from Cologne to Lübeck, of the Phoenicians' shift from the Levant to Carthage, of the many-sided moves of the various Soninke-derived or Wangara trade diasporas from the desert edge into many corners of West African trade. Some of these moves were in response to political or military pressures; others followed economic opportunity. But all were possible because the trading peoples had already learned how to carry out long-distance trade. The techniques of trade, in short, were transferable.

The very mobility of trade diasporas in the West African savanna country – south of the desert but north of the forest belt – meant that traders were in touch with one another over long distances. By the nineteenth century, a common culture of trade stretched from Cape Verde in the west as far as Lake Chad and even beyond. The institutional

[25] Paul Lovejoy, *Caravans of Kola* (Zaria, 1980), pp. 53–4.

relations between those who moved and those who stayed were remarkably similar over the whole area.[26]

The key figures were two: the landlord-broker as chief of those who stayed put and the caravan leader as chief of those who moved. The caravan leader (*madugu* in Hausa, *silatigi* in Malinke) was usually selected by the merchants traveling with a caravan. The selection process was complex in itself, involving elements of inherited prestige for sons of former caravan leaders, who were sometimes credited with special powers. Once a madugu was widely recognized, he tended to remain one until he retired. Once selected he had great authority over the caravan and the other merchants. He had a military force for direct protection; he bargained with local authorities along the road over indirect protection costs; and he often bargained collectively at the end of the journey on behalf of all the merchants under his charge, even though each individual merchant owned his own share of the goods.

The landlord-broker (*jaatigi* in Malinke, *maigida* in Hausa) normally came from the same ethnic group as the moving traders, but he had usually been established in alien territory for some years, often for several generations. It might take that long to build up the local knowledge, local roots, and local position that he could then put at the service of the traveling merchants – at a price. The most important things he had to offer were lodging and protection. This included facilities for the physical security of goods or slaves in transit, access to food supplies for his clients, protection against interference by local political authorities (or the means to pay them off), a possible line of commercial credit from local moneylenders, and a guarantee of good conduct and commercial probity from both sides. This was most important. Since the landlord would remain after the caravans had moved on, he could give assurance to the local people. At the same time, the caravan leader had an incentive to keep the moving traders as orderly as possible. Individuals among them might never pass that way again, but he himself was likely to return year after year.

The Hausa maigida in the kola trade did not necessarily act as a broker in the narrow sense of arranging particular transactions. If wanted, he could call on the services of an independent professional broker (*dillali* in Hausa, from the Arabic root, one more indication of the institutional borrowing back to the desert edge and beyond). Whether or not he also employed a dillali, the maigida received a commission on all goods sold

---

[26] For representative descriptions of the culture of commerce in Senegambia in the far west and of the Hausa trade diaspora based in northern Nigeria, see P. D. Curtin, *Senegambia*, esp. 1:271–308, and Lovejoy, *Caravans of Kola*, esp. pp. 81–3 and 101–112.

from his establishment, and he also bought and sold goods on his own account, both local products and those that arrived with the caravans.

A generalized account of the way people carry on their lives always runs the danger of making the normal appear to have been the universal practice. In fact, every trading event involved exceptions to the general pattern. Trade in West Africa, as elsewhere in the world, also involved warfare, brigandage, and a great variety of chicaneries on all sides. The dominant ethos of savanna trade was nevertheless in remarkable balance between the interests of the movers, the stayers, and the political authorities – all sharing the profits of what was to a degree a common enterprise.

The broker's role was quite different in some other parts of Africa. Whereas the West African savanna in the nineteenth century approached conditions of a competitive market in long-distance trade, this was by no means universal in Africa. In coastal ports on the horn of Africa, like Berbera, Zeila, and Massawa, landlord-brokers also existed, but the local authorities supported their demand for brokerage fees that were really protection payments in disguise – as much as 20 percent on the value of all transactions, compared with about 1 percent for a maigida in the Volta basin of West Africa. Collusion between landlord-brokers and local chiefs also helped to make these ports into a transit market, where foreigners were forced to sell their goods to local merchants who outfitted their own caravans to carry them on into the interior.[27]

In still other circumstances, brokers belonged to an ethnic group that sent out very few peddlers or moving merchants. This situation had developed on the Congo at Stanley Pool by the end of the nineteenth century. The pool was a natural breaking point between the riverborne trade upstream and the head-loading caravans that carried goods around the rapids to the coast. The Tio, the dominant ethnic group around the pool, were able to use this natural breaking point to establish their own position as landlord-brokers to all comers, serving both the Bobangi from upriver and the Vili and other traders from the seacoast.

In world perspective, this situation is unusual. The more common diaspora pattern was for some alien traders to settle down to serve their fellow-countrymen. But physical conditions around the pool made it a natural solution for the Tio to serve all comers. The optimum season for river trade and the optimum season for the coastal traders were different, and both involved large numbers of people for such a sparsely populated region. In the 1880s, when the Tio living near the pool were only about

---

[27] Mordechai Abir, "Brokerage and Brokers in Ethiopia in the First Half of the Nineteenth Century," *Journal of Ethiopian Studies*, 3:1–5 (1965); Richard Pankhurst, "The Trade of the Gulf of Aden Ports of Africa in the Nineteenth and Early Twentieth Centuries," *Journal of Ethiopian Studies*, 3:36–81 (1965).

10,000 people, as many as 4,000 to 5,000 Bobangi from upriver might be present as transients at any moment in the high season for trade, whereas an even larger number of porters from the coast might visit in the dry season. In this circumstance, it made sense for local brokers to hold goods six months so that moving traders would not have to wait a whole year to accumulate cargo for their return home.[28]

Coastal markets and European traders

Most of our present knowledge about precolonial African trade has been discovered since about 1960. Earlier knowledge was limited to European traders aboard ships or in the fortified trading posts and occasional trading towns like Saint Louis in Senegal or Luanda in Angola. Recent research makes it possible to recognize these posts as part of a number of European militarized trade diasporas – and to recognize the subspecies sent to Africa as part of a larger family of European seaborne and militarized trade diasporas that were the main vehicle of Europe's trade with Asia and Africa between the mid-sixteenth century and the late eighteenth. Recent research on trade within Africa makes it clear that these European trade diasporas, normally limited to coastal transit markets, dealt principally with African trade diasporas, which fed them with gold, slaves, ivory, and other products for export in return for European and Asian manufactures.[29]

Cross-cultural trade on the coast was organized in much the same way as cross-cultural trade at major transit markets in the interior. From their first visits to the African coast, Europeans recognized the need for some kind of cross-cultural brokers. Though they began with naive solutions, like kidnapping a few Africans for training in Europe as interpreters, they soon shifted. Even before the end of the fifteenth century, Portuguese shippers began to leave crewmen on shore between voyages to bargain with the "natives" and gather a cargo ready for loading at the next visit. These were the earliest "stayers" of the Portuguese African trade diasporas.

Before long, this pattern gave way to more elaborate shore establishments where European shore personnel performed the functions of African landlord-brokers, and African landlord-brokers soon appeared in these same port towns to serve the needs of African traders from the

---

[28] Jan Vansina, *The Tio Kingdom of the Middle Congo 1880–1892* (London, 1973), pp. 247–81, 283–312, and esp. pp. 259–65; Robert W. Harms, *River of Wealth, River of Sorrow: The Central Zaire Basin in the Era of the Slave and Ivory Trade, 1500–1891* (New Haven, Conn., 1981), esp. pp. 2–3 and 24–33.

[29] For a treatment of these alien trade diasporas over time in a single coastal region, see P. D. Curtin, *Senegambia*, 1:92–152.

interior. In the sixteenth and seventeenth centuries, the shore-based Europeans tended to learn the local language and to take local wives. Because the disease environment was extremely dangerous to newly arrived Europeans, few lived long enough to become really conversant with African ways of life. As a result, much of the actual cross-cultural intercession was carried out by Afro-Europeans and their descendants, many of whom became prominent merchants associated principally with African society.[30] The trade languages tended to be a Portuguese creole in early centuries and English-based creole or even English or French later on. Sometimes, not only Afro-Europeans but also local, coastal Africans learned enough about European culture to take over the role of broker, becoming, in effect, like the Tio of Stanley Pool, brokers who acted for moving traders from all directions.[31]

Because the modes of bargaining on the West African coast were drawn more often from African than from European culture, Western historians have sometimes misunderstood what was happening. In Senegambia and again in the region of Dahomey and the Gold Coast, prices quoted for European products in local currencies tended to stabilize in the early eighteenth century and to remain stable for decades on end. This created the impression that prices must have been controlled. This, in turn, suggested a pattern of "marketless" trade where prices were established by something other than the play of supply and demand, however modified by monopoly and imperfect competition.[32] In fact, this price stability was only apparent. Although the "price" attached to each type of European import was unchanging, both African and Eu-

---

[30] For examples see P. D. Curtin, *Senegambia*, 1:112–21, 1:136–9; Christopher Fyfe, *A History of Sierra Leone* (London, 1962), see index under "Caulker"; Margaret Priestley, *West African Trade and Coast Society: A Family Study* (London, 1969).

[31] For African-run brokerage institutions see Phyllis M. Martin, *The External Trade of the Loango Coast, 1576–1870: The Effects of Changing Commercial Relations on the Vili Kingdom of Loango* (Oxford, 1972), pp. 93–115; Werner Peukert, *Der Atlantische Sklavenhandel von Dahomey 1740–1797: Wirtschaftsanthropologie und Sozialgeschichte* (Wiesbaden, 1978), pp. 108–19.

[32] In particular, this led Karl Polanyi into an elaborate discussion of the Dahomean port of Whydah (or Ouidah) as a "port of trade," controlled by a powerful and centralized state in the hinterland. According to Polanyi, royal officials at the port arranged prices, administered the port and maintained it as a neutral zone from which Europeans were seldom allowed to stray. He saw this, in short, as the central feature of a complex, centralized, archaic economy, based on state slave raiding, with redistribution of the proceeds as a major support of the state. See K. Polanyi, in collaboration with Abraham Rotstein, *Dahomey and the Slave Trade: An Analysis of an Archaic Economy* (Seattle, 1966). Later research has shown, unfortunately, that Polanyi misunderstood the evidence. The state did not have a monopoly over the slave trade. Rather than being administered, the economy as a whole responded to market considerations with roughly the same social and economic complexity that might be found in early European market economies. See Peukert, *Atlantische Sklavenhandel*; Patrick Manning, *Slavery, Colonialism and Economic Growth in Dahomey, 1640–1960* (Cambridge, 1982).

ropean traders knew that they fluctuated in Europe and in local markets in Africa. Each therefore sought to adjust the assortment of goods he bought or sold to the true prices in European or African markets. Europeans tried to unload goods with low European prices. Africans tried to buy goods with a combination of high African and low European values.

The result was an elaborate form of assortment bargaining. Typically, the two parties or their respective brokers would meet and decide first of all the price to be paid for export commodities (slaves, gold, or whatever) expressed in whatever local currency of account might be in fashion – the fictional "trade ounce" of gold on the Gold Coast or Dahomey, "bars" of iron in Senegambia, and so on. This initial price decision was based on supply, demand, condition of the merchandise, and the like. The result of this first bargaining was a total value for the export goods, expressed in bars, ounces, or other local currency. Since the bar or ounce prices of these commodities were set by custom, the next step was to agree on the assortment of European goods that would make up the payment. And here supply and demand entered the bargaining about assortment of goods taken in payment, not about the price per unit.[33]

These African systems of assortment bargaining on the coast resembled other forms of quantity bargaining found widely in West Africa. The fact that they prevailed into the eighteenth century, wherever Africans and Europeans exchanged goods, probably reflects the dominance of Africans in the role of broker all along the west coast. That, in turn, no doubt reflects the difficulties of the African disease environment for European visitors at any time up to the second half of the nineteenth century.

Beginning in the late eighteenth century, however, customs began to change. New forms of currency and new forms of bargaining began to find their way into African trade, as the commercial culture of Europe in the early industrial age became ever more dominant throughout the global world of commerce. Some new trade diasporas were to be founded even later, but the worldwide era of the trade diaspora was coming to an end. In this sense, African trade diasporas of the nineteenth century were the last in a long process. It is now time to go back to look at its beginnings.

[33] Marion Johnson, "The Ounce in Eighteenth-Century West African Trade," *Journal of African History*, 7:197–214 (1966); P. D. Curtin, *Senegambia*, 1:233–70.

4

Ancient trade

Trade and exchange in human societies are certainly as old as the first human beings. A search for the beginning of organized trade, however, cannot and probably need not go back beyond the beginning of the agricultural revolution. About 10,000 B.C., the first agricultural communities began to emerge in the Middle East, leading by about 3500 B.C. to the first urban civilization in the river valleys of Mesopotamia. The rich, alluvial soils of the lower Tigris and Euphrates river valleys were ideal for farming, though the region was far too arid for farming without irrigation water from the rivers. The developed irrigation system that emerged in the fourth millennium B.C. included plows and a range of domesticated crops that made it possible to free as much as 10 percent of the population from the necessity of agricultural work. These people could then go into manufacturing, trade, the priesthood, political administration, or full-time military occupations.

This earliest urban society in Mesopotamia was followed shortly by other, similar societies. Early dynastic Egypt had joined by about 3000 B.C. A third riverine civilization flourished in the Indus valley of present-day Pakistan between about 2500 and 1500 B.C. All three of these western Asian or northeastern African societies had so much in common in their technology and in other aspects of culture that historians assume some degree of intercommunication at a very early date.

In China and the New World, agriculture and then urban societies came a little later, presumably with more independent development. In the New World, the major American centers of Middle America and the Andean region of South America apparently had little or no contact with one another until quite a late stage of their pre-Columbian history. In China the earliest urban society is usually dated to about 2500 to 1500 B.C. for the Huang Ho or Yellow River valley of northern China, with the earliest known written evidence dating to about the fourteenth century B.C. A Middle American agricultural revolution can be dated to about the second millennium B.C., only slightly later than China, and new archaeological evidence may well push both dates back a little.

Although Chinese and Middle American civilizations developed separately from those of the Middle East, Robert Adams has argued persuasively that early urban societies after the agricultural revolution tended to pass through stages of growth and development that have a good deal in common. As a demonstration, he used the examples of southern Mesopotamia and central Mexico to show similar processes, even though the possibility of significant direct influence of one on the other has to be considered impossible. And the absolute chronology was, in any case, quite different. The Mexican pattern of about 100 B.C. to 1500 A.D. paralleled what had already happened in Mesopotamia from about 3900 to 2300 B.C.[1]

Mesopotamian trade

The main lines of early urban society in Mesopotamia are knowable only through archaeology. The earliest urban civilization appeared in Sumer, in the far southeast of Mesopotamia bordering the Persian Gulf, and Sumerians continued as the dominant cultural force in southern Mesopotamia from before 3000 to about 2000 B.C. Political stability over such a long period would have been impossible, but a style of political life appears to have been consistent over a remarkably long time. The fundamental political unit was the city-state, with Ur, on the gulf, the most important of the Sumerian cities most of the time. Periodic invasions by people speaking Semitic languages swept over Mesopotamia, but the invaders were absorbed each time and converted to most aspects of the Sumerian culture.

From time to time, one city or another would establish a kind of hegemony over all or most of the two river valleys. Sargon, ruler of Akkad, in middle Mesopotamia near Babylon, did so in the 2300s B.C., though the political and military events of this period are so overlaid with legend they have to be accepted with a considerable margin for error. Sargon's descendants remained dominant until the mid-2100s B.C., when they, in turn, fell to newer "barbarian" invaders. A few decades later, from about 2125 to 2000 B.C., Sumer once more established its dominance over the rivers – a time period called the Third Dynasty of Ur.

The Third Dynasty of Ur marks the final appearance of the Sumerians on the historical stage. It was also the classical age for the civilization

---

[1] Robert McC. Adams, *The Evolution of Urban Society* (Chicago, 1965).

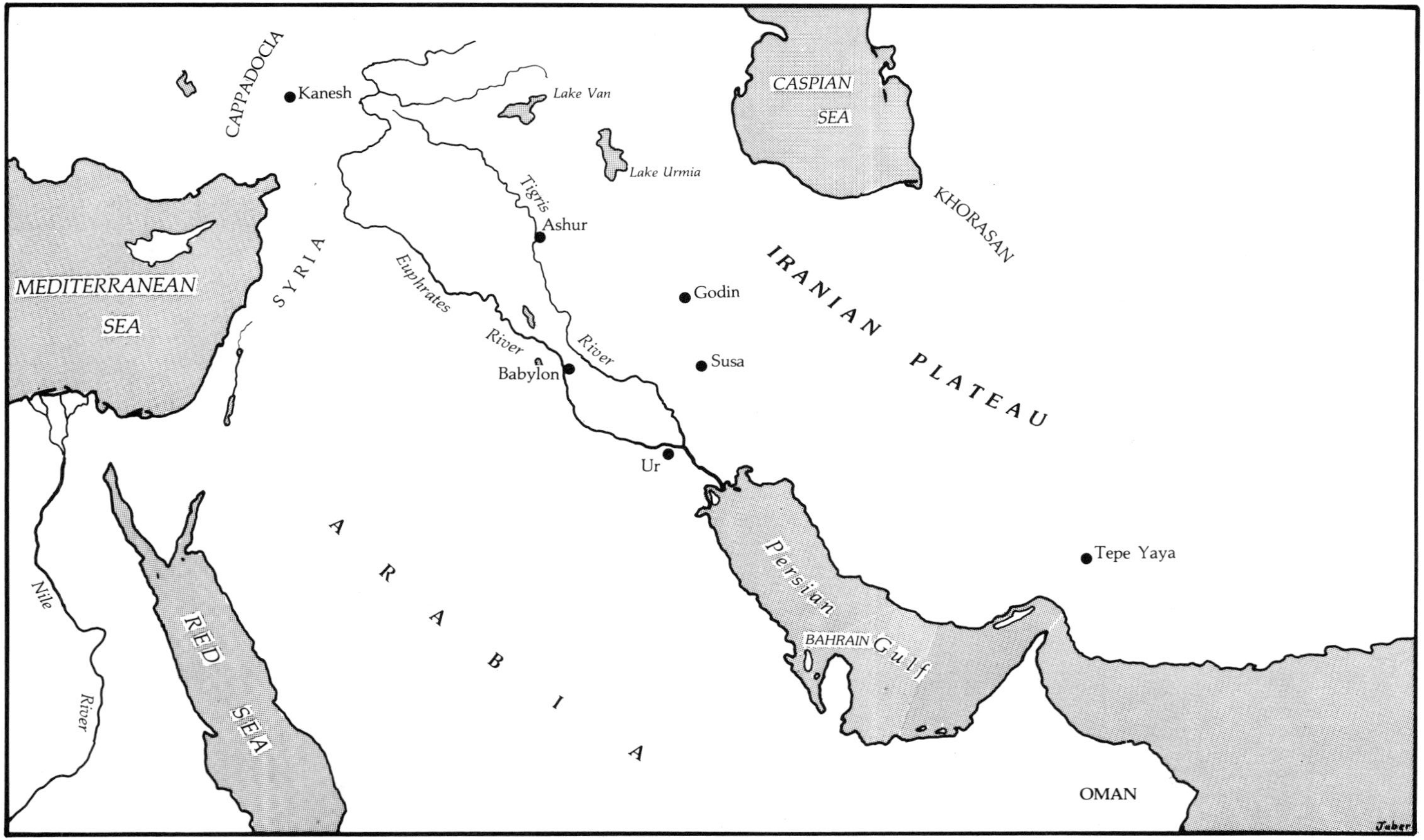

Map 4.1. The ancient Middle East

they had created and maintained through changing times for over a thousand years. It was, in addition, the first period of extensive written records. Tens of thousands of documents have survived on clay tablets of various sizes and shapes, written in the Sumerian language in cuneiform script.

These documents can now be read, though not many scholars actually do so. One effect is that narrow research results have sometimes led to broad interpretive hypotheses, which have then held the field for decades before new research appeared to challenge them. One such theory of special importance for early economic history is the hypothesis of the Sumerian temple economy. It was first developed by Anton Deimal in the 1920s, then modified by others over a half century, until it was finally demolished by a combination of archaeological and historical research in the 1970s.[2] It depicts a society run by the priests of the temples on bureaucratic and even despotic lines. The temples controlled most of the arable land. They recruited labor and allocated it to keep a complex irrigation system going. The system drew labor from the adult population as a whole, then redistributed the product to all, including the very old and the very young who could not support themselves. Barley was the principal crop, but the temple economy produced and redistributed oil, wool, dairy products, fish, vegetables, dates, fruit, beer, and wine. Nonagricultural workers also made textiles, leather goods, pottery, and metal objects in gold, silver, and bronze.[3]

Any economy of this complexity obviously involved a lot of exchange, but this theory held that exchange was controlled by the priesthood, who employed a staff of temple servants called *tamkaru* (sing. *tamkarum*) to carry out commercial functions – on the temple's account, not their own. The theory assumed that most exchange was either simple reciprocity, or redistribution by central authorities. Little or no place was left for operation of a market, with fluctuating prices responding to changes in supply and demand.

Recent research has demolished most important elements of this picture. Archaeological work, especially that of Robert Adams, has shown that large-scale irrigation works had not yet come into existence at this early period. Therefore, the need for bureaucratic organizations to run a "hydraulic" society was simply not there.[4] The hypothesis that virtually

---

[2] Deimal's research was mainly published in articles in *Analecta Orientalia* through the 1920s. It is summarized in his monograph "Sumerische Tempelwirtschaft zur Zeit Urukaginas und seiner Vorganger," *Analecta Orientalia*, 2(n.s.):71–113 (1931).

[3] This view dominated prominent texts like Tom B. Jones, *Ancient Civilization* (Chicago, 1960), or Jacquetta Hawks and Sir Leonard Wooley, *Prehistory and the Beginnings of Civilization* (New York, 1963), vol. I of the UNESCO *History of Mankind*.

[4] Adams, *Urban Society*, passim; Robert McC. Adams, *Heartland of Cities: Surveys of Ancient Settlement and Land Use on the Central Floodplain of the Euphrates* (Chicago, 1981), esp. pp. 243–8.

all land belonged to temples originated with Deimal's investigation of a single archive, one he took to be associated with a temple for the goddess Bau in the early twenty-fourth century B.C. Later research showed, first, that most land actually belonged to private individuals, including women. Private people had controlled land from the beginning of Mesopotamian history down through the Third Dynasty of Ur. State control over the economy become important only in later times.[5] Finally, new investigations showed that markets and fluctuating prices could be found in Mesopotamia at least as early as the end of the fourth millennium B.C., even though redistributive and reciprocal arrangements may also have existed.[6]

Other evidence shows long-distance trade, and not simply local exchange, far into the past, even though some detail is obscure before the Third Dynasty of Ur. Some of the recent evidence comes from new statistical methods in archaeology,[7] but older methods also turn up objects in Mesopotamian sites that could not possibly have had a local origin. Seashells from the Indian Ocean at least 1500 kilometers away have been found in datable fifth-millennium sites in northern Syria. Or, for about the same period, large quantities of obsidian have been found on the upper Tigris, where the closest possible source had to be eastern Anatolia about 600 kilometers away. Urban Mesopotamia developed some of the most skilled metallurgical craftsmen of the early Bronze Age, yet southern Mesopotamia had no local source of copper, which had to come from the part of the Iranian plateau just to the south of the Caucasus Mountains. Other goods of Iranian origin also found their way into Mesopotamia as early as 3000 B.C., including alabaster, carnelian, chloritite, mother-of-pearl, marble, obsidian, and turquoise.[8]

Without written records it is hard to be certain how this trade was carried on – through trade or relay trade, to mention only two possibilities. Harvey Weiss and T. Cuyler Young, Jr., however, found evidence on the Iranian plateau suggesting an early trade diaspora dating

[5] I. J. Gelb, "On the Alleged Temple and State Economies in Ancient Mesopotamia," in *Studi in Onore di Edouardo Volterra*, 6 vols. (Rome, 1969), 6:137–54; Benjamin Foster, "A New Look at the Sumerian Temple State," *Journal of the Economic and Social History of the Orient*, 24:225–41 (1981).

[6] C. C. Lamberg-Karlovsky, "Third Millennium Modes of Exchange and Production," in Jeremy A. Sabloff and C. C. Lamberg-Karlovsky (eds.), *Ancient Civilization and Trade* (Albuquerque, N. Mex., 1975); M. A. Powell, "Sumerian Merchants and the Problem of Profit," *Iraq*, 39:23–9 (1977); Benjamin R. Foster, "Commercial Activity in Sargonic Mesopotamia," *Iraq*, 39:31–44 (1977).

[7] See, e.g., the articles in Timothy K. Earle and Jonathan E. Ericson (eds.), *Exchange Systems in Prehistory* (New York, 1977).

[8] M. G. L. Mallowan, "The Mechanics of Ancient Trade in Western Asia," *Iran*, 3:1–9 (1965); T. W. Beale, "Early Trade in Highland Iran: A View from the Source," *World Archaeology*, 5:133–48 (1973).

to about 3200 B.C., apparently the earliest discovered so far. Their excavation of the mound at Godin V showed that people whose culture closely resembled that of Susa in lowland Mesopotamia inhabited the top of the mound, whereas people of the lower town surrounding the mound used artifacts typical of the local Iranian culture. Weiss and Young suggest that the Godin V enclosure was in fact a Susanian trading post, supported by a local agricultural village, and that the Susanian-appearing materials were made on the spot by resident Susanians. The trading post probably served as a stop along the road to Khorasan, where Susa traders would have gone to tap the northern sources of lapis lazuli and other minerals.[9]

Other Iranian excavations also help to illuminate patterns of Mesopotamian long-distance trade in these preliterate centuries. About 2800 B.C., chloritite or steatite stone bowls were produced in great numbers near the present Tepe Yaya in southwestern Iran, about 800 kilometers from the Mesopotamian centers of that time. Yet more of these turn up in archaeological finds in Mesopotamia than near the center of production, suggesting regular production for export in order to meet a Mesopotamian economic demand. The evidence also suggests that traders of the same culture that produced these bowls carried them for sale in the center of the economic world of that period, in much the same way that African specialized producers of dates or iron carried their products to the more multifunctional centers in *their* economic world (see Chapter 2).[10]

A little later in time, in about 2600–2500 B.C., similar stone bowls are found even more widely scattered through the whole region from present-day Soviet Uzbekistan in the northeast, to the Indus valley to the southeast, and west to present-day Syria. Some of these were certainly produced at Tepe Yaya, but many were not. They are so similar in style and so widely scattered, moreover, that they have been called the intercultural style. Their numbers and extent, taken with other evidence, suggest an elaborate network of trade, probably carried by professional traders and operating through market exchange, though some of the merchants may have acted as agents for temples or for political authorities who also wanted to profit from trade.[11] Available archaeological evidence suggests that the trade was probably indirect to some degree – that people from intermediate points like Tepe Yaya may well have

[9] Harvey Weiss and T. Cuyler Young, Jr., "The Merchants of Susa: Godin V and Plateau-Lowland Relations in the Late Fourth Millennium," *Iran*, 13:1–16 (1975).

[10] C. C. Lamberg-Karlovsky, "Third Millennium Modes of Exchange and Production," in Sabloff and Lamberg-Karlovsky (eds.), *Ancient Civilization and Trade*.

[11] Philip L. Kohl, "The Balance of Trade in Southwestern Asia in the Mid-Third Millennium B.C.," *Current Anthropology*, 19:463–92 (1978).

reached both directions and thus served as a trade diaspora connecting the Indus valley civilization with Mesopotamia, in circumstances where comparatively few Mesopotamians visited the Indus valley, or the reverse. Other possible intermediaries were seafaring people of the Persian Gulf, perhaps including the important group of maritime traders that was to use the island of Bahrain as their major entrepôt after the fall of Ur. Some archaeologists, indeed, have suggested that intermediary commercial links by sea and by land may well have been the *cause* of urban civilization in the Indus valley, not merely its result.[12]

One of the many fanciful stories about Sargon of Akkad in the late 2300s B.C. tells of an expedition to rescue a colony of merchants from Akkad, who were being mistreated by a local ruler somewhere in Anatolia. The story was long regarded as mythical, but recent excavations in northern Syria and again at Ashur in northern Mesopotamia indicate that Sargon's dynasty apparently maintained fortresses in the direction of central Anatolia, even though there is no evidence of Akkadian rule over these regions. The evidence suggests at least the possibility of a militarized trade diaspora or trading-post empire stretching overland to the northwest.[13]

Other traders came to Akkad by sea. Sargon boasted that ships from Oman sailed directly to the riverbanks of his capital, bringing copper and other exotic products, including beads, semiprecious stones, and ivory that may have come from as far away as India – most of these products coming by way of the entrepôt island of Bahrain.[14] Once again, the long-distance traders appear to have been from the less multifunctional society, carrying their goods to the economic centers of that time.

About 2000 B.C., when the Third Dynasty of Ur collapsed, Mesopotamia fell into a period of political disunity, only to be reunited after about 1900 B.C. by a new, Amorite dynasty of Semitic and probably nomadic origin. It established itself in Babylon and ruled over most of central and eastern Mesopotamia until a little after 1600. This Amorite period is also known as the Old Babylonian period. The most significant single piece of evidence about it is a legal code attributed to Hammurabi, the sixth of the Amorite kings, who may have ruled from about 1792 to 1750 B.C. By this time, Mesopotamian traders reached to the Mediterranean coast near Aleppo (now Haleb) in northern Syria. The seaborne trade of Ur also extended into the Persian Gulf as far as Bahrain, still an important center for the exchange of Mesopotamian foodstuffs and

---

[12] C. C. Lamberg-Karlovsky, "Trade Mechanisms in Indus-Mesopotamian Interrelations," *Journal of the American Oriental Society*, 2:222–9 (1972).
[13] M.G.L. Mallowan, "Mechanics of Ancient Trade," pp. 1–2.
[14] M.G.L. Mallowan, "Mechanics of Ancient Trade," pp. 1–7; A. L. Oppenheim, "The Seafaring Merchants of Ur," *Journal of the American Oriental Society*, 74:6–17 (1954).

textiles for copper, in particular. Minerals were always in short supply in the river valleys; they came not only by sea from Oman and beyond, but also from the Caucasus, Anatolia, and the Iranian plateau.[15]

The Amorite conquest led to drastic changes in the Mesopotamian economic organization. Whatever the past economic role of the state and of the temples, it was now greatly reduced. Temples were no longer a dominant source of capital and most royal monopolies ended. A class of *tamkaru*, now independent merchants, became dominant in trade, brokerage, and moneylending. Surviving contracts from Ur show something of the relationships between the capitalists of Ur and the merchants who actually took their goods to sea. Loans for a single voyage were customary, and it was sometimes possible to arrange ways of dividing the risk among a number of investors. Another way of reducing risk for the lender was to make the traveling merchant responsible for repayment of a loan, regardless of the outcome of the voyage.

Hammurabi's code shows the tamkarum sometimes traveling with his goods, sometimes staying in one place and sending his goods out with a traveling agent, sometimes financing the trade of others, as was possible in Ur as well. The government still participated directly in the trade in food, though it used the independent tamkaru as its agents. It also taxed trade and maintained some forms of commercial control, but most trade was carried out as private enterprise.[16]

Assyrian traders into Anatolia

Rich as the evidence is for the Old Babylonian period, it tells little in detail about the traders who went abroad and who may have encountered some of the problems of cross-cultural trade. For nearly the same period, however, in the twentieth century B.C., archaeological finds in the Cappadocian region of Anatolia provide extremely detailed evidence of a trade diaspora operating from Assyria into Cappadocia – the earliest documentary evidence of a trade diaspora.

The Assyrians were hill people, living on the northern fringes of Mes-

[15] Oppenheim, "Merchants of Ur," pp. 8–12; W. F. Leemans, *Foreign Trade in the Old Babylonian Period* (Leiden, 1960).

[16] Oppenheim, "Merchants of Ur," pp. 8–12; W. F. Leemans, *The Old Babylonian Merchant: His Business and His Social Position* (Leiden, 1950). Karl Polanyi, apparently under the strong impression of the now-discarded "temple economy," wrote an article on "Marketless Trade in Hammurabi's Time," in Karl Polanyi et al., *Trade and Markets in Early Empires* (New York, 1957). In spite of the title, he did not actually cite Hammurabi's code and therefore missed its contrary evidence. He also reached the conclusion that the Akkadian language had no word for market. That was not so. Because so much of Babylonian trade moved by river, the word for market is the word for quay (*karum*), which is also a root for the word for merchant. See Leemans, *Foreign Trade*, p. 1n.

opotamia, though related to the Akkadian, Amorite, and other Semitic-speaking immigrants. They were only occasionally incorporated into the various empires that controlled the river valleys from time to time. In the eighth century B.C., Assyria was to build an empire on its own – the one that appears in the Bible – though that was still a thousand years in the future. In the twentieth century B.C., Ashur was merely a city-state whose people were active in trade. Written records mention a ruler, who was also the principal judge and who ruled with the concurrence of three distinct bodies of citizens: one known as the elders, one as "the town," and the third as the *karum*, the Akkadian word for quay, hence market, but in this usage meaning the people of the market, that is, the body of merchants who administered the commercial center of the city. The karum levied taxes on the trade in copper. It bought and sold copper for its corporate account, and it made loans to private merchants as well. It kept a warehouse of karum property, and the warehouse was also available to private merchants who needed a place to store their goods. It also held goods or money on account for private merchants. The karum, in short, acted as a bank of deposit, a center for export and import, a clearinghouse, and a chamber of commerce all rolled into one.[17]

The records that make it possible to reconstruct the operations of an Assyrian trade diaspora, however, are not those from Ashur itself but an exceedingly rich collection of clay tablets discovered at Kultepe in Turkey, beginning in the 1920s and added to steadily through the excavations of the Turkish Department of Antiquities. By the early 1970s, some 3,000 were available in published form, and another 15,000 were awaiting publication. These documents show that Kultepe is the site of the ancient Kanesh, a settlement of Assyrian merchants. Kanesh was, indeed, the chief merchant settlement for a network of at least twenty other Assyrian commercial settlements in central and western Anatolia.[18]

Ashur's reason for commercial expansion in this direction was the fact that Anatolia produced gold, silver, and copper, but had no tin, which was also essential for making bronze. Ashur wanted metals, especially the gold and silver of the Anatolian highlands, and it had access to tin from the Iranian plateau and textiles from Babylonia, as well as its own craft products. The Assyrians in Kanesh bought copper as well as gold and silver, but they traded much of the copper in other parts of Anatolia,

[17] Paul Garelli, *Les Assyriens en Cappadoce* (Paris, 1963), pp. 172–7, 198.
[18] K. R. Veenhoff, *Aspects of Old Assyrian Trade and its Terminology* (Leiden, 1972), pp. xxi ff. The time span of the collection of documents is approximately 1940–1740 B.C. (Nimet Ozguc, "Assyrian Trade Colonies in Anatolia," *Archaeology*, 22:250–5 [1969].)

in effect using their commercial services to build up foreign exchange from what would now be called invisible exports.[19]

Asia Minor at this period was a mosaic of rival city-states. Even though one or another might rise in power from time to time and establish its hegemony over its neighbors, the resulting "empire" tended to be an incorporative state that left the annexed units under the control of their own princes, not under the continuous authority of a centralized bureaucracy. The position of foreign merchants was therefore much the same, whether the Anatolian states were grouped or completely independent from one another. The Assyrian commercial documents refer to local authorities as "the palace," and they leave no doubt that the local princes were masters in their own houses, whereas Assyrian traders were merely guests – welcome guests, no doubt, but guests that traded and traveled under the ultimate authority of the palace.

This meant that the palace was in a position to collect a variety of protection payments, and it may well have tried to collect as much as the traffic would bear. The Assyrians also had some bargaining advantages of their own. Too much pressure could send them elsewhere, since no one state could control all the sources of Anatolian metals. The visiting merchants also had their own corporate organization to act for the group. It took the form of a network of *karu*, hierarchically arranged. At the head was the *karum* in Ashur itself, below that the karum in Kanesh, and still further down the line a number of other karu in other Anatolian towns.

In Kanesh, for example, the karum dealt with the local prince in the name of all Assyrian merchants, and the palace was a large buyer of textiles, sometimes tin as well. When a caravan arrived, it had to go first to the palace, where the palace officials bargained collectively with the karum officials to set a special price, a price that obviously incorporated elements of "protection costs" and other charges. The palace, for example, stored some goods for merchants in its own warehouses. It had credit relations with Assyrian traders – more often as a borrower than a lender, but it did sometimes lend goods for commercial purposes. It also furthered trade in other ways, like policing the roads and helping creditors collect debts.

The bargained, official, or palace, price, however, applied only to a part of the total cargo, usually one-tenth. The Assyrians carried what remained down to their own quarter of the town, where it was sold on the open market. If the palace wanted to buy more, it had to pay the

[19] M. T. Larsen, *Old Assyrian Caravan Procedures* (Istanbul, 1967), pp. 3 ff.; Garelli, *Les Assyriens*, pp. 26–7, 233–40, 265 ff.

market price. At that level, trade was in the hands of individual merchants. The karum represented their collective interests but did not trade on its own account. It was not a commercial company but rather a guild organized to protect the interests of merchants who traded beyond the political authority of their own rulers. Nor were the tamkaru agents for the state or for temples, as may sometimes have been the case at the time of the Third Dynasty of Ur.[20]

Broadly speaking, the Assyrian merchants were divided into movers and stayers, as in many other trade diasporas. Some lived in the Anatolian merchant colonies and rarely returned to Ashur. Others moved back and forth with the caravans. Both types, however, traded on their own account and occasionally acted for third parties. Moneylenders in Ashur, who rarely went on the road themselves, put out capital to those who did. At times, groups would form to spread the risk of loss. They might entrust a sizable sum to a young, traveling merchant with the understanding that the loss would be theirs, but he would get one-third of the profits if there were any. In the same way, a stayer in Anatolia could use the travelers to do business for him in Ashur. Loans resembling loans at interest were also common, making it possible for a traveling merchant to take the whole risk and keep the whole profit beyond his interest payments. Temples sometimes financed trade, but not on their own account. The trader was the entrepreneur. The temple simply got back its capital plus interest.[21]

Karl Polanyi took the trading post at Kanesh as a prime example of marketless trade, a cross-cultural "port of trade" where prices were not allowed to fluctuate but were fixed by treaty. Unfortunately, he had to work from the early and incomplete studies of the Kultepe tablets. Even more, he was led astray by the dominance of the now-displaced hypothesis of a Mesopotamian temple economy. All later authorities who have studied the Kultepe tablets portray an economic order where merchants were extremely sensitive to small changes in price, where prices fluctuated rapidly, and where political authorities interfered in trade as much as they could to suit their particular interests – but never to the extent of successfully suppressing the underlying play of supply and demand, though here as elsewhere in the history of commerce, protection costs were an inescapable cost of doing business.[22]

[20] Garelli, Les Assyriens, pp. 233–40.
[21] Larsen, Caravan Procedures, pp. 4–5; Garelli, Les Assyriens, pp. 248–56.
[22] Garelli, Les Assyriens, pp. 265 ff.; Larsen, Caravan Procedures, p. 153; Veenhoff, Old Assyrian Trade, pp. 348–57; Robert McC. Adams, "Anthropological Reflection on Ancient Trade," Current Anthropology, 15:239–57 (1974).

Ancient trade in Egypt and the eastern Mediterranean

People began to move around by boat on the Mediterranean by about 7000 B.C., long before anything that could be described as an urban civilization had come into existence. Even without written records, physical remains tell a good deal about nonperishable goods they traded, but very little about the affairs of, or even the existence of, the merchants who must have done the trading. Obsidian, the black volcanic glass that flakes easily into blades, is an excellent indicator of early trade. In the absence of metallic tools, it was extremely valuable. It is also sufficiently rare in nature to be easily traced to a few sources. The island of Melos, about halfway between Athens and Crete, is the only Aegean source of obsidian. It begins to turn up in sites dated as early as 6500 B.C. on Crete and 6000 B.C. on the Greek mainland. Melos itself appears to have been uninhabited at this time, which suggests that strangers came there expressly to mine the obsidian.

Meanwhile, some of the techniques of farming and urban life that had first appeared in Mesopotamia appeared in Egypt as well, and from about 3600 to 3000 B.C. the different and characteristic civilization of the Nile valley began to take shape. Trade must have begun in this same period, since predynastic goods (from the period before about 3100 B.C.) have been found in Byblos on the coast of present-day Lebanon. Trade above the village level in the Nile valley itself appears to have been controlled by the state from the earliest dynastic period, but even this is uncertain. Egyptian records say nothing at all about merchants before about 2000 B.C., though historians assume that some large-scale trade was associated with the royal granaries and the officials who controlled them. Egyptian trade with other parts of the eastern Mediterranean was normally under tight government control, but it was also carried out by foreign merchants. Specialists in the history of the ancient Mediterranean tend to assume that here, as in recent Africa or ancient Mesopotamia, the most active of the early traders were not those from the multifunctional core area of the urban civilization but those from more specialized societies with something to sell and a desire for the products of "civilization." Thus, in the early phases of trade with the Nile Delta by sea, it was the Lebanese who brought their timber in return for Egyptian craft work, not Egyptians who went abroad looking for timber.[23]

Recorded Egyptian trade to the south, however, was carried by government expeditions, both up the Nile and up the Red Sea to the leg-

[23] William Culican, *The First Merchant Ventures: The Ancient Levant in History and Commerce* (London, 1966); Chester G. Starr, *The Economic and Social Growth of Early Greece, 800–500 B.C.* (New York, 1977).

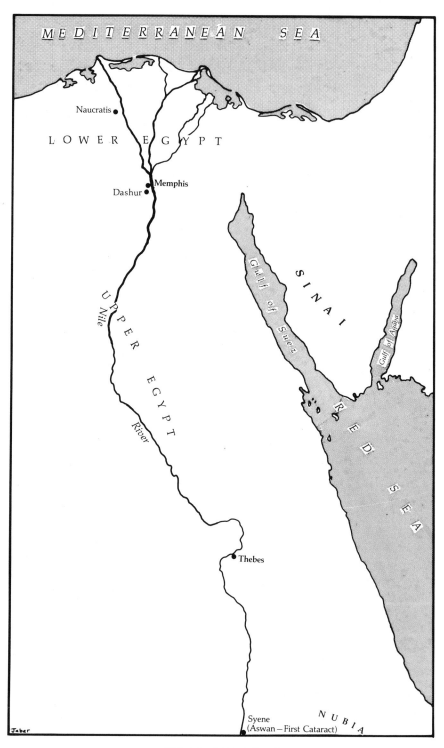

Map 4.2. Ancient Egypt

endary land of Punt, which probably meant both Yemen and the opposite shore in Africa. These official expeditions began about 2500 B.C., but they mainly dealt in exotics like frankincense, ebony, myrrh, and gold. Though individual expeditions often brought these products back in large quantities for that time and place, trade was not continuous. It could disappear for centuries on end only to reappear when the interest of the court changed.

After 3000 B.C. or thereabouts, trade at sea in the eastern Mediterranean also began to increase. Larger collections of obsidian, farther from their sources, turn up in archaeological finds. During the next millennium, an Aegean culture began to take form and to arrive, at about 2000, at social patterns that are at least proto-urban. That is, their principal remains are not cities on the Egyptian or Mesopotamian model, but palaces like the one at Knossos on Crete, or fortifications like those at Mycenae on the Greek mainland or Troy in Asia Minor. These changes, and general population growth around the edge of the Aegean Sea, were based on a new "Mediterranean" array of food crops – principally the combination of wheat, olives, and grapes – and different from those that were most productive in Egypt or Mesopotamia. Bronze technology also appeared, along with a culture ancestral to that of the later Greek civilization, including the Minoan script that is a recognizably early form of Greek.[24]

The period from roughly 2000 down to 1200 B.C. around the Aegean is known as the Minoan-Mycenaean age. Around 2000, trade in early Bronze Age products like wine and olive oil became common enough to suggest that professional merchants were now operating on some scale and presumably for the sake of profit. Remains of a Minoan colony on the island of Kythera suggest that it was an early trading post associated with professionalized trade. By about 1500 B.C., the Mycenaeans dominated the trade of the eastern Mediterranean, leaving the remains of what appear to have been trade enclaves in some of the port towns of the Levant.[25]

The sack of Troy in about 1200 B.C. is an event that can symbolize the end of Aegean prosperity – and of the Minoan-Mycenaean Age. It was only one of a whole set of disasters that seemed to hit the eastern Mediterranean at about this time. Some authorities talk of a Dark Age lasting down to about 750 B.C. In Anatolia, the Hittite government broke down. In the Aegean, piracy and anarchy increased. Egypt, Syria, and

[24] Colin Renfrew, *The Emergence of Civilization: The Cyclades and the Aegean in the Third Millennium B.C.* (London, 1972); C. Renfrew, *Before Civilization: The Radiocarbon Revolution and Prehistoric Europe* (London, 1973), pp. 211–34.
[25] C. Renfrew, *Emergence of Civilization*, pp. 441–60, 473; Donald Harden, *The Phoenicians* (London, 1962)

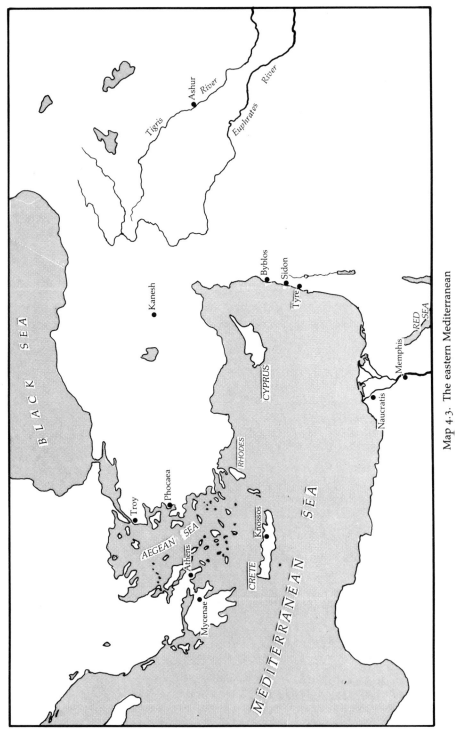

Map 4.3. The eastern Mediterranean

Palestine were all attacked by "barbarians" the Egyptian records refer to as the Sea People. In the European landmass to the northwest, this was a period of broad population movement, including some immigrant invaders of the Greek world. These various invasions and disturbances may not have been connected, but one common element could have been a shift in the climate that brought unaccustomed aridity to places like Crete and exceptional wetness to other parts of the Greek peninsula. Attica, on the other hand, was not touched by the climatic change, though it was certainly affected by the influx of those fleeing from it. Whether or not this particular hypothesis will hold up to further investigation, it is clear that a widespread destruction of peoples and cities and a breakdown of government institutions took place over a wide area.[26]

Greeks and Phoenicians

Literary sources for Aegean trade begin with Homer's oral traditions, probably written down in the eighth century, but pertaining to the Mycenaen world. Homer poses a problem, however, since his work may genuinely reflect the Mycenaean world, or it might have to do with the Dark Age, or even with the emerging world of the Greek city-states in the eighth century – or else all three in some mixture. In any case, the *Iliad* and the *Odyssey* both contain a very strong and negative view of commerce as an occupation. The noble ideal of that period was to gain from warfare or plunder, not by exchange. Trade was better left to foreigners. In the Homeric picture, the trade of the Greek world with the outside was left entirely in the hands of "Phoenicians," which, in the usage of the time, meant Levantines in general. The *agora*, later to become the Greek marketplace, was then only a meeting ground. The word *emporos*, which later meant a maritime trader, then meant only a passenger on a ship.[27]

These antimercantile views were to continue even after the Dark Age. They appear in the works of Aristotle, among other places, and they are reflected in the general Greek attitude toward occupations. That of a landowning farmer was at the top. Trade and nonagricultural manual labor were at the bottom. Trade was, even more, a distinctly dishon-

---

[26] N. K. Sandars, *The Sea Peoples: Warriors of the Ancient Mediterranean, 1250–1150 B.C.* (New York, 1978); Rhys Carpenter, *Discontinuity in Greek Civilization* (Cambridge, 1966); Reid A. Bryson et al., "Drought and the Decline of Mycenae," *Antiquity*, 48:46–50 (1974).

[27] Fritz M. Heichelheim, *An Ancient Economic History: From the Palaeolithic Age to the Migrations of the Germanic, Slavic, and Arabic Nations*, 2 vols. (Leiden, 1958–64), 1:246–7; M. I. Finley, *The World of Odysseus* (New York, 1954), pp. 62–9; M. M. Austin and P. Vidal-Naquet, *Economic and Social History of Ancient Greece* (Berkeley, 1977), pp. 43–4.

orable way to acquire goods, especially trade for the sake of profit rather than direct consumption. No wonder Hermes, the god of thieves, was also the god of merchants.[28] No wonder, either, that the Phoenicians, not the Greeks, emerged as the master traders of the Mediterranean world.

The Phoenicians were originally a Semitic people who had migrated into the Levant from the southeast at an early period, as many other Semites had come to settle in the Fertile Crescent. They were actually only a seagoing and commercial subdivision of the larger body known as Canaanites, and they were not distinguished from the other Canaanites until about 1500 B.C.

Evidence about the Phoenicians is limited, unfortunately, to archaeology and to what other people, often unfriendly witnesses, had to say about them. At the height of Phoenician prosperity, about 1200 to 700 B.C., Phoenician territory on the coast of present-day Lebanon was about 50 kilometers wide and 160 kilometers from north to south. After 700 or so, invaders from the east – like the Babylonians, Assyrians, and others who made life equally unpleasant for the neighboring Hebrews – began to cut into Phoenician territory and independence from landslide. Even after they lost their independence, however, these cities continued to be major maritime trading centers until they were captured by Alexander the Great in about 330 B.C. and merged into the wider Hellenistic world.[29]

The earliest Phoenician trade route linked the Levantine homeland to Egypt, the largest nearby center of economic activity. And the principal trade at this period was in Levantine products like timber, dyes, and textiles. Archaeological evidence of Phoenician trading posts is found in southern Palestine, in the Nile Delta, and up the Nile at least as far as Memphis.

By about 800 B.C., the main lines of the Phoenician trade diaspora to the western Mediterranean began to take shape, partly in response to local Levantine demand for Iberian metals, of which silver was the most important; but the scope of Phoenician trade also became much broader, adding slaves, pottery, and food products like wine and olive oil to the list. The western network centered on Carthage and Utica in present-day Tunisia, the island of Malta, Motya on Sicily, and Cadiz in southern Spain. Smaller settlements in southern Sardinia and the Balearic Islands were used at times.

It seems unlikely that the Phoenicians ever had a single, united state,

---

[28] Austin and Vidal-Naquet, *Ancient Greece*, pp. 11–12; Norman O. Brown, *Hermes the Thief*, 2nd ed. (New York, 1969).

[29] Harden, *Phoenicians*, pp. 44–56; Sabatino Moscati, *The World of the Phoenicians* (London, 1969), pp. 27–52.

even in the Levant. The home cities were independent of one another, even though they would sometimes act in concert. In the west, Carthage, founded about 800 B.C., soon became independent, and so were most of the other nodes in the network, though Carthage controlled part of its own African hinterland and some small enclaves on Sardinia and on the Spanish coast.

Little is known in detail about the Phoenician commercial operations, or about the decline of the system. Rivalry with Greeks in the western basin of the Mediterranean became serious after about 400 B.C. After the loss of the home cities in 330, the struggle between Carthage and Rome for the control of Sicily began in about 270, and Carthaginian influence in politics and commerce declined until the final sack of Carthage and destruction of Carthaginian power in 150–146 B.C.[30]

Meanwhile, the Aegean world had long since reentered the general commercial world of the Mediterranean. Archaeological evidence for the Dark Age after the fall of Mycenae shows comparatively few exotic objects on Aegean shores, and presumably little trade at a distance. Then, after about 800, products like ivory (which was certainly of non-Aegean origin) begin to reappear. Greek ceramics turn up in many different parts of the Mediterranean basin, and Greek goods reappear in the major markets of the Levant.[31]

In Greece itself the earlier Greek disdain for the commercial calling continued, but institutional arrangements evolved to deal with resident foreign merchants. In Athens (and other Greek cities with similar political constitutions) the population came to be divided into three groups: freemen, metics or foreigners, and slaves. By the fifth century B.C., metics, both Greek and non-Greek, were an important part of the Athenian population. One estimate of the fourth century puts them at 10,000, compared to 21,000 citizens, and they were probably more numerous in earlier centuries. Needless to say, all metics were not merchants. The group included artisans of all sorts, and city policy encouraged their immigration, even though metics were excluded from all political rights. They were subject to special taxation. In earlier times, each metic had to have a citizen-patron to represent him in the courts of law.

One further restriction was especially important. Metics could not own land. They were therefore excluded from agriculture and from the whole sphere of credit relations based on land. In time, they developed their own way of dealing with money, not land, and a whole separate sphere of credit and banking grew up – and apart from the anticraft, antimercantile attitudes of the traditional aristocracy. It was out of this part-

---

[30] Harden, *Phoenicians*, esp. 66–75.
[31] Starr, *Early Greece*, pp. 56–8, 60–1.

society of metic merchants that cities like Athens finally developed the commercial tradition that made it possible to enter into the broader world of Mediterranean commerce.[32]

As the Phoenicians had done, Greek cities also founded colonies overseas, but they were mainly for agriculture rather than commerce. A Greek *polis* or city-state would establish a colony settled by its own people, essentially to supply food for themselves and sometimes for the metropolitan city. Trade was secondary. The main areas of colonization were Cyrenaica in North Africa, the shores of Thrace and the Black Sea to the north of the Greek homeland, Sicily, and on the instep and on the toe of the Italian boot to the west.

Some settlements, however, *were* mainly commercial. Such a colony was called an *emporion*, rather than a colony in the usual sense. They were exceptional, and most were founded by the single Greek city of Phocaea, principally in what was to be southern France and northern Spain. The main western base was Massilia (later Marseilles), in much the same way Carthage served as a western base for the Phoenicians. The trading settlements still farther west in Catalonia were founded from Massilia.[33]

Much earlier, Greek merchants had begun trading in the Levant and Egypt. A trade settlement in northern Syria dates back to a little before 800. At Al Mina, they apparently had a trade settlement that was not a regular colony of a particular city, but for Greek merchants in general. A little after 700, another, similar trade settlement was formed in the Nile Delta. In this case, the Pharaoh assigned a site to Greek traders at Naucratis, as a place where the Greeks could build temples to their gods and live under semiautonomous rule by their own community. The Egyptian government required all Greek ships to trade at this point in the western part of the delta, just as it required all Phoenician ships to trade at an equivalent point in the eastern delta. This was, in short, a very early example of the Mediterranean *fundaco* or *funduq*. The town had both a Greek and an Egyptian quarter, but the Greek quarter was overlooked by an Egyptian fort. Ultimate Egyptian control was clear. The earliest political status was that of an emporion, not a polis. As traders came from all over the Greek world, however, a permanent community of Greek residents came into existence. In time, it gained some aspects of status as a polis under Egyptian overrule, though the resident Greeks were its only citizens. Traveling merchants retained their membership, whether as metic or citizen, in the polis they came from.

[32] Austin and Vidal-Naquet, *Ancient Greece*, pp. 99–101, 148–51.
[33] Carl Roebuck, "The Organization of Naukratis," *Classical Philology*, 46:212–20 (1951); M. M. Austin, *Greece and Egypt in the Archaic Age* (Cambridge, 1970).

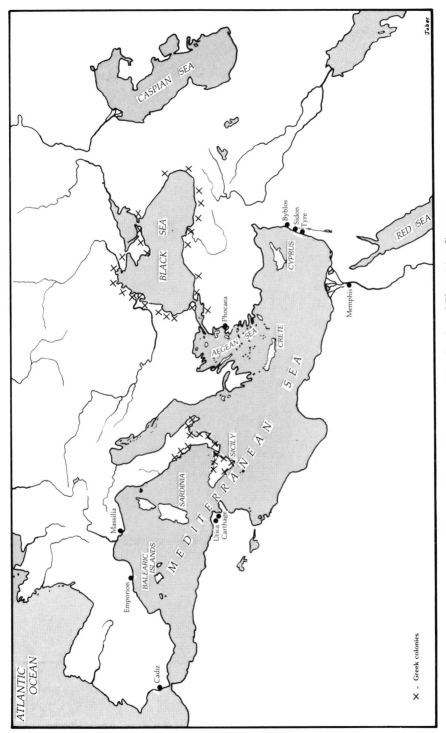

Map 4.4. The mediterranean of the Greek and Phoenician diasporas

X – Greek colonies

By the fifth century, similar and outlying Greek trading enclaves appeared elsewhere in Egypt, notably at Memphis and some minor points. After Alexander the Great conquered Egypt in the fourth century, Naucratis's transition from emporion to polis was complete, but the services of a cross-cultural trade enclave of that kind were no longer required. Trade moved elsewhere, leaving Naucratis as a local Greek community, the fossilized remnant of a trade diaspora that had gone out of business.[34]

By the fifth century, a generalized ecumenical or cross-cultural set of trade practices was coming into existence in the Greek world: Greek culture influenced the whole of the eastern Mediterranean coastline. Trade across the remaining cultural lines was simplified. Shipowners began to offer transportation services for hire, so that a regular professional group of traveling merchants (*emporos*) came into existence. By the beginning of the sixth century, another group called *proxemoi* began to function in the principal ports as professional guarantors and protectors of alien traders on short visits – suggesting the similar functions performed by the landlord-brokers of West Africa. Fragmented political jurisdictions remained a problem, but bilateral agreements between states appear in the fifth century and later, both in the Greek world and between non-Greek states in central Italy.[35]

Then, in the fourth and third centuries B.C., Greek culture began to expand throughout southwestern Asia, into Mesopotamia and what is now Iran, into Egypt as well. For the most part this expansion was peaceful, but Greek soldiers were now recognized as the best in the region and they were sought after eagerly by many Asian rulers. This Hellenization of southwestern Asia and northeastern Africa spread into Italy as well, where the rising power of Rome was also very much under Hellenic influence.

Alexander of Macedonia's conquest of most of this territory in the last decades of the fourth century was made possible in part by prior Hellenization, but it also put an even firmer Hellenic stamp on the cultures of all the peoples around the eastern basin of the Mediterranean and on to the Persian Gulf. With Alexander's conquests, the problems of political jurisdiction weakened, and trade became still more open in the Mediterranean world. In the eastern basin of the sea, Greek became the international language of trade, as Latin was to be in the west.

With these developments, trade diasporas in the sense of the term used here, ceased to exist as a major factor in Mediterranean commerce. They had contributed greatly to the homogenizing of Mediterranean

---

[34] Starr, *Early Greece*, pp. 62–5; Austin and Vidal-Naquet, *Ancient Greece*, pp. 61–8.
[35] Starr, *Early Greece*, pp. 71–6; M. I. Finley, *The Ancient Economy* (Berkeley, 1973), pp. 157 ff.; Heichelheim, *Ancient Economic History*, 1:224–6, 2:35–98.

cultures, but the very fact of cultural convergence meant that they were no longer required as they once had been. From the fourth century B.C. to about the third century A.D., maritime commerce in the Mediterranean passed through a period of nearly continuous technical progress, with changes in ship types, manning scales, and improved infrastructural support from dock facilities, warehouses, artificial ports, and the like.[36] With this, the culture of commerce had become so thoroughly homogenized in the Mediterranean region that open ecumenical trade was possible.

Pre-Columbian trade in the Americas

In spite of the long centuries of isolation from the Afro-Eurasian landmass, Amerindians discovered agriculture and developed urban societies and trade networks at an early date. Archaeological evidence of exotic goods at a distance from the point of origin carries back to 1600 B.C. for the state of Chiapas in southern Mexico, to 1500 B.C. for the Mexican Gulf coast, and a century or so later for the highlands of central Mexico.

From this period onward, archaeologists trace the growth of urban civilization principally through a sequence of style periods in art and architecture. For Middle America (Mexico and Central America taken as a single culture area), they conceive of a Formative Period beginning about 1500 B.C. and continuing to a little before the birth of Christ. A number of separate regions of internal intercommunication came into existence, each with its own style – and presumably a distinct culture. In the highlands of Guatemala and the tropical forests to the north, an early Mayan civilization came into existence. In the highlands from the vicinity of Mexico City southward into the present state of Oaxaca, a quite different civilization began to emerge. Perhaps the most impressive of these Formative cultures was that of the Olmec, who flourished on the gulf coast of Tabasco and southern Vera Cruz from about 800 to 400 B.C. Their jade statues and the gigantic stone heads like those found near La Venta are the basis for this spectacular reputation, though in fact we know next to nothing about their political system or other aspects of their culture.

The earliest known Middle American trade network, however, began at this period and it had connections. The principal evidence is the wide distribution of Olmec objects through other parts of Middle America. This distribution points especially to dense traffic along a corridor lead-

---

[36] For an account of this development see Jean Rougé, *Recherches sur l'organisation du commerce maritime en Mediterranée sous l'empire romain* (Paris, 1966).

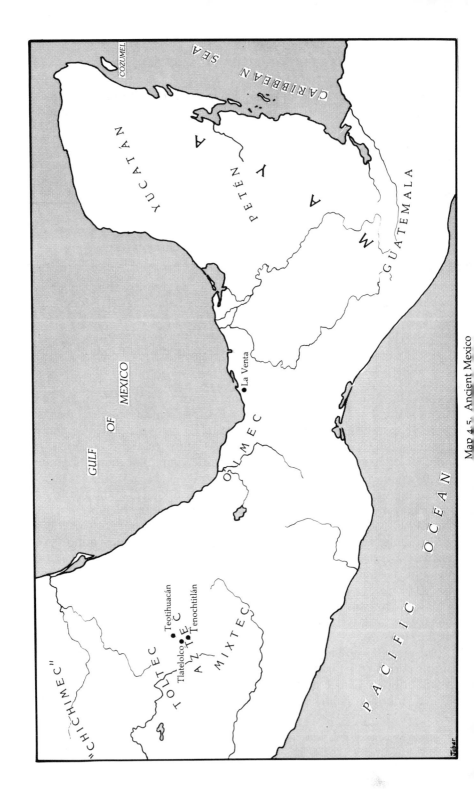

Map 4.5. Ancient Mexico

ing from the gulf coast to the central highlands. Early trade would be expected here, as in Africa when differences in altitude made different crops possible within a short distance. Jade and obsidian, the latter as important here for blades as it was in pre–Bronze Age Greece, were unevenly distributed in nature. Cacao beans from the tropical lowlands were the basis for an important stimulant and beverage. In later times, they also served as a small-change currency. Olmec trade reached many parts of the highlands, but Chalcatzingo, about 120 kilometers southwest of Mexico City, seems, on archaeological evidence, to have been a center for trade from the coast and distribution through the highlands. The ancient city at that location developed about 1600 to 1000 B.C. and flourished down to about 500 B.C. in a region of dense population and apparent wealth.[37]

The Formative Period was followed by one archaeologists label "Classic," which extended from a little before Christ up to about 800 A.D. Maya civilization in Guatemala and at the base of the Yucatan Peninsula reached its greatest achievements. Large urban centers appeared in the valley of Mexico, with Teotihuacán reaching a population in the fifty- to hundred-thousand range. From their artifacts, it appears that the Classic people reached a golden age for Middle America, with denser population and probably a higher income per capita than in the past or the immediate future. Along with this prosperity came a greater intensity of trade. Even people like the lowland Maya, who shared a relatively homogeneous environment and therefore had little reason to trade between nearby communities, traded extensively with the highlands in luxury goods and exotics.[38]

One of the most important trade items was obsidian, and the spatial distribution of obsidian blades in archaeological sites provides some important evidence about the economic sophistication of markets at this early period. Raymond Sidrys directed an ingenious research project in which he and his team measured the size of obsidian blades found in a number of Classic, lowland Maya sites. Blade size is important because of the way blades are flaked from the core of the obsidian by pressure.

[37] R. G. Hirth, "Interregional Trade and the Formation of Gateway Communities," *American Antiquity*, 43:35–45 (1978); Lee A. Parsons and Barbara J. Price, "Mesoamerican Trade and its Role in the Emergence of Civilization," in Robert F. Heizer and John A. Graham (eds.), *Observations on the Emergence of Civilization in Mesoamerica* (Berkeley, 1971). For another hypothesis about Olmec influence see Kent V. Flannery, "The Olmec and the Valley of Oaxaca," in *Dunbarton Oaks Conference on the Olmec* (Washington, D.C., 1968). For Middle American history in general see Eric R. Wolf, *Sons of the Shaking Earth* (Chicago, 1959); Frederick A. Peterson, *Ancient Mexico: An Introduction to the Pre-Hispanic Cultures*, 2nd ed. (New York, 1962); or R. C. Padden, *The Hummingbird and the Hawk: Conquest and Sovereignty in the Valley of Mexico, 1503–41* (Columbus, Ohio, 1967).

[38] Gair Tourtellot and Jeremy A. Sabloff, "Exchange Systems among the Ancient Maya," *American Antiquity*, 37:126–35 (1972).

If the blade maker worked carelessly, as he might do with a relatively cheap raw material, he could save labor time, but the resulting blades would be comparatively heavy in relation to the length of the cutting edge. If the worker took pains and spent longer per blade, it was possible – up to a point – to make blades thinner but just as efficient for cutting, thus economizing on the raw material. Sidrys took the average weight of blades per unit of cutting-edge-length as an index of the care taken in flaking blades. He found that this index decreased systematically with the distance from the source of obsidian, indicating that the individual blade makers responded to increasing costs. He concluded that this implied an efficient flow of market information and a sophisticated exchange network already in place over routes 400 kilometers long.[39]

About 800 A.D., the Classic Period came to an end throughout Middle America. The precise causes of this crisis are not known, and they may not have been the same everywhere. In central Mexico, the trouble seems to have been internal weakness at Teotihuacán combined with an external threat from the north. Semi-nomadic peoples from the more arid regions of northern Mexico began to come across the frontiers into the region of urban civilization, much as the nomadic Semites drifted into the civilized lands of Mesopotamia after the Sumerian period. Among the first were the Toltecs, who established their new highland center at Tula. From about 900 to 1100 A.D., they held off further invasions, but, as they weakened, new invaders called Chichimec (a term equivalent to "barbarians") began to cross the frontiers. A period of confused fighting, destruction, and migration followed, and the violence spread down to the coast and eastward into Yucatan.

By about 1200, the Toltec and Chichimec cultures in the highlands had blended and become a new set of interrelated cultures. The Aztec were dominant in the valley of Mexico, the Mixtec in the south and southeast, and the Toltec remnants and others in the north and west. About the middle of the fourteenth century, Tenochtitlán, an Aztec city-state in the valley of Mexico began to conquer central Mexico, first the valley itself and then a much broader region. The resulting dominion was not a tightly administered empire but the operations of a military machine that used its power to collect tribute. It was, nevertheless, the institution the Spanish found and called the "Aztec Empire" when they arrived in 1519.

That date also marks the effective beginning of written records that deal with trade. The early Spanish accounts of highland Mexico show a society with an extremely well developed market system. The largest

---

[39] Raymond Sidrys, "Supply and Demand among the Classic Maya," *Current Anthropology*, 20:594–7 (1979).

single market, at Tlatelolco near Tenochtitlán (the later Mexico City), had a daily market crowd as large as 60,000 people. Hundreds of different commodities were offered for sale, some local produce and others the result of long-distance trade. And the market network stretched throughout the densely inhabited regions of central Mexico. It must have taken several hundred years to develop, and it continued through the sixteenth century with comparatively little interference from Spanish authorities.[40]

Although the full development of this system cannot be traced, some bits of evidence suggest that a very old trade diaspora of coastal and probably Olmec origin played a significant role. The main evidence is the continued existence in the sixteenth century of a number of trade communities, culturally different from highland peoples, and still living in their separate wards in highland cities – Aztec, Mixtec, and some others. They had assimilated a good deal of highland culture by this time, but they maintained their individual identity and with it some elements of culture otherwise associated with the coast.[41]

The best reported of these commercial communities were the Pochteca, who lived mainly among the Aztec, especially in Tlatelolco and Tenochtitlán. Tlatelolco had only been conquered by Tenochtitlán in 1470. The Aztecs at that time took over the largest market of all, and with it the market people who dominated its long-distance trade as they had dominated the long trade routes for Tenochtitlán itself over some decades. The new rulers recognized the Pochteca as people with a special professional status, higher than the ordinary people, but lower than the Aztec aristocracy.

At the principal markets, many traders were simply local people who brought in their produce for sale. Tenochtitlán had an estimated population of 150,000 to 200,000 at the beginning of the sixteenth century, and much of its food necessarily had to come through the market system. The Pochteca were more concerned with goods to be sold at a distance, or that came from a distance. Following the common practices of other trade diasporas they were divided between a class of comparatively wealthy men who remained in one of the trade enclaves and financed the trade, and a second group who actually traveled the roads with their hired porters. Though they could act as agents for the Aztec state, or for individuals among the Aztec nobility, they normally traveled and traded on their own account. They moved in large groups that took on

[40] Charles Gibson, *The Aztecs Under Spanish Rule* (Stanford, 1964), pp. 352–60; Michael E. Smith, "The Aztec Marketing System and Settlement Pattern in the Valley of Mexico: A Central-Place Analysis," *American Antiquity*, 44:110–25 (1979); Elizabeth M. Brumfiel, "Specialization, Market Exchange, and the Aztec State: A View from Mexotla," *Current Anthropology,,* 21:459–78 (1980).
[41] Miguel Acosta Saignes, "Los Pochteca," *Acta Antropologica*, 1:1–62 (1945), pp. 34–50.

the character of a military expedition, once beyond territory that was tributary to Tenochtitlán. Thus, its protection costs were paid directly in military expenditures to guard caravans.

Many of the older authorities portray the Pochteca as spies, occasional ambassadors, and even a military arm of the Aztec state. This emphasis comes from the account of the sixteenth-century scholar, Bernardino de Sahagun, based on materials he was able to gather in Mexico, of which the Aztec document known as the *Florentine Codex* is especially valuable, devoting a whole, if brief, volume to merchants and craftsmen. The correct interpretation of this document, however, is uncertain. It shows the Pochteca as patriotic pioneers into non-Aztec territory, without clarifying their precise relationship to the Aztec state. Historians and anthropologists who read it with the hypothesis of a Sumerian temple economy as their background knowledge of early trade could view the Pochteca as equivalent to temple agents. Against a background of other trade diasporas and their role in world history, however, it reads more like praise for men who went out along the roads through dangerous territory at the risk of their lives – especially since the document itself makes clear that they acted on their own account as well as that of the nobility or occasionally of the state.[42] If the Pochteca did act militarily for the Aztec state, it may have been an exceptional phase in the centuries-long activity of that trade diaspora – more likely still, an incident in the inevitable need for protection, through self-help by the merchants or purchase from others. In other respects, their relationship to the state granted the Pochteca a fair degree of autonomy. They lived in their own wards in the towns, governed by their own magistrates. Like the karum of Ashur, some of the Pochteca helped to supervise the major markets, acting as appointed officials.[43]

---

[42] Fr. Bernardino de Sahagun, *Florentine Codex. Book 9 – The Merchants* (Salt Lake City, 1959). Translated by C. E. Dibble and A. J. O. Anderson.

[43] It may be surprising that the temple economy hypothesis regarding Mesopotamia could reach as far as the interpretation of Middle American history, but it happened. Anne Chapman took the Pochteca to be state servants on the model of the Mesopotamian temple servants who supposedly acted as trade agents. When the Pochteca went abroad to conduct cross-cultural trade, Chapman interpreted this as an administered trade, conducted in appropriate neutral, "port of trade" enclaves at nonfluctuating, nonmarket prices. (Chapman, "Port of Trade Enclaves in Aztec and Maya Civlization," in Polanyi et al., *Trade and Markets.*) The concept became popular in Middle American archaeological writing, in spite of the fact that Chapman herself later pointed out that her treatment of the Pochteca was a "descriptive model" based on Sahagun, but her discussion of Middle American ports of trade was a "logical model" based entirely on Polanyi's discussion of the ancient Middle East and on the assumption that people at similar levels of development will have similar institutions. It therefore stands or falls with the hypothesis of a temple economy. (A. Chapman, "Commentary on Mesoamerican Trade and its Role in the Emergence of Civlization," in Robert F. Heizer and John A. Graham [eds.].)

Though the Pochteca had assimilated many aspects of the cultures of their host societies, they kept their own god in preference to Huitzilopochtli, the high god of the Aztecs, whose thirst for human sacrifice has kept him in bad repute among non-Aztecs. Yiacatecutli, the Pochteca god, also demanded human sacrifice, but on a smaller scale. His other attributes suggest a variant of the Toltec god, Quetzalcoatl, the feathered serpent. Other merchant communities of the Mexican highlands also had Toltec features in their culture, but the Pochteca had cultural affinities to the gulf coast as well. It is possible, though not quite solidly demonstrable on present evidence, that the the Pochteca can be traced back to an Olmec trade diaspora into the highlands, which then became partly Toltec in culture at one phase in its history and was becoming increasingly Aztec at the time of the Spanish conquest.[44]

A similar group of commercial specialists lived scattered through Mixtec territory as well. They had their own towns in some instances. In others, they had wards in Mixtec cities. Like the Pochteca, their social status was higher than ordinary people but lower than the aristocracy, which nevertheless valued their presence for the sake of long-distance trade and foreign intelligence. These merchants also had cultural elements suggesting a Toltec origin, and they recognized their similarity to the Pochteca.[45]

A sequence in early forms of exchange?

The concepts of reciprocity, redistribution, and market exchange are widely used in the discussion of early trade.[46] All three are present in most economies to some degree. One remaining problem is to measure the degree in specific historical circumstances. Another is posed by a hypothesis that reciprocity, redistribution, and market exchange represent an evolutionary sequence of forms of exchange in human societies; that is, that reciprocity is naturally the first to appear, followed by

---

[44] Acosta, *Los Pochtecas*, pp. 34–50.

[45] Barbro Dahlgren de Jordan, *La Mixteca: Su Cultura e História Prehispanicas* (Mexico, D. F., 1954), pp. 241–9.

[46] Karl Polanyi is responsible for popularizing reciprocity and redistribution. Neil J. Smelser added mobilization, for the collection of wealth from the community, normally to be used in the political or material interests of the rulers, rather than being returned to the producers in any form – as it would be in a purely redistributive system. The fourth category, market exchange, goes back to the foundations of Western economic thought. See K. Polanyi et al., *Trade and Markets*, pp. 243–70; Neil J. Smelser, "A Comparative View of Exchange Systems," *Economic Development and Cultural Change*, 7:173–82 (1959).

redistributive systems, and finally by market exchange.[47] On the evidence surveyed here, they do not follow this sequence. Simple reciprocity has to be assumed for all periods, but market exchange occurs very early in human history. Redistributive systems, on the other hand, require bureaucratic governments to be effective. With the fall of the temple-economy hypothesis, it appears that redistribution was comparatively late in time, because elaborate bureaucracies developed comparatively late.

The apparent sequence in the pre-Columbian Andes is another case in point. The Incan state that dominated the whole Andean culture area before the Spanish conquest in the 1530s was a strong bureaucratic state. It operated a redistributive system in which surplus production of nearly self-sufficient villages was gathered into a vast system of state warehouses. Part was kept for the support of the state, including the court, the nobility, the army, and a variety of state services. Part was redistributed to the common people, and some was kept for security against future crop failures. The system may or may not have worked as it was supposed to do. In any event, market exchange existed alongside it. A market of sorts operated, for example, in Cuzco, the capital itself, if only as a kind of black market for the secondary exchange of state rations. An Incan system had, indeed, been superimposed in fairly recent times on a preexisting and well-developed marketing system, especially on the Pacific coast. There, dense urban populations lived in the oases formed where water flowed down from the highlands long before the Incas conquered their region. In the Incan period, they appear to have preserved many of the commercial habits of an earlier period, operating a sector of private enterprise in competition with the state redistributive system. Here, as in Sumer, redistribution appears to rise with the rise of a bureaucratic state, and to fall when that state weakens.[48]

If any general pattern of early trade emerges, it is the far simpler observation that contact between discrete cultures, partly through trade diasporas, led to spreading areas of intercommunication. These were sometimes, but not always, consolidated by military events like Alexander's conquests or political institutions like the Roman Empire. But these regions of ecumenical trade were not always sustained. They might be consolidated for several centuries, as Rome consolidated that of the

[47] Paul Wheatley, "Satyanrta in Suvarnadvipa. From Reciprocity to Redistribution in Ancient Southeast Asia," in Sabloff and Lamberg-Karlovsky (eds.), *Ancient Civilization and Trade*; George Dalton, "Introduction," in Dalton (ed.), *Primitive, Archaic and Modern Economies: Essays of Karl Polanyi* (New York, 1968).

[48] John V. Murra, *The Economic Organization of the Inka State* (Greenwich, Conn., 1980); Raymond J. Bromley and Richard Symanski, "Marketplace Trade in Latin America," *Latin American Research Review*, 9:3–38 (1974), pp. 4–5.

Mediterranean region. But there it broke down with the political fall of Rome, only to begin again on a broader scale with the rise of a new, ecumenical culture of commerce stretching from the Mediterranean in the west to the ports of southern China.

5

A new trade axis:
The Mediterranean to China,
circa 200 B.C.–A.D. 1000

In the last half-millennium before the Christian era, zones of intercommunication like the Hellenistic world began to develop elsewhere in the Afro-Eurasian landmass. On the Indian subcontinent, a new cultural synthesis had been in the making for centuries, built on elements of the older civilization of the Indus valley, local traditions elsewhere in India, and the cultural contributions of the Aryan-speaking invaders who came across the northwestern frontier during several centuries centered on 1500 B.C. or thereabouts. Buddhism, a new religion drawing on older Brahman religious traditions, was one of the main articulating elements in this new synthesis. It began spreading through the subcontinent from the time of the Buddha himself in the fifth century B.C. The Maurya Empire, reaching its apogee in the reign of Ashoka in the third century B.C., unified most of the South Asian world and guaranteed a broad, if temporary, victory for Buddhism as a religion. More important still, it helped to create a political framework for a common culture that began to be recognizably Indian in spite of great regional variation.

Still farther east, Confucius's teachings of the fifth century B.C. had their first political expression in the Han dynasty of China (ca. 206 B.C. to 220 A.D.), which united China for the first time and helped to integrate various local cultures in much the same way the Maurya and Hellenistic syntheses had done farther west.

Up to about the second century B.C., these centers had been separated by mountains, steppe, desert, and deep forests with very sparse populations. Overland contact was possible, but occurred only occasionally. Maritime contact was also possible along the whole southern coast of Asia and Europe – broken only by the land bridge at Suez – but navigation was short-range, from one port to the next with few long stages across the open sea. Then, with comparative suddenness, between about 200 B.C. and the beginning of the Christian era, regular overland trade came into existence across central Asia from China to the eastern Mediterranean. Seaborne trade also began over important segments of the whole route from Morocco to Japan. Trade now became a regular thing from the Red Sea and Persian Gulf to India, from India to Southeast Asia, and from Southeast Asia north to China and Japan. These trade routes, both overland and by sea, survived the fall of the Han and the Roman Empire, making possible a slow growth of cross-cultural trade, which continued to develop until the seventh and eighth centuries A.D., when the Tang dynasty in China and the Abbassid caliphate of Baghdad again provided imperial umbrellas over most of the trade routes between China and the Mediterranean.

Early Chinese trade and the opening across central Asia

The evidence about early Chinese trade so far available is disappointing, even though a recognizably "Chinese" urban civilization was already in place by the time of the Shang dynasty (1765–1122 B.C.). The earliest Chinese writing comes from this period, but the surviving writing on bones tells very little about Shang society as a whole and nothing at all about trade. Trade existed nevertheless. Shang tombs contain objects that must have come from a distance – like seashells and turtle shells from the South China coast, if not from the Malay Peninsula. Salt, turquoise, jade, and tin were also present and had no local source, but both the written and the archaeological records are too silent to permit speculation.[1]

In the third century B.C., the Chin dynasty united the core area of what was to be present-day China for the first time as a single empire. The dynasty's name is the root for the present name, but the Han dynasty that followed between 206 B.C. and 220 A.D. was even more important in establishing the forms of a Chinese empire. By the time of the Han, China was already a universal empire on the theory that the emperor was empowered by the "mandate of heaven" to rule over the whole world. In fact, individual emperors often failed to rule even over the whole of China, but the theory of universal rule persisted. Beyond the lands that were culturally Chinese were the realms of the barbarians. In theory they too were under the empire, but undeserving of full membership in Chinese society and not worth the trouble it would take to enforce their full submission.

The barbarians that were most important to the Han, to the Chin before them – and to most dynasties that followed – were the horse-riding, pastoral nomads who lived north and west of the Great Wall,

---

[1] C. K. Chang, "Ancient Trade as Economics or as Ecology," in Jeremy A. Sabloff and C. C. Lamberg-Karlovsky (eds.), *Ancient Civilization and Trade* (Albuquerque, N. Mex., 1975), pp. 211–14.

which the Chin had already built in its initial form more than a thousand miles long. They were both culturally and ecologically different from the sedentary farmers of the Chinese core area. In the longer sweep of history, these pastoralists, like those of North Africa, were probably an offshoot of the farming communities. They specialized in the herding of cattle, sheep, and horses – originally part of sedentary farming – on land too poor for year-round pasture, but rich enough to support animals that could be kept moving. Specialized nomadism appears to have begun in this part of the world between the fifth and third centuries B.C., and competition for land marginal to either ecology had already led the Chin to begin the Great Wall. From time to time, successful nomadic conquests of China would sweep across the wall, setting up new dynasties of nomadic origin, but in the longer run the sedentary society kept up a steady, if erratic, pressure on its nomadic neighbors.[2]

This ecological frontier, like the similar desert-edge frontiers in northern Africa, opened the possibility of profitable trade. As with many other commercial opportunities, frontier trade entailed protection costs, which could be met directly by employing military force on the frontier – as troops were always stationed along the Great Wall frontier of China – or they could be met by paying off the potential enemies, or, indeed, by a combination of the two policies.

The early Han emperors in the second century B.C. began with a general policy of paying protection money to the barbarians, but the barbarians sometimes raided the empire regardless, and the payments were burdensome. As the dynasty became stronger, it took the offensive against the most troublesome of the central Asian barbarians. After victory, it demanded tribute from the vanquished as a recognition of the empire's universal rule. On the surface, a reversal of roles seemed to have taken place, with China selling "protection" to the nomads, but the reversal was more ideological than real. The universal and moral quality of the empire required universal recognition of the emperor, but prudence made it worthwhile to pay off the barbarians as well.

After about 60 B.C., for example, when the Han broke the unity of the most threatening of the northwestern barbarians, the emperor demanded tribute payments, hostages to reside at court, and other guarantees of future security; but the Chinese reciprocated with gifts, and the value of the gifts was often greater than that of the tribute. The resulting two-way payments served symbolically to proclaim the emperor's supreme authority over humankind, while it gave the nomads

---

[2] Owen Lattimore, *Inner Asian Frontiers of China*, 2nd ed. (New York, 1951), pp. 163 ff. and passim.

a practical and material reason for not attacking the empire.[3] From one point of view, this was a clear example of marketless trade, embedded in a set of social and political relationships across an ecological frontier. From another point of view, it was an intricate fiction for controlling frontier trade and meeting protection costs while preserving the ideology of Chinese supremacy. In varying forms and with varying importance, it was to last into the nineteenth century.

At times the sheer quantities of goods passing back and forth as tribute trade could be significant. For the period of about 50 to 100 A.D., Ying-shih Yu has calculated that the flow of goods from Chinese to barbarians in a ring from Sichuan around to Manchuria amounted to 7 percent of imperial revenue, or about 30 percent of the value of the total government payroll, not counting other administrative and military costs of holding the frontier line. This was, of course, matched to some degree by the value of the barbarian tribute payments, though the balance of payments went in the other direction.[4]

For the later Han generally, tribute trade was only one of four different kinds of permitted trade with barbarians. Frontier markets were often associated with military camps. Trade by sea was also allowed. The role of Chinese shipping at this period is uncertain, though Chinese ships went as far as Malaya as early as 350 B.C.[5] Barbarian ships, however, were allowed to trade at designated Chinese ports, where they were confined to the port area and isolated as much as possible from Chinese society at large. Finally, in the middle Han, Chinese merchants also began to travel west across central Asia, in effect opening the "silk road" as a regular, overland route between Europe and East Asia, though Chinese merchants did not necessarily go all the way themselves.

The key to this opening to the West was in the geography of what was to be the Chinese province of Xinjiang. To take a caravan through uncontrolled nomad country would have been dangerous in the best of circumstances. The center of Xinjiang, however, is the Takla Makan desert, with the east–west mass of the Kunlun Shan to the south and the parallel range of the Tian Shan to the north. Both ranges were well watered, so that rivers flowed down toward the Takla Makan from the north and the south, creating a string of oases along the base of either mountain range. This combination of desert and oasis eased the passage for caravans. The oasis towns were a source of food and water, whereas

---

[3] Ying-shih Yu, *Trade and Expansion in Han China* (Berkeley, 1967), pp. 6–19, 45–6.
[4] Yu, *Trade and Expansion*, pp. 60–4.
[5] Joseph Needham, "Abstract of Material Presented to the International Maritime History Commission at Beirut," in M. Mollat (ed.), *Sociétés et compagnies de commerce en orient et dans l'océan indien* (Paris, 1971), pp. 140–1. Needham, *Science and Civilization in China*, vol. 4, part 3, *Civil Engineering and Nautics* (Cambridge, 1971).

the desert was so arid that potential raiders of the caravans were comparatively few. The original silk road ran along the southern string of oases, but the northern loop was available as an alternative in case of need.[6]

West of Xinjiang was another region of ribbon oases in a desert, where two major rivers flow westward out of the mountains into the Aral Sea. The rivers were the Oxus and Jaxartes of Hellenistic times, now the Amu Darya and Syr Darya of Soviet Central Asia. In the fourth century B.C., this became Alexander's conquered province of Transoxiana, the furthest reach of Hellenistic control into central Asia. By Han times, it was divided into a number of small kingdoms, of which Ferghana and Sogdiana were the most important. From Transoxiana, regular long-distance trade reached west to the Roman Empire. Or, travelers could move fairly easily across the Hindu Kush into plains of the Indus – and from there almost anywhere in the Indian subcontinent.

Some trade between India and China had been going on for a long time. Chinese silk was known in India at least as far back as the fourth century B.C., though it might not have come through central Asia. The sea route appears more likely, though the difficult overland route through Yunnan and Burma was also possible. In the second century B.C., however, China's push to the west brought Sogdiana and Ferghana into diplomatic relations with the Han court, including participation in the tribute-trade system. By the first century A.D., trade between India and China was extensive, and Chinese goods were widely sold in the Roman Empire, though few Chinese individuals traveled so far.[7]

Historians know very little about the merchants who carried this trade. Chinese merchants certainly came as far as central Asia on a regular basis. Merchants from central Asia and India alike carried their goods through to China. By the first century A.D., alien traders from the West had their own wards in the oasis towns fringing the Takla Makan, suggesting a trade diaspora, and merchants were certainly the carriers of Buddhism, first into central Asia where it became very common, if not dominant, in the early centuries of our era, both in Xinjiang and Transoxiana, and later on into East Asia, where it became and remained a major religion even after it had lost that position in its Indian homeland.

The silk road west of Transoxiana carried silk and lacquerware on to the Roman Empire, in exchange for woolen and linen textiles, coral and pearls, amber, glass, and various precious stones; but it was subject to shifting political conditions. At Alexander's death, Seleucus, one of the

[6] Lattimore, *Inner Asian Frontiers*, pp. 151–8.

[7] Yu, *Trade and Expansion*, pp. 137–8, 150–64. Tsung-fei Kuo, "A Brief History of the Trade Routes between Burma, Indochina, and Yunnan," *T'ien Hsia Monthly*, 12:9–32 (1941).

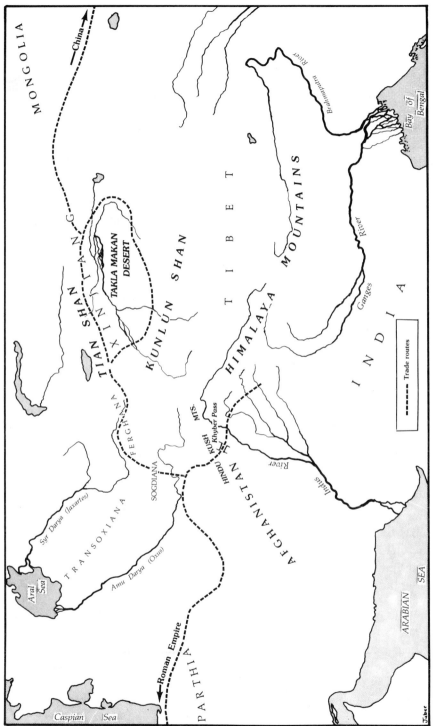

Map 5.1. Central Asia

Macedonian generals, made himself ruler of the region centered on Syria and Iraq – the Seleucid Empire, founded in about 312 B.C. It was still run by the Greek settlers at first, and it was very much a part of the Hellenistic world, but it gradually broke apart, as one region after another fell under the control of local magnates. One of these fragments grew to be the Parthian Empire, founded about 250 B.C. by Persian-speaking people of nomadic origin. Its original center was near the Caspian Sea, but it expanded to take in most of what had been Seleucid territory, reaching a peak of territorial extent about 50 B.C.

The Parthian rulers were no less Hellenistic in culture than the Seleucids had been. They were particularly solicitous about commerce, and they saw that caravanserais or rest stops were established at intervals along most of the important caravan routes. Both Chinese and Roman sources, however, complain that the Parthians reserved the Parthian sections of the silk road for their own merchants and caravaners, though they encouraged foreign trade as far as the Parthian frontier posts.[8]

The most important of the east–west routes in southwestern Asia ran from the Roman caravan center at Palmyra in Syria, eastward into Babylonia and on across northern Iran to Merv. There the route branched, one going southerly across Afghanistan to India, the other northerly across the Oxus to join the silk road across Xinjiang to China. At times when the Parthian hold over its outer provinces was weak, however, a southern detour around Parthia was possible. It took off from the Roman, desert-edge caravan city of Petra due east to lower Mesopotamia, then on through southern Iran and Baluchistan to India.[9]

Trade by sea in the western Indian Ocean

At the state of technology in Roman and Han times, nature provided three routes between India and the Mediterranean: the overland route through Parthia, the Persian Gulf plus overland to the Mediterranean, and the Red Sea plus overland, either to Egypt or to some part of the Fertile Crescent. The gulf and the Red Sea routes were already in competition for the carrying trade between the Roman and the Indian world, and they would remain so until the nineteenth century, in some respects on down to the present.

At first glance, the Red Sea seems superior, given the usual experience that sea transportation is cheaper than overland caravans. Compared to the narrow Suez isthmus, the gulf route required a long caravan crossing

---

[8] Malcolm A. R. Colledge, *The Parthians* (London, 1967), pp. 77–97; Yu, *Trade and Expansion*, pp. 198–9.
[9] G. C. Adhya, *Early Indian Economics: Studies in the Economic Life of Northern India and Western India c. 200 B.C. – A.D. 300* (Bombay, 1966), pp. 103–13.

to the Mediterranean, even if boats on the Tigris or Euphrates could be used part of the way. In fact, the Red Sea is not so favorably placed. Over the northern half of the sea, the wind blows from the north in all seasons. Early sailing vessels could not sail easily to windward. Beating north to the head of the Red Sea was slow and difficult. Even with the Suez Canal, sailing vessels rarely used the Red Sea route. Ships bound from Asian ports for Europe found it faster and easier to make the long detour around Cape Horn or the Cape of Good Hope. Before steam, mariners headed north up the Red Sea would usually stop about half way, either at a port on the Arabian side, like Jiddah, or on the Egyptian side at a port within reach of Aswan at the first cataract of the Nile. In either case the cargoes would go forward by camel. On the Egyptian side, they could be transferred to Nile boats, which could drift down to the delta whatever the wind – and prevailing northerlies made it an easy sail back upstream for the return trip. On the Arabian side, caravans could reach north to the Levant, or across the Suez land bridge to Egypt.

To the south, beyond the Straits of Bab el Mandeb at the entrance of the Red Sea, wind direction was no problem. This was the zone of the Indian Ocean monsoons, which blow from the southwest during the warm season and from the northeast in the cool. The actual period of steady, usable wind differs from place to place, but mariners are nevertheless assured at least four months of fair wind for passage either east or west along any part of the route between Arabia and Malaya. Temperature differences between the sea and the land to the north cause the alternation of easterly and westerly monsoons. Similar temperature differences also set up alternate northerly and southerly winds that help to carry shipping north and south at either end of the main east–west axis. In the west during the northern winter, winds are fair to reach south from Arabia to the Mozambique Channel and a little beyond. During the northern summer, mariners can expect southeasterly winds to carry them north over the same route. At the eastern end of the Indian Ocean corridor, similar monsoonal winds blow north from Malaya or Indonesia in the warm season, and south again in the cool, making for an easy sail between the ports of Southeast Asia and those of China and even Japan.

It was once widely believed that a certain Hippalus "discovered" the monsoons, making possible the sudden development of Indian Ocean trade about the middle of the first century A.D. The story is obvious Roman ethnocentric nonsense; people who lived on the shores of the northern Indian Ocean knew about monsoons all along, for the same reason Romans knew about winter and summer. For this part of the Indian Ocean, the monsoonal pattern was more complex than a simple east–west alternation. Between Arabia and Zanzibar, the "southwest"

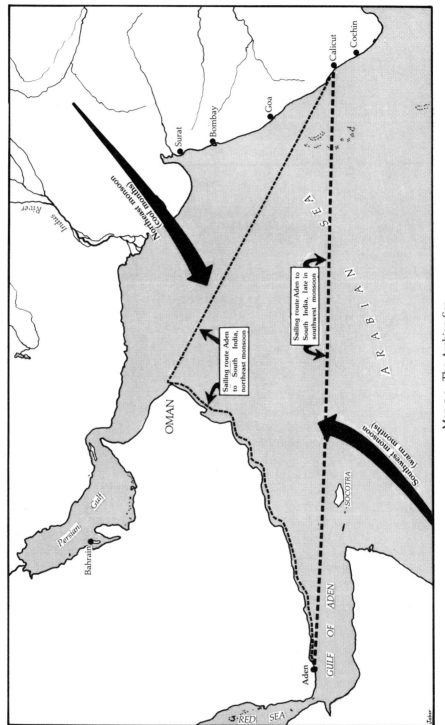

Map 5.2. The Arabian Sea

monsoon actually blows more nearly from the southeast or south on account of the intense heat of Arabia and the Horn of Africa in these months of the northern summer. In this season, winds are much stronger than they are with the northeast monsoon of the cool months. The northern summer is also the season when the intertropical front moves northward, bringing with it a belt of very disturbed atmosphere, high winds, and dangerous thunderstorms. The height of this monsoon in June and July can be a dangerous period for small craft; fishermen are sometimes forced to stay in port for weeks on end. Nor was it safe even for the largest of the Indian Ocean sailing craft of the pre-Christian era.

One possibility was to wait till the worst was over, making the crossing from Arabia to India in late August to October. Another solution was to take advantage of the fact that the northeast monsoon of the cool months blows from the northeast, not due east. An Arabian ship leaving from a port near Aden in the winter months could take advantage of coastal irregularities in wind direction to sail northeast up the southern Arabian coast to Oman. The compass bearing from the eastern tip of Arabia to the southern tip of India is southeast. It was therefore possible to cross to southern India in what was, in effect, a long tack against the northeast monsoon, with a favorable-enough wind and comparatively smooth seas. The same wind was also fair for a direct return to Aden without waiting for a reversal of monsoons.[10]

A significant change in the pattern of seafaring in the Arabian Sea appeared about 100 B.C. or a little earlier. Before that time, merchants of Mediterranean origin traded southward down the Red Sea using the combined caravan-and-ship operation. They would usually stop somewhere near the Straits of Bab el Mandeb, leaving Arabs or other Indian Ocean traders to carry on to India during the next favorable season.[11] About 100 B.C., they began to use the southwest monsoon for a through trip from ports midway up the Red Sea to southern India. By waiting long enough for the intertropical front to pass on north, they could time their crossing to arrive in India in late September, when the worst of the winds had abated. This meant that resident communities of Romans began to settle in the principal port towns of southern India. Similar Roman communities also settled along the non-Parthian portions of the overland route between the Mediterranean and India. It would be a mistake, however, to imagine these "Romans" as Italian. They were descendants of the same people who had been trading to the East before the Roman Empire came into existence: Jews from Egypt and the Fertile

[10] G. F. Hourani, *Arab Seafaring in the Indian Ocean in Ancient and Early Medieval Times* (Princeton, N. J., 1951), pp. 22–8.
[11] Adhya, *Early Indian Economics*, pp. 123–36; Hourani, *Arab Seafaring*.

Crescent, Greek-speaking Egyptians, and other Levantines from the ecumenical and Hellenized world of Mediterranean commerce. According to the Chinese records, the first Romans to arrive in China came by sea, not overland by the silk road, but the main Roman trade diaspora stopped in southern India, and it reached down the African coast only to the neighborhood of Zanzibar. These Roman trade colonies were nevertheless significant, as attested to by the large numbers of Roman coins found in southern Indian archaeological sites. After the Roman Empire had disappeared, evidence of the trade diaspora remained in the form of Jewish and Christian religious communities living in India long after Indian Ocean trade had passed into other hands.[12]

The cultural influence of these Mediterranean traders was less important for its impact on the broader Indian culture than it was in the Horn of Africa. There, Byzantine and Christian cultures were especially important for the kingdom of Aksum in the Ethiopian highlands near the Red Sea. Aksum rose to power in about 100 A.D. and remained important until the sixth century A.D. For a time, the Aksumite rulers conquered a good part of the Ethiopian highlands and parts of Yemen across the straits in Arabia, but their main source of wealth was trade – partly funneling local products into the Indian Ocean trade network, partly a carrying trade based on the Aksumite port of Adulis. This trade brought Aksum into the cultural world of Rome, especially the Greek half of the Roman Empire. But Byzantium was not alone. Aksumite architecture, for example, shows influences from India and from Merowe on the upper Nile, and Syrian influences were also strong. Many wall inscriptions are in Greek, though the Aksumites also developed their own alphabet that in time influenced others as far away as Armenia.

In the fourth century A.D., the rulers of Aksum converted to Christianity, not long after the conversion of Rome itself. Then, with the decline of the Aksumite economy after 600 A.D. or so, Aksum itself gradually withdrew from the greater trading world of which it had been a part, but the Christian religion lived on in the Ethiopian highlands. Greek gave way to Ge'ez as the principal written language, but the Christian Ethiopians maintained contact with Coptic Christianity in Egypt, even after the rise of Islam cut off easy contact with these closest Chris-

[12] Adhya, *Early Indian Economics*, pp. 123–36; Yu, *Trade and Expansion*, p. 145; E. H. Warmington, *The Commerce between the Roman Empire and India* (Cambridge, 1938); Romila Thapar, *A History of India*, vol. 1 (London, 1966), pp. 109, 115; K. A. Nilakanta Sastri, *A History of South India* (Madras, 1948), pp. 134–6. For a more detailed treatment of ancient Indian trade see also B. Srivastava, *Trade and Commerce of Ancient India* (Varanasi, 1968), and Moti Chandra, *Trade and Trade Routes in Ancient India* (New Delhi, 1977).

tian neighbors. And, after 1200 or so, Christian Ethiopians were to reenter the trading world of the Indian Ocean.[13]

Early trade to Southeast Asia

Maritime trade in the South China Sea and the Bay of Bengal began to flourish at least as early as it did in the Arabian Sea, and its long-term cultural consequences were even more important. Canton (more correctly Guangzhou) was already an important port for trade to the south in the early Han. Chinese merchandise reached Mesopotamia at least as early as 360 A.D., and Chinese merchants as well as Chinese goods were reaching India as early as the first century. Most shipping in the South China Sea appears to have been Chinese, but much of it could have come from Southeast Asia as well.[14]

Shipping across the Bay of Bengal, however, was dominated by merchants and shippers from India – part of a southern Indian trade diaspora based in a number of small Dravidian kingdoms on the southeast coast, of which the Chola kingdom was the most important. The Indians' first point of contact in Southeast Asia was a commercial settlement on the narrow Kra isthmus between Malaysia and Thailand. In earlier periods it was more used than the Straits of Melaka (Malacca) further south. Once across the isthmus, goods could be reshipped either to mainland Southeast Asia, to the Indonesian archipelago, or north to Canton. Still another trade diaspora, this time from northern India, moved overland across the mountains of eastern Bengal through Manipur and Assam to develop trade with the fertile plains of central Burma. A few Indian merchant settlements extended trade still farther north into the Chinese Yunnan Province.[15]

The cultural influence of India on Southeast Asia was so strong that some historians used to refer to a "Greater India" created by Indian migration and colonization and reaching its peak in the fourth and fifth centuries A.D. The importance of this influence is undoubted and is

[13] Y. M. Kobishanov, "Aksum: Political System, Economics and Culture, First to Fourth Century," in UNESCO, General History of Africa, 8 vols. projected (Paris, 1981), 2:381–99; Karl W. Butzer, "Rise and Fall of Axum, Ethiopia: A Geo-Archaeological Interpretation," American Antiquity, 46:471–95 (1981).
[14] Needham, "Abstract," p. 140; Yu, Trade and Expansion, pp. 172–83; K. A. Nilakanta Sastri, Foreign Notices of South India from Magasthenes to Ma Huan (Madras, 1939), p. 4; Paul Wheatley, "Satyanrta in Suvarnadvipa. From Reciprocity to Redistribution in Ancient Southeast Asia," in Sabloff and Lamberg-Karlovsky (eds.), Ancient Civilization and Trade; Tatsuro Yamamoto, "Chinese Activities in the Indian Ocean Before the coming of Portuguese," Diogenes, 111:19–34 (1981).
[15] R. C. Majumdar, Ancient Indian Colonization in South-East Asia, 2nd ed. (Baroda, 1963).

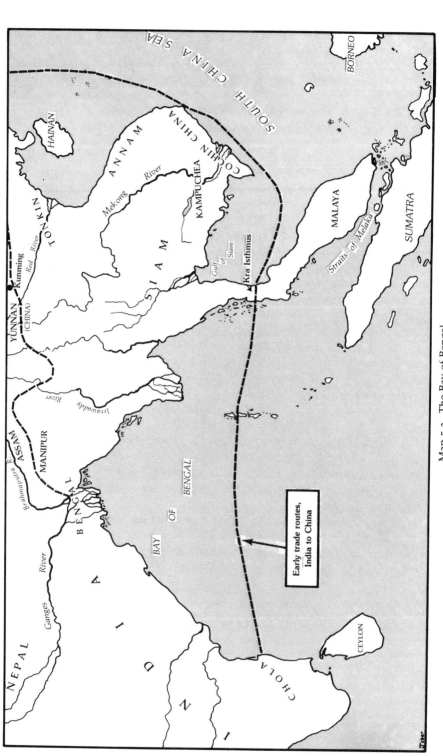

Map 5.3. The Bay of Bengal

clearly visible in the art and architecture of the period. It was even more important for political development. Bureaucratic states modeled on those of peninsular India sprang up on Sumatra, Java, and other of the islands, as well in the primary river valleys of the mainland. Recent historical writing, however, has tended to reduce the probable numbers of Indian immigrants, suggesting not a mass migration but a trade diaspora of Indian settlements at the principal points of commercial contact. Sanskrit inscriptions, for example, tend not to show a sudden shift to Indian forms, but rather a succession of local rulers whose names and titles became more and more Indianized with each passing generation.

Along with political change among the ruling class came a much broader conversion to Hinduism. In later centuries, Indians of the Brahman caste were opposed to crossing "the black water" for religious reasons, but this prohibition was not yet important. Many of the merchant entrepreneurs were themselves Brahmans. Southeast Asian conversion to Hinduism meant that their priestly function, as well as their merchandise, was in demand. Many Brahman immigrants appear to have come as young men who married local women and thus founded local Brahmanic families. In the longer run, however, Hinduism survived only on the island of Bali and a few minor centers.

Successive religious changes in Southeast Asia also followed from the work of later commercial missionaries. Just as Mahayana Buddhism spread along the trade routes of central Asia from India to China and Japan, Hinayana Buddhism was to spread, mainly from Ceylon, to become the dominant religion of Burma, Thailand, and Vietnam. Even later, the conversion to Islam of Malaya, Indonesia, and the southern Philippines was also the work of people who came with a Muslim trade diaspora.

The Mediterranean after the fall of Rome: the new universal empires

Trade diasporas had been unnecessary in Mediterranean Europe at the height of Roman power, but with the decline of Rome in the fifth century and later, they reappeared. More likely, they had been there all along as communities of commercial specialists who attracted little attention in an ecumenical world. From the fifth to the eighth century, however, they reappear in the former western Roman territory like France or Spain under the name *Syri*, implying Syrian or Lebanese origin. In fact, they came from many parts of the eastern Roman Empire, and their common language was Greek. Some were Jews, but Jewish or not, they were outsiders to the Romance-speaking world of the West. They were also outsiders in circumstances where trade was more and more a fringe

activity of the Western European economy. The result was a ghettoization of this merchant community, its religious separation from the body
social, and a return to conditions where trade diasporas, run by merchants who shared a common culture, were again required for trade
through regions where the common stamp of Roman overlordship no
longer existed.[16]

Meanwhile, two major military conquests remade the political map of
the Afro-Eurasian landmass, changing the patterns of possible trade
beyond recognition. One was the rise of Islam, traditionally dated from
the *hejra*, Muhammad's flight from Mecca to Madina in 622, but beginning more accurately with the Muslim conquest of the Middle East,
spread over several decades from the capture of Syria in 636 into the
660s, when the first Muslim universal empire was firmly established
with a capital at Damascus – usually called the Umayyad caliphate after
Umar, the conqueror. The resulting state was Arab, and it was to spread
the use of Arabic in much the same way the Roman Empire spread and
left a heritage of Latin as a written language for a large part of Europe,
lasting for centuries after the Roman Empire had disappeared. But, in
most important aspects of culture, it also picked up the heritage of the
two civilizations combined under the new empire, namely, the Byzantine
heritage in the West and the Sassanian heritage of Iraq and Persia in
the East. The territorial unit was thus close to the Hellenistic unity of
Alexander, even though Greece and Constantinople were left out. Although the unity of Islam under a single state was broken in 750, the
classical Islamic age of Abbassid rule from the new capital at Baghdad
continued on to about 1000 A.D.

The rise of Islam made two major differences as far as trade was
concerned. It tended to weaken, if not destroy, the former economic
unity of the Mediterranean basin. And it tended to establish a new kind
of unity that made trade easy under the cultural aegis of Islam – from
Morocco and Spain in the West to Persia and beyond in the East.

The second major reorganization was the emergence of the Tang dynasty in China. With the end of the Han about 222 A.D., China had
fallen into a long period of disunity, barbarian invasions, and short
dynasties controlling only parts of China. Then, after 589 A.D., the Sui
dynasty reunited China once more and prepared the way for the Tang,
which was to rule from 618 to 907, a period regarded as one of the most
successful and creative in all Chinese history. It was also an expansionist
period, especially in the seventh century, when Chinese forces first

[16] Guy Fourquin, *Histoire économique de l'occidente mediévale*, 2nd ed. (Paris, 1969); Georges
Duby, *The Early Growth of the European Economy; Warriors and Peasants from the Seventh
to the Twelfth Century* (Ithaca, N. Y., 1974).

established their control over Tibet, over the small states of Transoxiana, and briefly over what was to be northern Afghanistan. The Tang capital at Ch'ang-an became the greatest urban center in the world, with nearly two million people in the urban area and a million within the city walls. The long reach of Tang control to the west made it possible for many foreigners to visit China, including Muslims, Jews, and Nestorian Christians from India or Mesopotamia. The tolerant treatment of foreign residents ended for the time being with religious persecutions in 841–5, but even so Tang power had opened new possibilities in Asian trade.[17]

The simultaneous power of the Abbassids and the Tang made it comparatively easy for long-distance traders to make the whole journey across Asia and North Africa, in effect from the Atlantic to the Pacific. Relatively open trade across Asia had occurred once before in the Han-Parthian-Roman period at the beginning of the Christian era. It happened again in this Tang-Abbassid period of the seventh and eighth centuries. It was to happen for a third time with the establishment of the Mongol Empire over most of northern Asia after 1250 – the opportunity that made it possible for Europeans like Marco Polo to visit China freely for about a century afterward. And it would happen once more with the European maritime revolution of the fifteenth and sixteenth centuries that carried European shipping to all the oceans of the world.

Among those to take advantage of the Abbassid-Tang possibility were Jews, who could claim a degree of neutrality in the Muslim–Christian struggles in the Mediterranean. The Muslim conquest of the south shore did not cut off all communication across the sea, but north–south trade became insignificant until after 1000 A.D. Meanwhile, overland caravans ran from Morocco to Egypt, paralleling Muslim trade at sea. On the Christian side, coastal trade continued in the Adriatic and along the French and Spanish coasts to the west, and overland trade between Western Europe and the Byzantine Empire was difficult but not impossible.[18] The Franks (a generic term for Western Europeans at this period) were not especially fond of other religions, but Jewish communities were active in the east–west trade of southern Europe, being especially prominent in southern France. The Carolingians made them protégés of the monarchy partly for that reason. Jewish trade was still more widely tolerated in Abbassid lands, though they paid a special tax, just as the Coptic Christian minority did. The most prominent Jewish community in the world at this period was in Babylon, with a large settlement in

---

[17] As a reference work for East Asian history see Edwin O. Reischauer and John K. Fairbank, *East Asia: The Great Tradition* (Boston, 1960).

[18] L. Rabinowitz, *Jewish Merchant Adventurers: The Study of the Radanites* (London, 1948), pp. 24–34; Eliahu Ashtor, *A Social and Economic History of the Near East in the Middle Ages*, (Berkeley, 1976).

Cairo as well. Other Jews were scattered here and there along the trade routes and were able to move still farther as opportunity allowed.

For a brief period centered on the late eighth and early ninth centuries, a Jewish trade diaspora became the most important trade group over the whole network of routes linking Europe and China. The Jews who ran this trade were called *Radaniyya* in Arabic, or Radanites. Some authorities have suggested that they were a separate sect within Judaism, but the more plausible source of their name is the Persian *rha dan*, meaning "those who know the way," and Persian was the main trade language over many of the Radanite routes.[19]

Writing in about 845, the Persian geographer, Ibn Kurdadbeh, described the network of routes between the land of the Franks and China. In the Mediterranean, they had the alternative of coastal shipping along the Christian shores to the Levant, or else crossing into Muslim Spain to catch the North African caravan routes from Morocco to Egypt. For the passage into the Indian Ocean, they used both common alternatives: caravans to Jiddah and ships down the Red Sea, or else the overland trip to the Persian Gulf. From there they could continue to India by sea, or else catch the silk road in Transoxiana. Still another Radanite alternative made it possible to avoid Muslim territory altogether. They did this by taking their caravans overland from Europe through the still-non-Christian Slavic lands to the north of the Black Sea. There, in the Crimean peninsula and vicinity, Jews briefly exercised political control over the state of Khazaria (see map 5.1). From there, the route to the east went around the north end of the Caspian Sea and on into the Oxus valley and the silk road around the Takla Makan.[20]

Neither the Radanite routes nor the institution of a trade diaspora was new. What was unusual was a single trade diaspora with a shared culture carrying trade over such a long distance. It is hardly surprising that the enterprise lasted little more than a century. It ended not merely on account of Tang xenophobia, but also because the Abbassid power began to weaken and Tatars drifting westward across Asia blocked the overland route for a time. After that, the opportunity for cross-Asia trade would wait for another four hundred years till the Mongol conquests.

Indian Ocean trade and the rise of Islam

The rise of Islam, followed by the formation of the Abbassid caliphate in Baghdad, was more important for the future of Indian Ocean trade

---

[19] Rabinowitz, *Radanites*, pp. 108–11.
[20] Passage from "Book of the Roads and Kingdoms," quoted in Rabinowitz, *Radanites*, pp. 9–10. See also Nilakanta Sastri, *Foreign Notices*, p. 21; Ashtor, *Economic History*, pp. 105–06; Subhi Y. Labib, "Egyptian Commercial Policy in the Middle Ages," in M. A. Cook (ed.), *Studies in the Economic History of the Middle East* (London, 1970), p. 64.

than it was for the overland trade to China. Abbassid power provided a political cover for Muslim merchants, just as Tang power did for many merchant communities. Abbassid power did something more. By launching Muslim culture and religion onto the Indian Ocean, the Abbassids laid the groundwork for profound changes in culture throughout the basin of the Indian Ocean – changes that would continue after the Abbassid caliphate had disappeared.

In the broadest perspective of Afro-Eurasian history, in the period from about 750 A.D. to at least 1500, Islam was the central civilization for the whole of the Old World. Not only was it the most dynamic and creative of Rome's and Persia's successors; it was also the principal agency for contact between the discrete cultures of this period, serving as the carrier that transmitted innovations from one society to another. Arabic numbers are called Arabic because Europeans learned about them from the Arabs; but positional value notation was an Indian invention. Chinese inventions like the compass reached Europeans, and European inventions like artillery passed through the same hands. Nor was transmission limited to technology. The Muslim religion was also carried as part of a broad process of culture change – largely by traders, not conquerors. It is worth remembering that the two countries with the largest Muslim populations in the last quarter of the twentieth century are Indonesia and China, where Arab armies never trod.

Islam as a religion was also friendlier to trade and to traders than many other religions have been. Muhammad himself came from a trading town and had been a trader in his youth. The nomadic traditions that were also part of Islam in its formative decades tended to fade as the center of Muslim power moved out of Arabia and into the lands of the ancient sedentary civilizations of Egypt, the Fertile Crescent, Iraq, and Iran. In 750, the move of the Abbassid capital from Damascus to Baghdad was also a significant shift from a region that had looked to the Mediterranean toward one that had looked down the Euphrates and out onto the Persian Gulf.

Even before the rise of Islam, commerce in the western Indian Ocean had been largely in the hands of Persians and Jews from Mesopotamia. The new sultans in Baghdad did nothing to disturb these traders, though as the main language of trade Persian came to replace Greek during the early Abbassid centuries, say 750 to 1000. Persian also became the lingua franca for overland trade in central Asia, where the most important trade diaspora for western access to the silk road was based in the former Sogdiana – hence run by Iranians, in a broad sense of that term, who now began to use Persian as their everyday language. They also operated a route northward from Baghdad to the

Black Sea coast, where it made contact with the Jews who carried trade on west to Europe.[21]

Seaborne traders from the Persian Gulf also became more active with the rise of the Abbassids. A Muslim trade colony on Ceylon had been in business from about 700 A.D., and gulf traders now began to make the through voyage to China – a common practice in the eighth and ninth centuries, when the Tang were strong at one terminus and the Abbassids at the other. The voyage was possible by using the monsoons in a slightly unorthodox way. Ships leaving Persia or Mesopotamia would work their way down the gulf in September, then cross the Arabian Sea in the now-familiar quartering tack against the northeast monsoon to the southern tip of India. They could then catch the new southwest monsoon across the Bay of Bengal in December or so, which made it possible to use the southerly monsoon in the South China Sea, bringing them to Canton in April or May. They could then leave in the fall on the northerly monsoon, making it possible to catch the beginning of the northeast monsoon in the Indian Ocean and arrive back in the gulf by April or May. This timing made it possible to avoid the heavy winds of early summer, yet allowed about a year and a half for a round trip with stops for trade. Given time for repairs and the like, a ship could make a round trip every two years.[22]

In 878 A.D., rebels against the Tang government sacked Canton and killed most of the foreign traders resident there. The Tang dynasty was weakening in any event, and direct Muslim trade to China came to an end for the time being. In fact, it never again became the normal practice, and it may have been best suited to a trade in relatively small quantities of comparatively high value. Later Indian Ocean traders tended to sell their cargoes somewhere in Southeast Asia, letting others carry whatever part was to go north to China.[23] Meanwhile, new developments in the organization of maritime trade were to come in the early centuries of the new millennium.

---

[21] Berthold Spuler, "Trade in the Eastern Islamic Countries in the Early Centuries," in D. S. Richards (ed.), *Islam and the Trade of Asia: A Colloquium* (Philadelphia, 1970).

[22] Ashtor, *Economic History*, pp. 107–12; Hourani, *Arab Seafaring*, pp. 73–5.

[23] Hourani, *Arab Seafaring*, pp. 77 ff.; Rita Rose Di Meglio, "Arab Trade with Indonesia and the Malay Peninsula from the 8th to the 16th Century," in Richards (ed.), *Islam and the Trade of Asia*.

6

Asian trade in Eastern seas, 1000–1500

The eclipse of the Tang and the decline of the Abbassid caliphate after about 1000 were important events but not signs of decay in the general prosperity or creativity of either Chinese or Muslim civilization. They were not equivalent to the fall of western Rome in the history of Europe. Indeed, for China the eleventh century was to be one of outstanding economic growth, even though Chinese military power under central control declined from the levels reached under the Tang.

The "economic miracle" of early Song China

Between the foundation of the Song dynasty in 960 and the conquest of northern China by the Jurchen nomads in 1127, China passed through a phase of economic growth that was unprecedented in earlier Chinese history, perhaps in world history up to this time. It depended on a combination of commercialization, urbanization, and industrialization that has led some authorities to compare this period in Chinese history with the development of early modern Europe six centuries later.[1] At least for this brief period, China became the leading society in the world in terms of productivity per capita, and behind the achievement was a combination of technical capabilities and political circumstances.

The most general stimulant behind this development was an era of peace and a large internal market, linking cities that could be supplied from a distance with agricultural and industrial products. The key was the transportation network, the core of which was the Huang Ho River

---

[1] The process is summarized in William H. McNeill, *The Pursuit of Power: Technology, Armed Force, and Society since A.D. 1000* (Chicago, 1982), and Mark Elvin, *The Pattern of the Chinese Past* (Stanford, Calif., 1973). For further detail see John W. Haeger (ed.), *Crisis and Prosperity in Sung China* (Tucson, 1975); Robert Hartwell, "A Cycle of Economic Change in Imperial China: Coal and Iron in Northeast China, 750–1350," *Journal of Economic and Social History of the Orient*, 10:103–59 (1967); Laurence J. C. Ma, *Commercial Development and Urban Change in Sung China (960–1279)* (Ann Arbor, Mich., 1971).

in the north and the Chang Jiang (Yangtze) River in central China, joined
(as they had been for some time) by the Grand Canal, but now made
far more effective by new techniques for water transport and by feeder
roads and canals. Kaifeng, the capital of the northern Song, for example,
was probably the largest city in the world at this time, with 750,000 to
1,000,000 inhabitants. It is estimated that 80 percent of its grain supply
was rice, transported from the rice-growing regions of the south by way
of the Grand Canal.[2]

It was partly because of this large internal market that the Chinese
iron and steel industry was able to increase its scale of production. By
the tenth century, Chinese iron and steel makers knew about the blast
furnace for producing relatively cheap, if brittle, cast iron. They had also
learned to make iron with coke, rather than charcoal. By the eleventh
century the Chinese steel industry already had all the important technology the native Chinese iron and steel industry was to have up to the
nineteenth century. The size of the market made possible by the transport network meant that capital investment and economies of scale were
possible to an extent beyond any steel industry up to that time. One
smelter alone produced 14,000 tons of pig iron a year. (By comparison,
total English output of pig iron in the mid-seventeenth century is estimated in the range of 20,000 to 40,000 tons.)[3]

Nor were iron and steel alone. The eleventh-century prosperity brought
with it increased craft production throughout China, and with it increased foreign trade. The overland route to the west was comparatively
unimportant, but Chinese, as opposed to South Asian, shipping became
important over the sea routes to Southeast Asia. China exported silk
and other textiles, lacquerware, and some iron and steel in return for
spices and other tropical products. By the early twelfth century, government income from taxes on foreign trade amounted to 20 percent of
the total.[4]

Some of this achievement, however, was comparatively brief. The
high-productivity iron and steel industry in northern China disappeared
after the early twelfth century. The technical capabilities of the transport
network remained, but they were realizable only in periods of comparative political stability. Chinese technology for ocean shipping, however,
continued to be available and was important through the later Song and
into the Yuan period after the mid-thirteenth century.

[2] Hartwell, "Coal and Iron," p. 129.
[3] Hartwell, "Coal and Iron," p. 121.
[4] Ma, *Commercial Development*, p. 38.

Ecumenical trade in the Muslim Mediterranean, 970–1250

The pattern of history in the Middle East was less of a success story. The Abbassid caliphate was in political disarray from about 900 onward. Beginning in the eleventh century, the Islamic world had to stand off foreign invasions on several fronts. Frankish Crusaders in the Levant were one of these; a series of nomadic invasions from the Sahara and from central Asia were another threat. But the Muslim Mediterranean nevertheless also enjoyed a period of pronounced prosperity from about 970 to 1250 A.D. The political base was Egypt under the Fatimid dynasty, which, most of this time, controlled the Levant as well. The Fatimids had begun as a Berber dynasty ruling over Tunisia and associated with the Shi'ite sect. In 969, they conquered Egypt and moved their capital to Cairo. This not only took a major province away from the Abbassids in Baghdad; it also established Egypt as the new passageway for intercontinental trade. What had once passed through Mesopotamia and the Persian Gulf now passed through Egypt and the Red Sea.

Up to 1250 or so, Egypt was preeminent in the Muslim world, but this was not a period of unrelieved peace and stability. In 1171, the Fatimids gave way to the Ayyubid dynasty, and, in 1250, the Ayyubids gave way in turn to rule by the slave-soldiers who had made up the major part of their army. These were the Mamluks, who ruled over declining Egypt until the Ottoman Turks conquered the country and annexed it to the Ottoman Empire in 1517. In the eleventh-century nomadic crisis, Hilalian Arab nomads pushed past Egypt and on across North Africa in a destructive migration. Seljuk Turks advancing from the east captured Baghdad in 1055 and Jerusalem in 1071, which fell in turn to Frankish Crusaders in 1099. By 1125, the whole of the Levant had fallen to the Christians, but Sālih al-Dīn, or Saladin, the new Ayyubid leader, recovered Jerusalem in 1187. From then on the Franks were generally in retreat, though they could threaten new attacks even after Egypt was reasonably secure.

In spite of these political and military disturbances, a new zone of ecumenical trade came into existence in the southern Mediterranean, beginning in the eighth and ninth centuries, with the Islamization of the southern shore. It was not the same as the Roman commercial system, and allowance has to be made for the intrusive presence of the Franks and other enemies of Islam.

In spite of some deficiencies in the evidence, it is clear, however, that an important trade network centered on Fatimid Cairo was already operating before the end of the tenth century and that it extended well

beyond the range of Fatimid rule. It reached all of the Muslim Mediterranean, and it had ways of dealing with Frankish and Byzantine traders
as well. Historians are also fortunate in having documentary records for
Cairo's trade community that are richer than those for any other part of
the Muslim world before modern times. These records were kept by the
Cairene Jewish community because of a Jewish belief that no writing
that might contain the name of God should be intentionally destroyed.
Papers of this kind were put in a *geniza*, a room attached to a synagogue.
There, they could decay naturally, like a human body. With time, most
geniza papers did decay, but the dry Egyptian climate preserved those
of the principal synagogue of old Cairo until this century. They are now
scattered in many museums and libraries, but they are mainly open to
scholars and their information is much broader than one might imagine.
The Jewish community was not sharply separated from the Muslim
community. Most of the writing is in Arabic, though written with He-
brew characters. These records are indeed the best sources we have for
Muslim Egyptian society of this period, as well as for the Jewish community itself.[5]

In the relatively open trade of the Fatimid and Ayyubid periods, Jews
and Muslims were part of a single trading community. Jews were prominent in trade, but they were not the only traders; and they were free
to practice any other profession on an equal basis with Muslims or Copts.
They were a part of the Muslim world, speaking and writing in Arabic,
sometimes making the pilgrimage to Mecca, but keeping their own communities and their own law, even as the Muslims and Copts did – though
an area for common law also existed for cross-communal relationships.[6]

Toward the end of the eleventh century, perhaps 8,000 traveling merchants moved back and forth over the trade routes to Tunis and Sicily
by sea, farther west by sea, or by caravan paralleling the coast. The
oasis-hopping, desert-edge route was also available still farther to the
south, stretching all the way from Cairo to the distant desert port of
Sijilmasa in southern Morocco. These merchants worked together through
several forms of agency, and often across the lines separating religious
communities. A traveling merchant could handle goods for another who
stayed at home. Several kinds of partnerships were available, making
it possible to assign portions of the risk and profits. Some of these
agreements were written, but the common culture of the mercantile
community made many contracts possible simply "on a handshake," or

[5] Professor Solomon Dob Goitein has recently published the results of his research in
these records, stretching back over several decades, in *A Mediterranean Society*, 3 vols.
(Berkeley, 1967–78) and *Studies in Islamic History and Institutions* (Leiden, 1976).
[6] Goitein, *Mediterranean Society*, 1:59–74.

by the unwritten renewal of long-standing arrangements.[7] The complex and accepted nature of these practices suggests that they were already very old. Some, indeed, must represent survivals from the Roman period.

The Muslim Mediterranean had several important institutions that reduced the need for trade diasporas. One of these was the office of *wakil al-tujjar*, who served as a legal representative for foreign merchants in much the same way as an English commission agent was to do in the sixteenth century and later. In Cairo, if a foreign merchant needed to collect a debt, he could apply to a wakil to help him. Whereas a traveling merchant often had to store his goods in the caravanserai where he lodged – or to find a friend trusted enough to keep them – the wakil would store unaccompanied goods at his agency house. If the owner sent orders from a distance, the wakil could auction them off and forward the proceeds. Banking instruments were well developed so that money could easily be transferred without necessarily moving coins from one place to another, though the wakil would turn to professional bankers for these matters. Some wakil also owned and operated funduq or lodging houses for foreign merchants, recalling the combined functions of the landlord-brokers of West Africa.[8]

Even the way of becoming a professional wakil was similar to the Hausa way of becoming a professional maigida. The ideal man for the position was a merchant who had begun as a foreign trader, then, having done well in Cairo, had built up influence and reputation that he could use (for a price) in the service of others.[9] Though an earlier wakil may have served mainly traders of his own nationality, the Cairene wakil of this period was free to serve all comers. The wakil that emerges in the geniza papers may, however, represent a remnant of a trade diaspora that had worked its way out of business.

Trade diasporas still operated, especially in trade that reached beyond the zone of ecumenical trade centered on Fatimid Cairo. Most trade with the Franks, for example, came on Christian ships to Muslim ports, though Franks were not encouraged to remain as permanent residents. Nor were Orthodox Christians from the Byzantine north. The Byzantines had a trade colony in Alexandria, but not in Cairo, though Constantinople itself was host to many different merchant communities. For Constantinople in about 1060, the Spanish Jew, Benjamin of Tudela, listed merchant communities from Babylon, Sennar, Media, Persia, Egypt,

---

[7] Goitein, *Mediterranean Society*, 1:215–17; 1:183 ff.
[8] Goitein, *Mediterranean Society*, 1:186–92; M. D. Bratchel, "Italian Merchant Organization and Business Relationships in Early Tudor London," *Journal of European Economic History*, 7:5–32 (1978); Eliahu Ashtor, "Banking Instruments between the Muslim East and the Christian West," *Journal of European Economic History*, 1:553–73 (1972).
[9] Goitein, *Mediterranean Society*, 1:191–2.

Canaan, Russia, Hungary, and Spain – and a Jewish population of about 2,000. In Alexandria, Benjamin noted that people from Yemen, Iraq, Syria, and Constantinople, plus Turks and Franks, each had an assigned funduq. But these funduq were not so much autonomous communities like those of the ancient Greeks in Naucratis, nor were they the kind of lodging houses a wakil might operate for Fatimid subjects. Instead, they were caravanserais established by the Egyptian government for the better oversight of foreign merchants.[10]

Just as the ecumenical trade zone received traders from beyond its boundaries, it also sent out trade diasporas of its own. In Fatimid times and a little later, Jewish and Muslim Egyptians were especially active in the trade to India. Before the eleventh century, merchants from Iran, Iraq, and even central Asia had been habitual visitors to the Mediterranean. Now, with the new importance of the Red Sea route, Mediterranean traders traveled east.

The geniza records contain a wealth of information about this trade. Cairene merchants would go east with their goods for sale, often staying for two or three years. Goods in the eastward flow were textiles, clothing, glass, paper and books, ornaments and vessels made of brass, and other materials. But the most important exports were gold, silver, and copper for Indian industry. Westward, the main imports were spices, dyes, and drugs, as they had been since Roman times, with a minor current of Chinese porcelain and silk. The usual route outbound from Cairo was up the Nile to the vicinity of Aswan, then eastward by caravan to the Red Sea. Aden was a major entrepôt on the way to India. In India itself, however, a ship would call at only one of the several ports in western India to avoid multiple port dues. Shipping was relatively safe from pirates, though convoys sometimes formed, and two or more ships of the same owners often traveled together for safety – as, indeed, they did in the Mediterranean as well. Neither the Egyptian nor any other government furnished naval protection for merchant shipping in these seas. By the fourteenth century, however, merchant ships off western India normally carried soldiers for protection. Ibn Battuta traveled on one that carried fifty archers and fifty Ethiopian soldiers. (Ethiopians at this period made something of a speciality of seagoing warfare.)[11]

In foreign ports, merchants of the same origin often lived together, though formal ghettoization was not the rule. Merchants of dif-

[10] Subhi Y. Labib, "Egyptian Commercial Policy in the Middle Ages," in M. A. Cook (ed.), Studies in the Economic History of the Middle East (London, 1970), pp. 65, 71; Benjamin of Tudela, "The Perigrination of Benjamin the sonne of Jonas...," in Samuel Purchas, Hakluytus Posthumous or Purchase His Pilgrimes, 20 vols. (Glasgow, 1905), 8:523–93.
[11] Goitein, Studies, pp. 339–45; Tapan Raychaudhuri and Irfan Habib, The Cambridge Economic History of India, 2 vols. (Cambridge, 1982), 1:152 ff.

ferent religious communities seemed to deal with one another on cordial terms, and partnerships often crossed the lines separating Hindu, Muslim, Jew, and Christian. The Egyptian community overseas fell under the leadership of a specialized, export version of the office of wakil al-tujjar. He was not only a prominent landlord-broker like the wakil in Cairo itself; the local government also recognized him as head of a foreign community – a post he might combine with other government functions, like superintendent of the port or head of the customs house. A Jewish wakil in Aden had all these posts, along with that of chief justice for Jewish law, an appointment from the Head of the Diaspora, the secular leader of the Jewish people, whose headquarters was still in Baghdad. In much the same way, a Muslim wakil sometimes held the additional post of *cadi* or judge.

Up to the late twelfth century, this trade to the east was an extension of the relatively free and open trade patterns of the Mediterranean itself. Then, a particular group of Muslim Egyptian merchants, called *Karimi*, gained control over eastern trade with government support. They drove out the Copts and Jews who had also been involved. The historical record is somewhat cloudy. We do not know exactly how the Karim merchants operated or their relations with one another and with various governments. They clearly had government favor in Egypt and Yemen, and they lent these two governments considerable sums of money. Even the origin of the term *Karim* is uncertain, though it may be connected with the southern Indian Tamil word *Karyam*, meaning business or affairs. It may therefore indicate a connection to the southern Indian merchants' guilds that were also prominent in the twelfth and thirteenth centuries. In any event, the Karimi kept a semiofficial connection with the Egyptian government until 1429, when the sultan set up a royal monopoly over the spice trade, effectively ending their period of influence.[12]

The ways of trade: the Christian Mediterranean, 1000–1500

The Christian, north shore of the Mediterranean had much in common with the south in commercial practice, whatever the differences in religion. This was to be expected; both religious zones had inherited from their common Hellenistic-Roman past. The check, for example, an order to a banker to pay money held on account to a third party, was used on both sides of the Mediterranean. The term itself comes from the

[12] Subhi Y. Labib, "Karimi," *Encyclopedia of Islam*, 4:640–3 (1979); Goitein, *Studies*, 351–60; Eliahu Ashtor, "The Karimi Merchants," *Journal of the Royal Asiatic Society*, 1956:45–56 (1956); Subhi Y. Labib, *Handelsgeschichte Ägyptens im Spätmittelalter (1171–1517)* (Wiesbaden, 1965), pp. 339–45.

Arabic *sakk*, but the practice came into the Islamic world from Byzantine precedent, and it can be traced back to Roman Palestine.

In other matters the two zones diverged, and regional differences also existed within either. Annual international fairs, like those of Champagne for example, were important in the long-distance trade of northern Europe, but not in that of the Christian Mediterranean – less still in the Muslim world. Both the Christians and the Muslims used banking instruments similar to a modern bill of exchange for making payments at a distance. The forms and terms of payment were similar on either side of the Mediterranean, but they were different among Muslims in the Persian Gulf region, where they followed a pre-Islamic Persian model.[13]

But important differences in long-distance commerce *did* exist between the northern and southern shores of the Mediterranean. One of the most important was the way Christians dealt with relations between the commercial sphere and the political and military authorities – between those who sought profit through force and those who depended on peaceful exchange, more briefly, between plunder and trade. Venice, Genoa, and other Italian port cities organized trade diasporas that depended heavily on the use of force; commerce and coercion were closely linked, if not inseparable. Frederick Lane's important discussion of protection costs grew out of his observation of Venetian trade organization at this period.[14]

In the Muslim Mediterranean of Fatimid and Ayyubid times, on the other hand, traders and rulers were distinct groups of people with distinct interests in both theory and practice. Commerce was an honorable profession. Merchants had comparatively high status, in spite of the Koranic prohibition of usury and the suspicion of some moralists that merchants were too often tempted to cheat their fellow men. The state was supposed to protect traders, including foreign traders, but its control over economic life was limited in theory by such laws as the Koranic limitation on the kind and level of permissible taxation. Some Muslim governments, like the medieval Egyptian government, did at times engage in commerce on their own account; and they usually considered it their right to control commerce as the needs of the treasury dictated, but the political and economic spheres were supposed to be autonomous, as indeed they were in northern Europe.[15]

But Venice was different. It was a commercial republic that systematically used state power, not merely to increase state income, but also to increase the income of the Venetian merchants as a socioeconomic

[13] Ashtor, "Banking Instruments," p. 555, and passim.
[14] Frederick C. Lane, *Venice and History* (Baltimore, 1966), pp. 383–418.
[15] Ann K. S. Lambton, "The Merchant in Medieval Islam," in *A Locust's Leg: Studies in Honour of S. H. Taqizadeh* (London, 1962); Labib, "Egyptian Commercial Policy," pp. 74–6.

class. Venice began its maritime career as a Byzantine province, then as a Byzantine ally – protecting sea lanes or raiding other seafarers. Its first business was to collect "protection" payments as much as it was to carry goods. By the middle of the tenth century, it was already dominant in the northern Adriatic – after 1000 or so, along the Dalmatian coast of present-day Yugoslavia as well as into the central Adriatic. From 1082 to 1204, the Byzantine Empire recognized the value of Venetian naval services (and the threat of Venetian naval power, if unfriendly) by exempting Venetians from the duties normally payable in Byzantine territory. This fiscal recognition of Venetian coercive power brought Venetian shippers about 20 percent higher revenue than their principal competitors.[16]

About 1100, Venetian shipping emerged from the relative quiet of the Adriatic and Ionian Seas onto the contested waters of the eastern Mediterranean. Venetians quickly became involved in the politics of the crusading armies from Europe, partly as carriers of troops and supplies and partly also by using the threat of sea power to extort commercial concessions from the new Christian authorities in the Levant.

In 1201, as part of the preparations for the Frankish expedition known in European history as the Fourth Crusade, Venice embarked on a new policy. It entered into a contract with the Western European organizers of the movement, initially promising to transport the crusading armies if they in turn would help Venice to attack the Christian Adriatic city of Zara. In the end, as may have been planned from the beginning, the whole expedition turned from an attack on the Muslims of the Levant into an attack on the Byzantine Empire. In 1204, Constantinople itself fell to the Crusaders. From then until 1261, the Greek Byzantine Empire disappeared and a Latin Empire of the East took its place. In fact, the central control of Constantinople virtually disappeared and the actual control passed into the hands of the crusading leaders, who assigned themselves parts of the empire as fiefs.[17]

At that point Venetians had an important choice to make. They could have abandoned the standards and behavior of a commercial oligarchy in favor of those of the European feudal nobility – their allies in the conquest of Constantinople. They could have chosen, for example, to exercise territorial rule over some significant part of the Byzantine Empire, much as the Franks had done earlier in setting up the kingdom of Jerusalem. Instead, Venice used the victory to turn an incipient maritime trade diaspora into a full-blown trading-post empire with military control

[16] Lane, *Venice and History*, pp. 386–8, 392; Frederick C. Lane, *Venice: A Maritime Republic* (Baltimore, 1973), for a general treatment of the Venetian economy.
[17] Lane, *Maritime Republic*, pp. 312–43.

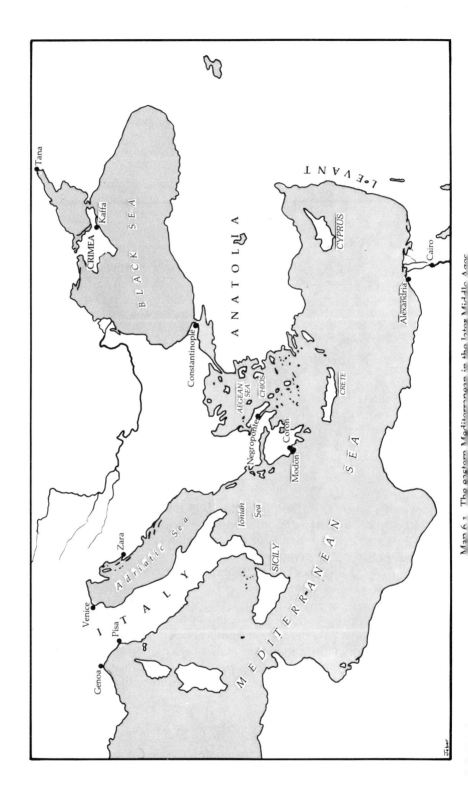

Map 6.1. The eastern Mediterranean in the later Middle Ages

over chosen centers. From the peace settlement, Venice got a reaffirmation of its old commercial concessions, plus the dock and shipbuilding sections of Constantinople (leaving the city itself to others) and a number of strategic strong points to protect and further Venetian trade. The key was the island of Crete, covering the routes to the Aegean and Black Seas as well as those to the Levant and Egypt. The route north to the Aegean was supported by strong points at Negroponte and at Modon and Coron at the southern tip of the Peloponnesian peninsula. A Venetian enclave at Acre in Palestine was added later, along with still other trade enclaves on the shores of the Black Sea. There, the Venetian trade diaspora met the overland traders who went northeast around the Caspian Sea and on through central Asia to link up with the silk road.[18]

Although Venice was a leader in this pattern of maritime trading-post empire, other Italian cities soon followed, for example, Pisa and Genoa, which were also involved in the profitable business of supplying the crusading armies of the Levant. Though Pisa dropped from the first rank during the thirteenth century, Genoa rose, by the 1250s, to threaten Venice, militarily as well as commercially. Venice won the early battles but, in 1261, Genoa helped to put Michael Paleologue on the throne of a revived Byzantine Empire as Michael VIII. In return, Genoa gained the kind of trading-post advantages Venice had seized a half-century earlier, including the Aegean island of Chios, Kaffa in Crimea, and fortified control over Pera, across the Golden Horn from Constantinople itself. Genoa thus gained superiority in the trade of the Black Sea, though Venice continued strong in the carrying trade to Egypt and the eastern Mediterranean.

Much later, this pattern of maritime trading-post empire was to spread into the Atlantic using Venetian and Genoese precedents, sometimes with Venetian and Genoese personnel as well. For the time being, however, it was an exception to the main pattern of commercial institutions over the long sea routes between the Mediterranean and China.

Readjustments in Asian trade, 1250–1500

The most important change in Asian maritime trade over these centuries was a marked improvement in maritime technology. The earliest trade had passed by short stages with little cargo and high crew costs. Even at the time of the Abbassid-Tang prosperity about 800, long-distance cargoes were limited to goods of high value and small bulk. By the eleventh and twelfth centuries, however, aromatics and drugs began to give way to textiles and condiments like pepper, destined for mass

[18] Lane, *Maritime Republic*, pp. 87–117.

consumption. By the thirteenth century, bulk commodities began to enter maritime trade. The pepper and spices that reached through to Europe were only a small part of the total Indian Ocean carrying trade that now included more manufactured goods, raw materials like timber, and large quantities of food as various as rice, sugar, wheat, barley, and salt.

These changes from luxury to bulk cargoes implied enormous increases in the sheer quantity of goods traded, made possible by nearly independent improvements in maritime technology in each of the main seas. For the Mediterranean, these included the development of ships like the Venetian galleys, as well as round ships capable of carrying 100 to 250 tons of cargo. The dhows that sailed the Indian Ocean increased in size as well, so that they too carried 100 to 400 tons of cargo. A large one could carry up to seventy war horses and a hundred fighting men along with other crew and passengers. Many in the Arabian Sea were built from the teak forests of western India. The most impressive shipping of the time, however, was the development of Chinese junks fostered by the early Song governments in the twelfth century. These vessels were larger and more seaworthy than any before this time, and they began using new devices like the magnetic compass early in the same century. Some were later built from tropical forests in Southeast Asia, but the type dominated trade in the South China Sea.[19]

Against this background in maritime Asia, the cataclysmic rise of Mongol power in the northern steppes was almost out of range at first, but it deeply influenced events everywhere. The Mongol conquests begin with Genghis Khan's unification of the steppe nomads in the first quarter of the thirteenth century, followed, in the years 1217 to 1280, by the conquest of all northern and central Asia from China to eastern Europe. The wars were enormously destructive, but the new rulers united so much of Asia that travelers could move securely under a single authority from the shores of the Black Sea to China. This relatively open route lasted only about a century, from approximately 1250 to 1350.[20] After that, the Mongol Empire split into a number of quarreling khanates. The

[19] See Richard W. Unger, *The Ship in the Medieval Economy, 600–1600* (London, 1980), esp. pp. 161–95; G. F. Hourani, *Arab Seafaring in the Indian Ocean in Ancient and Early Medieval Times* (Princeton, N.J., 1951); Archibald Lewis, "Maritime Skills in the Indian Ocean, 1368–1500," *Journal of the Economic and Social History of the Orient*, 16:238–64 (1973); Joseph Needham, *Science and Civilization in China*. Vol. IV, Part III, *Civil Engineering and Nautics* (Cambridge, 1971), pp. 359–656. For a summary of the treatment of Asian trade over this period I am indebted to John F. Richards, "Precious Metals and the Pattern of Commerce in the Late Medieval World Economy" (mimeographed, unpublished paper); Lewis, "Maritime Skills," pp. 258–60; and Raychaudhuri and Habib, *Economic History*, 1:125–59.
[20] For the Mongol episode in general, see Luc Kwanten, *Imperial Nomads: A History of Central Asia, 500–1500 A.D.* (Philadelphia, 1978).

through route continued in local use and sometimes for long-distance trade as well, but recurrent anarchy and warfare made the sea route preferable. Before 1400, most long-distance trade moved by sea. These changes in the north thus conspired with local developments in maritime Asia to make the fifteenth century the apogee of maritime trade along the coasts of Afro-Eurasia.

Individual trading groups met, or failed to meet, these changes, each in its own way; but some broader generalizations are also possible. The last centuries before 1250 or so had been centuries of unusual techno-logical advances for both China and western Europe. Both China and Europe experienced a crisis over the next century or so. For Europe, think simply of the Black Death and the Hundred Years' War; for China, of the Mongol invasions and its own epidemic of plague. But China and Europe were to recover in ways the old core area of Islam – the Abbassid caliphate – did not. After the Mongol capture of Baghdad in 1258, the old center of the caliphate in Iraq and Iran recovered very slowly. Egypt and Syria (under Egyptian control) held out against the Mongol advance, but they continued to fall behind western Europe in important tech-niques like textile production. With the Old World leader, the Muslim Middle East, no longer in the running, three new centers – Europe, India, and China – emerged as the most dynamic and economically productive of world regions during this quarter-millennium.[21]

This relative decline of the Middle East was partly a cause and partly a result of shifting trade routes. Neither the overland route through Iran and central Asia, nor the Persian Gulf route from the Mediterranean to the Indian Ocean, amounted to much. The Christians gained ground against Muslim shipping in the Mediterranean. The Red Sea route took as much as 80 percent of all trade passing to the east by sea – dominated by the Karimi merchants and the Egyptian government, just as Venice dominated the leg of the journey from Egypt to Europe.[22]

New commercial currents also appeared. After 1250 or so, the route southward down the African coast took on new importance. By the end of the fifteenth century, thirty to forty independent, stone-built towns, founded by Arabs and Persians, were scattered along the coast from Somalia to Sofala. Each was a separate city-state, controlled by the mer-chant community in an African setting without large political units in the immediate hinterland. These fortified urban centers invite compar-ison with a trading-post empire on the Venetian model, but the indi-vidual towns were not tied politically to a single center in Arabia *or* on the African coast. One or another would occasionally achieve a form of

[21] Ashtor, *A Social and Economic History of the Near East in the Middle Ages* (Berkeley, 1976), passim; Charles Issawi, "The Decline of Middle Eastern Trade, 1100-1850," in D. S. Richards (ed.), *Islam and the Trade of Asia: A Colloquium* (Philadelphia, 1970).
[22] Lewis, "Maritime Skills."

hegemony over its immediate neighbors, but the dominance was not lasting. A little before 1500, the annual northward flow of gold into the general commercial system of the Indian Ocean nevertheless reached at least a metric ton on the average. This linked Zimbabwe to the world economic system based on gold and silver, just as the western Sudan had already joined through the trans-Sahara trade.[23]

The trade pattern of the Arabian Sea also began to change with the economic shift from the Middle East to India. Toward the end of the thirteenth century, Arab and Persian seamen lost ground to Indians, as the northern Indian economy began to recover from the Muslim invasions and move on to new levels of productivity. The heartland of the Indus-Ganges plains could be tapped effectively from west coast ports in Gujarat, especially Cambay. Indian economic growth paved the way for the rise of Gujarati shippers throughout the Indian Ocean. Tome Pires, the early sixteenth-century Portuguese visitor, wrote that "Cambay chiefly stretches out two arms, with her right arm she reaches towards Aden and with the other towards Malacca, as the most important places to sail to."[24]

In the fifteenth century, Gujarat was the chief beneficiary of northern India's rise to prosperity, becoming the heartland of the most important single trade diaspora of the Indian Ocean, a position it held to the late seventeenth century, in spite of European competition. At this period, Gujarati were still mainly Hindu, with some Jains and growing numbers of Muslims among them. They had established trade communities in many ports, especially at Pudlicat in India and at Melaka in Malaya. As of 1500, about a thousand Gujarati merchants lived in Melaka, and four or five thousand Gujarati seamen visited there each year.[25]

In peninsular India, specialized merchant castes controlled most long-distance trade, especially the Kling, a Telagu-speaking group from the northern part of the Coromandel coast, and the Chettis, Tamil speakers from the southern Coromandel. Both took part in the dynamic expansion of south Indian commerce, as Indians replaced the Arabs and Persians who had formerly carried much of the trade across the Bay of Bengal. But south Indian port towns on both the Malabar and Coromandel coasts still held remnants of the earlier trade diasporas, including the Nestorian

[23] Neville Chittick, "East Africa and the Orient: Ports and Trade Before the Arrival of the Portuguese," in UNESCO, *Historical Relations Across the Indian Ocean* (Paris, 1980); Philip D. Curtin, "Africa in the Wider Monetary World, 1250–1850 A.D.," in John F. Richards (ed.), *Silver and Gold in the Medieval and Early Modern Worlds* (Chapel Hill, N.C., 1983).
[24] Tome Pires, *The Suma Oriental of Tome Pires*, 2 vols. (London, 1944), 1:42.
[25] Lewis, "Maritime Skills," pp. 243 ff; Raychaudhuri and Habib, *Economic History*, 1:127–8.

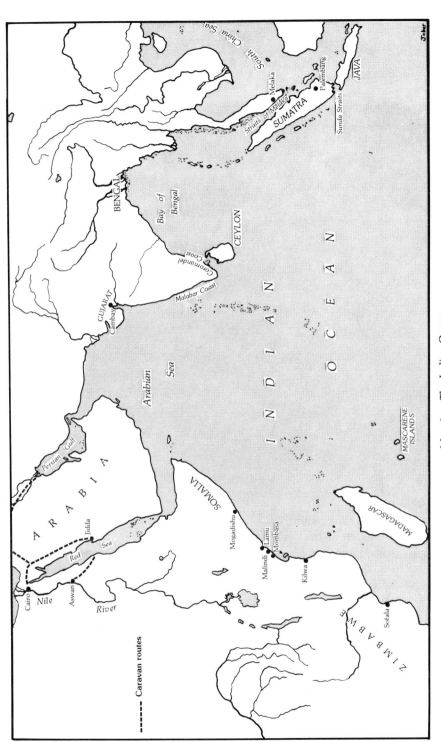

Map 6.2. The Indian Ocean

Caravan routes

or Thomas Christians, some Jews, and large Muslim communities descended from visiting Arab or Persian merchants who had married local
women.

For south India generally, this was a period when trade was less
restricted than it had been. In earlier centuries, on the evidence of wall
inscriptions from the eighth century onward, powerful merchants' guilds
controlled much of the trade from the region and within it. The most
powerful was the Ayyavole, with headquarters in the present-day Bi-
japur district. It had trade settlements throughout southern India and
as far afield as Persia to the west and Indonesia to the east. Its elaborate
military and social organization, along with more shadowy economic
controls, suggests that it might have acted as a militarized trading-post
empire, or perhaps more like the Karimi merchants of Egypt; but the
evidence is too thin to be sure. Like the Karimi themselves, strong
guildlike organizations were gone by the fifteenth century.[26]

In Southeast Asia as well, trade was freer than it had been. From the
seventh century into the twelfth, the state of Srivijaya had tried with
varying success to control the trade of the region from its capital at
Palembang in eastern Sumatra. At its peak it had controlled both the
Sunda Straits and the Straits of Melaka.[27] But it was now gone, and its
successor as the most powerful state in island Southeast Asia, the Hindu
state of Majapahit, was not principally a sea power. And it was in decline
after 1400 in any case. Political power on Java passed to a series of small
Muslim trading states. Fragmented power meant that traders could move
freely, often with the encouragement of rulers who hoped to profit from
their presence. This attracted Coromandel and Gujarati Indians from
the west, Chinese and Ryukyu Islanders from the north, and a variety
of Southeast Asians, including Burmese, Siamese, and Javanese, among
others.

China, on the other hand, had been and continued to be somewhat
exceptional in its trade policy and its attitude toward foreign merchants.
An older view of Chinese economic policy laid stress on an anticommercial tradition associated with Confucian political thought. China did
indeed have an antimerchant tradition, in common with most other
societies, but the main line of classical Confucianism was at least am-
bivalent, though it also favored keeping commerce under appropriate

[26] Lewis, "Maritime Skills," pp. 245 ff.; K. R. Venkatarama Ayyar, "Medieval Trade, Craft,
and Merchant Guilds in South India," *Journal of Indian History*, 25:269–80 (1947); A.
Appadorai, *Economic Conditions in South India, 1000–1500 A.D.*, 2 vols. (Madras, 1936–
51), 1:379, 391 ff.; Burton Stein, "Coromandel Trade in Medieval India," in John Parker
(ed.), *Merchants and Scholars* (Minneapolis, 1965).

[27] O. W. Wolters, *Early Indonesian Commerce: A Study of the Origins of Srivijaya* (Ithaca, N.Y.,
1967).

government control.[28] Under the Song, Yuan, and early Ming (from about 960 to 1430), China entered a period when its maritime trade flourished as never before. Some aspects of the old tribute-trade system survived, but it was comparatively unimportant. Most foreign trade was private, though under government control – and government encouragement. Foreign trade continued to be restricted to a few ports, often to only one, as it had earlier been restricted to Canton. Even though more ports were now open (as many as seven to nine under the Song), the port that Arabs and Franks called Zaitun (more properly Ch'uanchou or Quanzhou on the mainland opposite Taiwan) replaced Canton as China's most important port. Of his visit there in the late thirteenth century, Marco Polo reported:

Here is a harbor whither all ships of India come, with much costly merchandise, quantities of precious stones of great value, and many fine large pearls. It is also the port whither go the merchants of Manji [now Fukien], which is the region stretching all around. In a word, in this port there is such traffic of merchandise, precious stones and pearls, that it is a truly wonderful sight. From the harbor of this city all this is distributed over the whole province of Manji. And I assure you that for one shipload of pepper that goes to Alexandria or elsewhere to be taken to Christian lands, there are a hundred to this port of Zaitun.[29]

The growth of Chinese maritime trade also led to the first Chinese commercial settlements in Southeast Asia, especially in the seaports along the north coast of Java. Chinese founded other settlements along the whole arc of islands from Malaya and Sumatra in the west to Timor in the southeast and north to the Philippines.[30] Chinese ships also began to sail into the Indian Ocean as early as Srivijaya's decline in the twelfth century, but commercial voyages rarely went beyond India.

From 1405 to 1433, however, the Chinese court sent a series of seven major naval expeditions into the Indian Ocean. Several times, they reached as far as Aden and occasionally passed on to the East African coast. These were not small commercial ventures, though they brought

[28] Thomas A. Metzger, "The State and Commerce in Imperial China," *Asian and African Studies*, 6:23–46 (1970).
[29] Marco Polo quoted from Benedetto translation (London, 1931) by D. Howard Smith, "Zaitun's Five Centuries of Sino-Foreign Trade," *Journal of the Royal Asiatic Society*, 1958:165–77 (1958), p. 168. See also Jung-pang Lo, "Maritime Commerce and its Relation to the Sung Navy," *Journal of the Economic and Social History of the Orient*, 12:57–101 (1969); Edwin O. Reischauer and John K. Fairbank, *East Asia: The Great Tradition* (Boston, 1960), pp. 211–24.
[30] M. A. P. Meilink-Roelofsz, *Asian Trade and European Influence in the Indonesian Archipelago between 1500 and about 1630* (The Hague, 1962), pp. 25–6; Milagros C. Guerrero, "The Chinese in the Philippines, 1570–1770," in Alonso Felix, Jr. (ed.), *The Chinese in the Philippines*, 2 vols. (Manila, 1966); F. Hirth and W. W. Rockhill, "Introduction," in *Ju-kua Chau: His Work on the Chinese and Arab Trade in the 12th and 13th Centuries, Entitled Chuy-fan-chi*. First published 1911. (Taipei, 1970).

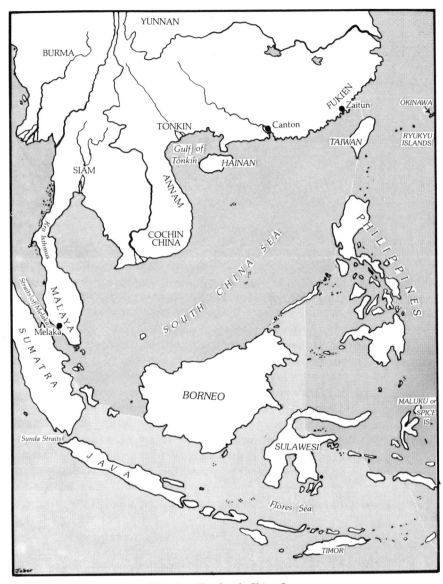

Map 6.3. The South China Sea

back gifts, tribute, and curiosities that might interest the court. Several consisted of more than sixty vessels and 25,000 men. Though they sometimes came into military conflict with local forces, their main purpose was not military and they made no effort to establish a permanent Chinese naval power in the Indian Ocean. If they expressed any interest beyond the personal curiosity of the court eunuchs who supported and led them, it was to extend the scope of the Chinese tribute system. (It is worth noting, however, that the opening up of the Indian Ocean commercial world had already influenced China, even Chinese court circles. The admiral who commanded most of these fleets was a court eunuch, but he was also a Muslim from the province of Yunnan; and his father had made the pilgrimage to Mecca.)

In 1433, the expeditions stopped as suddenly as they had begun. Ming officials went further still and tried to stop all Chinese participation in trade overseas. This anticommercialism had roots in neo-Confucian thought, in spite of its relaxation during the Song and Yuan periods. In the late Ming, it reemerged as part of an antiforeign reaction as well, and the combined antimerchant-antiforeign attitude remained a dominant theme in Chinese policy into the nineteenth century.[31] But imperial orders and commercial practice in Chinese ports were rarely identical. The government might try to keep its merchants at home, but the trade of the South China Sea was already part of a new region of relatively open commerce.

Outsiders soon appeared, willing and ready to take over China's maritime role, though some Chinese continued to sail as far as India, however illegally. Overseas Chinese, already domiciled in Southeast Asia, entered the China trade, along with other Southeast Asians. Off the Chinese coast in the late fifteenth century, the small kingdoms on Okinawa in the Ryukyu Islands stepped into the picture and began to play a commanding role in trade between China and Japan and Melaka, incidentally providing the economic base for a kind of Okinawan golden age.[32]

The way of trade in Eastern seas

By the fifteenth century, the Indian Ocean and the South China Sea formed a new zone of ecumenical trade, as had happened before in Hellenistic times and again under Fatimid aegis in the southern Mediterranean. But this time it was different. Hellenistic or Roman trade fell within a single zone of intercommunication, even as internal Chinese trade had done since the Han. It also fell under the protecting umbrella of a powerful state. Fatimid power reached less far than Rome's had done, but the new trade zone in the Indian Ocean world was one of

[31] Needham, "Abstract," p. 147; Reischauer and Fairbank, *East Asia*, pp. 321–5; Tatsuro Yamamoto, "Chinese Activities in the Indian Ocean Before the Coming of the Portuguese," *Diogenes*, III:19–34 (1981).
[32] Richards, "Precious Metals"; Shunzō Sakamaki, "Ryukyu and Southeast Asia," *Journal of Asian Studies*, 23:383–90 (1964).

dispersed military and political power. It was also a zone with many
and important continuing cultural differences – a culture far less homogeneous than that of either the Hellenistic or the Fatimid Mediterranean. In place of overwhelming cultural similarities, this zone of
ecumenical trade was a network of port towns related to inland caravan
centers, five or six major ports, with forty or fifty minor ones associated.
In some ways this network was not so much a zone of common culture
– though it had a common culture of trade – as it was an elaborate,
multifaceted trade diaspora with free entry for all who would carry on
business according to the unwritten rules of the club.

In these ports, traders were likely to find security for their goods,
banking facilities, marketing information, and a tolerable level of protection payments. Entry into the system was reasonably free, but not
without some reference to cultural origins. One leftover from the era of
past trade diasporas was the fact that most merchants in most of these
ports could find people of their own home culture to supply lodging
and cross-cultural brokerage. Among the most important of these entrepôts were Alexandria, Aden, Cambay, Melaka, and Zaitun. The others were interspersed or else scattered toward the fringes as far as Japan
to the northeast and Sofala to the southwest.

Since the twelfth-century decline of Srivijaya, no state had made a
serious effort to dominate any part of this system. Only China after the
mid-fifteenth century tried to regulate or limit the trade of its own people.
Pirates were a background problem in some regions, and in these circumstances ships traveled with soldiers as well as sailors. Trade was
free, however, of the kind of religious conflict that had split the Mediterranean after the rise of Islam. Remnant trade diasporas continued to
function, but militarized trading-post empires on the Venetian and Genoese model were emphatically missing or else so small as to be
unimportant.

The key articulating units in this system as a whole were cities –
sometimes, like Canton or Zaitun, set in the political framework of a
major empire, otherwise part of regionally strong states, like Cambay,
or else mere city-states like Melaka or Aden. These port cities and entrepôts served to integrate many smaller regions of supply and consumption. The remarkable traveler, Tome Pires, who visited in the early
sixteenth century when the system was largely intact, systematically
described the working of this international trade economy as the interaction of more than thirty-five subregions.[33] These can be set in a kind
of hierarchy that resembles the geographers' central-place hierarchy of

---

[33] The account here follows Pires, *Suma Oriental*, as extrapolated from and further organized by John F. Richards, "Precious Metals."

multifunctionality, but this one uses other factors as well to discriminate between levels. Europe, China, and the Indian subcontinent would fig-ure as core regions, marked by powerful and reasonably stable state systems. These three, and these three alone, also manufactured and exported industrial goods such as textiles, weapons, porcelain, glass, and metal utensils. In some respects, the Muslim Middle East might be included as a weak fourth on the list.

At a second level of economic multifunctionality came regions that did not manufacture or export industrial products. Southeast Asia would belong in this category, in spite of its great diversity – it contained no less than fifteen of Pires's subregions – and in spite of the fact that its scale of economic importance was otherwise nearly on the same level as India's.

Some of the subregions in Southeast Asia, however, belonged to a third category that was economically still less diverse, and often polit-ically more divided. Borneo would be one such region that supplied the larger market with products like wax, honey, sago, rice, camphor, and gold in return for manufactured goods.

Finally, at the fourth and lowest level were the extremely specialized territories of the pastoral nomads, who had little to sell but animal products or "protection" services to those who wanted to avoid trouble. Interior Arabia, Baluchistan (between the Indus valley and the Iranian Plateau) would fit into this category, perhaps along with some seaborne pirate communities in Southeast Asia. Whatever the nature of their com-modity exchanges, all of these regions and subregions were part of an international monetary system based on gold and silver, with copper and cowrie shells sometimes playing a subsidiary role.

Melaka is a convenient example of a commercial entrepôt city in South-east Asia to illustrate the way cross-cultural relations between merchant communities could be handled in the second half of the fifteenth cen-tury.[34] It had grown over the past century from a tiny center of fishing and piracy on the west coast of the Malay Peninsula into the most important trading city in its region. At first, its expansion was military. The Melakan rulers seized small enclaves elsewhere in Malaya and across the strait on Sumatra. Trade control may have been one motive, but in the longer run Melaka took another course. Instead of trying to profit from its coercive power, as Srivijaya had done, Melaka sought to attract any and all trade by offering neutrality and low duties. The neutral stance helped it to balance the potential threats of China and Siam against one another. The Melakan rulers, formerly Hindu, became Muslim early

---

[34] The crucial source is again Tome Pires, *Suma Oriental*. The best later use of his data is that of Meilink-Roelofsz, *Asian Trade*, on which this account is based.

in the fourteenth century. That too helped to attract Muslim traders from the west, and thus to balance Islam against the Chinese traders from the north. It also made possible alliances with other, similar Muslim trading states elsewhere in the archipelago. As a center of Islam at a major crossroads, Melaka played an important role in the further Islamization of the region.

Tome Pires's list of visitors and resident foreigners in the early sixteenth century is indicative:

> Moors from Cairo, Mecca, Aden, Abyssinians, men of Kilwa, Malindi, Ormuz, Parsees, *Rumes*, Turks, Turkomans, Christian Armenians, Gujaratees, men of Chaul, Dabhol, Goa, of the kingdom of Deccan, Malabars and Klings, merchants from Orissa, Ceylon, Bengal, Arakan, Pegu, Siamese, men of Kedah, Malays, men of Pahang, Patani, Cambodia, *Champa*, Cochin China, Chinese, *Legueos*, men of Brunai, *Lucoes*, men of *Tamjompura*, *Laue*, Banka, Linga (they have a thousand other islands), Moluccas, Banda, Bima, Timor, Madura, Java, Sunda, Pamembang, Jambi, Tongkal, Indragiri, Jappatta, Menangkabau, Siak, *Argua*, Aru, *Bata*, country of the *Tomjano*, Pase, Pedir, Maldives.[35]

All of these communities were assigned their own residential areas within the city, either individually or with related groups. The sultan's government chose four officials with the title *Shabandar* from among the merchant community to represent them in dealings with the government and with other merchants.[36] One shabandar took care of the Gujarati alone, the most numerous single community. Another represented other western merchants, mainly from India and Burma. A third was concerned with those from Southeast Asia up to and including the Philippines. The last served the East Asians as a group, including Chinese, Japanese, and Okinawans.

Through the shabandars, the sultan's government offered a variety of services, including warehouse space and elephants to carry cargo back and forth to ships. The government also tried to keep duties low. Where merchants had to pay 20 to 30 percent on the value of the cargo in Canton, the Melaka government kept "gifts" and formal charges to about 3 to 6 percent. To assure fair assessment, the value of each cargo was set by a committee consisting of five Klings and five members of any other community.

Although the Malay nobility came from a military tradition, with con-

---

[35] Pires, *Suma Oriental*, 1:268. Words in italics are those left by the translator in the original spellings.

[36] The term *shabandar* was originally Persian, with the literal meaning "ruler of the harbor." It spread throughout the Indian Ocean, with many later variant meanings. In the first shift, it came to denote a representative of Muslim merchants in a foreign port. Other variants made it equivalent to a minister of state, or even the head of a government in some places. W. H. Moreland, "The Shabandar in the Eastern Seas," *Journal of the Royal Asiatic Society*, 28:517–33 (1920).

tempt for commerce, the sultans of Melaka and some of the high officials traded on a large scale. The sultan owned some ships, chartered others, and sent out some part-cargoes with his agents. Some of these nobles were reputed to be immensely rich, one having a supposed fortune worth 140 Portuguese quintals' weight in gold – equivalent to 8.2 metric tons or 217,617 troy ounces. Other, private merchants had large capitals and also stayed put while their agents traveled and traded on their account. Klings and Javanese were the wealthiest communities. About a third of the ships that used the port were Melaka owned.[37]

Tome Pires makes it possible to reconstruct something about the kind and quantity of goods passing Melaka annually before the Portuguese arrived. As would be expected by this time, most of the goods had low ratios of value to weight. Melaka itself imported much of its food and almost all of the textiles in ordinary use. Most cargoes also originated comparatively near at hand. Leaving aside small-craft traffic in the Straits of Melaka itself, about half came from Burma or Siam on either coast of mainland Southeast Asia. Only about 10 percent came from China or Japan, the same from the Coromandel coast and Bengal in eastern India, and only 4 percent from western India or beyond. Island Southeast Asia other than Sumatra seems to have supplied about 12 percent. The remainder was presumably local traffic with Sumatra and Malaya.[38]

This distribution between long-distance and local traffic seems roughly what it would have been at any other point along the long route from China to the Mediterranean. Only comparatively small quantities of goods with high ratios of value to weight would make the whole trip economically. The trade from the Spice Islands of eastern Indonesia, which passed through Venice to the rest of Europe at the other end of the line, was therefore only a small part of the total quantity of goods passing Melaka, though its value was significant. Nor was the Mediterranean share of total spice production very great. Asian consumption was also important. The Chinese, Indian, and Middle Eastern markets all drew their cloves and nutmeg from this source, though pepper came from India as well as Sumatra. Pires estimated annual production at 100 metric tons of mace and 1200 of nutmeg from the Banda Islands, the principal source of those two spices. Cloves came from the Maluku Islands, with a total production of about 1200 tons there as well. These fifteenth-century production levels were apparently greater than they had been in the recent past – and about what they would be in the next century or so, when Europeans came to deal directly with the islands. If Pires's estimates are correct, Sumatra at this period already exported

[37] Meilink-Roelofsz, *Asian Trade*, pp. 27–59.
[38] Meilink-Roelofsz, *Asian Trade*, pp. 60–88.

as much pepper as it was to do at its eighteenth-century peak under European control.[39]

Many commercial practices in Melaka were common to other ports as well. One of the most universal was the recognition of resident aliens as communities entitled to autonomy from the direct control of local authorities. This was the case from Canton and the Philippines to Aden and Alexandria. Local practice differed, and so did the local forms of justification. In Canton, for example, the ancient distrust of barbarians combined with the Ming distrust of merchants to create a standoffish attitude. Foreigners were not normally allowed into Canton itself, but each nationality was assigned its own anchorage in Pearl River estuary downstream from the city itself.[40] Elsewhere, as in Calicut in western India, foreigners were encouraged with land grants and other privileges. There, the foreigners' own official had what amounted to criminal jurisdiction over his own group, but this practice was general for that part of India, associated with caste and guild autonomies in general. The local perception of foreigners also varied from place to place. Melaka had its four regional groupings. In western India, Arabs were often distinguished from Indian Muslims, just as Persians were distinguished from Parsees, the religious sect of more distant Persian origin. Throughout the Indian Ocean, Arabic and Gujarati were the international trade languages, supplemented by Tamil and Bengali on the Bay of Bengal.

At the other end of the line, in Alexandria, the lingua franca was literally that – the language of the Franks – in this case an Italian base with many Arabic and Greek loanwords. Egyptian authorities were also like the Chinese in their suspicion of foreigners. The Venetians, who carried the bulk of the spices and other Asian goods, had two large warehouses. Each competing European nationality (Genoese, French, and Catalan) had its own establishment, though on a smaller scale. The Europeans were allowed effective self-government over their own communities, but they were locked into their enclaves at night and on Muslim holy days. In other ways as well, the Egyptian authorities regarded the Frankish Christians (as opposed to the local Copts) as a potentially dangerous source of cultural and religious contagion, a sentiment the Franks fully reciprocated.[41]

Another widespread institution in the Asian commercial world was a form of collective price bargaining. It was similar to, but separate from, the collective evaluation for customs purposes of an incoming cargo by

---

[39] Meilink-Roelofsz, *Asian Trade*, pp. 70–93.
[40] Pires, *Suma Oriental*, 1:123–4; V. D. Divekar, "Maritime Trading Settlements in the Arabian Sea Region up to 1500 A.D." (Mimeographed, unpublished conference paper, Perth, 1979.)
[41] Lane, *Venice and History*, p. 287.

a committee of local merchants – the practice in Melaka, Canton, and many other ports. Collective price bargaining usually involved the ship's captain acting for all the merchants traveling with him and owning cargoes on his ship, while another individual or group acted for the local merchant community. Pires described it as it still operated in Melaka early in the sixteenth century:

It is an old custom in Malacca that as soon as the merchants arrive they unload their cargo and pay their dues or presents, as will be said. Ten or twenty merchants gathered together with the owner of the said merchandise and bid for it, and by the said merchants the price was fixed and divided amongst them all in proportion. And because time was short and the merchandise considerable, the merchants were cleared, and then those of Malacca took the merchandise to their ships and sold them at their pleasure; from which the traders received their settlement and gains, and the local merchants made their profits. And through this custom the land lived in an orderly way, and they carried on their business. And that was done thus orderly, so that they did not favor the merchant from the ship, nor did he go away displeased; for the law and the prices in Malacca were well known.[42]

This was clearly something less than perfect competition involving many buyers and many sellers in a free market. Nor could it be called an "administered" price assigned for social rather than economic reasons. Melaka was, after all, in competition with other possible entrepôts. By giving visiting merchants an assurance of prices that were known and competitive, and had some promise of being so from season to season, Melaka's rulers and traders could attract trade that might have gone elsewhere.

In other places, monopoly elements were stronger. Venetian shippers, for example, formed cartels to try to extract, at least temporarily, a monopoly profit over a particular route. The sultans of Egypt tried from time to time – and sometimes with temporary success – to monopolize the spice trade coming up the Red Sea, or to tax the trade as it passed through Egypt, making sure meanwhile that it could go no other way. But price fixing ad lib was simply not possible in the long run. Venetian shipping competed with other Europeans. Egypt usually had to deal with the possibility of overland trade from the Persian Gulf. Even when it controlled the Levant, other routes passed eastward from the Black Sea through Iran.[43]

Many Indian port authorities insisted on collective bargaining to redress the unfavorable position of many local buyers' having to deal with a single visiting ship's captain. Ma Huan, the scholar who went with several Chinese fleets into the Indian Ocean, reported that in the 1430s,

[42] *Suma Oriental*, 1:173–4.
[43] Lane, *Venice and History*, pp. 144–6, 186–8.

the zamorin, or ruler, of Calicut sent an official and a Chetti trader to go over the Chinese account books as well as examine the cargo that was to be placed on sale. Once a price was set for a particular item, it was unchanged as long as the ship remained in port, and each new export commodity offered for sale to the Chinese had to be evaluated in the same way.[44]

That, at least, is what happened in theory. As with any cartel, the temptation was considerable to agree to price or quantity restraints, but later to break them in private. This is one reason why the tight trade restrictions in Canton so seldom worked in practice. The sixteenth-century experience of the Spanish in the Philippines illustrates the problem. In Manila in the 1590s, shortly after the Spanish took over the city, they accepted the time-honored form of collective bargaining, which came to be called *pancada* in Philippine Spanish. The master of an incoming junk from China was obliged to bargain with a committee of merchants acting under the authority of the municipality of Manila, ultimately that of the governor himself. Merchants who wanted to participate committed themselves in advance to invest a stated sum. The purchases were then shared in proportion to investment.

The intent was to improve the bargaining position of the Manila merchants, but it never worked as intended. The longer the Chinese ship stayed in port, the easier it became for a Manila merchant and a Chinese merchant to make their own deals on the side.[45] Given the fact that most of Asia's seaborne trade at this period was a peddler's trade, where merchants rented space on a ship and went along with their goods, there were, in fact, many potential buyers and sellers on both sides. From what we know of Asian merchants' competitiveness, through Pires and others, it is hard to avoid the conclusion that side deals in such situations were probably the rule rather than the exception.[46]

On the eve of the European incursions, a zone of ecumenical trade had come into existence, larger than any that had been created before. The

---

[44] Ma Huan, *The Overall Survey of the Ocean's Shores* (London, 1970), pp. 140-1. Translated and edited by J. V. G. Mills.

[45] Guerrero, "Chinese in the Philippines," in Felix, Jr. (ed.), 1:24.

[46] Some authorities once held that most Indian Ocean seaports from the beginning of the Christian era down to the sixteenth century were "ports of trade" in the special substantivist definition of that term. That is, goods exchanged were elite goods only, not objects of common consumption; price-fixing markets were absent in long-distance trade; prices were established by government agencies according to political, not economic, goals. See, for example, A. Leeds, "The Port of Trade as an Ecological and Evolutionary Type," in *Proceedings of the 1961 Annual Meeting of the American Ethnological Society. Symposium: Patterns of Land Utilization and Other Papers* (Seattle, 1961). As should be clear by now, this view will not stand up to a careful reading of Tome Pires, much less to the more recent and careful research by scholars like Goitein, Meilink-Roelofsz, or Labib.

Europeans were to change all that. Their arrival in the Indian Ocean world was not such a generally revolutionary event as some historians used to believe, but it forced important changes in the ground rules by which Asian trade was conducted. It put off the further development of an ecumenical trade zone for at least two centuries. By then, the common culture of trade that did develop was very different from that of the late fifteenth century.

7

The European entry
into the trade of maritime Asia

European voyages around the Cape of Good Hope and across the Atlantic brought revolutionary changes in world history, but the full consequences were slow to appear. European shipping, like other European technology, had developed remarkably during the Middle Ages, but it was not yet vastly superior to Asian shipping. It was not yet what it was to become when industrial power made Europe the unquestioned world leader. Europeans of the sixteenth century were much stronger than they had been in military and naval power, but they were not dominant.

The European "maritime revolution" of the fifteenth and sixteenth centuries was not so much a revolution in ship design as the discovery of the world wind system. Prevailing winds vary with latitude in the Atlantic, Pacific, and the southern Indian Ocean. Strong and regular trade winds blow from the east over about twenty degrees north and south of the equator – from the northeast north of the line, from the southeast south of the line. Still farther north or south, from about forty to sixty degrees north or south, the prevailing winds are from the west. By the middle of the fifteenth century, Portuguese mariners had discovered this pattern off the Saharan coast of Africa. They learned to sail south with the northeast trades and then, on the return, to make a long tack to the north-northwest sailing as close as they could to the prevailing northeasterly winds. In time, this would bring them to the westerlies in the vicinity of the Azores. Columbus had sailed down the African coast before he considered crossing the Atlantic. He therefore knew that he could sail west with the tradewinds, in full confidence that farther north, he would find westerlies to bring him home.

Even before 1500, Europeans discovered that this pattern was also true of the South Atlantic. In 1498, with the help of local pilots, Vasco da Gama learned the basic workings of the Indian Ocean monsoons. By 1522, when Del Cano brought one of Magellan's ships back to Spain after the first European voyage around the world, the wind system of the Pacific was known as well. From then on, the Europeans could sail to virtually any coast in the world, though the full implications of this new ability were not immediately recognized.

The Portuguese trading-post empire

When the Portuguese arrived in Eastern seas, they brought a new current of trade and, even more, a new way of organizing commerce and protection costs. Asian trade diasporas before this time had operated with comparatively low protection costs, in spite of local piracy problems. Merchants traveled on ships that were often only lightly armed. Seaborne cannon were virtually unknown. Political authorities held coercive power and sometimes extorted what amounted to protection payments (or their officials did so as a private matter), but trade was generally open to all.[1]

Historians in the past, however, depicted a "Muslim monopoly" over Indian Ocean trade, taking it for granted that if Western Christians were to enter that trade at all, they would have to come "with guns blazing," as they actually did. Muslims were no doubt the most important single religious community in Asian maritime trade, but they were not a monolithic group. Even the Muslims were divided into many different and separate trade communities, and they rarely tried to interfere with trade by other religious communities. Jews, Jains, Parsees, and Hindus were important traders. So were Asian Christian communities like the Ethiopians, Armenians, and Nestorians from India. It is safe to assume that peaceful Portuguese shipping could have joined in free competition with existing traders.

In fact, the Portuguese had at least three options. One was to pay off Asian authorities as necessary. The second was to furnish their own protection. They could have seized a few port towns, fortified them, and used them as bases for secure storage of goods awaiting shipment, either back to Europe or outward through the Asian trade network. Instead, they pushed the coercive element one step further – not merely protecting their own trade but also selling "protection services" to others, forcing Asian merchants to pay for the privilege of sailing the seas in peace.

On the face of it, this was a curious choice. It was not the Asian way of trade, nor was it normal for Portuguese trade in Europe itself. The Portuguese crown had supported the diaspora of Portuguese traders in

---

[1] See Chapter 6 and, for the Asian organization of protection costs or redistributive enterprises, see Niels Steensgaard, *Carracks, Caravans and Companies: The Structural Crisis in the European-Asian Trade of the Early 17th Century* (Copenhagen, 1973), pp. 60–113.

Europe through factories or *feitorias*, in the familiar Mediterranean pattern. One in Flanders dated from the fourteenth century, located first in Bruges, but moved to Antwerp in 1488. Other royal factories were located in England, at Seville, and at Venice. The royal official in charge had duties a little like those of a present-day consul: to encourage Portuguese trade and watch out for the interests of Portuguese merchants.[2]

For its overseas operations, however, the Portuguese government chose another model, namely, that of the Venetian and Genoese trading-post empires in the Mediterranean. The Portuguese not only knew of the Italian trade practices, but many Genoese and Venetians also were settled in Lisbon. Several had been involved in sugar planting on Madeira, others in the Portuguese push down the African coast in the fifteenth century. Still others were active in the further Portuguese drive into Indian trade at the beginning of the sixteenth.[3]

These Italians functioned in some ways as technical instructors, who naturally taught their own way of doing things; but Portuguese society had its own predisposition toward coercive forms of commercial enterprise. Lines between feudal nobility and the merchant class were a little more fluid than they were in most of northwest Europe. There, the nobility were sharply distinguished from other classes. They were ranked after the clergy for theological reasons, but far above the peasantry. Merchants were even further down the line in prestige, in spite of their wealth and occasional power. This anticommercial ideology had the usual background. Nobles ruled; clergy intervened with God; peasants produced food for all; but merchants merely exchanged goods without apparently producing anything. As late as the eighteenth century, a French nobleman could lose his status by merely engaging in trade; but theory and fact were rarely completely aligned. Many a noble family had originally risen through trade. In Portugal, however, nobles, even members of the royal family, were openly involved in all kinds of commercial undertakings. It was only natural for them to bring the military traditions of the feudal aristocracy into these new enterprises.[4]

Between the 1410s and his death in 1460, Prince Henry sponsored a number of voyages down the African coast, and his career highlights the way Portuguese society could mix functions kept separate farther north. He was Administrator of the Order of Christ, an important crusading order, theoretically still dedicated to the anti-Muslim cause, and simultaneously a member of the feudal aristocracy, holding certain lands

---

[2] António Henrique de Oliveria Marques, *History of Portugal*, 2 vols. (New York, 1971), 1:171.

[3] Charles Verlinden, *The Beginnings of Modern Colonization* (Ithaca, N. Y., 1970), pp. 98–112.

[4] Marques, *History of Portugal*, 1:180–1.

from the crown on feudal title, and an important merchant as well. He invested his own fortune along with funds belonging to the Order of Christ in all kinds of commercial ventures, including privateering, surely one of the most coercive forms of private enterprise. And he was not alone. Though he sponsored as many as a third of the Portuguese voyages down the Sahara coast before 1460, various feudal lords, private merchants, and the king himself also invested in these enterprises.[5]

This mixture of feudal and commercial activity continued through the late fifteenth century, with the crown especially active under Dom João II in the 1480s. The mixed social origins of the investors and directors were reproduced among those who actually navigated and commanded trading posts, where the combination of feudal background and desire for wealth through commerce was especially strong. The combination of trade and plunder came naturally. It was indicative that Dom Manoel "the Fortunate," the king who gained the first wealth from trade with India, took the grandiose title, "Lord of the Conquest, Navigation, and Commerce of Ethiopia, Arabia, Persia, and India" (little of which actually ever fell under Portuguese control). His contemporary fellow-monarch, Francis I of France, called him "the grocer king" – it was not a compliment.

The pattern of trade and empire that emerged during the African voyages, as well as the more distant Mediterranean precedent, helped to form the pattern that would emerge in the Indian Ocean after da Gama's voyage to India in 1498. By the 1480s, the earliest pattern of more-or-less peaceful trade had shifted to the model of a trading-post empire. The territorial bases were islands, sometimes islands well off shore like the Cape Verdes or São Tomé in the Gulf of Guinea, where African armies were no threat. Otherwise they were coastal islands where surrounding water formed a natural moat. The main island fortresses of this type were Luanda on the coast of present-day Angola and Elmina in Ghana, though there the fort was on a long peninsula separated from the mainland by a lagoon. The Portuguese also tried and failed to capture the island that would later become Saint Louis du Sénégal.

These precedents were clear in the instructions given in 1505 to Francisco de Almeida, the new viceroy of Portugal's Indian Ocean possessions. He was ordered to seize and fortify strategic points, giving precedence to island locations. Garrisons in these forts were to provide security for the fleets that were to begin patrolling the Indian Ocean, first of all, for the protection of Portuguese maritime trade, but second to sell protection to Asian shippers in the form of permits called *cartazes*,

---

[5] For a recent treatment of early Portuguese exploration see Bailey W. Diffie and George D. Winius, *Foundations of the Portuguese Empire, 1415–1580* (Minneapolis, 1977); Marques, *History of Portugal*, 1:144.

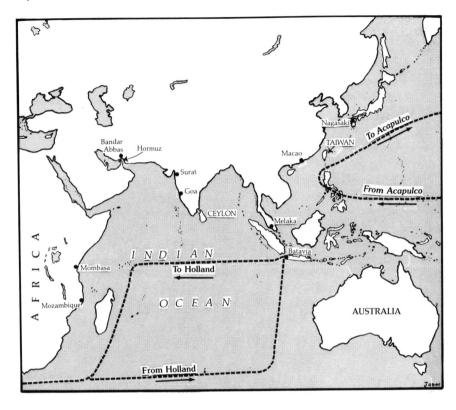

Map 7.1.   The Indian Ocean

which were to be required of all non-Portuguese vessels engaged in local Asian trade.[6]

The trading-post empire that emerged took the shape of earlier Asian trade networks. The Portuguese quickly picked up Asian knowledge of winds, currents, routes, and ports, looking for a pattern of strong points that would give command over the sea lanes. In the northwestern sector, these were the island of Hormuz guarding the narrow straits at the entrance of the Persian Gulf and Aden at the entrance of the Red Sea. The Portuguese seized Hormuz, but they failed to take Aden; and they could never correct this initial failure. The Red Sea remained under Muslim, mainly Turkish, control. Portuguese sea power only occasionally reached into the Gulf of Aden.[7]

In southeastern Africa, the Portuguese were more successful. They

---

[6] Marques, *History of Portugal*, 1:232 ff.; Diffie and Windus, *Foundations*, pp. 243–300.
[7] Robert Bartram Serjeant, *The Portuguese off the South Arabian Coast: Hadrami Chronicles* (Oxford, 1963), esp. pp. 1–40.

sacked Kilwa, the old entrepôt for the gold trade of Zimbabwe, and they set up as their own equivalent a fortified post on the island of Mozambique. From there, they tried to dominate trade from the goldfields to the port of Sofala and northward along the coast. Portuguese fleets sometimes operated north of Mozambique, but it was only in the 1590s that they seized and fortified the island of Mombasa on the Kenya coast, providing a northern anchor for their African operations.

On the Indian mainland, they needed a strong point that could serve as their equivalent to the ports of Gujarat. After an initial effort at Cochin, they switched to Goa, another island partly defensible by seapower and convenient to the pepper-growing Malabar coast in the south.

Southeast Asia was especially important, since the spice trade was the main Portuguese objective. In 1511, they seized the key port of Melaka, and for a time they had a fortified trading post at Ternate in the Maluku (Molucca) Islands where the spices actually grew, though neither of these tradings posts gave them a genuine superiority over neighboring Asian powers – nor put them in a position to monopolize the spice trade. In 1557, they rounded out the pattern when Chinese authorities allowed them to fortify the island of Macao in the mouth of the Pearl River below Canton.

It is significant that these port towns were either key entrepôts before the Portuguese came or could be made the functional equivalents of the five or six main port towns of the pre–da Gaman commercial order. This was important for the Portuguese program of selling protection to Asian merchants. The fees charged for the cartazes were quite modest, but one condition of the sale was that ships granted permission to trade over a certain route were also obliged to call at Portuguese-controlled ports. Once there, any cargo that was unloaded or transshipped paid a duty of about 6 percent, rising to 10 percent in the seventeenth century.[8] The income from such charges at a port like Melaka, a normal breaking point between China Sea and Indian Ocean trade, could be important.

The Portuguese crown sought to control these operations through two separate organizations. One was the Casa da India, a royal trading firm located in Lisbon and endowed with royal monopoly over the principal imports from Asia. This included pepper, mainly from the Malabar coast of India, cinnamon, mainly from Ceylon (now Sri Lanka), and the luxury spices: cloves, nutmeg, and mace from the Maluku and Banda Islands of eastern Indonesia. Ginger, lacquer, silk, and borax were also on the monopoly list, but pepper was by far the most important.

The second organization was the Estado da India for the political

---

[8] M. N. Pearson, *Merchants and Rulers in Gujarat: The Response to the Portuguese in the Sixteenth Century* (Berkeley, 1976), pp. 133–54.

administration of the trading posts, control of military and naval forces, and economic regulations governing trade in Asian waters. Its headquarters was theoretically in Lisbon, but the effective center of power and authority was the viceroy in Goa with command over all posts, military, and naval forces from the Zambezi valley in Africa to Macao in China. Both the income and the expenditure of the Estado da India were higher than those of the Casa, since they included the military and naval expenses that made the Casa's profits possible, along with the tariffs, tolls, cartaz receipts, and other government income collected in the East.

In a sense, the Casa da India's revenues were commercial – drawn from the sale of commodities and shipping services, at monopoly prices where possible. The Estado da India's revenues, on the other hand, came mainly from the sale of protection – partly by the crown for the crown's own revenue, but even more by the crown's eastern officials for their own pockets. These officials drew far more income from the bribes and gifts of Asian traders and Asian rulers than they did from salaries. This corruption was so extensive that it was not merely a source of bureaucratic inefficiency. By the late sixteenth century, the whole structure rested on it. The pattern of private payments outweighed the importance of official channels many times over. Corruption had become, in Niels Steensgaard's phrase, "constitutionally determined."[9]

Pepper sales in Europe brought the crown a handy profit, but the operations of the Estado da India rarely did; and the fiscal balance for the Portuguese government over the long run was negative. For the crown, then, the initial decision for coercion rather than simple trade was certainly a mistake. For individual Portuguese in the East, however, it was probably, on balance and over the long run, profitable to sell "protection," since the individual pocketed the proceeds, while the crown paid the cost.[10]

In other respects as well, the reality of Portuguese empire in the East was less than the words "Lord of Conquest, Navigation, and Commerce" might suggest. Part of the problem was technological. The maritime revolution was in its early decades. Ships could sail to India and return, but the voyage remained extremely dangerous. Even today, the southern coast of Africa is a region of high winds, rocky shores, and few harbors. Of all the ships that sailed from Portugal for the Indian Ocean between 1500 and 1634, 28 percent were lost at sea. Nor were

[9] Steensgaard, *Carracks*, pp. 81–95.
[10] Steensgaard, *Carracks*, pp. 81–95; Pearson, *Gujarat*, p. 56; M. N. Pearson, "Corruption and Corsaires in 16th Century Western India: A Functional Analysis," in Blair B. Kling and M. N. Pearson (eds.), *The Age of Partnership: Europeans in Asia before Dominion* (Honolulu, 1979).

they many to begin with. The average number of departures for this whole period was only seven ships a year. They were monsters for their time, a thousand tons or more – several times the size of ordinary deep-water Asian ships. But Asian ships still carried most Asian trade, and the return cargoes around the Cape to Europe were limited. Over this whole period from 1500 to 1634, only 470 ships made it back from the East, less than four a year. This means that, even discounting outbound losses at sea, about a third of the ships that reached the Indian Ocean stayed there for the remainder of their useful lives.[11]

This permanent migration of shipping highlights an important aspect of this Portuguese trading-post empire. It was more Goa centered than it was Lisbon centered. In a hierarchy of urban multifunctionality, Lisbon was clearly at the top of formal hierarchies in government, economy, and religion; but it was a distant top. Goa, though lower, had more intimate control over its subordinate cities than Lisbon had over Goa. Both Goa and the lesser cities were also closely involved in patterns of Asian trade and relationships with other Asian cities. Just as royal officials made their fortunes by allowing Asians to corrupt them, other Portuguese – soldiers, clergymen, and even a few private traders – entered Asian trade on much the same terms as Asian traders. They sometimes shipped their goods on the royal ships, but they could also ship on the Asian-built (and sometimes Asian-owned) ships of European design manned by Asian or mixed crews. Partly because the return to Europe was so risky, most Portuguese trade consisted of carrying Asian goods to Asian destinations.

Portuguese culture reached deeply into the ecumenical patterns of Asian commerce, just as other new trade diasporas had influenced it in the past. The Portuguese language, for example, became an important, perhaps the dominant, lingua franca in Asian maritime trade, and it held that position till nearly the end of the eighteenth century, when it was gradually supplanted by English.

But the Portuguese were not successful in their effort to monopolize the traffic in pepper and spices between Asia and Europe. Their greatest success came in the first few decades of the sixteenth century, when their shipping reached all the way to the Maluku islands, and they even built a trade fort on the island of Ternate in the 1520s. But they bought spices in competition with Chinese, Malay, and a variety of traders from island Southeast Asia, including Javanese, and Makassarese and Bugis from South Sulawesi (South Celebes). Before the century's end, the Spanish appeared as well, by way of their own string of fortified trading

---

[11] Vitorino Magalhães-Godinho, *L'économie de l'empire portugais aux xve et xvie siècles* (Paris, 1969), pp. 663–709.

posts reaching from Seville to Mexico, then from Acapulco across the Pacific to Manila and south to the Spice Islands. After the 1570s, the Portuguese even lost their post at Ternate and fell back on the alternative policy of buying spices in Melaka from Asian traders who operated over the 3,500 kilometers that still separated Melaka from the Spice Islands. The port of Makassar on South Sulawesi became increasingly important as the center of South Sulawesi trade diasporas, which included the spice trade among other concerns of interisland shipping.[12]

It was much the same with the pepper trade on the Malabar coast of India. In the beginning, the Portuguese tried to monopolize the purchase of pepper through military and diplomatic pressure on petty rulers, supported by a maritime blockade to prevent pepper from being "smuggled" north to Gujarat, and on to the Persian Gulf for transshipment by caravan to Europe. These measures certainly discouraged some of the competition and may actually have created monopoly conditions for short periods, but, in the early seventeenth century, the Portuguese were only able to buy and ship about 10 percent of total Malabar production, even in a good year.[13]

Although quantities carried around the Cape were small in comparison with Asian trade, or with trade in European waters, they were nevertheless significant compared to those that got through to Europe by caravan. In the early decades of the sixteenth century the Portuguese crown had been able to charge prices based in part on the monopoly element in its operations. Later in the century, the monopoly weakened, but the crown still did well charging a price that was competitive with alternate routes. By the 1560s, the Portuguese appear to have imported about half of all the spices that got through to Europe. For pepper in the best decades of the century – the 1550s, and again in the 1570s and 1580s – the Portuguese may well have supplied about three-quarters of Europe's imports and perhaps the same in spices as well.[14]

Sixteenth-century responses of the Asian traders

Historians of Europe often write about the Portuguese trading-post empire in ways that distort unintentionally by keeping the Portuguese at the center of the Indian Ocean stage. In spite of Portuguese naval power,

[12] M. A. P. Meilink-Roelofsz, *Asian Trade and European Influences in the Indonesian Archipelago between 1500 and about 1630* (The Hague, 1962), pp. 136–72; Anthony Reid, "The Rise of Makassar" (in press).
[13] Anthony B. Disney, *Twilight of the Pepper Empire: Portuguese Trade in Southwest India in the Early Seventeenth Century* (Cambridge, Mass., 1978), pp. 32–6.
[14] C. H. H. Wake, "The Changing Patterns of Europe's Pepper and Spice Imports, ca. 1400–1700," *Journal of European Economic History*, 8:361–403 (1979).

the Portuguese were only one among a number of different trade diasporas that continued to operate, either with or without Portuguese permission. Asian traders met Portuguese at many different points, not
least in Goa itself, where the Portuguese were always outnumbered by
Asian traders. As elsewhere, some were residents who helped their
fellow-countrymen find their way in an alien setting. More were moving
traders who came with their goods, made their exchanges, and then
departed. As might be expected from the Portuguese tendency to oppose
Muslims wherever possible, the largest single community was Hindu.
Others were Asian and African Christians – Nestorians from nearby
parts of India, Ethiopians, and Armenians as well. Muslims were present, in spite of Portuguese disfavor, from Africa, Persia, Arabia, and
from the old Muslim settlements on the Malabar coast south of Goa.
Hindus and Jains came partly from Gujarat and partly from the nearby
parts of India. They dealt partly in local food, textiles, and handicrafts
for the supply of the fort, but they also brought in goods from China,
Bengal on the other coast of India, or Arabia and the Persian Gulf. As
of 1546, an estimated 30,000 Gujarati lived in Portuguese-controlled towns,
compared to a Portuguese population in these same trading towns that
never exceeded 10,000.[15]

Gujarati predominance continued outside India as well. About 1600,
the Portuguese-controlled port of Hormuz at the entrance of the Persian
Gulf had 17 percent Portuguese residents, 10 percent Indian Christians
and Indo-Portuguese, 27 percent Hindu, 7 percent Jewish, and 40 percent Muslim. Most of the Hindus and some of the Muslims would have
been from Gujarat, since Gujarati still dominated the trade between India
and the Persian Gulf. As late as the 1570s, the value of Gujarat customs
revenues was still three times the total revenue of the Portuguese empire
in Asia, though many Gujarati merchants worked within the Portuguese
cartaz system. In effect, where the Portuguese had decided to invest in
arms so as to collect protection payments, the Gujarati decided to pay
protection money instead. This made it possible for them to continue
trading in their own right. Gujarati capital also helped to finance trade
that was legally Portuguese, and Gujarati predominance, measured in
value of trade carried, continued on into the seventeenth century, when
Dutch and English competition was also present.[16]

[15] John Huyhgen van Linschoten, *The Voyage of John Huyhgen van Linschoten to the East
Indies*, 2 vols. (London, 1885), 1:256; Meilink-Roelofsz, *Asian Trade*, p. 130; Holden
Furber, *Rival Empires of Trade in the Orient, 1600–1800* (Minneapolis, 1976), p. 315.
[16] Jean Aubin, "Le royaume d'Ormuz au début du XVI⁴ siècle," in Aubin (ed.), *Mare
Luso-Indicum*, 5 vols. (Geneva, 1971–   ), 2:2–63; Pearson, *Gujarat*, pp. 4–5, 92–117; Tapan
Raychaudhuri and Irfan Habib, *The Cambridge Economic History of India*, 2 vols. (Cam-
bridge, 1982), 1:432–3.

Elsewhere, local Asian trading communities reacted in a number of different ways. Our present knowledge cannot illustrate the whole range of possibilities, but examples that *have* been exposed by recent research show some of them. One place of special concern for the Portuguese was the Malabar coast of southwest India, the center of Indian pepper production. It was also a region of ancient and interrelated trade diasporas with a complex past. That region, the present Indian state of Kerala, was wet tropics with several crops of rice possible each year. The low tropical coastal belt was also hemmed in by mountains to the east, which cut it off from easy contact with the rest of southern India. Ancient patterns of long-distance trade had linked it by sea with both western and Southeast Asia.

The local society was Hindu, but the two dominant castes were uninterested in trade. Their wealth came from land, their prestige from religion. They tended to be rural based, leaving the cities to outsiders who had been coming to buy pepper since Roman times. For nearly that long, Kerala society had recognized its need for foreign merchants in long-distance trade. Local rulers had issued grants of autonomy to religious and ethnic communities defined in local law as *Nagara*, trading corporations related conceptually to the ancient Indian trading guilds. They enforced their own law within the community, lived apart from the rest of the population in their own wards, and sometimes enjoyed freedom from taxation or other privileges.[17]

For a long time before the sixteenth century, four merchant groups had dominated Kerala's trade. Two were Hindu, the Chetti from the Coromandel coast and the Gujarati from the north. Two were Muslim, the temporary visitors from Persia or Arabia, and a group descended from transients but now taken root in Kerala. This local Muslim community was called Mappila. It began to take shape at least by the twelfth century. Merchants from the west came across the Arabian Sea in seasonal trade. These Muslims practiced the Arabian form of temporary marriage, acquiring families in one or more Indian ports. The new social group was Muslim in religion, Arabian in some aspects of culture, but Indian by descent. It also had cultural associations with the lower Hindu castes, and with the untouchables who had converted or married off their daughters as a way of moving up in society. Nestorian Christians and Jews were also present as less prosperous trading communities.

Politically, power in the early sixteenth century was fragmented in fact, though concentrated in theory in the hands of four Hindu states,

---

[17] Genevieve Bouchon, "Les musulmans du Kerala à l'epoque de la découverte portugaise," in Jean Aubin (ed.), *Mare Luso-Indicum*, 2:18–27; Stephen Frederick Dale, *Islamic Society on the South Asian Frontier: The Mappilas of Malabar, 1498–1922* (New York, 1980), pp. 19 ff., 29.

which the Portuguese identified by the names of their chief cities: Calicut, Cannanore, Cochin, and Kollam (Quilon). Mappila Muslims, like
the other merchant communities, operated in all four, making up as
much as 20 percent of the regional population. When Vasco da Gama
first arrived in 1498, his pilot took him to Calicut, then the greatest
Malabar entrepôt for the spice trade from Southeast Asia. The Portuguese soon alienated the zamorin, or ruler, of Calicut, partly through
violent behavior toward his Muslim subjects. Local rivalries, however,
made possible Portuguese access to Cochin in return for military and
other support against Calicut over decades of chronic warfare.

Portugal also tried to monopolize the pepper trade of this region,
working where possible through local rulers. Hindu peasants actually
produced the pepper. They sold it first to middlemen, normally Nestorian Christians, who traveled into the hinterland, made contact with
individual growers, and bulked the product for shipment. As Christians,
they might be expected to find favor with the Portuguese, but the In-
quisition thought otherwise, because they were not Catholic. Muslims
in most ports bought the pepper and either sold it to the Portuguese or
shipped it north to Gujarat in fleets of light, fast vessels that could stay
close to shore and take refuge on land or in shallow water if the Portuguese should try to intercept.[18]

The Portuguese called these Muslim traders "corsairs," and the Calicut
Muslims no doubt called the Portuguese some equivalent name in their
own language. The more significant point is that by the early seventeenth
century, the Portuguese military threat had brought about a thorough
militarization of Mappila society. By that time, Mappila shipping had
turned into an armed trade diaspora that made little distinction between
the legitimacy of trade and plunder after a century of maritime guerrilla
warfare. The new emphasis on armed trade included an ideological shift
in local Muslim thought, built on the ancient belief in *jihad*, or struggle
against unbelievers.

Here, as elsewhere, the Portuguese impact had no such simple con-
sequence as destroying the existing trade networks, nor even using those
that seemed to further Portuguese aims. Portuguese naval power reinforced some Asian trade opportunities while it suppressed or distorted
others. The Portuguese carried their anti-Muslim bias into attempted
trade regulation for the Bay of Bengal. Where they might trade with
Muslim Gujarati in some places, they wanted Muslims out of the trade
between India and Southeast Asia, if at all possible. One way to accom-
plish this was to encourage Kling merchants from the Coromandel coast

---

[18] Pearson, "Corruption and Corsaires," in Kling and Pearson (eds.), pp. 27, 32–9; Furber,
Rival Empires, p. 315; Disney, *Pepper Empire*, pp. 32–9.

to take their place. This called for opposition to Gujarati trade in the Bay of Bengal and favors to encourage Kling traders already settled in other ports to use Melaka instead.[19]

But Portuguese opposition was hardly enough to drive the Muslim traders from the Bay of Bengal. They could simply substitute another entrepôt for Melaka. When the Portuguese captured Melaka in 1511, the ex-sultan had moved down the coast to become sultan of Johor, the hinterland of the later port of Singapore. Johor welcomed Portugal's enemies, but its main trade contacts ran east and north in Southeast Asia itself. Traders approaching from across the Bay of Bengal found a more favorable entrepôt in the sultanate of Aceh, on the northwest end of the island of Sumatra. Aceh was already a major pepper producer, and its own traders began to carry pepper around the Portuguese blockade. This could be easily done on the northeast monsoon, sailing directly to Aden but passing well to the south of Ceylon. Portuguese cruisers rarely patrolled so far south, and at most times the Gulf of Aden was more secure for Muslim ships than it was for Portuguese. Even Hindu Gujarati sometimes used this same route, sailing first from Gujarat to Melaka with a cartaz, then loading pepper in Sumatra and making directly for Aden without one.[20]

From Southeast Asia north to China, the sixteenth-century strategy was again different. The Chinese prohibition of foreign trade by Chinese was first issued in the 1430s and still in effect, though Portuguese were permitted to settle at Macao after 1557. The Okinawans were still important over these routes in the early sixteenth century, and Japanese shipping became important in the second half, using aspects of European ship design and navigational techniques under direct Portuguese tutelage until the closing of Japan after 1635. But a great deal of the China trade was carried illegally by Chinese from the province of Fujian or by overseas Chinese from Southeast Asia, who could sail with papers, easily purchased in Melaka or Macao, making them officially Portuguese.[21]

In the Indonesian archipelago, of course, the Portuguese simply lacked the power to act effectively over the thousands of miles of trade routes stretching along the main chain of islands from Melaka to Java and eastward to the Spice Islands. Those routes were shared by many, with special and growing prominence for the trade networks centered on the city of Makassar (the present Ujung Pandang) in South Sulawesi.

---

[19] Dennys Lombard, "Questions of Contact between European Companies and Asian Societies," in Leonard Blusse and Femme Gaastra (eds.), *Companies and Trade: Essays on Overseas Trading Companies during the Ancient Regime* (The Hague, 1981), pp. 79–87.
[20] Meilink-Roelofsz, *Asian Trade*, pp. 138–46; Pearson, *Gujarat*, pp. 92–117.
[21] Meilink-Roelofsz, *Asian Trade*, esp. pp. 124, 157–69.

North European competition for the Portuguese

Between about 1570 and 1600, other Europeans began trading to the Indian Ocean. Their coming marked a new phase, a new and heavier weight of Europe on Asian affairs, but it was still less than it was to be with the next increase of available European power toward the middle of the eighteenth century. The "European Age" in world history had not yet dawned. The Indian economy was still more productive than that of Europe. Even per capita productivity of seventeenth-century India or China was probably greater than that of Europe – though very low by recent standards.[22] Europe's clear technological lead was still limited to select fields like maritime transportation, where design of sailing ships advanced enormously through the sixteenth and seventeenth centuries. Otherwise, Europe imported Asian manufactures, not the reverse.

These major economic trends have to be seen as somewhat distant background for more immediate political shifts like the rise and fall of states and dynasties. In the last decades of the sixteenth century, China was passing through the last and weakest phases of Ming rule. Disastrous decline in governmental authority at the center foreshadowed the end of the Ming and the foundation of the Manchu or Qing dynasty in the 1640s. In the Muslim lands of South and Southwest Asia, major political reorganizations were also taking place in the sixteenth century. This new era in Muslim affairs has been characterized as the "Age of Three Empires,"[23] and this last period of Muslim imperial greatness reached its apogee in the seventeenth century, when the northern Europeans entered the Asian stage.

The earliest of the three empires was Ottoman Turkey, neighbor of Europe and rival of European sea powers in the Mediterranean all through the sixteenth century. Its peak of military power had already passed by 1600, but the Ottomans could still threaten Vienna and the middle Danube to the end of the seventeenth. The second of the three empires was the Safavid dynasty in Persia. It had gained control over the Iranian Plateau by about 1500, but the peak of its power came during the reign of Shah Abbas the Great (1587–1629). The last of the three was Mughal India. It began with a conquest of northern India by invaders from central Asia in the first decades of the sixteenth century, but its peak of power came only with the reign of Akbar (1556–1605) and Mughal culture continued to flourish through most of the seventeenth century.

[22] Raychaudhuri and Habib, *Cambridge Economic History*, 1:458–70.
[23] The term is Marshall Hodgson's. The period and its significance are summarized in his book, *The Venture of Islam: Conscience and History of a World Civilization in Three Volumes*, 3 vols. (Chicago, 1974), 3:1–162.

Even though much of the trade from Asia to Europe passed up the Red Sea or the Persian Gulf, the reputed wealth of trade by sea was enough to attract European competition for the Portuguese. The earliest in time and least significant in the long run were the Spanish from their base in Manila. The union of the Spanish and Portuguese crowns from 1580 to 1640 saved both Iberian powers from attack by the other – and strengthened both against the Dutch and English.

Manila thus became a transit market linking a Chinese trade diaspora with the Manila galleons from Acapulco. Like Goa, Manila was under European control, but the trading population there was largely Asian. One estimate for 1571–1600 put the annual average of seasonal Chinese visitors at 7,000, compared with a resident Spanish and Mexican population of less than a thousand. By 1600, the resident Chinese population had reached 8,000. Since the Chinese visitors were almost all male, intermarriage soon produced a mixed-race, mixed-cultural community able to act as cross-cultural brokers. It was indicative that the Philippine Spanish word for Chinese was *sangleye*, derived from the word for trade in the Xiamen (Amoy) dialect of Chinese. Relations between Spanish and Chinese, however, were hardly more peaceful than those between the Portuguese and Muslim traders. The outnumbered Spanish greatly feared Chinese influence; periodic "insurrections" were followed by massacres of the Chinese residents. Outbreaks in 1603 and 1639 were especially serious.[24]

The Dutch and English entered Asian trade in circumstances that included the prior arrival of the Portuguese. That in itself changed the Dutch and English options. To enter peacefully was no longer possible, especially when the king of Portugal was also king of Spain – perhaps the strongest monarch in Europe and certainly determined to defend what his predecessors had seized. In the last decades of the sixteenth century, he was chronically at war with France, England, and the Dutch provinces. For these north European enemies, the Iberian empires overseas were an inviting target.

International anarchy among Europeans overseas was confirmed by a peculiarity of international law. The various treaties that separately ended the wars between Spain, on one hand, and France, England, and the United Provinces, on the other, provided for peace in Europe only. The European zone of peace was bounded by the "lines of amity," that is, the Tropic of Cancer to the south and an imaginary north–south line

[24] Rafael Bernal, "The Chinese Colony in Manila, 1570–1770," in Alonso Felix, Jr. (ed.), *The Chinese in the Philippines*, 2 vols. (Manila, 1966); Milagros C. Guerrero, "The Chinese in the Philippines, 1570–1770," in Felix, Jr. (ed); John F. Cady, *Southeast Asia: Its Historical Development* (New York, 1964), pp. 238–40; William L. Schurz, *The Manila Galleon* (New York, 1939).

in mid-Atlantic. Beyond these lines, the European powers were neither at peace nor at war; it was an internationally defined zone of anarchy. This anomalous situation lasted into the 1680s, when a new series of bilateral treaties gradually brought it to an end. Meanwhile, it complicated the protection problem for European merchants beyond the lines. Plunder did not automatically replace trade, but unarmed trade was out of the question.

As sea powers, England and the United Provinces had a number of options. One was interloping, entering Asian or American trade in hopes of being able to evade Hispanic patrols. Both began their attacks on the Spanish and Portuguese in this way in the second half of the sixteenth century.

A second possibility was to organize enough military power to attack and capture the Hispanic empires. For the Indian Ocean, at least, both maritime powers decided against a major attack by government forces. Instead, each chartered a joint-stock company endowed with a monopoly over that nation's trade beyond the Cape of Good Hope. Each company also had the legal right to raise armies and navies, to fight wars, and make peace within their zone. Both charters recalled, in short, the mixture of feudal-military traditions with commercial aims that marked the first Portuguese efforts more than a century earlier. These arrangements were now justified in both England and Holland on grounds that merchants who would make profits overseas should also pay the protection costs, which might otherwise fall to the state, hence to the ordinary taxpayer.

In fact, neither company ever attempted a wholesale seizure of the Portuguese posts. Evidently it was no more an economic proposition for the companies than for their governments. As of 1600, the Portuguese held Mozambique, Mombasa, and Hormuz in the west, Goa in the center, and Melaka and Macao in the east. The only one that fell to either Dutch or English attack was Melaka, captured by the Dutch in 1641. Some of the others were lost to Asian powers (Hormuz to Safavid Persia in 1622, Mombasa to Omani Arabs in 1697), but the rest remained Portuguese to the middle of the twentieth century. A Portuguese trading-post empire therefore continued alongside whatever new elements the northern Europeans might introduce.

A third possibility was to create a new trading-post empire, parallel to the Portuguese and with about the same compromise between open competition and force. That is, it would include the use of force where necessary to secure commercial advantage.

A fourth possibility was similar, but with the use of force limited to self-defense. Successful trade would depend on purely commercial competition, though this would include as always the necessity of paying for protection or supplying it with the company's own forces. This option, in short, approached the mode of operation of the Indian Ocean traders before 1500 – with the major difference that any new European entrant had to be prepared to fight the Portuguese, who were not yet willing to sell protection to other Europeans.

Any of these options implied a further consideration. The trade diasporas of the Europeans were not to follow the Asian pattern of organization, where congeries of small firms worked in competitive cooperation with one another. As economic entities, the north European companies kept at least a large part of their trade under the same centralized, bureaucratic control their military-political operations necessarily followed. This newer and larger-scale commercial firm had begun with the Casa da India and other government trade. With the new companies of the seventeenth century, centralized control over a whole trade diaspora became much more evident. Indeed, it became typical of many of the European subfamilies of trade diasporas of the seventeenth, eighteenth, and into the nineteenth century, in other parts of the world as well.

As with all formal models, none of the European options became a reality in a pure form. All Europeans had to operate with a mixture, though one option or another would be dominant. And the mixture also tended to change with time. This proposition can be illustrated by taking the Dutch and English companies one at a time.

The VOC in practice

In 1602, the government of the United Provinces chartered the Vereenigde Oostindische Compagnie, the Dutch East India Company, or VOC. It was a new departure after a period of free-lance and aggressive Dutch interloping in the late 1590s, and the choice of a restrictive, monopolistic company was a curious one for the Dutch at this time. They themselves were the leading maritime power in Europe. Their ships dominated the European sea lanes, because they could carry goods more cheaply than anyone else. They specialized in bulk cargoes like fish, salt, Baltic timber, southern wine, and English and Flemish cloth. They were also the European leaders in commercial skills like bookkeeping, exchange services, and the marketing of securities. One might have expected VOC policies designed to capitalize on these advantages.

Instead, its first intent was to seize the Portuguese trade system by frontal assault. This policy is partly explained by the structure of the VOC itself. The company was subdivided among the various Dutch provinces, with an internal structure that gave capitalists a chance to invest, with some say in policy, but left the final decision to the state.

The VOC therefore began with its military force more important than its trade goods. It was less a capitalist trading firm than it was a syndicate for piracy, aimed at Portuguese power in Asia, dominated by government interests, but drawing its funding from investors rather than taxpayers.

Once in Asian waters, the VOC found that it lacked the power for a frontal assault. The Portuguese in Asia were few, but they had already accommodated such a variety of Asian interests that they were extremely hard to dislodge. The VOC therefore abandoned its first choice and fell back to the second option of setting up a parallel system. The main base was the fortified city of Jakarta, renamed Batavia, on the northwestern coast of Java. It was the functional equivalent to Melaka, though it used the Sunda Straits, not the Straits of Melaka, for its main passage between the Indian Ocean and the South China Sea. The VOC then tried to seize Taiwan, as its functional equivalent of Macao or Manila for entry into the Chinese market. It seized parts of coastal Ceylon as functional equivalents to southern Indian ports like Goa or Calicut, while Cape Town near the southern tip of Africa served as the equivalent of Mozambique and Brazil as way stations between Europe and India. All this was not, of course, the work of a few decades or careful planning from scratch. It was a sequence of gradual changes that took up much of the seventeenth century. Many people in VOC management regarded these posts as mere stopgaps until they might have power enough to seize all the Portuguese entrepôts as well.

The Dutch made one significant innovation in routes from Europe to the east. While they kept with the monsoonal crossings of the Indian Ocean for their inter-Asian trade, they found that ships outbound from Europe could stay far south so as to cross the southern Indian Ocean in the belt of prevailing westerlies, which blow all year long. They could then come north through the Sunda Straits. For the return to Europe, they could drop a little south of the equator to catch the southeast trade winds, which also blow all year. These routes through the South Indian Ocean kept Dutch shipping away from Portuguese naval patrols and saved it from the tyranny of seasonal winds.

As the Dutch developed their centers of trade and power, they also imitated the Portuguese attempt to monopolize trade. They too sold passes equivalent to a cartaz, and so did the English East India Company. At first, a pass made a ship safe only from capture by the fleet of the issuing nationality. With time, however, the companies began to honor the passes issued by the others. But where the Portuguese were willing to issue passes over most Asian routes, the Dutch company entered inter-Asian trade as well as the trade between Asia and Europe. It therefore restricted passes as a way of keeping down competition. At times, it tried to reserve the textile trade between the Coromandel coast and Java for its own shipping. It also tried to eliminate Asian shipping in the spice trade of the Maluku and Banda islands. At one period, the VOC tried to keep Gujarati ships out of Southeast Asian ports altogether. As with the Portuguese before, these moves simply pushed Asian competition onto alternative routes. Gujarati and Armenian ships, for example, could sail from India to Manila and there find a favorable entrepôt for distributing Indian cloth to the thousands of islands farther south.[25]

The Dutch succeeded in one way the Portuguese had failed; they created a genuine monopoly over the nutmeg and cloves production of the Maluku, Banda, and Ambon islands by controlling production itself, not merely trying to suppress "smuggling." On orders from Amsterdam, they sent soldiers to destroy the trees on shore so as to reduce supplies to other potential buyers. Between the 1640s and the 1680s the VOC realized a monopoly profit.

Elsewhere, the Dutch demanded a variety of privileges from the Asian authorities, though some of them granted privileges voluntarily as a way of attracting valuable trade. The Mughal Empire, for example, gave both the VOC and the English company concessionary duty payments and freedom from internal tolls as a way of attracting their silver. On the Malabar coast, the Dutch company succeeded to the sole right to purchase pepper in Cochin, once held by the Portuguese, and on Ceylon, it came close to the complete monopsony it had over trade in eastern Indonesia. Elsewhere, however, the Dutch were forced to operate within a trade system that was for most purposes open to all comers in spite of a good deal of individual chicanery and corruption.[26]

The Dutch drive for monopoly, however, was not a financial success. The cost of coercion was greater than the return, and this problem became more and more serious for the VOC in the eighteenth century.[27] Restriction also implied low turnover at a time when Asian trade was increasing by leaps and bounds. Because the VOC restricted trade in spices, they became a smaller and smaller part of the total value of exports to Europe. Spices and pepper were 75 percent of Dutch returns in 1620, 33 percent in 1670, and 23 percent in 1700, when textiles had already reached 55 percent. Willy-nilly, the VOC was gradually working its way back toward the competitive advantage in shipping services that

[25] Om Prakash, "Asian Trade and European Impact: A Study of the Trade of Bengal, 1630–1720," in Blair B. Kling and M. N. Pearson (eds.); Furber, *Rival Empires*, pp. 266–9. For the Dutch in general see also Charles R. Boxer, *The Dutch Seaborne Empire, 1600–1800* (New York, 1965).

[26] Om Prakash, "European Trade and South Asian Economies," in Leonard Blusse and Femme Gaastra (eds.).

[27] Furber, *Rival Empires*, pp. 52–3.

had built Dutch prosperity in European waters before the Asian adventure had begun.

The English East India Company

In the early 1590s, the English commercial community had the same options the Dutch had, and roughly the same information about Asian trade. Knowing of Portuguese weakness in the Spice Islands, it saw the greatest opportunity in eastern Indonesia. But the English East India Company, chartered in 1600, worked with different home conditions. Its charter gave it a monopoly over all English trade east of the Cape of Good Hope, along with the right to exercise force, but the similarity ended there. It was not under government control, as the VOC was. In its early years, it only had about one-tenth the capital of its Dutch rival, and the capital was raised from shareholders one voyage at a time, returned along with any profit at the end of the voyage. This meant that it lacked the ability to conquer anything. After 1613, capital was subscribed for a three- or four-year period, but the company had no permanent capital fund until 1657. This meant that a fortified trading post like Goa or Batavia was simply out of the question, though the company set up factories on shore to manage its Asian affairs between voyages. In fact, it held no sovereign territory at all until the English crown acquired Bombay from Portugal and passed it over to the company in 1669.

Long before, it had had to shift its objectives from the spice trade to the trade of western India, where its most important early factory was located in the Gujarat town of Surat, then part of the Mughal Empire. Until the 1620s, it kept its eye on the spice trade as well, with a factory on the island of Ambon. In 1623, however, the Dutch captured the factory and put the factors and most of their servants to death in the "Amboina massacre." The incident was more shocking to the English public than it was decisive in the East, but the English company pulled back from the Spice Islands to a factory at Banten (Bantam) on western Java. Meanwhile, English fortunes had improved in the Arabian Sea. In 1622, the company sent a naval force to help the Persian Empire capture Hormuz from the Portuguese. The Persians then founded a new mainland port of Bandar Abbas, which they opened to all friendly shipping.

The English company was thus comparatively late in acquiring fortified trade enclaves in India. By the 1680s, Madras on the Coromandel coast had become sovereign company territory, for all practical purposes. The Mughal court gave the company permission to fortify its post at Calcutta in 1696. Thus, by the end of the century, the three cities that were to become the seats of the three presidencies of British India were already in place – Bombay, Madras, and Calcutta – along with a number of less permanent factories and forts. In spite of the slow start, England at last had its own trading-post empire equivalent to those of the Portuguese and Dutch.

Even then, the English company moved carefully to get the greatest value from its comparatively small capital. Unlike the VOC, it left the inter-Asian or "country" trade to private merchants, both Asian merchants and some of the company's own officials acting in their private capacity. Even the ownership of ships to carry the company's cargoes back and forth between England and India was left to a separate but associated group of English capitalists. By the end of the seventeenth century, the company's business had settled down to the export of silver, originally from the Americas, in return for imports of cotton piece goods, raw silk, pepper, some indigo, and ultimately coffee and tea, though neither beverage was to be really important until the middle of the eighteenth century.[28]

Though the English company held a legal monopoly over all English trade to the east, it was never able to act like a textbook monopolist. Dutch, and later French, Danes, and other Europeans, also traded to India. If the English company tried to raise prices to monopoly levels, other English merchants were perfectly free to import Asian goods from Holland or elsewhere in Europe. Indeed, in its search for foreign exchange to buy silver, the company normally had to reexport Indian goods to the Continent, where they competed directly with those of the other East India companies.

Most of the time, the English company could compete effectively because its protection costs were comparatively low in the early decades. It had to pay protection costs, of course, even in the seventeenth century, for naval forces and a few soldiers on shore. It was therefore in a position to try from time to time to extract money from Asian merchants. It also paid protection money to a variety of different authorities, including the British government itself, which borrowed money from the company on favorable terms as a tacit quid pro quo in return for the monopoly grant. It also paid off important Asian powers, like the Mughal Empire, though the presence of an English post in a Mughal port town was often an advantage to both parties. The company's servants in the East also paid and received bribes for many purposes. But the English operations as a whole nevertheless mark a step away from the kind of trading-post empire the Portuguese had set up in the sixteenth century – and an even

[28] For the company's business affairs see K. N. Chaudhuri, *The Trading World of Asia and the English East India Company 1660–1760* (Cambridge, 1978), esp. pp. 215–410.

more drastic departure from the tougher, more successful Dutch monopoly over the sale of spices.[29]

Plunder is an effective, but potentially very expensive way to acquire wealth. It was a lesson the European trading companies were slow to learn, but they did gradually learn. The Asian trade the Europeans tried to control or suppress continued to grow through the sixteenth and into the seventeenth century. The seventeenth century was, indeed, a kind of golden age for Indian maritime trade. Then, with the early eighteenth century, stagnation and then decline began to set in. It was partly brought on by the decline in centralized power for both the Mughal and Persian empires, but it was also a matter of increasing European power from the middle of the eighteenth century. By the second half of the century, the Asian-European relationship began to change dramatically as the trading-post empires on Java and in Bengal turned into full territorial empires with the dawn of a "European Age." Meanwhile, alongside these European trading-post empires, Asian traders continued to operate their own trade diasporas, though often in new ways designed to accommodate the Europeans' presence and the ongoing problems of cross-cultural trade.

[29] Chaudhuri, *Trading World*, esp. pp. 453–62; Raychaudhuri and Habib, *Cambridge Economic History*, 1:432.

8

Bugis, banians, and Chinese:
Asian traders in
the era of the great companies

One of the historian's chronic problems is uneven source material. For certain times and places, the almost-accidental generation and preservation of historical records make possible a detailed reconstruction of the past. The geniza records of medieval Cairo are a good example. For other times and places, records are scarce. It is often hard to arrive at a balanced judgment between well-described and ill-described aspects of the past. It is therefore difficult to balance the Asian against the European contribution to the commercial history of maritime Asia before the late eighteenth century. The records of the great European companies are admirably preserved in the centralized archives of Europe. Those of Asian merchants were mainly private, and no one saw much use in keeping them beyond the era of the voyages and transactions they recorded. Asian, as well as European, historians have had to work from the European records, because they are the best we have for describing Asian commerce, even where Europeans were not directly involved.

As a result, the historical literature on maritime Asia in these centuries conveys the impression that the Europeans were the dynamic factor, directing and dominating trade, perhaps carrying most of it. That was simply not the case before the eighteenth century, a kind of transitional century into the "European Age" that was to come, even though the Dutch and English of the early seventeenth century *did* come to dominate the spice trade to Europe so effectively that spice caravans to the Mediterranean virtually disappeared.[1] But the overland caravans on these and other routes still ran. They simply carried different goods. In the Indian Ocean proper, total trade increased enormously in these centuries – for European and Asian carriers alike. But our knowledge is not so reasonably balanced. This chapter and the last are similar in length; but that one condenses an enormous body of literature, whereas this one

---

[1] Niels Steensgaard, *Carracks, Caravans and Companies: The Structural Crisis in the European-Asian Trade of the Early 17th Century* (Copenhagen, 1973).

is necessarily drawn from sparse, random, and mostly very recently published research. It is possible to discuss examples, but not yet to present a broad survey of what happened.

Trade diasporas from South Sulawesi

Another aspect of uneven sources for Asian history is the comparative neglect of Southeast Asia. Widespread literacy came later there than it did in India or China. Chinese and Indian culture have been so obviously important in the area that Southeast Asian cultures are easily neglected. Some Southeast Asian peoples nevertheless took the initiative in commercial affairs and built important and militarized trade diasporas at precisely the period when the Dutch appeared to be sweeping all before them in the Java Sea.

South Sulawesi is the southwestern peninsula of the peculiarly shaped island that used to be called Celebes. It was not an important trade center before the sixteenth century – only a place of visit for Javanese merchants making eastward to the Maluku and other spice islands. It was neither culturally nor linguistically unified, having on the southwest peninsula alone two quite separate language groups – one Makassar, the other Bugis and related languages. In addition, its coasts had long been frequented by the Bajau, a maritime people who speak languages belonging to still another group. The Bajau lived principally on their boats, and widely scattered along the coasts of Sulawesi, Borneo, the southern Philippines, and the Maluku islands. Some of their oral traditions suggest an early origin in Johor near the tip of the Malay Peninsula. By the early sixteenth century, however, they were especially associated with Makassar and South Sulawesi. As Tome Pires described them:

These islands trade with Malacca and Java and with Borneo and with Siam. They are men more like the Siamese than other races. Their language is on its own, different from the others. They are all heathen, robust, great warriors. They have many foodstuffs.

These men in these islands are greater thieves than any in the world, and they are powerful and have many *paraos*. They sail about plundering, from their country up to Pegu, to the Moluccas and Banda, and among all the islands around Java; and they take women to sea. They have fairs where they dispose of the merchandise they steal and sell the slaves they capture. They run all round the island of Sumatra. They are mainly corsairs. The Javanese call them *Bujuus* and the Malays call them this and Celates. They take their spoils to *Jumaia*, which is near Pahang, where they have a fair continually.

Those who do not carry on this kind of robbery come in their large well-built *pangajavas* with merchandise. They bring many foodstuffs: very white rice; they bring some gold. They take *bretangis* and cloths from Cambay and a little from

Bengal and from the Klings; they take black benzoin in large quantities, and incense . . . They all wear krises.[2]

The Bajau sea nomads lived symbiotically with the more land-oriented kingdoms on South Sulawesi, especially with the culturally Makassar kingdoms of Gowa and Tallo, and with the Bugis kingdom of Bone. During the course of the sixteenth century and into the seventeenth, Bugis and Makassar also took to seafaring as merchants and sometimes raiders. In the process they absorbed some of the Bajau, while the rest sank into poverty on the fringes of whatever land-based kingdom accepted their presence. The Gowan port of Makassar became an increasingly important entrepôt. Malay merchants, among others, came to settle here under the ruler's written guarantees of their autonomy and safety, and Makassar soon took a commanding position in the trade of the central Java Sea, with trade farther eastward to the Spice Islands increasingly important. In the 1610s, Spanish, Chinese, and Danes appeared as traders and established factories on shore. When Melaka fell to the Dutch in 1641, Portuguese refugees came to settle here as well, and the port soon had some 3,000 Portuguese residents. A substantial Indian merchant also came to settle and soon established himself as one of the leading financiers and traders of the town. Asian rulers, like the sultan of Aceh at the northern tip of Sumatra or the raja of Golconda in India, also sent their agents to Makassar to help traders of these nationalities. Makassar grew wealthy, in short, on a policy of welcome for all foreign traders – not unlike the policies Melaka had followed two centuries earlier.[3]

The economic base was partly the entrepôt trade, but South Sulawesi

---

[2] Tome Pires, *The Suma Oriental of Tome Pires*, 2 vols. (London, 1944), 1:126–7. The translator wrongly identified the "Bujuus" as Bugis, rather than Bajau, which is here corrected. See Anthony Reid, "The Rise of Makassar" (in press).

The Bugis are the most prominent of seafaring trade diasporas in island Southeast Asia, but they were related to other people with a maritime orientation whose history is only beginning to be unraveled. See David E. Sopher, *The Sea Nomads: A Study Based on the Literature of the Maritime Boat People of Southeast Asia* (Singapore, 1965); James Francis Warren, *The Sulu Zone, 1768–1898: The Dynamics of External Trade, Slavery, and Ethnicity in the Transformation of a Southeast Asian Maritime State* (Singapore, 1981).

It is wrong to make too much of a coincidence of terminology, but it is striking nevertheless that people of a maritime culture similar to that of the Bajau still live from fishing and ocean shipping, having an island base along the coast of Somalia and northern Kenya, and that they go by the Swahili name, Bajun, which might well be pure coincidence. Vinigi L. Grottanelli, *Pescatori del Occeano Indiano* (Rome, 1955); A. H. J. Prins, *Sailing from Lamu: A Study of Maritime Culture in Islamic East Africa* (Van Gorcum, 1965).

[3] For the political history of South Sulawesi in the seventeenth century, see especially Leonard Andaya, *The Heritage of Arung Palakka: A History of South Sulawesi (Celebes) in the Seventeenth Century* (The Hague, 1981); Reid, "Makassar," 18–21; Anthony Reid, "A Great Seventeenth Century Indonesian Family: Matoaya and Pattingalloang of Makassar," *Majalah Ilmu-Ilmu Sosial Indonesia*, 8:1–28 (1981), p. 10.

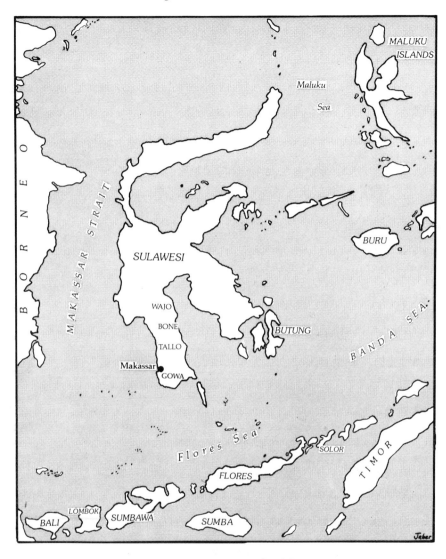

Map 8.1. Sulawesi and vicinity

also produced a rice surplus that was shipped to the Malukus, to Timor and Solor in the Lesser Sunda Islands, and even to northern Australia. Timor and Solor produced sandalwood, in great demand in China for incense. Spices went both to China and westward toward India and Europe. Since the voyage from Makassar to Timor, or to a port like Ternate in the Spice Islands, was just over 1,000 kilometers, this was a trade in high-bulk, low-value commodities over a considerable distance.

Whatever the piratical tendencies of the Bajau and other South Sulawesi navigators who learned from them, they were clearly highly skilled mariners.

Tome Pires used the Malay term *parao* for their vessels, more commonly *prau* today. Whatever it once meant, it is now the generic term for any Malay or Indonesian type of ocean-going sailing vessel not clearly either European or Chinese in derivation. The most famous praus in recent centuries are those of South Sulawesi sailed by the Makassar, Bugis, and others. They vary greatly in size from the large cargo praus with a broad beam and a rectangular sail hung from one or more tripodal masts, down to the smaller and faster fighting vessels of the sixteenth through eighteenth century, depending for victory on speed of maneuver by sails and oars alike.[4]

The seventeenth-century rise of the port of Makassar also encouraged what the twentieth century was to call "modernization," that is, the effort to acquire foreign technology that appeared to be valuable. It was especially encouraged by two outstanding leaders, Karaeng Matoaya of Tallo and Pattingalloang, who served as chancellor of Gowa. Together the two men ruled Makassar and its vicinity through the first half of the seventeenth century. They set out to borrow what they found useful from the knowledge of their European and Chinese visitors, including shipbuilding techniques, the European manner of making and using nautical charts, and coined money. (Makassar and Aceh were the only precolonial Indonesian states to have their own gold coinage.) The period of Matoaya's effective rule (1593–1610) was also when Makassar adopted Islam, which can be regarded as still another form of modernization, largely for commercial purposes. Nor were all these changes simple imitation. Some change came through stimulus diffusion, where the knowledge of the *kinds* of things others could do prompted local innovation more suited to local needs or resources. The Makassar and Bugis were alone in island Southeast Asia to invent their own alphabet to make their language a suitable vehicle for the new demands of law and commerce. They had the alphabet in common, though the Makassar and Bugis languages are quite different.[5]

Given the Dutch concern to master the trade of the Spice Islands, and given the clash of commercial policies between the open trade of Makassar and the monopolistic system the VOC was seeking to create, it was only a matter of time before Makassar and the company would come to overt military conflict. The opportunity came in the mid-1660s,

---

[4] C. C. MacKnight, "The Study of Praus in the Indonesian Archipelago," *The Great Circle*, 2:117–28 (1980).

[5] Reid, "Matoaya and Pattingalloang," esp. pp. 12–23.

when the VOC was able to intervene militarily in a war between the Bugis kingdom of Wajo and the two Makassar kingdoms of Gowa and Tallo – all three fighting the Bugis kingdom of Bone. With Dutch help, Bone won, and it allowed the Dutch to seize and fortify the port of Makassar. The Dutch then set out to exclude all other traders from the port, and the VOC was strong enough to do this, as it was also strong enough to bring the trade of the Spice Islands under its sole control. But this also meant cutting off the existing Makassar and Bugis trade diasporas from their center on South Sulawesi, and that had wholly unexpected results.[6]

As the Dutch began to exclude Bugis and Makassar from the trade of Makassar and the Spice Islands, the Bugis of Wajo in particular compensated for their defeat at the hands of Bone and the Dutch by putting their energy into trade; while the Makassar fell behind as merchants in a vain effort to recapture Makassar City from the Dutch. Bugis, Dutch allies or not, began to leave South Sulawesi in a movement that reflected aspects of their earlier trade diaspora. Now, however, they began to move in larger numbers, from family-size groups on up. Leadership often came from individuals of the chiefly class in the home country. The new migrants were not merely merchants, but merchants with whole families and others capable of becoming a fighting force whose power lay in its mobility built on the maritime culture of the Bajau. By the early eighteenth century, the migration had become a set of interconnected, militarized trade diasporas of a size and complexity as least as great as that of the Dutch intruders who had set it in motion. The Wajo Bugis were so successful that the diaspora-based Wajo were able to return and recapture Wajo itself from its Bone overlords, though it never again became their principal base.[7]

In time, the movement reached from the northern coast of Australia to the southern Philippines, and from western New Guinea to Burma. Its main centers, however, were islands south of the Java Sea, parts of coastal Borneo, and especially the coasts of Malaya and Sumatra on either side of the Straits of Melaka. There, the wandering Bugis and Makassar became important both in trade and as mercenaries in the service of local princes – occasionally in that of the VOC as well. Many settled in the sultanate of Johor at the eastern entrance of the straits, especially in

---

[6] Holden Furber, *Rival Empires of Trade in the Orient, 1600–1800* (Minneapolis, 1976), p. 85.
[7] Jacqueline Lineton, "Pasompe' Ugu': Bugis Migrants and Wanderers," *Archipel*, 10:173–201 (1975), esp. pp. 173–7; Leonard Y. Andaya, "An Outline of the Social and Economic Consequences of Dutch Presence on South Sulawesi Society in the Late 17th and Early 18th Centuries," (Paper presented at the Symposium on the Western Presence in South-East Asia, Manila, January 25–8, 1982, consulted through the courtesy of the author). Anthony Reid, personal communication.

the strategic archipelago of Riau, near the still-undeveloped island of Singapore. From the Bugis point of view, this was an excellent place to settle. They could govern their own affairs under the rather distant overrule of the sultan on the mainland. They could trade, and they could expand their influence over subsidiary bases farther west in the straits, especially at Lynggi and in Selangor. These ports were to be increasingly important in the course of the eighteenth century, since they were the main outlet for the export of tin that began to be mined in the hinterland.[8]

By the 1710s, however, relations between the Bugis visitors and the sultans of Johor began to deteriorate into open warfare, and the Bugis prevailed. They then established their firm control over Malay ports in Selangor and elsewhere. And here they were no longer tolerated guests; they were rulers, just as the VOC ruled nearby Melaka. This brought on several decades of Bugis–Dutch conflict in the region of the straits, in which each of the two alien trade diasporas, relatively well balanced in military and naval power, tried to increase its advantage by alliance with various Sumatran and Malay rulers along either side of the straits. The competition was asymmetrical, of course, since the VOC was a tightly controlled, centralized, and militarized trade diaspora with head-quarters in the Netherlands. The Bugis and Makassar had no political control at all from their homeland in South Sulawesi. In the straits area, they operated mainly as semiindependent bands, though occasionally unified enough to control one or another of the comparatively small sultanates along either shore.

The principal VOC tactic was to use force or threats of force to coerce Malay rulers into permitting their subjects to trade only with the Dutch – at least in certain desirable commodities. For a time in the second quarter of the century, the Dutch seemed to be winning. In 1756, how-ever, the Bugis counterattacked with a force that very nearly captured the key Dutch post of Melaka, and Bugis fortunes recovered for a few decades, based on a new strategy of setting up their own entrepôt at Riau to compete with Dutch Melaka. The Bugis won easily in price competition with the Dutch, whose long-term policy was based on high unit profit but low turnover. The Bugis opened Riau to all comers. It attracted not only Bugis and Makassar but also Chinese, English, Thai, and Javanese commerce to become for a time the most important port

---

[8] Leonard Y. Andaya, *The Kingdom of Johor 1641–1728: Economic and Political Developments* (Kuala Lumpur, 1975), pp. 202–41; Sinnappah Arasaratnam, "Dutch Commercial Policy and Interests in the Malay Peninsula, 1750–1795," in Blair B. Kling and M. N. Pearson (eds.), *The Age of Partnership: Europeans in Asia before Dominion* (Honolulu, 1979), esp. 163–4.

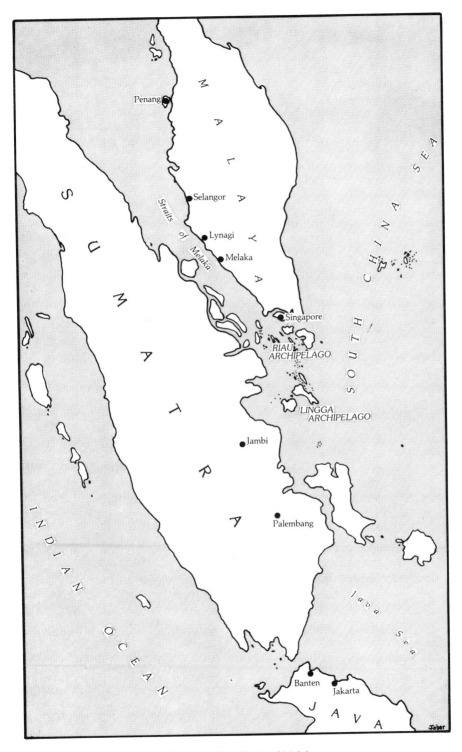

Map 8.2. The Straits of Melaka

linking the trade of the South China Sea and the Java Sea with that of the Indian Ocean.[9]

This success of an Asian trading-post empire was brief. Europe was already beginning to industrialize. The weight of the new European military technology had already begun to shift the European–Indian balance of force on the subcontinent as early as the 1740s and 1750s. In 1784, the Dutch sent a major naval force to Indonesian waters. Among other things, it drove the Bugis from Riau and ended their threat as a rival trade empire. But any chance either Bugis or Dutch may once have had to dominate the Straits of Melaka ended once and for all in 1795, when, as an incident of its struggles with revolutionary France, Great Britain sent an even more powerful fleet, which captured all the Dutch posts in Southeast Asia.

After the fall of Napoleon in 1815, Britain returned Java to the Dutch, but it kept Melaka as part of a new colony, later called the Straits Settlement. In time, it became the nucleus of a British Malaya. More important still, Britain founded the new port of Singapore near the Riau archipelago, based from the beginning on a policy of open trade – in effect an even more successful continuation of the policy the Bugis had followed in Riau.

The first and most important group of foreign traders to take advantage of this opening was the Chinese, but the Bugis community was also important in Singapore, numbering between two and three thousand by the middle of the nineteenth century. They reoriented their commerce to the new conditions. Their fleets and far-flung trading posts now began to supply Singapore with the island products suitable for reexport to China and elsewhere. In return, they supplied island Southeast Asia with Chinese goods and with the products of European industrial technology as they began to be available in Singapore. The VOC had long since failed financially. Bugis trade could now penetrate Java and other islands the Dutch controlled, often in successful competition with Dutch merchants and Dutch sources of supply.

In the twentieth century, the Bugis trade diaspora was to be transformed once more, as the network of Bugis sailors and traders made it possible for ordinary peasants from South Sulawesi to migrate as well. Especially after Indonesian independence in 1949, many left seeking better material conditions. After the great South Sulawesi religious rebellion of 1951–65, others fled as refugees from the fighting and government repression. Even though the numbers moving overseas annually in this century are in the tens of thousands, as opposed to the hundreds

---

[9] David Joel Steinberg et al. *In Search of Southeast Asia* (New York, 1971), pp. 134–5; Arasaratnam, "Dutch Commercial Policy," in Kling and Pearson (eds.), pp. 172 ff.

or even a few thousands of the preindustrial centuries, the basis for this intense migration was laid by the voyages of the Bajau sailors 500 years ago and more.[10]

The trade of the China Seas

Although the ships of the VOC, the English company, and English-owned "country" ships all sailed north from the straits toward China, they were comparatively few before the middle of the eighteenth century, in spite of the Dutch factory at Nagasaki in Japan and the Portuguese at Macao. Most of China's trade was in the tropical products of Southeast Asia, exchanged for Chinese manufactures destined for the islands or for Indian Ocean trade. The little that went as far as Europe was carried in European ships, but most was carried, legally or illegally, by the long-established Chinese trade diaspora in Southeast Asia.

The Chinese tended to think of their overseas trade in two divisions – more distinct in concept than in geography. One, called the "western ocean," was roughly mainland Southeast Asia from Malaya north through Siam (now Thailand), Cambodia (now Kampuchea), and Annam (roughly the present Vietnam). The other, the "eastern ocean," covered the whole island range from Japan, through the Ryukyus, the Philippines, and the islands of present-day Indonesia.[11]

The second half of the sixteenth century and the early seventeenth was a period of remarkable growth in the international trade of the China Seas, in spite of disorders that accompanied the weakening of the Ming dynasty on the mainland. Part of this trade was in Chinese hands, though illegally. Much of the slack was picked up for a time by Japanese, while Okinawans fitted in as they could. Like the Europeans and Bugis, the Japanese could shift back and forth between plunder and trade. They could trade with or attack the Chinese mainland as the opportunity presented itself. Japanese merchants also went out to Southeast Asia in large numbers, establishing Japanese trade-diaspora communities in the Philippines, Makassar, and especially in Siam. Between 1604 and 1635, 355 ships sailed from Japan for destinations in Southeast Asia.

In Siam in the 1620s, tension between Siamese bureaucrats and Chinese merchants created an opening for the Japanese, and a large commercial colony came to settle in Ayudhya, the capital and chief port of the Thai state, even though it was almost 90 kilometers upriver from the seacoast. For a time, the king had a Japanese bodyguard and exchanged embassies

---

[10] Lineton, "Bugis Migrants," passim.
[11] Sarasin Viraphol, *Tribute and Profit: Sino-Siamese Trade, 1652–1853* (Cambridge, Mass., 1977), p. 7.

with the shogun. A Japanese adventurer managed briefly to make himself a power at the Siamese court, and Siam's trade with Japan was more valuable than all other foreign trade combined. In 1629, however, a new ruler came to the Siamese throne and reintroduced the previous royal monopoly over foreign trade. In the 1630s, the Japanese shogun also began restricting foreign trade until he formally closed Japan to foreign merchants in 1639, and prohibited all foreign travel by Japanese. The only Europeans permitted were the Dutch, confined to a small island in Nagasaki harbor. Chinese were also confined to Nagasaki, though Koreans were sometimes allowed to trade elsewhere. Japanese authorities set an annual export quota for copper and silver, the Chinese having double the Dutch allowance.[12]

China, as always, controlled and restricted its foreign trade, especially through the ancient system of tribute-trade convention, revived by the Ming and continued by their Qing successors. Trade with the Chinese mainland was cumbersome if not illegal, hence the role of offshore entrepôts like Manila, Okinawa, Siam, and sometimes Taiwan. The Dutch factories in Siam and Cochin China, for example, were established more for the sake of Chinese goods to be bought there than for the products of Siam itself. Among other things, this meant that the Chinese trade community in Siam was one of the oldest and most important in Southeast Asia.

One center of sixteenth-century Chinese trade to Siam was Pattani on the northern Malay Peninsula. The Chinese may indeed have been the original discoverers of Malay tin, and Chinese tin miners and mine owners were certainly present in southern Siam by the fifteenth century. By the seventeenth, however, the largest Chinese community was at Ayudhya, the capital, which had three or four thousand of the ten thousand or so Chinese resident in Siam. Muslims from western Asia and Chinese were the only foreigners permitted to live within the city walls. They had their own quarter, the finest in the town, with large and elaborate houses. Most other foreign merchants had separate wards outside the walls – where Portuguese, Javanese, Malays, Makassarese, and people from Pegu, in what is now coastal Burma, each enjoyed autonomy under their own chief, following long-established practice in Asian ports.

From the 1630s onward, trade between Siam and China increased rapidly, based on Chinese manufactures like porcelain and silk in return for Siamese rice and timber. By the eighteenth century, Bangkok had

[12] Viraphol, *Tribute and Profit*, pp. 15–17; G. William Skinner, *Chinese Society in Thailand: An Analytical History* (Ithaca, N.Y., 1957), pp. 8–9; Edwin O. Reischauer and John K. Fairbank, *East Asia: The Great Tradition* (Boston, 1960), pp. 598–600.

also grown into the largest center anywhere for the building of Chinese-style junks, drawing on the nearby teak forests. Sino-Siamese trade, however, had to be carried on through a curious institutional structure. On the Siamese side, foreign trade was a royal monopoly. On the Chinese side, it was theoretically limited to goods that entered as tribute and to the gifts the tributaries carried home with them.

On the Siamese side, the royal trading company was a department of the treasury. It bought Siamese export goods and resold them to foreigners who called at the ports. It collected import and export duties, and it had the right to buy imported goods at any price it chose to set – on the face of it, a tough situation for foreign merchants like the Chinese. In fact, however, the royal officials who administered this system were themselves foreign merchants, mostly Gujarati on the western side of the peninsula and Chinese on the eastern side. By the mid-seventeenth century, the Siamese court also began a policy of hiring ships to carry its cargoes overseas on its own account. Again, the ships' captains and owners were local Chinese. This was extremely favorable for the Thai Chinese, who could rise, in effect, to become mandarin merchants – an impossibility in China, where officialdom was recruited from the gentry, not from the merchant class.[13]

In China by the 1650s, the new Qing or Manchu dynasty had finally established its authority even in the far south. In the way of new dynasties, it laid out new regulations covering matters as diverse as the sizes of ships and crews, prohibited exports, proper conduct of port officials and alien tribute bearers, and the mode of storing landed cargoes. All private trade was strictly prohibited, but a convenient fiction slipped into Cantonese practice. All cargo in excess of the official tribute was landed with it and labeled "ballast on board tribute ships," to be held until permission to sell it arrived from Beijing. That could take several months. Meanwhile, if the foreign ship needed to leave, it had to take on ballast in order to assure a safe passage. It therefore bought Chinese goods for ballast on its voyage home. In this way, the "ballast" ships carried in both directions was more important than the tribute that justified it.[14]

By the 1660s and 1670s, a new fiction made its appearance and lasted into the early nineteenth century. The Cantonese regulations provided that each ship arriving on a tribute mission was to send the tribute on to Beijing with a party of no more than twenty-one foreigners. Since Beijing and Bangkok were nearly the same distance from Canton, this

[13] Skinner, *Chinese in Thailand*, pp. 12–14; Viraphol, *Tribute and Profit*, pp. 4, 11–12, 18–22, 24-7.
[14] Viraphol, *Tribute and Profit*, pp. 30–1.

was a time-consuming journey. Cantonese officials were kind enough in their interpretation of the law not to require tribute ships to wait in port, allowing them to return to Siam for refitting. Needless to say, they needed to load ballast for a safe voyage. A single tribute mission could thus justify two ballast cargoes in each direction. With due allowance for auxiliary shipping, the official limitation of Siamese trade to three tribute ships each year could be parlayed into as many as ten cargoes in each direction, or around 3,000 metric tons of capacity each way.[15]

Given the fact that the theoretical trade partners were a royal monopolist on one side and a universal emperor receiving tribute on the other, this might seem to be a prima facie case of marketless cross-cultural trade. Sarasin Viraphol, however, who studied these commercial contacts through both Thai and Chinese sources, concluded that the Chinese merchants who dealt with the Canton end as well as the Chinese merchants who conducted the "Siamese" trade operated for the most part as market-oriented entrepreneurs, even though they were forced to do so within the legal fictions of the tribute trade and the fictional monopolies of the Siamese court.[16]

Chinese trade was also extremely important for island Southeast Asia. In the sixteenth century, the Chinese trade community was far larger and did more trade than the Portuguese did. The island of Sumatra was the chief source of pepper for China, as it was for Europe. With the fall of Melaka to the Portuguese, Sumatran trade split. The part headed west across the Bay of Bengal and beyond tended to move through Aceh at the northern end of the island. The part headed eastward along the island chain or up the South China Sea tended to pass through the port of Banten (Bantam) at the western end of Java, though some Gujarati and Tamil merchants used that port as well.

Banten had a substantial community of Chinese middlemen in the pepper trade. They not only served their fellow Chinese; they were also buyers and bulkers for any overseas merchant who wanted to use their services. Some were involved in local seaborne trade as well, sending their junks throughout the archipelago. Still others offered brokerage and other commercial and financial services. Intermarriage and cultural interaction had already created a mixed culture similar to the later Javanese-Hokkienese mixture called *peranakan*, and the sultan of Banten favored the foreign merchants, placing both a Kling and a Chinese on his council and using Chinese brokers, interpreters, and weighers in government service.

When English and Dutch factors also appeared in the early seven-

---

[15] Viraphol, *Tribute and Profit*, pp. 30–9.
[16] Viraphol, *Tribute and Profit*, p. 8.

teenth century, European notions of monopoly came into conflict with the older tradition of open trade. Over several decades, the sultan, with the support of the local Chinese, fought a running battle to keep the pepper trade centered on Banten, while the Dutch used various forms of coercion to move as much of it as possible to their own port town of Batavia, only a few miles away on the northwest corner of the island.[17]

On Sumatra itself, Chinese also performed many of the same bulking and brokerage functions they did in Banten. In Jambi, the chief pepper port, they were the principal merchant community, dealing with ship captains from Siam, Java, and Melaka as well as Holland, England, or China. Their small ships sailed up and down the coast, calling at river-mouth ports to buy pepper from the Minangkabau growers, who brought it downriver in small craft, to sell it at the river mouth for cloth from India. Indian cloth was extremely important in this respect, so that the India-to-Indonesia trade was an integral part of the pepper trade, whether the ultimate destination of the pepper was China, Europe, or elsewhere. As Europeans became important in the cloth trade from southern India, the complexity of cross-cultural exchanges increased – Indian–European in India, European–Chinese in the pepper ports, Chinese–Minangkabau to deal with the producers. On Sumatra, as in Banten, the Chinese cross-cultural brokers had already modified their own culture to accept many features of local practice and belief. Several, for example, had converted to Islam; some served in the royal administration, and at least one was accepted into the Jambi nobility and served as a diplomatic intermediary between the sultan of Jambi and the Dutch.

The Europeans found it difficult to bypass the Chinese middlemen, and the Chinese found it profitable to deal with the Europeans, who could advance Indian cloth against future deliveries of pepper. But in Jambi, as in Banten, Dutch pressure ultimately forced most overseas shipping, from China as elsewhere, to call only at Batavia. The Jambi people then had to take their pepper there for sale.[18]

These changes were not necessarily all to Chinese disadvantage. As elsewhere in Asian trade of these centuries, European pressure in one direction often opened opportunities in another. By the 1630s, the VOC introduced tighter restrictions on the role of "free burghers" in the "country trade," that is, Dutch citizens resident in the East, but not company employees. It was part of the general VOC objective to carry as much of the country trade as possible on its own account. In practice, however, the company lacked the capacity to carry much more trade

[17] For Chinese trade to the islands see M. A. P. Meilink-Roelofsz, *Asian Trade and European Influence in the Indonesian Archipelago Between 1500 and about 1630* (The Hague, 1962), pp. 245–66.
[18] Meilink-Roelofsz, *Asian Trade*, pp. 258–66.

than it already had. The result was to open the country trade of Batavia to the Chinese resident in Java or Sumatra. Batavian free burghers, no longer able to trade on their own, were often willing to finance the Chinese who could. In effect, the new policies unintentionally allowed Batavia to annex part of the ancient Chinese trade diaspora, which expanded its trade to supply Batavia, while the VOC concentrated on the cloth trade from Coromandel and on the export of pepper and spices to Europe.[19]

Renegades and banians

Superficially, the Asian world of maritime trade was clearly divided into compartments containing legal entities like the great chartered companies, cultural units among the Asian trade diasporas, or areas of Asian sovereign jurisdiction. In actuality, many of these clean distinctions faded away like Chinese tribute trade or the Siamese royal monopoly. National and cultural barriers in particular were looser than historians used to suppose. Individuals crossed the culture line for many reasons, principally for trade, but mercenary soldiers were also a large group floating between cultures. Portuguese had served in sixteenth-century Burma and elsewhere outside the sphere of the Estado da India. Many Asians, like the Bugis, fought for Europeans at times, and still more served in "European" forces all through the Indian Ocean region.

Portuguese and "black Portuguese" (which is to say a variety of Luso-Asians) were widely scattered. Some of their communities survived for centuries – up to the present on eastern Timor. The Portuguese community on Timor originated with a sixteenth-century community of people who cut sandalwood for the trade to Macao and maintained a Portuguese identity over the centuries, even though Lisbon sometimes sent out no Portuguese officials for decades at a time. Eastern Timor was finally reannexed and remained a Portuguese colony into the 1970s, long after the other half of the island had become part of independent Indonesia. A similar community persisted from the sixteenth century into the seventeenth in the twin ports of Gresik (Grise) and Jaratan on the northern coast of Java, keeping commercial contacts with Melaka through the early seventeenth century. Local Portuguese often traded in partnership with Javanese merchants for the voyage eastward to the Maluku and Banda islands – till the Dutch tightened their blockade and cut off access.[20]

---

[19] Meilink-Roelofsz, *Asian Trade*, p. 237.
[20] Charles R. Boxer, *Fidalgos in the Far East, 1550–1770* (The Hague, 1948), esp. pp. 174–98; Meilink-Roelofsz, *Asian Trade*, pp. 269 ff.

A number of individual Portuguese country merchants settled outside Portuguese-controlled ports and dealt with anyone willing to trade with them, the Dutch included. C. R. Boxer's research has illuminated the career of Francisco Vieira de Figueiredo, who settled in 1648 at Makassar after some wandering. From that notoriously open port, he sent his ships to China, the Philippines, and Sumatra. He dealt with English, Chinese, Dutch, and a variety of Southeast Asians. His ships carried not only his own cargoes, but sometimes those belonging to the ruler of Makassar or to Spanish merchants resident there. As for the Dutch, he sometimes had to fight them, but he also traded at other times with their officials in Batavia – illegally, of course. When the Dutch closed down the open port at Makassar in the early 1660s, he simply moved on to Timor and continued his trade from there for a few more years.[21]

Vieira was not alone. Other, more shadowy Western figures also appear on the trading landscape of Southeast Asia in the seventeenth century. A Greek named Constantine Phaulcon served the king of Siam as an adviser in the third quarter of the century. West Asians also appear. One important official of the kingdom of Mataram on Java was a Turk; another was either Gujarati or Persian. The ancient Jewish trade diaspora not only continued; it also received new recruits from the West – partly from the Levant and partly Sephardic exiles from Portugal, who reached Asia by way of either England or the Netherlands.[22]

Even the country trade of the Europeans was less European in fact than it might appear to be in theory. In trying to keep certain routes to itself, the VOC nevertheless hoped to make a profit from carrying the cargoes of Asian merchants, and from carrying the merchants themselves as passengers. Asian merchants not only traveled on European-style ships; they also owned such ships and sometimes hired European officers to run them, just as the European companies hired Asian crews. By the 1770s, only about half the sailors on Dutch East Indiamen were actually Dutch.[23]

Asian rulers also participated in trade, even as they had done before the Portuguese appeared. The kings of Siam were not only active in the trade of China. They also used their other seacoast for trade on the Bay

---

[21] Charles R. Boxer, *Francisco Vieira de Figueiredo: A Portuguese Merchant-Adventurer in Southeast Asia, 1624–1667* (The Hague, 1967), esp. pp. 7 ff. and 52.

[22] Viraphol, *Tribute and Profit*, pp. 9–10; Meilink-Roelofsz, *Asian Trade*, p. 244; Furber, *Rival Empires*, p. 25; Dennys Lombard, "Questions on the Contact between European Companies and Asian Societies," in Leonard Blusse and Femme Gaastra (eds.), *Companies and Trade: Essays on Overseas Trading Companies during the Ancient Regime* (The Hague, 1981).

[23] Om Prakash, "Asian Trade and European Impact: A Study of the Trade of Bengal, 1630–1720," in Kling and Pearson (eds.), *The Age of Partnership*, pp. 47–9; Furber, *Rival Empires*, p. 302.

of Bengal, and some of the king's ships, managed by an agent in Bengal, were active in the trade between the east and west coasts of India. The sultan of Banten was another active shipowner in the 1660s and 1670s. His ship, the *Bull*, sailed under European officers as far west as Madras and north to Manila, and Asian ships often carried European goods, just as European ships carried Asian goods. That pattern was notable in Philippine trade, where Spanish authorities permitted Asian but not other European shipping. English-owned goods therefore entered Manila on vessels belonging variously to Hindus, Muslims, Armenian Christians, and Parsees.[24]

Whatever ideas the European companies might have had about keeping trade in their own hands, they always had to deal with Asian suppliers. Each Indian port supported merchants of varying wealth and importance, and some of them were very rich indeed by European standards. A powerful European company might try to push its advantage in price bargaining, but the Indian sellers could do the same. Two merchants of Belasore, in Bengal, were often able to organize rings of potential buyers to bargain collectively with the English East India Company, and in 1681, one merchant alone supplied nearly half the goods the English bought in that port. The company sometimes tried to avoid this concentrated power by dealing only with a greater number of middling merchants, but that solution was not always possible.[25]

In these circumstances of interlocking trade diasporas, either Asians or Europeans might find themselves in the role of cross-cultural broker, but it went more often to Asians with long residence in the same port and accumulated knowledge of local affairs. The Europeans, as strangers, needed tactical advice about the local commercial scene, as well as the more obvious information and translation services. As with the Hausa *maigida* or the medieval Egyptian *wakil*, cross-cultural brokerage was often best performed by a foreign merchant of long residence. Indeed, the overlay of trade diaspora was such that most merchants in many parts of India were foreigners. In Bengal, for example, the most prominent merchants were from Gujarat or Rajasthan on the other side of India. The Dutch post at Kasimbasar at one point dealt with eighteen different and prominent merchants, and not one of them was a Bengali.[26]

Some of the Gujarati merchants in Bengal may have come by sea, but

[24] K. N. Chaudhuri, *The Trading World of Asia and the English East India Company 1660–1760* (Cambridge, 1978); Serafin D. Quaison, *English "Country Trade" with the Philippines, 1664–1765* (Quezon City, 1966), p. 41 and passim.

[25] Chaudhuri, *East India Company*, pp. 67–8, 148–9.

[26] Dilip Basu, "The Banian and the British in Calcutta, 1800–1850," *Bengal Past and Present*, 92:157–70 (1973); Pradip Sinha, "Approaches to Urban History: Calcutta (1750–1850)," *Bengal Past and Present*, 87:106–19 (1968).

the Guarati trade diaspora also reached overland across northern India. Gujarati merchants and bankers dominated much of the economic life of the whole region, but not from the port towns. Their main center was Murshidabad in the interior, and their network extended to Mirzapur, Benares, Nagpur, and Multan. But to treat the Bengal setting as a simple intersection of a European and a Gujarati trade diaspora disguises the enormous complexity of a point of exchange where resident merchant communities included Portuguese, Dutch, English, French, Armenian, central Asian, Marwaris, and various northern Indians from the interior, as well as Gujarati Hindus and a variety of different Muslims, including some Muslim Bengalis.[27]

In Madras and in Bengal, in particular, the need for cross-cultural assistance led to the formation of a professional class of cross-cultural guides and advisers, called *dubash* in Madras and *banian* in Bengal. The Bengali term is confusing, since it recalls the Gujarati *vanya*, meaning a caste of merchants. That was, in fact, the ultimate origin of the term, but it passed first into Portuguese, to signify any Indian merchant at all, then into Bengali English to mean a personal Indian agent to assist in the commercial affairs of a particular European official or merchant. Mughal aristocrats appear to have employed similar agents, and the Portuguese no doubt did the same, though perhaps without the elaborate development the institution passed through in eighteenth-century Bengal.[28]

The typical banian of that period was something more than a mere broker; he was also a capitalist and sometime partner of his European principal. An older stereotype shows the banian as a man of humble origins who rose to wealth and power through "collaboration" with the British. In fact, banians often supplied the initial capital for an East India Company official to enter trade on his own account, and they shared in the profit. By the late eighteenth century, an English official could do things an ordinary Indian could not do. He could, for example, pass his personally owned goods through the tollgates of the Mughal Empire without having to pay the tolls Indian merchants paid. This privilege had originally belonged to the East India Company, for company goods only, but in Bengal company servants had secured the right to the *dastak* or seal of exemption for their own personal goods as well. In these circumstances, both the banian and his English partner could gain from their relationship.

The typical banian attached himself to one English official at a time,

[27] Chaudhuri, *East India Company*, p. 98.
[28] Peter Marshall, "Masters and Banians in Eighteenth-Century Calcutta," in Kling and Pearson (eds.), *The Age of Partnership*; Basu, "The Banian and the British," pp. 159–60.

though he might later change to another. He was usually a man of substance, with money to invest, and it was usual to begin at the lower range of the company hierarchy, moving to higher officials as he gained in capital and experience. In time, he might offer his services to a government department for its Indian dealings, or even to an agency house doing cross-cultural business for principals abroad. The most successful banians finally moved out of collaborative enterprises to set up on their own in insurance or banking shares.[29]

In the 1760s and afterward, agency houses began to provide some of the service the banians had done in the past, and still continued to do. When a company servant first came to India, he needed the cross-cultural agency of a banian, and he needed the Indian capital a banian could supply. Later on, however, if he had been successful, it was usual to retire to England. He then needed some way to get capital back to Britain, or else a way to keep it active in the East after he was gone. The agency house filled this need. It could buy or sell goods for a small commission, could receive or pay money in a variety of currencies, and could hold nonperishable goods till such time as the owner ordered their sale or shipment. Meanwhile, the owner could borrow against their value.[30]

With the rise of agency houses in the late eighteenth and early nineteenth centuries – and of similar institutions outside of British India – cross-cultural trade became far more institutionalized than it had been. As cross-cultural brokers, agency houses had become, in effect, common carriers, ready to take on the affairs of almost anyone with money to pay for their services. With that, the gradual homogenization of Asian commercial cultures moved ahead in a giant step of the kind that had been taken in Europe itself about the sixteenth century. The great monopolistic companies were still around till the failure of the VOC and its abolition in 1799, or the English company's loss of its monopoly rights for India in 1813 and China in 1833. Long before that, however, the agency houses were carrying far more of total British trade in Asia than the company was.

Urban networks

The dominant framework for historical writing about Asian maritime trade in the seventeenth and eighteenth centuries is still that of the great European companies. In addition to the Dutch and English, the largest and most representative, there were several French companies, an Os-

[29] Basu, "The Banian and the British," p. 160; Marshall, "Masters and Banians," in Kling and Pearson (eds.), pp. 195 ff.
[30] Furber, Rival Empires, pp. 189–200.

tend company, a Scottish, a Danish, a Swedish, a Prussian, and a Russian company – all operating for varying lengths of time and with varying success. But it remains important to remember that, for any date before the second half of the eighteenth century, Asians carried more of Asian trade than Europeans did. The last decades of the seventeenth century were the pinnacle of importance for Indian shipping. The trading fleets out of Gujarati ports then dropped off in the first half of the eighteenth century, balanced somewhat by the rise of partly Indian "country" shipping from Bengal.[31] But the Bugis could still compete effectively against the Dutch company into the second half of the century and were still able to challenge Dutch military power with power of their own. But somewhere in the decades between about 1740 and 1790, effective power in Eastern seas, and on land in India, had shifted to the Europeans.

Before this dawn of the European Age, however, the European companies were only one articulating element in Asian trade. The Asian trade diasporas were a second, and the network of Asian port cities that was already important before 1500 continued as a major factor. It still provided the place and the institutions for cross-cultural exchanges. Some were dominated by the political authorities, notably, as always, Canton by imperial China, but now also Batavia by the Netherlands, and Goa by the Portuguese. Whatever the political control, all these cities included large communities of foreign traders. They were not exclusive trading posts for the dominant power alone, even when that power was itself a trading company. Other cities were much more open, like Surat, Bandar Abbas, or Banten at some periods.

The rough hierarchy of multifunctionality that was already detectable before 1500 remained, though the individual ports might well shift position within it. During this period Melaka lost, first to Batavia – as Batavia would lose out to Singapore by the middle of the nineteenth century. Gujarati ports like Surat gradually lost a little to Bombay, while on the east coast of India various Bengali ports rose in importance and finally gave way to the preeminence of Calcutta.

And the port cities themselves were only an interrelated subsystem of a greater whole. Seaborne trade was not all trade, or even most trade. Behind Canton lay the extensive canal and road network of China. Similar overland networks operated all through the Indian subcontinent. Nor were the sea links from the Indian Ocean to Europe the only links. A set of overland routes also ran from India and Persia through to the seaports of the Mediterranean and Black Seas, north from the Caspian to Russia, and even overland through eastern Europe to cities like Am-

[31] Tapan Raychaudhuri and Irfan Habib, *The Cambridge Economic History of India*, 2 vols. (Cambridge, 1982), 1:424–33.

sterdam. The silk road still carried trade at most times, and the eighteenth century was the period of China's most impressive political expansion to the west. Evidence for overland trade is less extensive than it is for seaborne trade, but overland trade was important nonetheless.

9

Overland trade of the seventeenth century: Armenian carriers between Europe and East Asia

Seaborne trade was probably the leading sector of commercial growth in the world economy – perhaps going back as far as the ninth century, certainly from the fifteenth-century maritime revolution well into the nineteenth. The seventeenth century, however, and at least the first half of the eighteenth, marked a period of intense development in overland trade as well. This chapter will deal with overland connections between Persia and Europe, between Persia and India and East Asia, and especially with the Armenian trade diaspora that was active in the overland trade as well as the maritime trade of the Indian Ocean.

In addition, and in these same centuries, new trade diasporas began to carry Euopean goods overland into regions previously served only by indirect relay trade. Siberia was one such region, as European, Chinese, and Ottoman demand for furs sent Russians eastward through the forests of northern Asia. This movement began in the middle of the sixteenth century. By the 1640s, the fur traders had found ways to use the large rivers of Siberia so as to reach the Pacific Ocean with only occasional need to portage goods from one river to another. Continuing by sea, they reached Alaska by the early eighteenth century and had explored down the North American coast to California by the early nineteenth.

The same demand for furs sent European fur traders and their local agents into the North American forests with a similar timing. French trading posts on the lower Saint Lawrence from the early seventeenth century became the anchor for a trade network westward along the line of the Great Lakes to reach the Mississippi and beyond by the end of the century. In the 1670s, the English entered the North American trade as well, partly through New York, recently seized from the Dutch, partly by a direct sea route to the southern and western shores of Hudson Bay and then south and west. About the end of the eighteenth century, North American fur traders began to encounter the Russians coming around the world from the other direction.

Both the Russian and the North American fur trade followed the

179

pattern of overland trading-post empire, using force to protect goods in transit, to control strong points, and sometimes to make local people deliver furs as tribute, but not to control or administer the territory as a whole.

Similar penetration by European or part-European traders took place on other continents during these same centuries. One of the most spectacular was that of the *bandeiras* in the Brazilian hinterland. These were armed companies that made interior expeditions combining slave raiding, commerce, exploration, and prospecting. The word *bandeira* came from a Portuguese word for a particular kind of military company, and the *bandeirantes* were, in the long run, responsible for the exploration and settlement of the Brazilian interior. They set out from a number of centers in settled Brazil, but their most prominent base point was the plateau country of the present state of São Paulo, where intrusive Portuguese had already begun to mix with the Tupi native Americans of the region before the end of the sixteenth century. Those who became bandeirantes were therefore racially and culturally mixed, and they continued to speak the Tupi language far into the eighteenth century. Their combination of raiding and trading suggests some aspects of the Bugis diaspora around the Java Sea, but the raids led to permanent settlements that in turn became the nuclei for colonial towns. During the transition, they were strong points in an overland trading-post empire that resembled the trading-post empires simultaneously coming into existence in North America and northern Siberia.[1]

Long-distance traders penetrated other parts of the Americas as well in these centuries, following a variety of different forms. On either side of the Plata River, well south of the *bandeiras*, cattle from Europe escaped onto the open grassland of the pampa. As they became "wild" they were a free resource, to be hunted by anyone who cared to do so. Traders entered the region to commercialize the export of hides from the pampa zone that covered parts of Argentina, Uruguay, and the Brazilian state of Rio Grande do Sul. It was not, perhaps, cross-cultural trade in the mode of the classic trade diasporas, though cultural differences played a role. Unlike most European settlers in the Americas, the cattle killers crossed the frontier line in their way of life as well as their geographic location. They often mixed biologically as well as culturally with the sparse native American populations of the grasslands. Similar communities of "trans-frontiersmen" developed not only in the Plata region, where they went by the name of *gaucho*, but also on some of the larger Caribbean islands as the "cow-killers" or buccaneers, in the Orinoco

---

[1] See Richard M. Morse, *The Bandeirantes: The Historical Role of the Brazilian Pathfinders* (New York, 1965).

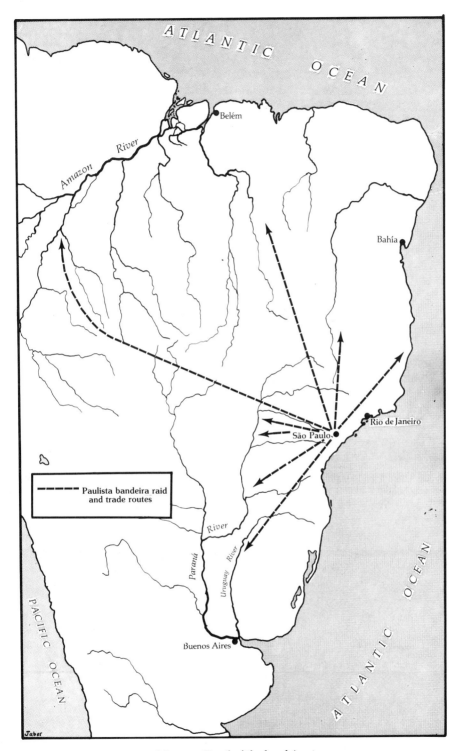

Map 9.1. Brazil of the bandeirantes

valley of Venezuela as the *llaneros*, or in the developing *vaquero* subculture of northern Mexico (north of the old *Chichimec* frontier).

During the transitional period between the establishment of these communities and their suppression under the weight of further European migration and settlement, their commercial needs were often observed by a form of trading-post empire. The pattern in northern Mexico of the eighteenth century is the most familiar. The Spanish pushed north, not in continuous settlement behind a frontier line, but through setting up enclaves of Spanish control in territory that was otherwise not under their administration. They reached north from central Mexico by stages up to Santa Fe in New Mexico. They pushed into California with the chain of missions spotted along the Camino Real as far as San Francisco. Here, as in the fur trade of Canada or Siberia, the trade centers and missions were centers of cross-cultural exchange in ideas and goods alike. The Spanish had coercive power, and they were controlled from a central place in Europe itself, but for the time being they made no effort to run a regular colonial government as they had done in central Mexico since the sixteenth century.[2]

This chapter will be concerned with a much older kind of overland trade diaspora, but one that flourished into the century when these other kinds of trade diasporas were coming into existence on other continents.

The Armenians in early commerce

Historical Armenia is the region where the present Turkey, Iran, and the Soviet Union join; Armenians still live in all three, though the Socialist Soviet Republic of Armenia is the only residual political unit that bears the name, and ethnic Armenians are widely scattered about the world. They are estimated today at about six million, half still living on the high plateau of the Armenian homeland and half living elsewhere in Asia, Europe, or the Americas.[3]

Armenians have been and still are united by a common language and religion, regardless of the political frontiers of the moment. The language belongs to the Indo-European group, where it constitutes a one-language language group. Some linguists once classified it with Persian because of the large number of Persian loanwords, but its separate status is now established. It was one of the earliest languages in its region to be written, and it still has its own distinctive alphabet. The Armenian religion is also a distinctive form of Christianity. In the early centuries after Christ, Armenia was in contact with the Christianizing Roman Empire,

---

[2] See Edward H. Spicer, *Cycles of Conquest: The Impact of Spain, Mexico, and the United States on the Indians of the Southwest, 1553–1965* (Tucson, 1962).
[3] For a recent general survey see David Marshall Lang, *Armenia: Cradle of Civilization*, 2nd ed. rev. (London, 1978).

but outside its frontiers. Partly for this reason, it looked for religious authority to its own hierarchy, separate doctrinally from both the Orthodox Byzantine Empire and Nestorian Christianity that spread along the trade routes between Rome and China. With the rise of Islam in the Middle East generally, Armenia managed to maintain its position as a Christian island in a Muslim sea – much as Ethiopia did in Africa, which may help to account for the long history of cordial relations between Armenia and Ethiopia. Isolation as a separate religious community among Muslim neighbors also underlined the need to deal tactfully with Muslims and may help to account for Armenian commercial success as long-distance traders through Muslim lands.

The Armenian homeland was strategically placed for overland trade between the Mediterranean basin and points east, in spite of the fact that it had no seacoast at all. It lay, instead, landlocked within the triangle formed by the Caspian, the Black Sea, and the Mediterranean proper. At most periods in history, however, trade passing eastward from either the Black Sea or the Mediterranean was forced through or near Armenia in order to pass south of the Caspian Sea. Once east of the Caspian it could go northeast through Transoxiana on the way to the silk road and China, or more southerly through Afghanistan to the Indus-Ganges plains of northern India. Trade did occasionally move around the northern end of the Caspian Sea, but this was the land of the steppe nomads – unsafe for caravans except in times of unusual political stability, like those of the Mongol Empire.

Other, more southerly, routes were, of course, beyond the Armenian sphere. One such was the combined caravan-water route from the vicinity of Aleppo to the upper Tigris or Euphrates, then downstream to the Persian Gulf. A second was the "desert route," which stayed away from irrigated fields of Mesopotamia as a matter of choice rather than necessity. It ran parallel to the rivers, but kept 30 to 50 kilometers south of the irrigated land, partly for the sake of the camels' health, but mainly as a way of avoiding high protection payments to a large number of petty authorities along the river. Caravaners had to pay off nomadic chiefs south of the rivers, of course, but these authorities were sometimes able to guarantee a measure of safety over a considerable stretch of the route. Camel caravans could pass from the Mediterranean to the Persian Gulf in about forty-five to seventy days. Even though the desert route did not pass through Armenia, Armenians were often among the most important overland traders on this route as well.[4] Needless to say, the nomad problem could also exist here as it did north of the Caspian. The

---

[4] Douglas Carouthers (ed.), *The Desert Route to India: Being the Journals of Four Travelers by the Great Desert Caravan Route Between Aleppo and Basra 1745–1751* (London, 1929), pp. xi–xxxv. John Huyhgen van Linschoten, *The Voyage of John Huyhgen van Linschoten to the East Indies*, 2 vols. (London, 1885), 1:46 ff.

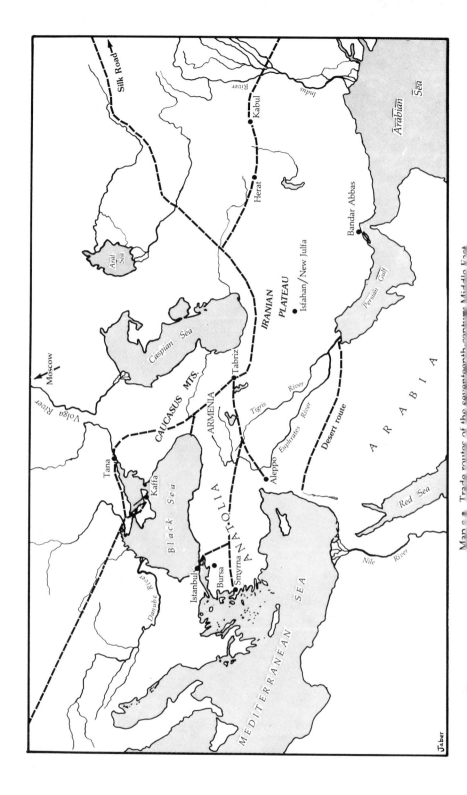

Map 1. Trade routes of the seventeenth-century Middle East

routes available at any point in time depended, in short, on political conditions – as the alternative water routes by way of the Persian Gulf and the Red Sea had done for centuries.

Armenian commercial success also depended on Armenia's setting in international relations, and that varied greatly through time. At least three times in history, Armenians rose to unusual territorial power. The first was in the ninth to the sixth century B.C., where the Armenian kingdom of Urartu was an important stopping point for trade between Asia and the Mediterranean world. This was probably too early for long-distance through trade, but fragments of Chinese silk dated to 750 B.C. indicate that this region must have been one of the earliest to receive goods from China.

The second century B.C. marked a second period of Armenian political success, when an Armenian empire beyond Rome's imperial frontiers controlled a corridor reaching from the Caspian to the Levantine coast of the Mediterranean, giving Armenia an important role in the silk trade from China by way of the Parthian Empire.[5]

Once again in the tenth century A.D., Armenia became comparatively powerful and prosperous, and again reached out to the Mediterranean – a situation made possible by the simultaneous weakness of the Abbassid caliphate in Baghdad and the Byzantine Empire in Constantinople. In the early eleventh century, this success was challenged, first by the Byzantines, who rolled back the Armenian advance to the west, then by the Seljuk Turks, who conquered Armenia along with the rest of the Levant and its hinterland. By 1070, the conquest was complete and Armenia lost its important political role, if not its possibility of reviving as an independent state.

The Armenian diaspora to the sixteenth century

Like other traders, the Armenians formed trade colonies along their routes. With a time span of well over a thousand years, and complex political and economic changes, many of these trade colonies were no doubt assimilated by the host population among whom they had settled. Others, however, maintained their identity as an Armenian community and could sometimes recover their sense of Armenianness with a revival of more intense contact with the homeland. Some remnant communities have survived, for example, along the trade route from Armenia proper toward the Levantine coast of the Mediterranean, but this was close

---

[5] Lang, *Armenia*, pp. 96, 130–1.

enough to the homeland to maintain contact or permit refoundation of these communities when trade prospered.[6]

An equally ancient trade route directly west to the Byzantine capital at Constantinople rose and fell with changes in Byzantine-Armenian relations. Even before Byzantium weakened and then fell to the Turks in 1453, the Armenians had established cordial relations with the Ottomans. They had an Armenian trade settlement and a Christian patriarchate at Bursa, the Ottoman capital. When it moved, first to Adrianople and then to Istanbul, the Armenians moved with it and became one of the chief mercantile elements at the Ottoman capital until the Turkish anti-Armenian pogroms in the early twentieth century.[7]

The Armenian trade northwest around the Black Sea was harder to maintain over long periods of time. In the fourteenth and early fifteenth centuries, for example, it was very active. Armenians who settled at Crimean ports like Kaffa carried the overland trade to feed the Genoese seaborne trade diaspora to the Black Sea. These Crimean Armenians not only carried goods back toward their homeland; they also ran caravans still farther west through present-day Rumania and Poland and beyond to Nuremberg in Germany and Bruges in the Low Countries. Their colonies in Crimea were so large that the Genoese sometimes called it *Armenia maritima*. In that new base, Armenians also began to take on elements of the local, Tatar culture. They kept their Armenian identity, and loyalty to the Armenian church, but they began to speak Tatar as the home language and even to write it with Armenian script.

With the Turkish seizure of Crimea in 1475, many of the Crimean Armenians were forced to move west as refugees into Moldavia, Transylvania, and mainly to Galicia, now in southern Poland. In central Europe, they made contact with other Armenian communities in closer touch with the homeland. They therefore changed their culture once more – back to norms more nearly those of contemporaneous Armenia. In spite of many vicissitudes, the Polish and other Armenian settlements in central Europe kept their position in the overland caravan trade till they were finally displaced by railroads in the nineteenth century.[8]

The Armenians and Safavid Persia

Armenian trade diasporas of the sixteenth century and earlier also stretched northward up the Volga from the Caspian (of which more

[6] Lang, *Armenia*, pp. 190–1.
[7] R. W. Ferrier, "The Armenians and the East India Company in Persia in the Seventeenth and Early Eighteenth Centuries," *Economic History Review*, 26:38–62 (1973), p. 38.
[8] Frederic Macler, "Les Arméniens de Galicie," *Revue des études arméniennes*, 6:7–17 (1926); Keram Kevonian, "Marchands arméniens au XVIIe siècle," *Cahiers du monde russe et sovietique*, 16:199–244 (1975), pp. 208 ff.

later) and eastward toward India. Even before the Dutch and English appeared in the Indian Ocean, a few Armenian traders had made their appearance in Agra, the Mughal capital of northern India, perhaps by overland trade across Afghanistan, perhaps by Gujarati or Portuguese shipping from the Persian Gulf to Gujarati ports. In any event, the oldest readable date in the Armenian cemetery at Surat is 1579.[9]

In the early seventeenth century, however, Armenians began to spread in larger numbers into the commercial world of the Indian Ocean and west toward Europe. Part of the explanation lies in their special relationship to Safavid Persia. It may be recalled from Chapter 6 that Persia under the Safavid dynasty was one of three Islamic empires in "the Age of Three Empires." They and other states of that period are sometimes called "gunpowder empires" as well. After about 1450, political authorities all through the Afro-Eurasian intercommunicating zone could exercise a new kind of central control. Efficient seige cannon gave a new edge to offensive warfare against private fortifications. Powerful subjects could no longer defy central governments as easily as they had done in the past.

The original center of Safavid power was northwestern Iran, and the early capital was Tabriz. By 1503, the Safavi family had conquered much of present-day western Iran and Iraq as well, creating in the process an empire based mainly on loyalty to the shi'ite version of Islam. Then, in the middle decades of the sixteenth century, the Safavids lost many of the original western conquests, but Shah Abbas the Great (ruled 1587-1629) restored the size of the empire through new gains in the east. More important, he created an efficient centralized bureaucracy, largely staffed by non-Persians, mainly Georgians and Armenians who had converted to Islam. As a symbol of his new power, Abbas built a new capital at Isfahan, which was to become, for the next century, one of the great centers of Muslim art and architecture.

Christian Armenian merchants came to be involved with Isfahan partly because of the shah's general confidence in their fellow countrymen, but also through an incident of his wars against the Ottomans. In 1605, during an Ottoman advance into Armenia, the shah responded with a scorched-earth policy and a mass evacuation of the population north of the Araks River. Many died during the forced evacuation, but the peasantry that did survive were sent to settle in the silk-producing province of Ghilan, immediately to the south of the Caspian. Urban Armenian refugees, especially the professional merchants, were resettled directly outside the walls of the new capital at Isfahan. This Armenian suburb

---

[9] Lang, *Armenia*, pp. 210–11; M. H. Seth, *The Armenians in India*, (Calcutta, 1937), pp. 102–03, 151–2.

was called New Julfa, after a city in the evacuated zone. The result was a double town, a Muslim political center alongside a Christian and Armenian commercial center. This new base, and the shah's patronage, gave the New Julfa Armenians an opportunity to further their own commercial interests by helping the shah with his. After 1622, it also gave them access to the Indian Ocean through the new port at Bandar Abbas at the entrance of the Persian Gulf, a port founded after the Portuguese lost their post on the island of Hormuz to Persian assault, with naval assistance from the English East India Company.[10]

Not all Safavid rulers were so favorable to Armenian traders, but their occasional patronage gave Armenians a political base from which to operate both overland and overseas. They did so with great success through the seventeenth and into the eighteenth century. But the eighteenth century was a period of increasing difficulty. Even before the last effective Safavi ruler died in 1722, the shahs began to be less favorable to the New Julfa community. Catholic missionaries appeared and made many converts among the Christian Armenians, and the shi'a state was even less friendly to their new religion than it had been to the old. Political conditions in Persia remained anarchic through most of the century to the foundation of the new Qajar dynasty after 1799, so that many New Julfa merchants went elsewhere. Many of the wealthiest moved to India and entered Indian trade in varying relationships to the East India Company or its servants. Others moved north, following the lure of the silk trade in that direction. Still others moved west into the Ottoman lands or beyond into Europe. Meanwhile, the seventeenth century had brought unusual opportunities.[11]

Overland trade from Persia through Russia

The sixteenth- and seventeenth-century rise of the Ottoman, Safavid, and Mughal empires took place at a period when Christians posed new threats to the integrity of Muslim civilization. One such threat was the already familiar maritime drive into the Indian Ocean, though the seriousness of the challenge to Muslim powers was not always evident until the eighteenth century. The second threat came from the north, from Russia, or Muscovy as it was then called. From the fifteenth cen-

[10] R. W. Ferrier, "The Armenians"; John Carswell, *New Julfa: The Armenian Churches and Other Buildings* (Oxford, 1968); Carswell, "The Armenians and the East-West Trade through Persia in the XVIIth century," in M. Mollat (ed.), *Sociétés et compagnies de commerce en orient et dans l'océan indien* (Paris, 1971); Niels Steensgaard, *Carracks, Caravans and Companies: The Structural Crisis in the European-Asian Trade of the Early Seventeenth Century* (Copenhagen, 1973), pp. 209–414. For Safavid Persia in general, see Roger Savory, *Iran under the Safavids* (Cambridge, 1980).
[11] Carswell, *New Julfa*, pp. 14–15.

tury, the Muscovites began to conquer southward along the course of the Volga River, establishing their domination over some of the Tatar people who already lived there and sending colonies of Russian settlers to help maintain their control over the new territory. These Tatars were some of the first Muslims anywhere to fall under Christian rule, but their numbers were few and the Muslim world at large was not alarmed. International relations of Muscovy, Poland, the Ottomans, and the various Tatar hordes in the steppes north of the Black Sea were more often grounded on a search for power and advantage than on the dictates of religion. The Russian advance, indeed, opened opportunities for Muslim commerce. Muslim Tatar merchants from the Volga were able to establish a trade diaspora reaching southeast to the markets of Bukhara and elsewhere in the old Transoxiana, with comparative security because they were Muslim. In the other direction their trade could reach north and northwest into the heart of Muscovy – with relative security because they were subjects of the tsar.[12]

Although the early phases of the Russian advance down the Volga were slow and often reversed for short periods, the Russian conquest of the khanate of Kazan in 1552 and of Astrakhan in 1556 opened the whole river, and the Caspian Sea as well, to Russian shipping. After Astrakhan had become a forward base and the main point of transfer between the Volga and the Caspian, Russian naval power could raid the Persian shore as well, and Muscovy found it possible to enter as a Christian third party into the existing struggle between the sunni Ottomans and the shi'ite rulers of the new Safavid Persia.

Neither the Russians nor the Persians had a large trade community anxious to enter the trade of the newly opened Caspian–Volga axis. Even before the final fall of Astrakhan to Muscovy, Armenians were engaged in the Volga trade alongside local Tatar merchants and a variety of other foreigners. Before the end of the seventeenth century, this would include Crimean Tatars, Nogai Tatars, Russians, Persians, and Hindus, a few of whom settled in trade communities as far north as Moscow.[13]

The most improbable entrant into this competition was England. As early as the 1550s, the London-based Muscovy Company had opened seaborne trade to Archangelsk, rounding the North Cape into the Arctic

---

[12] Marshall G. S. Hodgson, *The Venture of Islam: Conscience and History of a World Civilization in Three Volumes*, 3 vols. (Chicago, 1974), 3:221–2.

[13] Lloyd E. Berry and Robert O. Crummey (eds.), *Rude & Barbarous Kingdom: Russia in the Accounts of Sixteenth-Century English Voyagers* (Madison, Wis., 1968); Adam Olearius in *The Voyages and Travels of J. Albert de Mandelslo ... into the East Indies* (London, 1669), p. 12; Jan Struys, *The Voyages of I. Struys through Moscovia, Tartary, India, and Most of the Eastern World* (London, 1684), p. 17; Holden Furber, *Rival Empires of Trade in the Orient, 1600–1800* (Minneapolis, 1976).

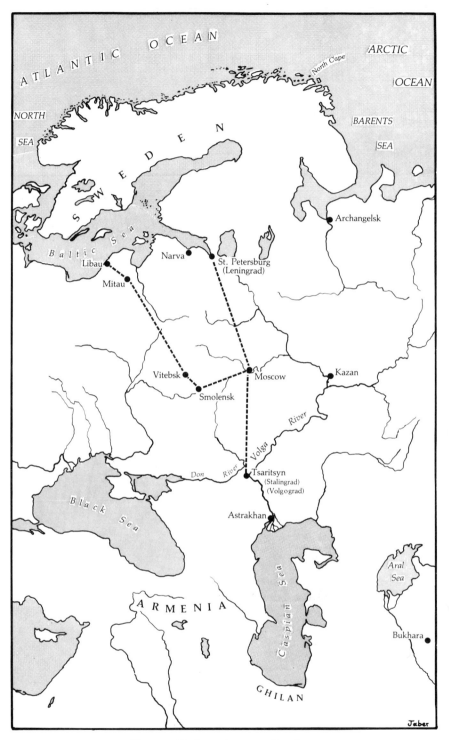

Map 9.3. Trade routes across Russia

Ocean. From there it sought to extend its trade diaspora southward by the rivers and portages of northern Russia, first to Moscow, then joining the Volga to the Caspian. One goal was to tap the Persian market, but the ultimate, if distant, objective was to reach through central Asia and on across Afghanistan to India. Some Persian and Central Asian goods did indeed pass to Europe in this way in the sixteenth century, and a certain Anthony Jenkinson in the employ of the English Muscovy Company actually made the full trip from Archangelsk to Bukhara in central Asia, and back by way of Persia. But Armenians were already carrying most of this trade.[14]

The Volga River route was clearly the preferred way of shipping goods between Russia and Persia whenever political conditions permitted, but overland transportation was not out of the question. At times when the Volga was subject to bandit raids, the preferred route was overland from Moscow to Tsaritsyn by sledge in winter or cart in summer. The carts used in the mid-eighteenth century were about 3 meters long and 0.8 to 1 meter wide, pulled by one or sometimes two horses. Somewhat surprisingly, travel in winter was cheaper and faster than in summertime, with an estimated advance of 65 kilometers a day in winter, as against only about 50 in the summer for the run between Moscow and Saint Petersburg. Below Tsaritsyn, the goods were put on river boats capable of hauling about 45 tons with a crew of fifteen to twenty. From Astrakhan, the final stretch across the Caspian was made in light-draft sailing vessels.

The viability of the route onward to Western Europe was more problematical, though the apparent distances in northern latitudes are much exaggerated on maps based on the familiar Mercator projection. The usual estimate of the 1740s allowed 30 days for the trip northward from Ghilan to Astrakhan, then 45 days from Astrakhan to Moscow, then 20 days on to Saint Petersburg (now Leningrad) – a total of 95 days in all. By contrast, the trip from Ghilan westward to Mediterranean ports was estimated at 70 days to Smyrna (now Ismir) or 60 days to Aleppo (now Haleb). But the rivalry between the two routes was governed more by political factors than by physical problems of transportation. Not only were the Safavid and Ottoman empires chronically at war, but the Ottomans were also sometimes at war with Russia, and the route from Moscow to the Baltic was often blocked by warfare between Russia and Sweden, at least until 1721.

Although the trade between Russia and Persia was often discussed in the West as though it was an exchange of silk for woolen cloth and

[14] T. S. Willan, *The Early History of the Russia Company 1553–1603* (Manchester, 1956); Berry and Crummey (eds.), *Rude & Barbarous Kingdom*, passim.

little more, that part was only the through trade that left from, or arrived in, Western Europe. The actual quantities carried over shorter sections of the route were mostly items of comparatively low value for weight. Fish from the Caspian was consumed all over Russia, even at Saint Petersburg on the Baltic. Caviar also entered trade in the eighteenth century, made from Caspian sturgeon eggs by Armenians on both sides of the sea. They mixed the roe with brine and pressed it to remove as much of the oil as possible. In that form, it would last two or three years without other canning or preservatives. They shipped most of it north to the Russian market, normally about 100 tons a year, but in 1749 production rose to a new height of 330 tons. The overland route to the Mediterranean also took some caviar, which was eaten as far west as Italy.

Estimates of the silk trade for the early eighteenth century suggest that the Armenians carried about 130 tons a year up the Volga route, about one-third for sale in Russia, the rest for reexport to Western Europe. By midcentury, however, Ghilan production was down to only about 110 tons, of which about 20 percent was consumed in Persia itself; 70 percent passed north up the Volga, and the remainder went west to Aleppo and Mediterranean ports.

Trade from Muscovy westward to the Baltic was possible at some periods. It was important especially in the 1670s and 1680s, though it had to pass westward through either Sweden or the Duchy of Kurland, which controlled what was later to be Latvia. Trade through the Arctic ports revived in the 1730s and 1740s, when English traders were able to take advantage of an Anglo-Russian commercial treaty of 1734 to establish once more a briefly effective English trade diaspora through Russia to Astrakhan and on to Ghilan. The actual transporters, interpreters, and cross-cultural brokers were – as one might expect by now – Armenian.[15]

Relations within the Armenian community

These long-distance trade contacts required elaborate institutional arrangements. Normally, the principal merchants at centers like New Julfa dealt through younger people, who traveled the roads. They preferred family members where possible, but trade was a regular profession; and professional training was available in New Julfa. Several different texts describing trade practices and foreign conditions were available. The

---

[15] Jonas W. Hanway, *An Historical Account of British Trade Over the Caspian Sea*, 2 vols. (London, 1754), 1:57–9, 94–5, 200, and passim; Douglas K. Reading, *The Anglo-Russian Commercial Treaty of 1734* (New Haven, Conn., 1938).

author of one of these, Kostand Joughayetsi, also ran a school for apprentice merchants.[16]

Another, similar manual was published in the Armenian language in Amsterdam in 1699. It dealt with weights, measures, tariffs, regulations, and prices over a good part of the Eurasian landmass. The list of places for which this information was available tells something of the range of trade by Amsterdam Armenians. As might be expected, coverage was best for nearby European points; weights and measures were given for Antwerp, Amsterdam, Ancona, Krakow, Cadiz, Danzig, Denmark, Frankfurt, Florence, Genoa, Hamburg, London, Leipzig, Lisbon, Marseilles, Messina, Nuremberg, Naples, Oran, Paris, Riga, Seville, Venice, and Vienna. Outside Europe, it provided information on Agra, Surat, and Hyderabad in India; for Pegu in Burma, Manila in the Philippines, for a number of points in Armenia itself and in Persia, along with Basra at the head of the Persian Gulf, Baghdad, Aleppo, and Smyrna. Other sections dealt with trade practices and prices through Russia and north to Archangelsk, and with the trade of Egypt, Ethiopia, and southward down the East African coast.[17]

A unique document illustrating commercial relationships within the Armenian community has recently been translated and published in both English and French.[18] It is an account of commmercial transactions and travels, made by a traveling agent from New Julfa for the benefit of his principals. It covered more than ten years, beginning with the original contract between the agent, Hovannes Ter-Davtian, and his principals, Zakharia and Embroom Guerak, sons of one of the wealthiest merchants in New Julfa and members of a family whose commercial dealings reached north to the silk-growing region of Ghilan and west to Venice. These particular members of the family, however, specialized in the trade to India, on to Lhasa in Tibet, and still farther to Xining, the capital of Quinghai province in western China.

The form of the contract was similar to the ordinary partnership or *commenda* agreement in use by merchants in both the Christian Mediterranean and the Muslim world. The principals supplied the capital, which Hovannes took with him half in cash and half in cloth for the Indian trade. At the end of the trip, the principals were to receive three-

[16] John Chardin, *Sir John Chardin's Travels in Persia* (London, 1927), p. 281. First published in 1686. Lvon Khachikian, "Le registre d'un marchand arménien en Perse, en Inde et en Tibet (1682–93)," *Annales: économies, sociétiés, civilisations*, 22:231–78 (1967), p. 235.

[17] Kevonian, "Marchands arméniens," presents a partial translation, including the Table of Contents.

[18] Lvon Khachikian, "The Ledger of the Merchant Hovannes Joughayetsi," *Journal of the Asiatic Society* (Calcutta), 8:153–86 (1966) or "Le registre"; Pierre Jeannin, "The Sea-borne and Overland Trade Routes of Northern Europe in the XVIth and XVIIth Centuries," *Journal of European Economic History*, 11:5–59 (1982).

194 Cross-cultural trade in world history

quarters of the total profit, while Hovannes would keep one-quarter. In fact, Hovannes also traded on his own account, so that he was able to build up his own capital along with that of his principals.[19]

Part of his obligation under the contract was to keep a logbook of all his transactions, which he did from 19 December 1682 to 3 December 1693, when the account breaks off without explanation. On his arrival in India, he spent the period from 1683 to 1686 traveling back and forth in what was essentially a peddling trade, returning to Surat from time to time to receive new supplies from Persia by sea. His account often mentions the principal Armenian residents by name – thirteen for Surat, nine for Agra, and so on – but these were certainly only the leaders of a larger community. Their names, however, tell something of the scope of the Armenian connection. The chief of the Agra community was Avetik, son of Petros of Shiraz (in southeastern Persia). Another prominent merchant in Agra was Poghos of Kazan, the distant trading center far up the Volga in Russia. In these Indian trading cities, he always found an Armenian church and priest in residence.

As his experience increased, Hovannes's role as an agent became more complex. He began dealing on the account of Avetik of Agra, as well as on his own account and on that of his principals in New Julfa. Avetik, in turn, acted as agent for Hovan of Shiraz, another merchant of New Julfa. All these transactions were duly reported in his journal, so that his principals were fully informed and presumably allowed such multiple agency.[20]

In 1686, Hovannes and Avetik planned a venture for Hovannes to Tibet, under an agreement for multiple agency. Both remained bound to their principals in New Julfa, but for this venture each put up his own capital in equal shares, to a total of 9,370 rupees, a sum equivalent to 106.3 kilograms of silver. The investment, however, was in precious stones and Indian textiles, by now a considerable store, so that Hovannes had to hire two Armenian servants, and all three went armed. They left Agra in February 1686, passing by stages down the Ganges to Patna, then north to Nepal, where they traded locally in the vicinity of Khatmandu for three months before passing on to Lhasa, where they arrived toward the end of September.

Even in a place as remote as Tibet from the main centers of trade, Armenians formed a substantial permanent community. Hovannes was able to board with a resident Armenian family. At that point he changed functions from those of a traveling to those of a resident merchant – and without dropping his financial relationship to his principals in distant

[19] Khachikian, "Registre," p. 233.
[20] Khachikian, "Registre," pp. 238 ff.

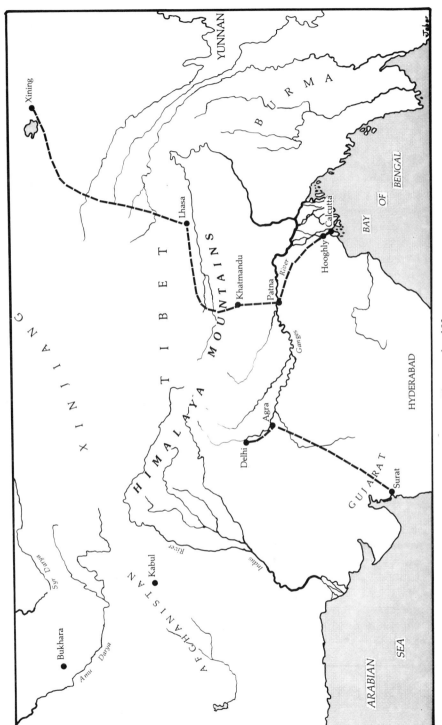

Map 9.4. The travels of Hovannes

New Julfa. Some of his commercial operations were performed within Lhasa itself. Others led farther afield. The longest reach was to entrust some of his own capital to traveling Armenians bound for Xining, some 1,700 kilometers to the northeast. For this expedition, Armenians joined together with some local Tibetan merchants and some Kashmiri for a journey that took a full year.[21]

In 1693, Hovannes finally decided to leave Tibet with cargo that included 4,583 kilograms of musk, 5.1 kilograms of gold, plus porcelain and other Chinese products. He made his way with numerous adventures, back to Khatmandu and Patna, then to Hooghly on the lower Ganges. There, he resumed his earlier pattern of short-range trade in the vicinity until the account breaks off suddenly in December 1693.

Although this document is a lone survivor from a thousand similar accounts that must once have existed, it helps to set off the role of the traveling merchant and of the Armenian community as a subgroup within the wider society of Mughal India. Conflict was settled within the Armenian community alone. In Lhasa, where it may have been too small for this, the Kashmiri and Armenians acted together as the group within which conflicts were resolved.

Such intergroup cooperation is yet another indication of the growth in ecumenical forms of commerce within the Indian trading world toward the end of the seventeenth century. Armenians still preferred to deal with Armenians, or even with members of their own families, but it was possible to use other agents. Where trade by sea a century or so earlier had been essentially a peddling trade, where the merchant had to travel with his goods, this was no longer required. Hovannes was able to send goods back and forth to his principals in New Julfa without actually making the trip himself. Money had been easy to transfer in Mughal India since the late sixteenth century. None of the Armenian merchants appear here to carry large sums in cash, since money could be transmitted through money changers, merchants, or even through government officials. This service was secure and the charge was modest, about 1 or 2 percent. Interest on bills of exchange was also comparatively low at about 0.75 percent per month when the risk was not considered to be very great. Hovannes, and no doubt others as well, practiced a kind of arbitrage between low- and high-risk enterprises by borrowing on his personal security at 9 percent per annum and then lending the money for higher-risk operations at 27 percent.[22]

In Europe as well, the settled Armenian merchants operated some-

[21] Khachikian, "Registre," pp. 242–3.
[22] Khachikian, "Registre," p. 263.

thing like a commission house for other Armenians at a distance, as well as performing the typical functions of a landlord-broker for travelers who happened to visit centers like Amsterdam. Like the Armenians in India, they were able to make credit available to other traders, with little paperwork or formality. Within the Armenian community, contracts could be made on a handshake.[23]

Other Armenians up and down the trade routes acted as agents for non-Armenians and used non-Armenians as their own agents. The fact that Armenians were Christian, yet skilled in traveling through Muslim lands, made them useful as diplomatic agents. The Ethiopian court had an ancient connection to Armenia through mutual pilgrimage to Jerusalem. As early as 1519, the Ethiopian court at Gondar sent an Armenian envoy to Portugal, by way of the Portuguese posts in India. In the second half of the seventeenth century, a certain Khoja Murad served Ethiopia on a variety of diplomatic missions: to Surat and Delhi in 1663–4 and to Batavia on Java to deal with the Dutch on three different occasions between 1674 and 1697. These voyages are reported in detail, and it is clear that Khoja Murad was a professional merchant who took on diplomatic work as another form of agency for a distant principal.[24] Armenians also used Western agency on occasion. In 1702, a group of Armenian merchants in Calcutta joined to charter a ship from the English East India Company for a voyage from Calcutta to the Persian Gulf. Company servants often sent their goods on board Armenian-owned ships as well.[25]

In other circumstances, Armenians served as agents for state trading operations. They acted in this capacity for Shah Abbas before 1629, when the silk trade was a royal monopoly – much as the Chinese in Siam acted for the king in a period of royal monopoly. Surviving records for this period show at least twelve trade missions that went beyond the Levant to European ports, often only as far as Venice, but sometimes to England, France, or the Netherlands. After the royal monopoly ended, the Armenians in this trade were well placed to carry it on their own.[26]

[23] Silvio van Rooy, "Armenian Merchant Habits as Mirrored in the 17th–18th Century Amsterdam Documents," *Revue des études arméniennes*, 3(n.s.):347–558 (1966).
[24] Richard Pankhurst, "The History of Ethiopian-Armenian Relations," *Revue des études arméniennes*, 12(n.s.):174–345 (1977); E. J. van Donzel, *Foreign Relations of Ethiopia, 1642–1700: Documents Relating to the Journeys of Khodja Murad* (Leiden, 1979).
[25] K. N. Chaudhuri, *The Trading World of Asia and the English East India Company 1660–1760* (Cambridge, 1978), p. 83; Om Prakash, "Asian Trade and European Impact: A Study of the Trade of Bengal, 1630–1720," in Blair B. Kling and M. N. Pearson (eds.), *The Age of Partnership: Europeans in Asia before Dominion* (Honolulu, 1979).
[26] Steensgaard, *Carracks and Caravans*, pp. 68–74 and passim.

Communities of the Armenian diaspora

The trade communities of the Armenian diaspora lived in many different relationships to the host societies, but never controlling their hosts and never militarized beyond the needs of personal self-defense. Hovannes's resort to arms for protection on his Tibetan trip was about as far as it went. Other Armenians bought protection as called for, rather than supplying their own.

Armenian strength came, rather, through mutual self-support, mainly expressed and organized through the church. One of the first privileges Armenian traders asked for was the right to build a church and worship in their own way. This was true in New Julfa itself, which was also a diaspora town, and its Christian churches are recognized architectural monuments. The New Julfa Armenians also enjoyed political autonomy from the shah's government – these outward forms being strengthened by commercial privileges passing from the shah to the community, and by taxation passing back from the community to the shah.[27]

In the Ottoman Empire, Armenians had a long tradition of friendship with the sultan, even though the Safavid and Ottoman empires were normally hostile to each other. In the Ottoman case, this friendship drew support from the long Ottoman tradition of allowing alien communities, called *millets*, a good deal of autonomy under their own leaders. Thus the Armenian Christians enjoyed privileges similar to those of the local Greek Orthodox or the local Jewish population, which also continued active in trade. These were all Ottoman subjects. The Western Christians who came to trade in the port towns were not. Their conditions of life were consequently more circumscribed. In Istanbul and Ismir, they could live in ordinary houses, though confined to a particular part of the city. In Aleppo, Cairo, and a number of other cities, they were confined to a specific building in the ancient tradition of the *funduq*. In either case, they were cut off from the life of the country and forced to trade through designated non-Muslim Ottoman subjects – Greeks, Jews, or Armenians mainly – in any dealings with the sultan's Muslim subjects. These measures, in effect, assigned the role of cross-cultural broker to particular groups.[28]

Armenian caravans from Persia might make for Istanbul or Ismir, but most commonly for Aleppo (now Haleb, Syria), the nearest point of exchange even though it was not an actual seaport, but a town about 100 kilometers inland and served by the port of Iskanderun (Alexan-

---

[27] Carswell, *New Julfa*, passim.
[28] Alexander H. de Groot, "The Organization of Western European Trade in the Levant, 1500-1800," in Leonard Blusse and Femme Gaastra (eds.), *Companies and Trade: Essays on Overseas Trading Companies during the Ancient Regime* (The Hague, 1981), pp. 231–44.

dretta). Before about 1630, by which time the cape route had diverted the former caravan trade in spices, Aleppo had been a major entrepôt for all Asian goods entering Mediterranean circulation. The silk trade from Persia continued to be important, however, till the middle of the eighteenth century. Armenian carriers brought Persian silk from the East. Camel caravans brought European goods, mostly cloth, from Iskanderun. The European factors then sold their goods to Jewish or Armenian brokers, trying to make a direct exchange of European woolens for Persian silk whenever possible. But it was rarely possible, so that money and credit were both involved – credit sometimes granted by the Armenians, sometimes by the Europeans. At its height, this trade was reputed to have attracted as many as 10,000 Armenians into Ottoman territory, though the Ottoman Empire already had an Armenian community of far older derivation.[29]

In Western Europe as well, the Armenian diaspora from New Julfa overlaid a much older trade diaspora, which had apparently been assimilated long before the seventeenth century. In France, it dated from the period of the Crusades, when the Armenian kingdom of Cilicia reached to the Mediterranean coast. It had good relations with the Frankish crusading states, but the Muslim counterattack ended both the Frankish and the Armenian hold on the Levant. Part of the fallout, however, was a sizable Armenian refugee migration into Mediterranean Europe, especially to the Italian trading cities, where Armenians established their own quarters and their own churches for a time.[30]

Toward the end of the sixteenth century, a new wave of Armenians began to arrive in Europe, first in Venice and Leghorn, then Marseilles – towns attached to seaborne trade with the Levant. Many of the new arrivals were Ottoman subjects from port towns like Ismir, but a contingent from New Julfa joined them in the early seventeenth century.

As with other trade diasporas, some Armenian merchants settled down, married European wives, and began to act as brokers and intermediaries for traveling Armenians less acquainted with European ways. The Marseilles notarial records show particular individuals appearing again and again as legal intermediaries for other, foreign Armenians. As the community began to assimilate French culture, it also had a cultural influence of its own on French life. Coffee was introduced in the 1650s by merchants from the Levant, not necessarily Armenians, but an Armenian

---

[29] Steensgaard, *Carracks and Caravans*, pp. 154–210; Ralph H. Davis, *Aleppo to Devonshire Square: English Traders in the Levant in the Eighteenth Century* (London, 1967), pp. 27–31; Hanway, *Caspian Sea*, 1:28–9; G. Ambrose, "English Traders at Aleppo (1658–1756)," *Economic History Review*, 3:246–67 (1931–2), pp. 253–4.

[30] C. D. Tekekian, "Marseille, la Provence, et les arméniens," *Mémoires de l'Institut Historique de Provence*, 5:5–65 (1929), pp. 5–9.

from Marseilles opened the first public coffee houses in the 1670s, first
in Marseilles, then in Paris and other towns. Armenians were, indeed,
the proprietors of most of the early cafés in France. By the early eighteenth century, Armenian culture passed through a phase of voguish-
ness. Chardin's account of his travels in Persia served Montesquieu as
inspiration for his *Persian Letters*, a fictional account of Europe and Persia
seen through the eyes of Armenian travelers, and the picturesque Persian dress of the Armenian visitors appears in contemporaneous paint-
ings of French port towns. A few Frenchmen even wore Persian Armenian
clothing themselves.[31]

The legal position of Armenian communities in western Europe differed greatly, depending on support or opposition from European governments and the rivalries with local merchants. In France, both Richelieu
and Colbert favored the Armenian community, while the French merchants in port towns like Marseilles tried as much as possible to restrict
their commercial activities. European merchants trading abroad within
Europe were already protected by the web of diplomatic and consular
representation. This was not necessarily so for non-Westerners. Persia's
first consul at Marseilles was not appointed until the 1710s, and the first
appointee was, as one might suspect, a New Julfa Armenian. Ottoman
subjects were still outside the range of formal representation. Whether
Armenian Christian or Turkish Muslim, they found it hard to stay in
business in France except for short periods of favorable relations.

Ottoman subjects, on the other hand, were better received in the
Netherlands. Armenians came there by sea from the Levant, but also
overland through central Europe or by way of the Baltic. Several settled
and established themselves as shippers to the Levant, their ships flying
the Dutch flag and bearing names like *Coopman van Armenien*. After the
middle of the eighteenth century, however, the silk trade to the Levant
collapsed and with it the fortunes of merchants involved.[32]

Meanwhile, some of the Armenian community in Western Europe
wandered still farther afield. In the 1730s, the Royal African Company
in London, looking for someone to facilitate their dealings with the
Muslim slave traders of the Gambia, hired Melchior de Jaspas, an Arabic-
speaking Armenian then in London, who shifted over, in effect, to an
English trade diaspora and served the company in Africa till he died of
disease, like most outside visitors to that part of the world. His record
as a cross-cultural broker in Africa, however, was neither better nor
worse than that of his English colleagues.

Elsewhere, the position of the Armenian community could vary from

---

[31] Tekekian, "Marseille," pp. 30, 34.
[32] Tekekian, "Marseille," pp. 35, 54–5; Kevonian, "Marchands arméniens," pp. 208 ff.

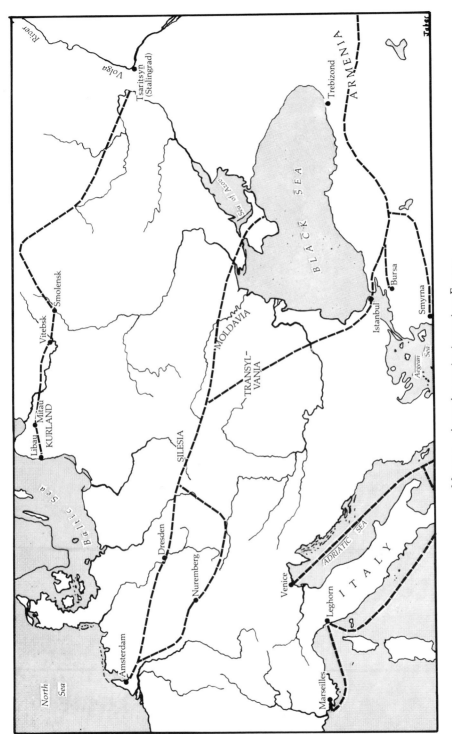

Map 9.5. Armenian routes to western Europe

official favor, simple grants of autonomy, or official disfavor. In most places, Armenians profited from residence long enough to become subjects of the local government, and they had no powerful homeland to appear threatening. The Armenian community in Astrakhan, for example, was Russian in nationality and tended to be favored by the Russian government. In Poland, the large Armenian community in Galicia had a grant of autonomy from the Polish crown, including the right to take judicial cases before special Armenian judges enforcing Armenian law.[33]

The kind of relationship Armenian traders regarded as ideal emerges from the unusually detailed record of negotiations between Philippe de Zagly, an Armenian merchant and self-styled plenipotentiary, and the duke of Kurland, ruler of what was to become Latvia. The Armenian cut quite a figure in Europe and left a reputation as a con man, which he no doubt was. He was also a serious, if atypical, merchant of the Armenian trade diaspora. He came to France from New Julfa in 1669 and managed within a very short time to marry the sister of Madame Tavernier, wife of the famous French traveler to Persia and the East. He also obtained a military commission, converted to Catholicism, and was baptized with Louis XIV's own brother as his godfather. De Zagly converted easily. He later joined both the sunni and the shi'ite versions of Islam in quick succession. He ended an adventurous career in 1707, when the ruler of Erevan in the Armenian homeland ordered his head cut off.[34]

In his European years, de Zagly was concerned with trade between Baltic ports and Western Europe. In the 1680s and 1690s, that trade passed first to Narva, then under Swedish control but now in the Estonian SSR, and from there overland to Moscow and down the Volga. The Armenian merchants were unhappy about the Swedish section. Tolls were high, and Swedish officials were often unpleasant, no doubt because of the old connection between the Armenians and the tsar. De Zagly proposed to divert this trade to the Kurland port of Libau (now Liepaja), then due east through Mitau (now Jelgava), the capital of the duchy, and onward with a combination of river and cart travel through Vitebsk and Smolensk to Moscow.

De Zagly approached the duke with a proposal that could serve as a

[33] John Carswell, "The Armenians"; Jacques de Morgan, *The History of the Armenian People* (Boston, 1965), p. 335; Reading, *Anglo-Russian Treaty*, pp. 223–5; Macler, "Arméniens de Galicie," p. 12; Philip D. Curtin, *Africa Remembered: Narratives of West Africans from the Era of the Slave Trade* (Madison, Wis., 1967).

[34] Roberto Gulbenkian, "Philippe de Zagly, marchant arménien de Julfa, et l'établissement du commerce persan en Courlande en 1696," *Revue des études arméniennes*, 7(n.s.): 361–99 (1970).

model for maximum demands by diaspora traders. He asked the duke to furnish his countrymen with three stone houses in three appropriate towns along the route and to guarantee protection for their goods in transit and freedom for the practice of their religion. For the first four years of the agreement they were to pay no tolls, and the duke was asked to set up a loan fund at low rates of interest, to help Armenian merchants get started. Each of the three houses was to have an interpreter, salary paid by the duke. In case any ducal ships were sailing westward, they were asked to carry such Armenian goods as they had room for, and at a low freight rate specified in advance. The proposal also spelled out the rates that would apply after the first four years and would have granted the duke the right to preempt the purchase of goods in transit at specified, but favorable, prices.[35]

The outcome may be a surprise. The duke actually granted most of the requests. He promised the houses, the free tolls for four years, moderate tariffs thereafter, and permission to use ducal ships when available. He turned down the loan fund and made a few other changes in his own favor, but de Zagly got most of his request. This was, in short, a concession to passing merchants that resembled some of the earlier concessions from the Russian court for the Volga route, but it was not quite the free gift it might appear to be. The duke of Kurland gave free protection, but in return he gained the right to tax trade that would not otherwise have entered his duchy at all. Unfortunately, the surviving record says nothing about the outcome, but the region was so badly disrupted by the Russo–Swedish wars of the next two decades, it could hardly have lived up to expectations. After the wars, trade resumed in the 1720s along the route from Narva or Saint Petersburg to Moscow – now entirely in Russian hands.

The Armenians were not the only small-scale traders on the overland routes of this period. Inscriptions on the churches of New Julfa indicate the death and burial there of Greeks, Russians, Portuguese, French, Swiss, English, and Dutch. A writer on the Amsterdam of 1664 noted the presence not only of Armenians and the familiar European traders from Germany, Poland, Hungary, Wallonia, France, Spain, and Russia, but also Turks and occasional Hindus. And in the overland trade of Eastern Europe, Jews were certainly far more important than the Armenians were.[36] The Armenians must nevertheless have been the most successful of trading groups in the broader Asian trade, and the indi-

---

[35] Philippe de Zagly to duke of Kurland, Mitau, 8 September 1696, quoted in full in Gulbenkian, "de Zagly," pp. 379–91.
[36] Carswell, *New Julfa*, p. 13; Violet Barbour, *Capitalism in Amsterdam in the Seventeenth Century* (Baltimore, 1950), pp. 56–7; Jeannin, "Overland Trade Routes," pp. 5–6.

vidual fortunes they accumulated were at least as great as those of the most successful merchants in London or Amsterdam.[37]

One of the most remarkable aspects of Armenian trading success was the low level of coercive power available to them, in a world where their European competitors traded with an army and navy close at hand. They paid for protection, but they also managed to work under the patronage of powerful rulers like the shah, the tsar, the grand mughal, and even that of the English East India Company. Part of the secret of that success was a willingness to work in the interstices not occupied by the commerce of their more powerful rivals.

The Armenians were also skilled in using many different kinds of transportation. The whole passage of a shipment of silk from Ghilan to Amsterdam could be made to the account of a single Armenian merchant, even though it crossed many different jurisdictions and involved ocean transportation on the Caspian and Baltic, river shipping on the Volga and other north Russia rivers, and overland cart or sledge routes in between. Elsewhere in the trade of Asia, as many as five or six different trade-diaspora groups might well be involved in the movement of goods from producer to consumer. The pepper trade of Sumatra or of southern India is an example.

The Armenians also cultivated and passed on to younger generations the accumulated skills in diplomacy and cross-cultural brokerage. As one English competitor put it with a combination of envy and cultural arrogance, the Armenians

are likewise educated in all the servilities of ASIA, and understanding how to accommodate themselves to indignities which the genius of a free nation will hardly submit to are in some measure the better qualified to carry on a commerce through foreign dominions.[38]

Like other trade diasporas in Asian commerce, however, decline began in the middle decades of the eighteenth century, partly on account of political troubles in Persia, partly on account of the decline in the Persian silk trade, but more generally because the Europeans had a new kind of power that gave them greater leverage in all of their dealings with Asians. Armenians responded in several different ways. Many of those in New Julfa converted to Catholicism, and many diaspora communities became Westernized. Many moved into Western spheres of Asian trade. Armenians in India, for example, could work more closely with the English and thus profit from the new power of the Europeans. The career of a certain Edward Raphael and his descendants is a case in point. His family had been merchants in New Julfa, who converted to

---

[37] Chaudhuri, *Trading World of Asia*, pp. 137–8.
[38] Hanway, *Caspian Sea*, 1:300.

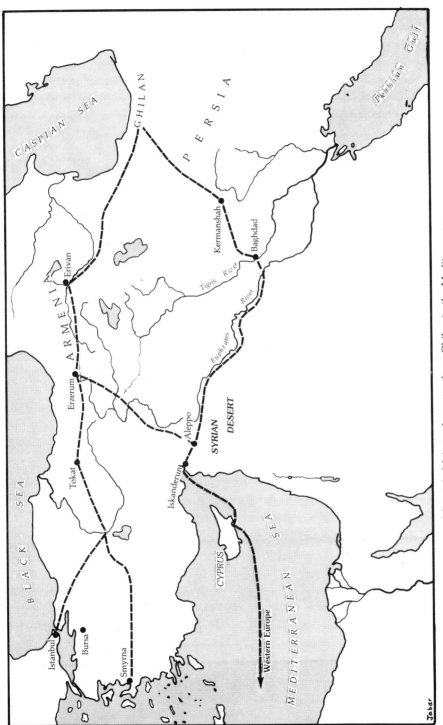

Map 9.6. Main trade routes from Ghilan to the Mediterranean

Catholicism. He moved to India, where he founded the Carnatic Bank in Madras in 1788, the first joint-stock bank in southern India. His son Alexander, by now thoroughly anglicized, moved to England, apparently left trade, and sat in the unreformed House of Commons as the M.P. for St. Albans.

Some of those who went north for trade had similar careers. One New Julfa family, whose son went north into Russia with the declining trade of the mid-eighteenth century, succeeded in earning titles of nobility from both Catherine II of Russia and from Joseph II of Austria. In 1815, still another member of that same family founded the Lazarev Institute of Oriental Studies in Moscow, the first such institution in the Russian Empire. By that time, the era of the Asian trade diasporas was giving way to a new, more ecumenical pattern under the heavy impress of Western norms. One way to survive was to accept the inevitable.

10

The North American fur trade

The fur trade of North America was part of a broader movement of European expansion into the northern forests of Asia and America. Its two branches started with similar timing near the beginning of the seventeenth century and continued until they changed form drastically in the early nineteenth. Both were driven by European economic demand for fur garments, and both were carried out within the institutional forms of a trading-post empire. This chapter will be concerned principally with the North Amerian fur trade, but with the Siberian fur trade in the background to help maintain the perspective of world history. The two branches of the movement were similar in many ways, but different in others.

The North American setting: epidemiology and culture

The most striking difference was epidemiological, arising from the long separation of the Americas from the disease environments of the Afro-Eurasian landmass. The Americas were originally populated from Asia, but regular contact was then broken for tens of thousands of years before it was reestablished by Columbus and his successors after 1492. In the interval, people in the Americas developed their own food crops, their own domestic animals, and their own patterns of culture. These American cultures lacked some of the technology that was crucial to Old World civilization. They lacked large animals capable of pulling carts; hence they had no need for applications of rotary motion like the wheel.

More important, they lacked the patterns of disease that had become generalized through the Afro-Eurasian intercommunicating zone. A few diseases were peculiar to the Americas, but the serious problem was the lack of acquired immunities to the common diseases of Europe, Africa, and Asia. This included diseases that were devastating even in the Old World, like smallpox, malaria, and yellow fever, but it also included the usual European childhood diseases like measles, whooping cough, mumps, scarlet fever, and diphtheria. These are childhood diseases *because* most people get them in childhood and then carry a lifelong immunity. Children also suffered less from these diseases than adults did, even in the Old World. In the Americas, these Old World diseases infected people of all ages, and the result was demographic disaster.

The impact of the new diseases, however, came gradually, as each new region of the Americas came into contact with the Europeans. It began in the sixteenth century with the populations of the tropical lowlands, most of which had simply disappeared as organized communities by the middle of the seventeenth century, under the combined impact of a broad spectrum of European diseases combined with tropical diseases from Africa. The populations of the tropical highlands of Middle America and the Andes also dropped, beginning in the sixteenth century, till they finally leveled out after a century or more at something like 15 to 30 percent of the original level.[1]

In northern North America, native American populations were sparser. Europeans came in smaller numbers, and they came later. These epidemics therefore began about a century later than they had in the Caribbean. And they moved inland with the European settlers, till the last struck only in the nineteenth century, long after populations in the South had already passed through the crisis of nonimmunity and begun to grow again. In the northern forests, the Europeans and their diseases moved inland with the inland movement of the fur trade, bringing a series of demographic catastrophes. A similar demographic loss took place in Siberia as well, since the hunting and fishing populations of the Siberian forests were also comparatively sparse, with a narrower range of endemic disease, and hence of acquired immunities, than would be found at the centers of the intercommunicating zone. At least among peoples of eastern Siberia, the population losses appear to have been close to North American levels. The hunting Yukagirs of the Lena River country, for example, declined from about 5,000 people to 1,500 by the turn of the nineteenth century, and only 443 were recorded in the Soviet census of 1926–7.[2]

The physical isolation of eastern Siberia, however, was not so absolute as the centuries-long isolation of the Americas. Intrusive peoples could push in from the other parts of Asia, even as the Russian fur traders were to push in from the west. But people the Russians found as "native"

---

[1] For a general treatment of these biological transfers see Alfred W. Crosby, Jr., *The Columbian Exchange: Biological and Cultural Consequences of 1492* (Westport, Conn., 1972), esp. pp. 35–63.

[2] Nelson H. H. Graburn and B. Stephen Strong, *Circumpolar Peoples: An Anthropological Perspective* (Pacific Palisades, Calif., 1973), pp. 38–49.

to Siberia had also been intrusive from southern Asia some centuries earlier. The most important of these were the Turkic-speaking Yakut who had come from the south with a pastoral economy based on cattle and horses. In their new home along the Lena River, they added fishing. And they amazed early European visitors by sometimes feeding their cattle on fish, when no other food was available. But more important than their material culture was the fact that they were already immune to a wide range of diseases. As a result they became the largest culture group in the whole of the circumpolar region in Europe, Asia, or North America, with a quarter of a million people in the mid-1920s. By the eighteenth century, the Russian fur trade had developed a symbiotic relationship with the Yakut horsemen, who carried most of the supplies and furs by pack horses over the trails between Yakutsk on the Lena River and the Okhotsk on the Pacific Ocean.[3]

The depletion of fur-bearing animals was another destructive concomitant of the fur trade that struck both continents. The level of economic demand was so high, and the rate of capture was so great, that the supply of animals in any region was seriously depleted within a few decades. Fur traders then moved on to new territory – incidentally to infect new populations with their diseases. This economic phenomenon of depleting a natural resource and moving on is common enough in mining, but fur-bearing animals are potentially renewable if they are not overhunted. Fur traders had a material interest in trapping out and moving on, but the native Americans and Siberians did not. Their apparent interest was to conserve the resource by limiting the catch, but they made little or no effort to do so.

Economists have theoretical explanations of the way people behave when confronted by what are known as "open-access" resources, that is, those that are not owned or, if owned, are nevertheless open to public exploitation. It is sometimes called the "fisheries model," since its most prominent application is to deep-sea fishing. Where a resource is there for the taking, with potential captors in competition with one another, the individual fisherman or hunter will try to capture all he can. If he does not overfish, other fishermen will. His future loss from failing to conserve will be the same, whether or not he fishes now. If he does not, he will have no present profit to set against future loss. The history of sea fisheries is full of examples, down to the present plight of certain whales. On land in Africa, the phenomenon of an "ivory

[3] Graburn and Strong, *Circumpolar Peoples*, pp. 33–7; James R. Gibson, *Feeding the Russian Fur Trade: Provisionment of the Okhotsk Seaboard and the Kamchatka Peninsula, 1639–1856* (Madison, Wis., 1969).

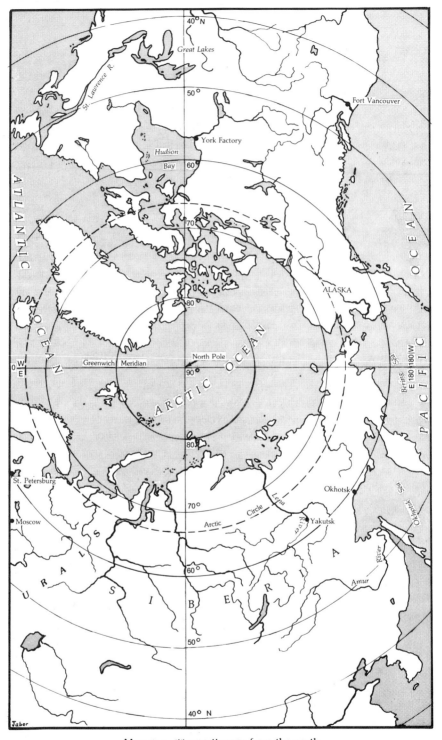

Map 10.1. The earth seen from the north

frontier" driven farther and farther into the heart of the continent during the eighteenth and nineteenth centuries is another case in point.[4]

The speed of depletion depended on a number of factors. One was the specific animals being trapped. In Siberia, the principal animal from the beginning of the fur trade was the sable (*Martes zibellina*), a kind of marten. At first, sable were found all through the northern forests as far west as Finland, but after the 1670s they could be trapped only in Siberia, and after the mid-eighteenth century, only in the far southeast of Siberia. At that point, the principal animal for the Russian trade became the sea otter (*Enhydra lutris*), taken mainly from the waters of the North Pacific. It produces an extremely valuable fur, partly on account of its size. A prime skin before drying could be nearly two meters long and a meter wide. The Russian American Company in 1817 valued a prime sea otter skin at ten times the worth of a prime beaver and forty times that of a prime sable.[5]

For the North American trade, the most important fur-bearing animal was the beaver, principally used for making beaver-felt hats. Curiously enough, these hats came into popularity in the late sixteenth century, when beaver first became easily available to Europe, and their popularity lasted to the early nineteenth, just when beaver began to be scarce. European fashion then turned to hats made of silk and other materials.[6]

The trappers' tools also played a role in the trade's rate of advance. Before the Europeans arrived, native Americans had no iron tools. Iron and steel spear points and axes immediately made it easier to kill animals, speeding the rate of depletion. The shores of the lower Saint Lawrence began to be depleted even before the end of the sixteenth century. By the mid-seventeenth, depletion had reached into what became upstate New York. Trappers' tools changed little between the early seventeenth and the early nineteenth century, but they changed many aspects of life

---

[4] See James A. Crutchfield and Giulio Pontecorvo, *The Pacific Salmon Fisheries: A Study of Irrational Conservation* (Baltimore, 1969), pp. 11–36; J. R. Gould, "Externalities, Factor Proportions, and the Level of Exploitation of Free Access Resources," *Economica*, 39:383–402 (1972). The relations of human beings and animals in North America have been subject to another kind of explanation, depending much more on noneconomic factors – mainly psychological and religious and related to specific cultural conditions in North America. See Calvin Martin, *Keepers of the Game: Indian-Animal Relationships and the Fur Trade* (Berkeley, 1978). Since the same phenomenon of overhunting also took place in Siberia during these same centuries, and in Africa a little later, a more generalized kind of explanation seems to be called for. See also Shepard Krech III (ed.), *Indians, Animals, and the Fur Trade: A Critique of Keepers of the Game* (Athens, Ga., 1981).

[5] Gibson, *Fur Trade*, pp. 24–7.

[6] Harold A. Innis, *The Fur Trade in Canada* (Toronto, 1956), pp. 3–6; Arthur J. Ray and Donald Freeman, *"Give Us Good Measure": An Economic Analysis of Relations between the Indians and the Hudson's Bay Company Before 1763* (Toronto, 1978), pp. 18–20.

and culture among the people who began to use them – aspects that went far beyond the immediate sphere of hunting and trapping.

In the early nineteenth century, new techniques began to spread. First came the steel trap, increasingly important through the century. New modes of transportation began to replace native American techniques like birchbark canoes and snowshoes. Carts began to be used for overland transportation in northern Minnesota and southern Manitoba. Planked York boats, which could be rowed or sailed with smaller crews per ton than the bark canoes of the *voyageurs*, began to be used on the Canadian rivers that flowed northward into Hudson Bay. On the Great Lakes and the western rivers, large sailing vessels and steamboats replaced the canoes.[7]

These changes cut costs and altered the economics of trapping; new kinds of skin now came to market. In the early decades of the trade, marten, fox, wolf, and bear were important along with beaver; they came from the same habitat and their rate of depletion was parallel. Muskrats had also been present, but their value was not enough to justify the cost of transportation until the nineteenth century. Buffalo robes also played little role until the nineteenth century. Bison were prairie animals, in any case, and their natural outlet was by way of the Mississippi-Missouri river system. Demand in the eastern United States and Europe rose just as steamboats became available, so that prices trebled between the 1820s and the 1850s; and exports from the Great Plains reached more than 100,000 robes a year through the 1850s and 1860s. At that rate the buffalo were effectively finished off before 1890.

In spite of the similarities between the northern forests of America and Asia, the two environments were different in significant ways – both physical and cultural. People in central and western Siberia had practiced agriculture even before the fur trade began, though most of those in Pacific Siberia did not. Asians north of the forest, however, had reindeer herds, which were missing in North America. Asians to the south of the forests were the steppe nomads so important to Asian history as a whole. Much of this semiarid region was and remained fit only for nomadic occupation, whereas the equivalent region of the Plains nomads in North America later became some of the richest agricultural land in the world.[8]

The steppe nomads in Asia had ancient contact with the intercommunicating zone. So did many of the Siberian forest people, but the contact was distant and tenuous, and it decreased with movement from

---

[7] Innis, *Fur Trade*, pp. 10–22; Ray and Freeman, *Good Measure*, pp. 19–23.
[8] Gibson, *Fur Trade*, pp. xvi–xvii.

west to east. Some people west of the Sea of Okhotsk, for example, made iron tools, but the Kamchatka Peninsula was still in the Stone Age. The line between the technology available in the Eurasian inter-communicating zone and that available in pre-Columbian America was not a sharp division at the Bering Straits. It was a transitional zone stretching from the straits westward into northern Asia.

Northern Asia in the seventeenth century was far closer than northern America to its present population density. Neither continent could sup-port a dense population in the northernmost forest zone or farther north in the tundra country, except where mineral deposits could be exploited. But the southern forest in what was to be Ontario, Michigan, New York, and Wisconsin was potentially rich. In these earlier centuries, however, it was very sparsely settled indeed. This sparseness alone meant that political organization was sketchy. Political units were small and largely kinship based. Military organization followed the political pattern; a major war band was more likely to be numbered in hundreds than in thousands.

The native Americans also differed culturally among themselves. Those who were to be involved in the fur trade can be divided by ecology into three groups. First were the woodland hunters, mainly migratory people who moved frequently in search of game or fish, breaking into small bands for hunting, reuniting for other purposes. This group included the Eskimo and many different Algonkian-speaking peoples. It stretched from the present Nova Scotia and New Brunswick, north of the Gulf of Saint Lawrence, north and west to the northern shores of the Great Lakes. The second group was the agricultural, eastern woodland people with much denser populations. It included the Iroquois confederation of northern New York State from Lake Champlain to the west and south and the Huron of Ontario south of Georgian Bay. The final group con-sisted of the nomadic Plains Indians like the Sioux, Blackfoot, and Chey-enne. These people had already passed through the "horse revolution" before the eighteenth century. When horses of Spanish origin escaped to the Great Plains, the Indians learned how to use them and developed from sparse and inefficient hunters and gatherers into the prairie people whose whole new way of life was based on horse nomadism and buffalo hunting.[9]

Though the Huron and Iroquois were long-term enemies, they were both important in the early penetration of the fur trade. Outsiders first described the Huron in about 1615, when they numbered twenty to thirty thousand people east of Lake Huron and south of Georgian Bay. They were divided politically into four separate units, which joined to

[9] For reference, see Diamond Jenness, *Indians of Canada*, 7th ed. (Ottawa, 1977).

form a confederacy like that of the Iroquois in New York. The Petun and others had a similar culture but were not members of the confederation. Huron settlements could number several thousand, defended by palisades and growing maize, beans, and squash. Inside were as many as fifty long houses, made of light wooden frames with bark for covering. Each house could be up to 40 meters long, inhabited by eight or ten families closely related through the female line.

In spite of these dense settlements, much of southern Ontario was completely uninhabited, though part was regarded as Huron hunting grounds and served as a buffer between them and the Iroquois to the south. As elsewhere, ecological differences encouraged trade between these farmers and the forest hunters farther north, where little agriculture was possible – or is possible today. Algonkian-speaking hunters sent down surplus furs, dried fish, copper, and charms in return for maize, tobacco, Indian hemp, fishing nets, and other minor products.[10]

The North American setting: geography and the strategy of access from the ocean

Two factors governed the strategy of the fur trade, namely, the location of the animals and the potential ways to reach them by using the waterways. Given available technology, these were the natural avenues in North America, as they were in northern Asia. Another factor governed the location of the best furs. The farther north, the colder the winters and the thicker the pelts. But also, the farther north, the thinner the food supply and the fewer the animals. In eastern Canada and parts of the northeastern United States, this pattern was complicated by the Laurentian Shield, a geologic formation of crystalline rock, mostly granite. It was, and is, a land of lakes, bogs, rich mineral deposits, and very little soil. Although some agriculture is barely possible, the shield is fundamentally unsuited to agricultural occupation. This is why most Indians north of Huron country could not have become farmers, even if they had wanted to do so. And the conditions that made the shield tough for humans also made it tough for fur-bearing animals. Furs existed there, but the richest source of furs in eastern Canada was the forested region just to the south of the shield.

Three water routes led into this region. The Europeans began with the Saint Lawrence, a comparatively easy extension westward from the sixteenth-century fisheries off Newfoundland, and it was navigable by

---

[10] The authoritative work on the Huron is Bruce G. Trigger, *The Children of Aataentsic: A History of the Huron Peoples to 1660*, 2 vols. (Montreal, 1976). See also Trigger, "The French Presence in Huronia: The Structure of Franco-Huron Relations in the First Half of the Seventeenth Century," *Canadian Historical Review*, 49:107–141 (1968), pp. 109–12.

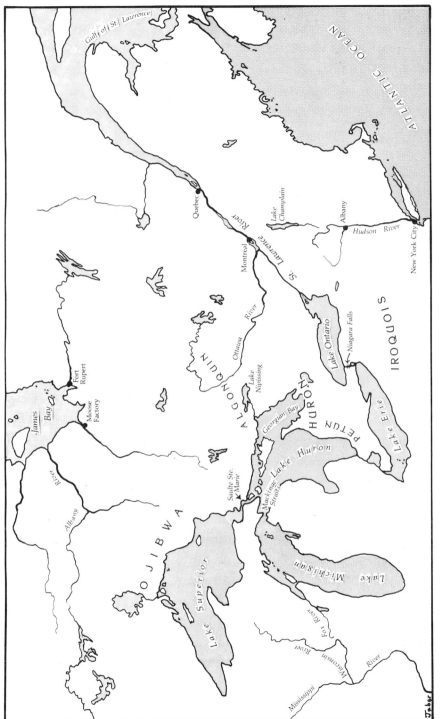

Map 10.2. The Great Lakes and the Saint Lawrence valley

oceangoing vessels as far as the Lachine Rapids, just above the present city of Montreal. Farther west, smaller craft could follow the line of the Great Lakes to Niagara falls and beyond, but the lakes route was secondary to the early fur trade. The Ottawa River flows into the Saint Lawrence just above Montreal, and it provides the most direct route to the west. With a short portage from the Ottawa into Lake Nipissing, canoes could reach northern Lake Huron. With a comparatively short lake passage they could reach on to Michilimackinac and Sault Sainte Marie, and on west by way of Lake Superior or southwest into Lake Michigan and across Wisconsin to the Mississippi by way of the Fox and Wisconsin rivers. The French began trading on the lower Saint Lawrence as early as the 1530s, but this route was little used before 1600.

The Hudson River provided a second entry. Oceangoing ships could pass New York to reach as far as Albany. From there, the Mohawk River provided a westward passage to Niagara, and the line of the lakes carried on southwest to Detroit and beyond. The Dutch set up their first trading posts on Manhattan Island in 1613 and at Albany in 1614. By 1615, when the first French explorers reached Huron country, they found that competition with the Hudson route had begun. The Dutch at Albany were already buying furs from an established Iroquois trade network that stretched west and north. The Iroquois country was not ideal for furs, but as farmers, the Iroquois had maize to trade with northern hunters, who *did* have furs. The Saint Lawrence had the northern advantage of better furs, but it also had the northern disadvantage of icing over in the winter, whereas the Hudson was free enough of ice to be used most winters.

The route by way of Hudson Bay was even farther north and even more seasonally limited, but it provided the shortest route of all into the heart of the continent. The distance by sea from Liverpool to Fort Churchill on Hudson Bay was no greater than that from Liverpool to Montreal.

A fourth route by way of the Mississippi was theoretically available but little used until the late eighteenth century. The Mississippi furnished a north–south route to the sea, and, combined with the major tributaries, the Ohio and the Missouri, it provided an east–west route as well; but it came into use only in the last decades of the fur trade. Then, in the mid-nineteenth century, furs from the Rocky Mountains and buffalo robes from the northern Plains moved down the Missouri to Saint Louis, then either south to New Orleans or up the Ohio to the canals and roads that already linked the upper Ohio to the Atlantic coast.

In addition to the choice of routes, European fur traders had a choice of strategies to follow in securing the furs and getting them to Europe.

One possibility was an all-European operation, without native American help. Europeans from existing settlements could sometimes make seasonal trapping expeditions into the fur-bearing regions. A second possibility was to leave European trappers behind to gather furs on a year-round basis. A third alternative was to stay put in the European settlements, advertise a willingness to buy furs, and let the native Americans do the trapping and transporting. This policy would have paralleled that of European trade diasporas on the African coast in these same centuries. A fourth possibility was to push the trading posts into the interior, so as to have closer contact with Indian trappers and Indian middlemen in long-distance trade. This option shifted the transit market inland and increased the European share of the long routes. It also involved the protection costs of an overland trading-post empire, with control over strong points and transportation routes, but not over the surrounding countryside.

All four of these possibilities were tried in North America, though not in the order given. The first two, the all-European possibilities, came only in the nineteenth century, mainly in the trade from Saint Louis up the Missouri, where the "mountain men" were the trappers who stayed all year to supply the annual summer expeditions up the river.[11] The alternative of waiting for Indian trappers to bring in the furs was the first to be tried, but the depletion of furs near the settlements soon pulled Europeans into the interior. The usual pattern by the second half of the seventeenth century was for Europeans to set up permanent fortified posts in the interior, while Indian trappers caught the animals and Indian middlemen carried them to the posts – in effect, a series of European trade diasporas meeting a series of native American trade diasporas at convenient sites on major waterways.

In North America, furs were normally purchased, though in Siberia forced deliveries were common in much the same pattern as that of the VOC in the Spice Islands. The practice of collecting furs as tribute began with Tatars of the steppe, who demanded tribute called *iasak* from the forest peoples to the north, just as they also collected tribute when they could from the sedentary peoples to the south. The Russians took over the practice and carried it eastward through the forest. The practice differed enormously through Siberia, but the required tribute was usually defined as so many sable skins, other skins being evaluated by that standard. These tribute payments were an important source of income for the Russian state, and the state was always important in the Russian

---

[11] Joseph Jablow, *The Cheyenne in Plains Indian Trade Relations, 1795–1840* (New York, 1951); David J. Wishart, "The Fur Trade of the West, 1807-1840: A Geographical Synthesis," in David Harry Miller and Jerome O. Steffan (eds.), *The Frontier in Comparative Studies* (Norman, Okla., 1977), pp. 160–7.

fur trade; but private traders were nevertheless present as well, and the total value of private trade was far greater than state trade and tribute combined.[12]

The fisheries model suggests that a farsighted royal monopoly might have held off the depletion of fur-bearing animals in Siberia, but the Russian state never tried to go that far. In Alaska after 1799, however, government-sanctioned private monopolies began to take over the fur trade. After 1817, they merged into the Russian American Company with effective monopoly powers that lasted until annexation by the United States in 1867. The company was able to limit the catch of fur seals and sea otters. As a result, the depletion that had driven the Russians forward thus far stopped, at least temporarily. The sea otters in Alaskan waters were to be killed off by the Americans, mainly in the 1880s and 1890s, when the fisheries model was allowed to resume.[13]

Although monopoly in the rest of North America might have spared the fur-bearing animals for more rational long-term harvest, lack of monopoly meant that Europeans could rarely exact tribute. Most of the time, they were forced to pay prices that were in some degree competitive. No one European group ever managed to control all of the routes of entry into the interior of the continent. Each therefore had to compete against the others for the good will of the Indian trappers and traders. Through most of these centuries, the main competitors were the French on the Saint Lawrence, the English on Hudson Bay, and the Dutch and their successors on the Hudson River. Even after the British seized Quebec in 1759, Montreal traders organized as the Northwest Company competed as fiercely with the Hudson's Bay Company as their French predecessors had done. It was not, in short, so much a matter of national interests as locational interests or the rivalry between places at approximately the same level in the hierarchy of urban multifunctionality (see Chapter 1).

In spite of the fact that European fur traders used less violence against the Indians than the European farmer-settlers were to do later on, the fur trade had a comparatively high incidence of violence. Part of the explanation has to be found in Amerindian political organization, which was weak among the agricultural peoples and both weak and transient among forest hunters and Plains nomads. It was therefore hard to locate an authority with power to make a lasting agreement or one that would cover a wide territory.

Still another source of violence came from the cultural overtones of

[12] Raymond Henry Fisher, *The Russian Fur Trade, 1550–1700* (Berkeley, 1943), pp. 49–51, 178–83.
[13] Lydia T. Black, "The Nature of Evil: Of Whales and Sea Otters," in Krech (ed.), *Indians, Animals, and the Fur Trade*, pp. 118–20.

trapping. Hunting and trapping were associated with warfare and were performed by the same social groups that did the fighting. The furs were captured, not produced. Goods that *were* produced, like maize, were often grown by women and other nonwarriors and fell into another category.

Part of the violence also came from the workings of the European state system. France and England were as often at war as at peace from the last quarter of the seventeenth century to Waterloo – nearly a century and a half. War in Europe meant war overseas as well. Even in peacetime, traders and officials knew that war had to be expected. Harold Innis, in his classic work on the Canadian fur trade, emphasized the economic nature of Anglo–French competition in North America. W. J. Eccles has suggested more recently that Innis got the causal directions reversed. After 1700 or so, he argues, the European governments, as opposed to private traders, were not concerned with the North American fur trade for its economic value but for the leverage it gave them in seeking alliances with the Indians. And Indian alliances could help to win colonial wars, because the Indians had the only significant military force west of the Appalachians. Eccles argued that French government fiscal interests would have dictated a complete abandonment of the fur trade in the early eighteenth century, but strategic interests kept it going.[14] In any case, neither the Hudson's Bay Company nor the French fur operations as of about 1700 were as important to their home governments as the Siberian fur trade was to Russia, which was estimated to draw as much as 10 percent of government revenue from that source.[15]

The first phase on the Saint Lawrence, 1600–49

The earliest North American fur trade was little more than a by-product of the European presence on the Gulf of Saint Lawrence, in search of fish. Trade within native American societies up to that time had been comparatively short range, like the trade between the Huron and their northern hunting neighbors. Trade over longer distances could reach as far as a thousand miles, but it was relay trade. When the fur trade began, it had a profound impact on Indian societies, most obviously because it diverted them from their old occupations and led them to catch the fur-

---

[14] Innis, *Fur Trade*, passim; W. J. Eccles, "A Belated Review of Harold Adams Innis, The Fur Trade of Canada," *Canadian Historical Review*, 40:420–41 (1979); Hugh M. Grant, "One Step Forward, Two Steps Back: Innis, Eccles, and the Canadian Fur Trade," *Canadian Historical Review* 62:304–22 (1981); W.J.A. Eccles, "A Response to Hugh M. Grant on Innis and the Canadian Fur Trade," *Canadian Historical Review*, 62:323–9 (1981).
[15] Gibson, *Fur Trade*, pp. 24–7.

bearing animals in return for the iron tools and weapons the Europeans could furnish.

And the new tools and weapons led to further social and political changes, one of the most immediate of which was to create new ways of working out economic and military rivalries within Indian society. One new pattern appeared almost at once and recurred frequently. Any Indian group that first made contact with a European post might then try to monopolize trade by force. Resulting conflict helped bring on a new level of violence beginning in the late sixteenth century and continuing into the seventeenth. The Iroquois monopolized the fur trade reaching the Dutch in Albany, whereas the Huron and Algonquin did nearly the same in alliance with the French on the Saint Lawrence.[16]

At times these conflicts drew support from preexisting ideas about property rights in trade routes. The Huron, for example, regarded any trade route as the property of the extended family or subfamily that had pioneered its use. Others could use it only by permission. By the early seventeenth century, a small number of Huron chiefs controlled most Huron trade. The Huron sexual division of labor simplified the problems of reaching distant French posts. Men were needed for the heavy agricultural work of clearing fields in the winter and early spring. By late spring, they were then free to leave for long trading expeditions, while the women did the lighter work of keeping the fields clear of weeds during the summer.[17]

It was the Huron who initiated commercial contact with the French. They wanted the European products for their own use, but they also wanted to act as middlemen, bringing the European goods into their existing trade network. They passed the French goods on to the north and west, to their old trade partners, the hunting peoples. Huron maize also passed north and west in return for furs. Everyone became more specialized. The Huron grew more maize; the hunters trapped for fur, rather than hunting for meat alone. The Huron concentrated on long-distance trade, even selling some of their maize to the French in distant Quebec.[18]

The scale of Franco-Huron trade increased greatly with Samuel de Champlain's visit of 1615–16. He cemented an informal Franco-Huron alliance against the Iroquois and invited a number of young Huron men

---

[16] George T. Hunt, *The Wars of the Iroquois: A Study in Intertribal Trade Relations* (Madison, Wis., 1960); Bruce G. Trigger, "Trade and Tribal Warfare on the St. Lawrence in the Sixteenth Century," *Ethnohistory*, 9:240–56 (1962); Conrad E. Heidenreich and A. H. Ray, *The Early Fur Trade: A Study in Cultural Interaction* (Toronto, 1976); Freeman and Ray, *Good Measure*, pp. 19–21.

[17] Trigger, "Franco-Huron Relations," pp. 112–13; Conrad E. Heidenreich, *Huronia: A History and Geography of the Huron Indians* (Toronto, 1971), pp. 220–3.

[18] Trigger, "Franco-Huron Relations," pp. 116–18.

to live in Quebec, promising in return to send Frenchmen to live in Huron country. This followed the Huron custom of exchanging a few people with a trading partner as a token of good faith. It was, incidentally, also a way to build up the kind of cross-cultural experience that would be of value in future trade. In this case the exchange brought Jesuit missionaries and the beginning of religious as well as economic change.[19]

The 1620s marked the peak of the Huron fur trade, though its size is hard to estimate. In 1623, sixty Huron and Algonquin canoes came down to Lachine Rapids, forty-five in the following year. This was substantial, since the Huron canoes on this route were seven meters long, paddled by five men. Still, only about 200 Huron men were involved in these annual trade expeditions, out of an estimated Huron population of 21,000. If the Huron contribution to total French fur exports from Quebec was about two-thirds of the whole, Huron fur trade may have been in the vicinity of nine to ten thousand beaver pelts in an ordinary year, perhaps as many as fifteen thousand in unusual circumstances. This brief florescence of Franco-Huron trade and cultural exchange, however, ended abruptly after the mid-1630s.

By the early 1630s, both the Huron and their Iroquoian enemies had depleted the supply of beaver in their own territory. Future furs would have to be found to the west and north. Then, in 1635, the Huron began to experience the disastrous consequences of nonimmune contact with European disease, with smallpox, influenza, and perhaps measles as well, all sweeping through in short order. By 1641, half the Huron were dead.

The economic disaster of depleted beaver then prompted the Iroquois to use their military power to secure a larger share of diminishing trade. In the 1640s, they turned north in a series of raids against the Huron trade route to Quebec and against the Huron country itself. By 1649, all of the former Huron territory had fallen to Iroquois war parties, and the Huron themselves were either dead or scattered. Some joined the Iroquois as subordinates. Some fled to live among their former trade partners to the northwest.[20]

The Ottawa and Ojibwa inherited the Huron role of feeding the French fur trade, but the new source of furs was much farther west, around Lake Michigan and Lake Superior and north toward James Bay and the Arctic. One group of Huron, however, managed to keep a hand in the fur trade. This was the small community that had gone to live in the

[19] Trigger, "Franco-Huron Relations," p. 115; Heidenreich, *Huronia*, pp. 237–50.
[20] Trigger, "Franco-Huron Relations," pp. 127–30; Heidenreich, *Huronia*; Bruce G. Trigger, "The Ontario Epidemics of 1634–40," in Krech (ed.), *Animals, Indians, and the Fur Trade*.

French settlements on the Saint Lawrence and now attracted Huron refugees as well. They had learned enough of French culture to act as cross-cultural brokers. Those that survived the epidemics also had a degree of acquired immunity to European disease. As a result they were able to set up a new trade diaspora, based on the river but trading north into the boreal forest, using their ability to deal both with the northern Indians and with French newly arrived from Europe.[21]

The opening of the bay

The destruction of the Huron drew French explorers as well as Indian middlemen to the West. Groseilliers reached Green Bay in Wisconsin by 1654–6. He and Radison came back to Lake Superior in 1659 and learned from the Indians that Hudson Bay was not far away to the north. They then set off for France in search of financial support for a direct approach by sea. Failing in France, they sought English support and finally reached the lower bay in 1668–9. The expedition was a financial success. In 1670, their supporters formed the Hudson's Bay Company, with a royal charter granting a legal monopoly over all English trade into Hudson Bay. This sequence of events is significant because it meant that the precedents of the Saint Lawrence trade were carried to the bay as well, even though the traders there were to be mainly of a different nationality.[22]

The Hudson's Bay Company (HBC) began with annual, summer-season voyages, returning to Europe before the freeze. In 1679, however, it shifted to year-round, fortified trading posts located where major rivers flowed into the bay from the south and west. But the HBC departed from the precedent of the French fur trade in one regard. Company personnel went no farther than the shores of the bay. They waited there for business to come to them, in direct and conscious imitation of British trading practices in India and on the African coast.

The French contested this move with voyages into the bay itself, but they were forced out and agreed by treaty in 1713 to leave that route to the English. The main French response was to reach out overland toward the bay from their base on the Saint Lawrence – more important still, to send French traders, the famous *coureurs de bois*, to deal directly with the Indian suppliers of furs in the Far West. A chain of trading posts led west from Lake Superior along the line of the present U.S.-Canadian boundary, then northwest through Manitoba into central Alberta. The

---

[21] Heidenreich and Ray, *Early Fur Trade*, pp. 12–33; Heidenreich, *Huronia*, p. 279.
[22] Ray and Freeman, *Good Measure*, pp. 121–5; Innis, *Fur Trade*, pp. 43–83; Edwin E. Rich, *The Fur Trade and the Northwest to 1857* (Toronto, 1967), pp. 24–44.

Montreal-based French changed, in short, from the policy of encouraging Indian traders to visit them. They now extended their own trade diaspora into the interior. In spite of the longer distances they had to travel, French coureurs were effective competitors with the HBC men in the North, especially in the 1740s and 1750s.[23]

In this new competitive situation, the pattern of Indian groups seeking to establish their monopoly over the supply of furs to the European posts reappeared. In the 1670s, the Ojibwa who supplied the French on the Saint Lawrence began to supply the HBC men on the bay as well. When the French reached into the interior, therefore, the Ojibwa lost out. Meanwhile, especially after about 1720, Assiniboine and Cree, forest hunters living south and west of the lower bay, became the main suppliers to the HBC posts. They had two advantages over their Indian competitors. First, they were close enough to the bay ports for an assured round trip between spring thaw and fall freeze. More distant traders risked being caught by an early winter. Then again, their contact with the English gave them, first, access to European weapons and tools and, hence, a military advantage over the Indians farther away. The French toyed with the idea of forming a counteralliance with some of the Plains horse nomads, especially the Dakota Sioux, who were already in chronic conflict with the Assiniboine and Cree. The possibility recalls the earlier French intervention in Iroquois–Huron disputes, but the French gave it up this time as more likely to hinder trade than otherwise.[24]

In 1763, the British annexation of Quebec took the French out of the North American fur trade, but it made little difference in the rivalry between points of entry. Recognizing the potential rivalry between routes, the British government sponsored what amounted to a cartel agreement. In theory, New York was to control Niagara and Detroit and the trade along the main line of the Great Lakes. Montreal – meaning in practice Scottish and New York fur traders who now moved north of the old border – was to have the old main line of the Ottawa River, Lakes Huron and Superior to Grand Portage and beyond, whereas the HBC sphere was to be as it had been.

The upshot of an intricate conflict was that New York lost access to the best of the remaining fur-bearing territory. Individual Montreal traders competed among themselves for a time, but in 1804, they had merged into a single firm, the Northwest Company.[25] That move set the scene for a final struggle between two monopolies and two points of entry. The HBC changed tactics and began advancing its posts up the rivers

[23] Ray and Freeman, *Good Measure*, pp. 17–36.
[24] Ray and Freeman, *Good Measure*, pp. 39–43.
[25] Rich, *Fur Trade*, pp. 130–42.

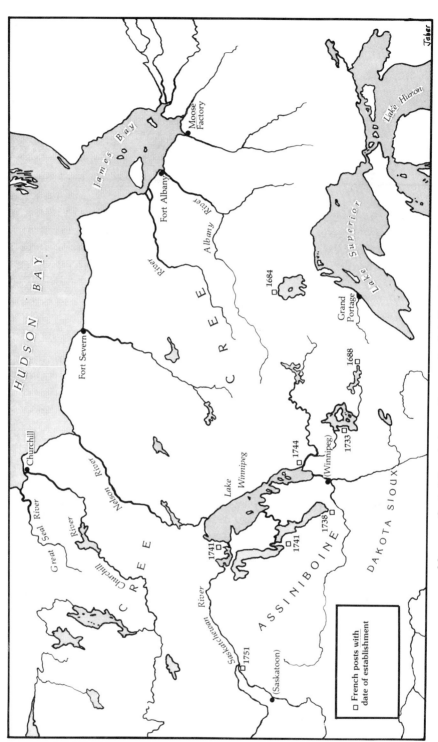

Map 10.3 Central Canada (names in parentheis indicate later establishment than text references)

flowing from the south and west into the bay. It shifted from the bark canoes of its Indian suppliers to wooden, oar-driven York boats that could carry heavier loads at lower cost. Sometimes the forward posts of the two companies were side by side, and sometimes their rivalry turned to armed violence; but the HBC gradually gained the advantage. In 1821, the two companies merged under the name of the Hudson's Bay Company, with a legal monopoly over the whole Canadian fur trade.[26]

By that time, the North American fur trade was nearly finished. Its farthest reaches were then approached by sea from the Pacific coast, encountering the Russians in the process. Perhaps the final reach into virgin territory was the episode of the mountain men of the Rockies, where altitude replaced latitude in assuring the quality of the furs. From the early 1820s into the 1830s, several hundred Euro-American trappers scattered into the mountains, but the effort died out nearly as rapidly as it began. In the course of the 1830s, the best of the Rocky Mountain beaver were trapped and gone.[27]

The fur trade and the price-fixing market

The North American fur trade was clearly different from most cross-cultural trade we have encountered so far. It involved a meeting between market-oriented Europeans and native Americans, who had been isolated for many centuries. Their economies were far more self-subsistent than those in most of Africa or Asia. Their technology and their pre-contact trade systems were less developed. Cross-cultural trade before and after the European arrival ran a broad gamut of possible relationships, from mutual raiding and plain robbery, through a variety of ritual ceremonial exchanges with important social and political functions. Sometimes exchanges with mainly commercial significance took place simultaneously with others where the ritual significance was uppermost. Among the Cheyenne Plains nomads, for example, two groups would sometimes assemble for trade "on the pipe," where the ceremonial exchange of gifts between the men was combined with the ritual smoking of the pipe of friendship, but private trade was carried out on the side, often between women from the two parties.[28]

---

[26] Innis, *Fur Trade*, pp. 49–165; see Ann Carlos, "The Causes and Origins of the North American Fur Trade Rivalry: 1804–1810", *Journal of Economic History*, 41:777–94 (1981), for a recent revision of older views based on her "The North American Fur Trade, 1804–1821: A Study of the Life Cycle of a Duopoly" (Ph.D. dissertation, University of Western Ontario, 1980).

[27] Wishart, "Fur Trade," pp. 169–83.

[28] Jablow, *The Cheyenne*, pp. 46–8. See also Richard I. Ford, "Barter, Gift, or Violence: An Analysis of Tewa Intertribal Exchange," in Edwin N. Wilmsen (ed.), *Social Exchange and Interaction* (Ann Arbor, Mich., 1972), for further illustration of exchange possibilities.

Historians of the fur trade in recent decades have also been impressed by the variety of modes of exchange. Several have argued that the North American fur trade was based on political and social or on intellectual and religious considerations – not on supply and demand or the market principle. Though broadly substantivist, these authorities take somewhat different points of view. Abraham Rotstein and Edwin E. Rich argue, with slightly different emphases, that the fur trade was mainly a matter of political and military alliances between the European powers and the Indians: a treaty trade with material considerations secondary. There is something in this; European trade all over the world at this period involved coercion for protection and extortion of various kinds. It was, after all, the age of mercantilism in economic thought, which insisted on a close link between economic and political advantage.

But politico-military alliances were not strikingly more important here than they were in European trade with Asia. Arthur Ray and Donald Freeman have argued recently and persuasively against the Rich-Rotstein point of view. They concede that the French furnished arms to the Huron, the Dutch to the Iroquois, and that the French toyed with a Dakota connection. But the Hudson's Bay Company never engaged in hostilities against any of the Indian groups living on the shores of the bay. After the fall of the Huron, native Americans tried to avoid trading exclusively with a single European nationality; they preferred to play one against another. For that matter, a treaty was an alien concept. None of the forest hunters had leaders with the authority to make a binding agreement covering future trade relationships.[29]

The second recent antimarket study of the fur trade is that of Calvin Martin. It also has substantivist overtones, but the main contention is that the Indians had a special attitude toward animals, and one with strong religious overtones. The underlying idea was that the spirits of the animals would help human beings, so long as the humans killed no more animals than were absolutely necessary for their own survival. When the Indians began to die in the great epidemics of European diseases, they thought the animals had failed them. They therefore turned on the animals, according to Martin, in an uncontrolled slaughter, of which the fur trade was a part. This position too has been answered persuasively in a recent response by Shepard Krech and his associates.[30]

With these two lines of revision laid to rest in most respects, the fact remains that people of different cultures *do* often have different attitudes toward material goods. And this was certainly the case of the European

[29] Rich, *Fur Trade*; Abraham Rotstein, "Fur Trade and Empire: An Institutional Analysis" (Ph.D. dissertation, University of Toronto, 1967); Ray and Freeman, *Good Measure*, esp. pp. 32–3.
[30] Martin, *Keepers of the Game*; Krech (ed.), *Indians, Animals and the Fur Trade*.

fur traders and the native Americans. For many Indian groups, mutual gift giving was important in establishing friendly relations, both between groups and within groups. Wealth carried prestige, but only when the wealth was redistributed in the form of gifts. The Indian reputation for light fingers came from this attitude. Indians often thought that any apparently surplus goods ought to be theirs for the taking, which led to enormous misunderstandings around trading posts all across North America. This did not mean that native Americans disdained the possession of material goods. Why else travel hundreds of miles in search of trade with Europeans? Trade was, indeed, a prime way to acquire the goods that built prestige and influence. The result was a system of diffused reciprocity, which worked because gift giving was a way to attain a desirable high status; and the giver could give willingly because he himself might someday receive an equivalent gift in time of need.[31] The system can be explained in terms of normal economic theory, based on the need to allocate scarce goods and services, as well as in substantivist terms that would insist that this diffused reciprocity was imbedded in a social order.

These native American attitudes have been widely reported, from Iroquois and Huron to the famous custom of potlatch on the Pacific coast. They were curiosities European visitors would write about. Reporting of the commonplace is much harder to come by. In spite of Jesuit relations and other reports on the coureurs de bois, surviving sources rarely deal with the actual forms of bargaining or exchange. Most early trade from the Saint Lawrence was in the hands of private traders, who had no obligation to report to anyone – no Hovannes here. The HBC, however, had the kind of bureaucratic structure that led to reporting and record keeping, hence to a picture of the actual form of cross-cultural exchange on the bay.

Neither Indian nor English trading precedents could be followed completely, but the tendency was to lean toward native American ways. The HBC even adopted a special accounting system to fit Indian practices. Instead of using pounds, shillings, and pence, the factor at an HBC post translated the value of goods received from Britain into a currency of account called "made beaver," abbreviated MB and originally the value of a good beaver pelt. The transposition of currencies followed a price list evaluating each type and quality of import in terms of MBs. This list, which differed for each individual post, was called its *Standards of Trade*. Each post also had a second list, the *Comparative Standard*, which

---

[31] Heidenreich and Ray, *Early Fur Trade*, p. 17; Ray and Freeman, *Good Measure*, pp. 242 ff.

evaluated each kind of animal pelt in MBs. Neither list changed very much over time.

Superficially, these lists suggest an administered trade at fixed prices, but this was not the case. Neither standard represented actual exchange values of particular transactions. They were designed to serve as a guide to the factor and his superiors. The factor negotiated with Indian sellers as best he could. His objective was to obtain a total quantity of furs, by gift and exchange combined, that would produce a difference between the MB value of goods sold and that of furs bought. That difference was called the "overplus," and the size of the overplus measured the success of the trading season. But it was an index, not a measure of actual profit. The true profit depended on the European cost of trade goods, the sale value of the furs, and the company's expenses.

The actual bargaining at the trading posts followed native American practice, similar to the Cheyenne pipe trade. In the mid-to-late eighteenth century, trading parties came in under a recognized trade captain who acted collectively for his group, while the chief factor of the post acted for the HBC. The two opened negotiations with an exchange of gifts. The values were not fixed but changed according to the advantage each hoped to gain. Factors, for example, often varied the gift according to the number of canoes a trade captain brought with him, in effect, a personal gratuity for quantity. The furs presented to the factor were an inducement to give good measure and fair dealing in the trade that was to follow. Both sides made speeches along with the gifts. They then smoked the peace pipe, and trade could begin.[32] Bargaining over the equivalents of skins to trade goods took place in the trade room of the fort, but only for the trade captain. Indians with their own furs to trade came instead to a hole in the wall of the fort.

The supply of furs had a low price elasticity. Individuals apparently worked with an implicit supply schedule that responded little to price changes, once a fairly small quantity of European goods had been acquired. Part of the explanation may be that hunting peoples moved frequently, setting physical limits on the quantity they were willing to carry around with them. One by-product is that trade captains were often more concerned about quality than they were about price alone.

After this individual bargaining, which could take several days, the factor and the trade captain presented another round of gifts, and the Indians set off for home. Once away from the HBC post, the trade captain was supposed to redistribute the gifts he had received, whereas the factor merged the gifts and furs traded and reported his overplus to the London office. The factor and the trade captain were clearly key people

[32] Ray and Freeman, *Good Measure*, pp. 54–7.

in a complex trading ceremony, no doubt marked by a good deal of misunderstanding but effective in making cross-cultural trade possible when both sides had come a very long distance.[33]

This trade relationship was clearly not administered trade, and it was somewhat short of free competition. The HBC held a government monopoly over English trade, and the French were excluded by treaty after 1713. In form, the HBC was a monopsonist-monopolist, but the Montreal interests were active and highly competitive in the region south of the bay. HBC prices in James Bay, the "bottom of the bay," were set in recognition of those the French were paying farther south.[34] But the Indian trade parties had little competitive choice in a single season. After spending several months to arrive at an HBC post on the bay, they could hardly withdraw to go elsewhere that year. But alternatives for future years were available, and the HBC personnel knew that they had to make their range of offerings attractive, or the traders would simply not come back. In general, then, though reciprocity and redistribution were both present, and monopoly elements were strong, the North American fur trade ultimately responded to the market principle.

This adjustment of a European trade diaspora to the needs of cross-cultural trade bears an interesting resemblance to the exchange system used on the West African coast at this same period. In both cases, the Europeans overseas abandoned the pounds, shillings, and pence of the home accounts in favor of accounts kept in MB, bars, or trade ounces of gold. In both cases, the "prices" assigned to European goods in these new currencies were relatively inflexible, so that flexibility to deal with the play of supply and demand had to come from some other source. In West Africa (see Chapter 3) it was through assortment bargaining. Along Hudson Bay, it was more often through barter without a currency, the terms of the exchange being adjusted to something closer to European measures by the concept of the overplus.

This, at least, gave the European bookkeepers a point of departure. The accounting system at the West African factories made it extremely difficult to know how much profit or loss a factor was actually making on a particular transaction. The disadvantage was apparently worth the price for the sake of having a cross-cultural medium of exchange that could satisfy some European and some non-European norms. As with so much else in world trade after the late eighteenth century, these practices too began to shift toward European norms. The era of the trade diasporas was nearing its end.

[33] Ray and Freeman, *Good Measure*, pp. 57–8, 74–5, 218–23.
[34] Harold Innis's classic work on the fur trade tended to show the French as comparatively weak competitors. This view is no longer common. Both the French and the Northwest Company were strong and active. See Eccles, "Belated Review"; Ray and Freeman, *Good Measure*, pp. 198–217.

11

The twilight of the trade diasporas

It is often said that trade diasporas tended to work themselves out of existence, as commercial ties reduced the cultural differences that called them into being in the first place. But the Westernization of world commerce between about 1740 and 1860 was something new. It not only deprived the existing Western trade diasporas of an effective role; it ended once and for all the long era in history when trade diasporas had been the dominant institutional form in cross-cultural trade.

Industrialism and the shifting balance

The root cause of all this was not just the long-term trend toward more and larger areas of ecumenical trade; it was even more the birth of the industrial age. The new technology made possible a fundamentally new kind of human society, with much higher levels of production and consumption than ever before – but bringing with it new problems, environmental pollution, pressure on nonrenewable resources, weapons powerful enough to wipe out most of the human race.[1]

In the first instance, the new industrial age was also the "European age," if only because the Europeans got the new technology first, and with it the ability to conquer and dominate others at comparatively small cost. The balance of military power had begun to shift somewhat earlier. The "gunpowder empires" of the sixteenth century were a general Afro-Eurasian phenomenon. By the middle of the eighteenth century, a second innovation in artillery gave the Europeans a lead over others, based on field artillery that was light, cheap, and could be fired by a crew of trained artillerymen as rapidly as a single soldier could load and fire a musket. Field artillery in conjunction with volley firing by trained in-

---

[1] For a recent treatment of the technological aspects, see David S. Landes, *The Unbound Prometheus* (Cambridge, 1969); or for a more general treatment see volume III of Carlo M. Cipolla (ed.), *The Fontana Economic History of Europe* 5 vols. (London, 1973).

fantry meant that European troops – or European-trained troops appropriately armed – could now defeat Asian or African armies several times
their size.[2]

As early as the 1740s, these new military techniques began to influence
the way European trading-post empires could behave toward their Asian
neighbors. And that shift in relative power began a transition away from
the trading-post empires of the recent past, toward the kind of territorial
rule represented by British India in Bengal or the Netherlands Indies
over Java. The trading firms had used force principally as a way of
increasing profits. They had paid protection money and they had collected it, but they had rarely made important decisions on mainly political grounds. This began to change as the comparative power of the
Europeans increased. It also began to change as the frequent wars between France and Great Britain spread overseas; war in Europe meant
automatic war between the French and the English East India companies
in Indian waters and on the Indian subcontinent.

It was this rivalry between English and French that set the English
East Indian Company on the course that led to a gradual transition from
trading-post empire to real, territorial control – first over parts of India,
then (directly or indirectly) over all of it. Anglo-French competition became serious in the 1740s, as the French Compagnie des Indes in southern India began to play on the rivalries between Indian states. It began
arming and training Indian troops in European methods of warfare,
including the use of field artillery and volley firing. It also brought more
European troops to India, and the English Company was forced to do
the same in self-defense. These military commitments were expensive.
One obvious way to pay for them was to do what Indian rulers did to
raise money for *their* armies, that is, to collect taxes, especially land taxes
from the peasantry.

The English company increased its authority by stages, in step with
its increasing military power. Its military supremacy in Bengal is usually
dated from the battle of Plassey in 1757, but the date is more symbolic
than real, and the battle itself was little more than a very impressive
artillery bombardment. It nevertheless opened the way for gradual but
steady encroachment by the company on the authority of its Indian
neighbors. It first began to collect certain land rents on the authority of
the *nawab*, or ruler, of Bengal, who had become a company puppet.
Then, by 1765, it forced the nawab to make the company, in its collective
capacity, his chief revenue officer, or *diwan*. At first it exercised the

---

[2] Carlo M. Cipolla, *Guns and Sails in the Early Phase of European Expansion 1400–1700*
(London, 1965), esp. pp. 143–8; Gale B. Ness and William Stahl, "Western Imperialist
Armies in Asia," *Comparative Studies*, 19:2–29 (1977); William H. McNeill, *The Pursuit of
Power: Technology, Armed Force, and Society since A.D. 1000* (Chicago, 1982).

powers of the office of diwan through Indian agents, but in 1772 it began to do so openly through its own paid officials, collecting the revenue and managing the financial affairs of the three provinces closest to Calcutta: Bengal, Bihar, and Orissa. This was a considerable area, including all of present-day Bangladesh as well as West Bengal, which remained part of the Republic of India. With that, the East Indian Company was no longer a mere trading firm. It was also a government, and the British Parliament recognized as much in 1773 by passing a "Regulating Act." This was, in effect, the first in a series of measures that gradually took the company's political functions away from its board of directors and gave them to royal officials.

This transition from trading-post empire to territorial empire over India lasted to 1858, in theory. In practice, British officials ruled most of India much earlier, even though the conquering armies were officially those of the East India Company, and the bureaucrats who ruled were officially its servants. Indeed, in 1813, it lost its right to monopolize trade between India and Europe, having long since given up the effort to monopolize the trade of the Indian Ocean itself. In 1834, it lost its monopoly over British trade to China, and for all practical purposes, it stopped being a trading company at all. It became, instead, the branch of the British government designated to rule over British India. The British government finally disbanded the company in 1858, after a serious mutiny by its Indian soldiers – the soldiers whose European armament and training had made Britain dominant over India in the first place.

Meanwhile, British rule had long since begun to spread British commercial culture throughout the country. The old trade diasporas and commercial contacts continued, but their methods followed the Western mode more and more closely. And a new Western-run, Western-style economy grew up alongside the old commercial order, with banks, insurance companies, railways, telegraphs, and a growing sphere for such new institutions as the managing agency. The old patterns occupied a smaller part of the growing economy, even though some aspects have continued to the present.

The VOC passed through a similar transition from trading-post to territorial empire, with a similar basis in the new European military power. The transition grew out of local circumstances on Java. In the first half of the seventeenth century, one kingdom, Mataram, ruled virtually the entire island. It was outwardly centralized and strong, and the king's theoretical power was limitless, but centralized power barely survived the death, in 1645, of Agung, its founder. Even earlier, considerable authority remained with local subrulers, who would not always obey the central government. From Agung's death, power shifted even more decisively to potential successor states with a local base – including the VOC in Batavia and a few centers of Bugis and Chinese power, which had also begun as nodes of a trade diaspora.

In spite of the VOC's desire to avoid territorial rule, it had military power available in Batavia, and political disorder was bad for business. From the 1670s, a patterned interaction came into existence. When a sultan of Mataram was unable to suppress rebellion he called for Dutch help. Out of gratitude, or under Dutch pressure, he would cede territory to the VOC. The Dutch then ruled it through the same chronically in-subordinate officials who had ruled it for Mataram. In this way, over a century or so, one territory after another passed from the control of Mataram to that of Batavia. By 1757, the Dutch were masters of almost the entire island. But their territorial rule over Java was even more indirect than early British rule in India. Most of the island was admin-istered by men the Dutch called regents – still the descendants of those who had ruled under Mataram. In effect, the Dutch could give orders in certain spheres, mainly those affecting their economic interests, such as the production and export of coffee. Otherwise, the regents ruled as they chose. The VOC thus had made a kind of transition to territorial empire, but not to the kind of territorial empire that was to come with nineteenth-century colonialism. It was still more Javanese than Western. In 1799, the VOC sunk to its end in commercial failure in spite of (per-haps, because of) its territorial rule on Java.

In the first decades of the nineteenth century, the former territories of the VOC passed through a sequence of different jurisdictions, in-cluding a period under Napoleonic France and a few years of British rule. In 1816, the Dutch government took over and set up a colonial regime called the Netherlands Indies. These various European masters tried to make something real out of their fictional dominance over Java, but their efforts were neither systematic nor successful. They were enough, however, to arouse a Javanese reaction against Dutch control and foreign ways. The result was a major rebellion that ran through the period 1825 to 1830 – a crisis of empire like the Indian mutiny. But more than the Indian mutiny, this war combined what had been, for India, the initial takeover with a later, xenophobic reaction to European rule. The Dutch faced a choice between pulling out or fighting a real war of conquest. They chose to fight and then created for the first time a true colonial administration that could give orders and see they were obeyed.[3] In the commercial sphere, this led to a near-monopoly over the export

---

[3] Michael Adas, *Prophets of Rebellion: Millenarian Protest Movements against the European Colonial Order* (Chapel Hill, N.C., 1979), pp. 3–11 and passim.

trade, vested in a Dutch government trading company. It therefore differed from the gradual introduction of Western commercial institutions, as in India where Indian merchants were still allowed to operate. Here, local merchants were left with local trade only, which meant in effect that it fell into the hands of a few local Muslims, Chinese, and Bugis left over from the earlier diasporas.

These transitions to territorial empire in Bengal and Java are only two of many possible examples of the way Europe's new industrial power impinged on the non-Western world. The new strength of European influence was less obvious in commerce than it was in politics, but it was immense. Where, in the era of the companies, the Europeans had been involved in elaborate forms of cross-cultural brokerage, cross-cultural brokerage was no longer in much demand, when one party could call the tune.

Distant reflections of the industrial age: secondary empires in Africa

Nor were the European trading companies the only institutions to receive a windfall of power as a result of European industrialization. Between about 1780 and 1880, Africa passed through a transition analogous to the economic and military transition in Asia, only in Africa the Europeans were fewer on the ground. Increasing trade and supplies of arms from Europe tended to go, in the first instance, to those who controlled trade and had access to arms. We have already seen how increased trade, increased traffic in slaves, and more arms imports into East Africa led to rising levels of violence from the 1780s onward (see Chapter 2). These tendencies increased through the first half of the nineteenth century. After about 1850 and especially after the 1870s, African traders began to turn themselves into rulers, even as the European traders had done in parts of Asia almost a century earlier.

European weapons, rather than a European presence, underlay these changes. After the 1860s European firearms changed rapidly, from muzzle-loading muskets at midcentury, through variant innovations in rifling, cartridges, breech loading, and rapid-fire magazines. All of these found their way into African hands – though the machine guns the Europeans began using in the early 1880s did not. An African trader or ruler who could acquire a supply of the latest European weapons before his neighbors had them at his mercy. One result was that African political boundaries, especially in eastern and central Africa, were redrawn by the creation of new political units, which are sometimes called secondary empires because they drew their strength indirectly from the industrial technology of Europe.[4]

Afro-Arabs were among the builders of secondary empires in these decades, but they were not alone. Yao traders set up a small kingdom in Tumbuka, west of Lake Malawi, even before Swahili merchants appeared in the vicinity.[5] A Nyamwezi trader-adventurer founded a kingdom in the copper-bearing region of Shaba in Zaire, and an Afro-Arab founded one on the upper Congo centered near the present city of Kisangani. Even nontraders like the kings of Buganda could become expansionist, so long as they could persuade traders to sell them later model guns. But the phase of secondary empire was comparatively brief in East Africa. The first wave of the European invasions reached even into the heart of Africa by the 1890s.

At least one variant of the several ways a trade diaspora could become a secondary empire can be illustrated with the example of a trade network that began on the Nubian reaches of the Nile to the north of Khartoum and ended with conquests in the late nineteenth century that extended south into present-day Zaire and west to Nigeria. The Nubian stretches of the Nile were typical of the date-camel complex (see Chapter 2), and this passage of the Nile through the desert had been a corridor between Mediterranean and sub-Saharan Africa for centuries. It had been ruled by Pharaonic Egypt, by Rome, and later by Islamized and assimilated settlers from Arabia. By the eighteenth century, the people of southern Nubia thought of themselves as Arabs, though they remained more Nubian than Arabian in descent. Those of the southernmost reach of the Nubian Nile, the first long reach after the White and Blue Niles join at Khartoum, identified themselves as Arabs. More specifically, they were Ja'alīyīn, tracing their descent back not only to Arabia but to Abbas, the Prophet's uncle.

The first decades of the nineteenth century were especially prosperous. Southern Nubia was politically independent as a kingdom centered at Shendi. The Ja'alīyīn operated trade routes in all directions: south to the borderlands of Ethiopia, east to the Red Sea at Suakin, west through Kordofan to the sultanate of Darfur. Darfur was, indeed, a secondary center for their activity, with one branch route running directly south to the equatorial forest and another northeast across the desert to the westward bend of the Nile and continuing on north to Egypt. This was the historic Forty-Day Road from Darfur to the Nile. Both this route and the one along the Nile itself were important for a

---

[4] For secondary empires generally see Philip D. Curtin et al., *African History* (Boston, 1978), pp. 332–61, 404–17.
[5] Leroy Vail, "Suggestions Towards a Reinterpreted Tumbuka History," in B. Pachai (ed.), *The Early History of Malawi* (London, 1972), pp. 148–67.

northward flow of goods from the Sudan, the forest, and the desert –
ivory, ostrich feathers, slaves, copper, tamarind, gum arabic, and camels
for the Egyptian market.[6]

After 1820, the situation changed rapidly. First, the Egyptian government conquered Nubia and the Sudan immediately to the south. These
conquests marked the first success of a new Egyptian secondary empire,
built with the new power of troops trained in the European fashion,
using the latest European weapons, and often serving under European
mercenaries as well. The first result was favorable to Ja'alī trade. Many
Nubian merchants moved to Khartoum, the new capital of the Egyptian
Sudan and the center for an expanding trade that attracted many other
merchants, such as Copts from Egypt, Levantines, and even a few
Europeans.

In 1839, the Egyptians discovered a new opening to equatorial Africa.
Up to this time, the Nile south of the Sudan was an extensive papyrus
swamp, called the *sudd*, and it seemed impassable by boat. At first the
new route was confined to government boats, but after 1851 it was open
to all merchants. In this period of rising ivory prices, traders spread
along the maze of waterways above the sudd, into the Bahr al-Ghazal
district of the Sudan and farther south into the present northeastern
Zaire and northern Uganda. Beyond the sudd, however, the Egyptians
made little effort to establish civil government, and the preexisting local
governments were too weak to control the influx of alien traders. As a
result, the merchants of the diaspora began first to govern their own
trade enclaves, like a conventional trading-post empire, and then to
govern the surrounding region till they had created, in effect, a secondary empire on the frontiers of the Egyptian secondary empire.

The process moved by stages. First, the traders set up armed camps,
called *zariba* and protected by their own military force of slave-soldiers
armed with the latest European weapons. Then the men of the zariba
moved from self-defense to intervention in local affairs, which brought
new levels of violence and local anarchy, and an increase in the numbers
of slaves for sale. But anarchy was bad for trade, and at the next stage,
the rulers of the zariba began to establish order in the vicinity, thus
shifting gradually from the forms of a trading-post empire to those of a
small secondary territorial empire.[7]

These militarized trade diasporas of the 1850s and the early 1860s were

---

[6] P. M. Holt, "Egypt, the Funj, and Darfur," in Richard Gray (ed.), *The Cambridge History of Africa*, vol. 4 (Cambridge, 1975).

[7] P. M. Holt, "Egypt and the Nile Valley," in John E. Flint (ed.), *The Cambridge History of Africa*, vol. 5 (Cambridge, 1976), pp. 35–7; Richard Gray, *A History of the Southern Sudan 1839–1889* (Oxford, 1961), pp. 45–69; Richard Hill, *Egypt in the Sudan 1820–1881* (London, 1959).

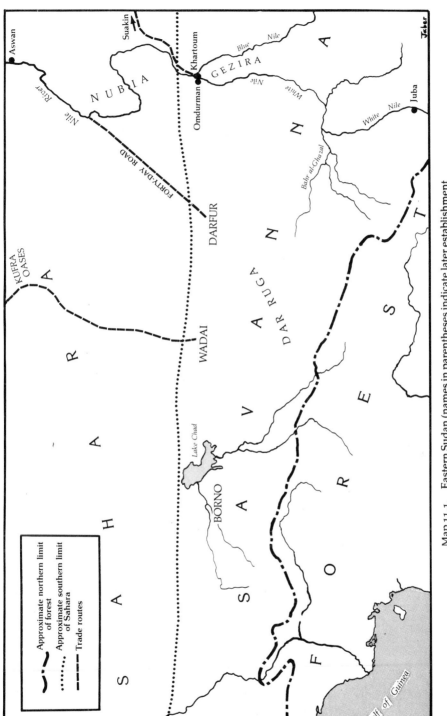

Map 11.1.   Eastern Sudan (names in parentheses indicate later establishment than text references)

international in management, though most were based in Khartoum and recruited most of their personnel from the Ja'alīyīn living there – this being the reason they were sometimes called "Khartoumers." By the second half of the century, other Ja'alīyīn found themselves forced to leave the Nubian Nile because of population pressure. They often joined the secondary empires as subordinates of the original merchant founders. By the late 1860s and 1870s, their penetration to the southwest had gone so far that they began to compete with other Ja'alīyīn who had earlier established themselves in Darfur. In the schematic model of central-place hierarchy, Darfur and Khartoum were equally subordinate to Cairo and at about the same level in the commercial hierarchy, though Darfur was still an independent sultanate. One result was bitter competition between the two second-level cities, as each tried to strengthen its control over its own hinterland. The conflict was heightened somewhat as the leadership of the Khartoum network became more Levantine and Coptic, which meant that they had closer ties to Cairo than Ja'alī were likely to have.[8] Figure 11.1 illustrates these tensions in schematic form as of about the 1860s.

Given the fact that all participants were armed with European weapons, and none were under close control of the Egyptian government, it was only natural that some of these tensions should lead to violence. The attack came from the traders on the frontier south of Darfur, in effect, those at a third level in the hierarchy of dependence on Cairo. The leader was a Ja'alī named al-Zubair Rahma Mansur, who began as a merchant in the Bahr al-Ghazal in the mid-1850s. During the 1860s, he shifted from commerce to political and military leadership over the other Ja'alī of the region. In 1874, he was strong enough to turn north and conquer the sultanate of Darfur.[9] In effect, he began to build a secondary empire, not merely within the shell of the Eygptian secondary empire, but completely independent of it. That was too much for the Egyptian government. In 1878, it sent a force that captured him and ended once and for all both his trade network and his political sphere.

His followers still had the option of escape, and they had the modern weapons that made them invincible against those who still did not. Al Zubair's son, Rabih Fadlallah, mustered a force that had a core of Ja'alīyyīr augmented by slave-soldiers purchased or captured in his father's campaigns. They set out for the west with their breech-loading rifles, into a zone where even smooth-bore, muzzle-loading muskets were rare.

---

[8] Gary, *Southern Sudan*, pp. 70–86; Holt, "Egypt and the Nile Valley, "in Flint (ed.), *Cambridge History of Africa*, 5:35–8; Jay Spaulding, "Slavery, Land Tenure and Social Class in the Northern Turkish Sudan," *International Journal of African Historical Studies*, 15:1–20 (1982).

[9] Gray, *Southern Sudan*, pp. 120–5.

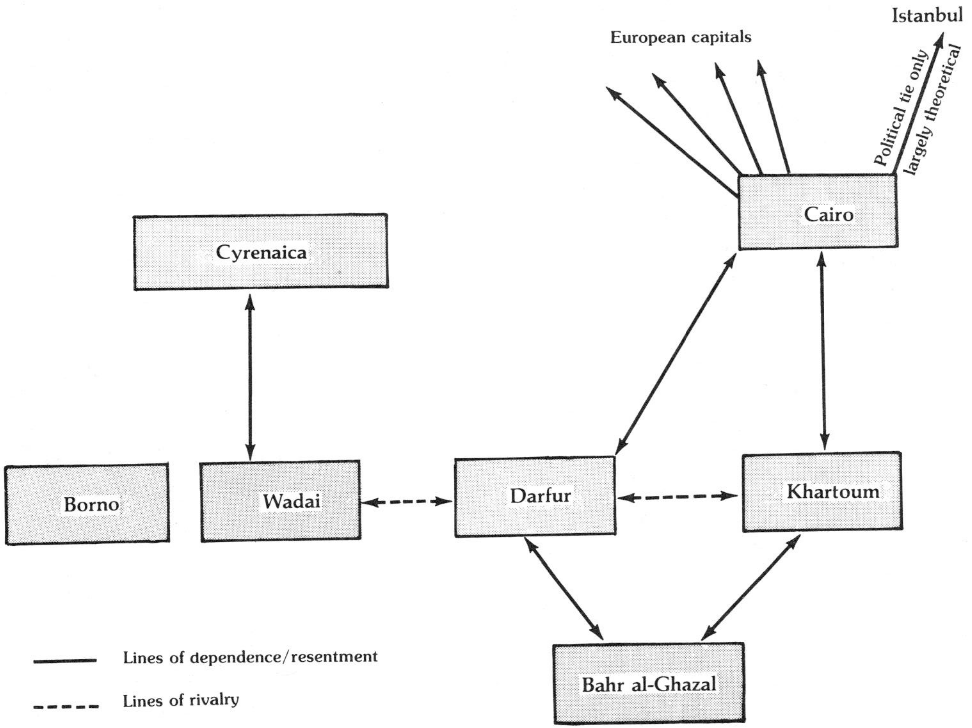

Figure 11.1. Relations between nodes of Sudanese trade diasporas, circa 1860

Istanbul

Political tie only
largely theoretical

Cairo

European capitals

Khartoum

Bahr al-Ghazal

Darfur

Cyrenaica

Wadai

Borno

——— Lines of dependence/resentment

- - - - Lines of rivalry

Rabih made first for the slave-supplying region south of Wadai (the next kingdom to the west of Darfur, now in eastern Chad). There he remained until 1893, with a tenuous political hold over a small territory, and supported by slave raids beyond its frontiers. This kind of quasi-state, however, threatened local stability and the position of others farther up the central-place ladder of multifunctionality. As Egypt had rooted out his father, Wadai sent a force to root him out. He defeated the Wadai army and escaped to the west, this time to seize the kingdom of Borno, west of Lake Chad. But success was short lived. The era of independent African states was coming to an end. A French force defeated Rabih in 1900 – with much the same timing as the British takeover of the Egyptian secondary empire in Nubia and the Sudan in 1898. The Ja'aliyyīn were already too militarized to survive in the new, colonial conditions. Only a few African trade diasporas, for that matter, were able to adjust to the Western commercial culture that was about to be imposed on them.

Informal empire and the new trading posts: Singapore

Somewhat earlier in the nineteenth century and in spite of the territorialization of trading-post empires in Bengal and Java, the Europeans overseas were moving in new directions. Just as they avoided overt conquest in Africa until the 1880s, conquest and administration were not the normal goals of European powers anywhere in the non-Western world until late in the nineteenth century. One possibility – and probably the dominant goal through the first three-quarters of the century – was to exert influence based on the new European power, but without the forms of a colonial government. The Europeans of this period preferred "informal empire" because it seemed to protect all interests that were really vital or profitable without the considerable cost of ruling over an alien society.[10]

The ways and means of informal empire could vary greatly. Sometimes, the economic power of the industrialized countries was enough by itself to give them inordinate influence in the capitals of less fortunate countries overseas. If required, suggestions could be backed by implied threats – or real threats. The most skillful "gunboat diplomacy" succeeded without actually using force, though all parties knew it was available in case of need.

One new device for exerting power and influence with minimal force

---

[10] John Gallagher and Ronald Robinson, "The Imperialism of Free Trade," *Economic History Review*, 6(n.s.):1–15 (1953).

was a new kind of trading-post empire, developed most effectively by Great Britain in East Asia. Instead of using a chartered company as a semiofficial but armed trade diaspora, it was even more effective, in the new context of European power, to establish government-run trade entrepôts. They could serve as a naval base, a point of safety for warehousing and distributing the new output of the industrial revolution and for bulking raw materials for European industry. Incidentally, they furthered the new patterns of ecumenical trade in the Western mode.

In Southeast Asia, the British returned Java to the Netherlands, but they kept Melaka and seized the island of Singapore. Sir Stamford Raffles, who had ruled Java for the British, was the chief architect of the new policy. Seeing the sultanate of Johor under confused cross-pressures from Dutch, Bugis, and other interests, it was no great problem to detach the island itself, initially as the property of the East India Company. The British government's interest was clear, however. The base was not to further the company's trade alone, it was to protect all British trade. Raffles wanted Singapore to be a place for "the resort of independent trade and trade of our allies."[11] Partly through his influence, as well as Bugis precedent, Singapore was a free port from the beginning. It sought prosperity by maximizing the trade, in Singapore, of all nations, not the exclusive trade of one. In the early nineteenth century, however, it was taken for granted that a fair proportion of the goods traded would be British made.

In 1826, the British government transferred Singapore from the East India Company to the Colonial Office, to serve as the capital of the new colony, namely, the Straits Settlements, including Melaka and Penang. Singapore soon became the most important of the three, with more than 35,000 people by 1840. Only a small minority was British. The rest were representatives of all the trade diasporas that had recently traded in the region: Arabs and Parsees from the far west, Bengalis and Klings from eastern India, Bugis and Javanese from what was to be Indonesia, but most of all Chinese. These were mainly merchants at first. Then they began to invest in plantations just beyond the frontiers of the Straits Settlements, and in tin mining elsewhere in peninsular Malaya. Economic growth quickly outran the available labor supply. The Chinese merchants then turned to their own homeland for contract workers, and the Chinese trade diasporas became the takeoff point for a much larger stream of Chinese contract emigration under private sponsorship.

British Singapore thus moved through stages. It first became a major node for Cantonese and Fujianese trade diasporas, among others. Sec-

---

[11] Raffles, quoted in Rupert Emerson, *Malaysia: A Study of Direct and Indirect Rule* (New York, 1937), p. 81.

ond, it began to serve as a base for the economic enterprise of local Chinese capitalists exploiting the resources of mainland Malaya. Third, it became a place of settlement and farther movement into Malaya for colonists from southern China. These stages moved on Chinese, not European, initiative, but even though the capital and labor were Chinese, the ultimate consumer was industrial Europe. At a later stage, the Straits Settlements became the springboard for a British advance to territorial empire over Malaya, though that step came only in the last third of the century. From the 1870s, British informal influence became more and more formal, till Singapore's informal empire became the Malay States governed from Kuala Lumpur.[12]

Hong Kong and the treaty ports

The evolution of a trading-post empire along the Chinese coast took a different course. In the eighteenth century, the Chinese system of tribute trade with the outside world continued in theory, if not in practice. It had been a legal fiction for centuries, but now the vast majority of trade through Canton, still the official port of entry, passed through other channels. It was the Chinese custom to regulate many forms of economic enterprise by assigning them to specific merchant guilds, which were then collectively responsible to the imperial officials. Three different groups of licensed brokers (*ya-hang* in Chinese) were appointed to deal with aspects of Canton trade. One of these, which the English called the *hong* merchants, was charged with the trade of the Europeans, giving the hong, in effect, a monopoly over cross-cultural brokerage with Europeans at that port.

Chinese officials imposed many other restrictions on foreign merchants in Canton. They could not live within the city walls but had to live in a merchants' quarter along the Pearl River. At certain times of the year, the Chinese ordered them to leave Chinese territory altogether, which was done easily enough by retreat to the conveniently nearby but officially non-Chinese territory of Macao – still under Portuguese control in the late eighteenth century.

At that time, foreign merchants were more numerous than ever before, largely on account of the tea trade. The East India Company was the largest purchaser of tea, which meant that its local representative could act as an English equivalent to the head of the hong merchants. But the company was only active in the trade to Europe. Imports into Canton that gave it the capacity to buy tea were carried by the "country" trade from India – much, but not all, in the private hands of the company's

[12] See Steinberg et al., *In Search of Southeast Asia* (New York, 1971), esp. pp. 134–40.

officials. Cotton from Bengal was the main import, though silver was also significant, and opium from India grew in prominence with the passage of time.

By the 1790s, the old system no longer fitted in well with the new facts of power in the world. Both Britain and the Netherlands tried to get the Chinese court to recognize them as equals, but failed. In the early nineteenth century, the old Canton trade system came under increasing strain. The number of private traders grew, and some of the most important British firms began to act under the cover of being tributary representatives of minor European states like Sardinia or Denmark, which confused the fictional aspects of tribute trade still more. Innovations came from abroad, such as the Indian system of agency houses, which were willing and able to buy, sell, bribe appropriately, arrange for insurance, or provide banking services. As trade grew, the trade in opium grew fastest of all, even though it was illegal to import or to use opium in China. Opium became important to the East India Company out of all relationship to its actual value, though that value was enough to pose a threat to the health and well-being of the Chinese Empire. For the company, it provided the main source of foreign exchange for the return trade in tea bound for Europe, which was, in turn, its primary source of commercial revenue. The company also profited from taxes on the production of opium in India and on its export overseas.

When Chinese restraints on trade frustrated the foreigners, they, and especially the dominant British, were tempted to threaten military action. In 1834, the British sent Lord Napier to Canton as superintendent of trade with orders to end the fictitious tribute system and to insist that Britain be recognized as an equal of the Chinese Empire. The Chinese rejected the demand, even though Napier backed it with a naval assault on the Chinese shore batteries at Canton. The British and Chinese merchants in Canton arranged a compromise and resumed their trade, but the old trade system no longer worked, not even as badly as it had done in the recent past. European traders were now to be found in many different Chinese ports, but without legal recognition and with increasing friction between foreign sea captains and local officials, bribed or not.

By the late 1830s, the scene was set for a more forceful "opening" of China to the new, Western system of open trade, relatively free from restriction by non-Western authorities. But the change required force, not just the threat of force, and the resulting violence erupted as the Opium War of 1839–42.

Behind the conflict was a double opposition. The Chinese were apprehensive about the inflow of illegal opium, not only for its own deleterious effects, but also because these rising imports had begun, in the late 1830s, to produce an alarming outflow of silver. That, in turn, seemed to threaten a monetary crisis. The British, meanwhile, became more and more resentful of the Chinese refusal to treat their diplomats as representatives of an equal government. China was determined to stop the opium traffic. Britain was determined to do away with the ancient fiction of tribute trade, not merely for the sake of opium sales, but also to achieve free entry into the Chinese market for British manufactures in general.

The resulting war was extremely lopsided, even though the British fought it mainly with the forces of the East India Company, without bothering to call in royal troops or the Royal Navy. It was a clear confrontation between the new military technology of the industrial age and the comparatively old-fashioned equipment available to the Chinese. The differences had become so great that the British won with a few thousand men and one or two crucial warships. The significant innovation was the first appearance of steam-driven, iron warships, notably the shallow-draft iron steamer, *Nemesis*, which could move up the Chinese rivers with impunity, silencing the shore batteries as it went. In the opening of China to Western trade, "gunboat diplomacy" was more than a figure of speech.[13]

The peace settlement gave the British the right of entry they had wanted, including special privileges associated with informal empire in the nineteenth century. The initial Anglo-Chinese treaty of 1842 ceded the undeveloped island of Hong Kong, granted the British rights of residence and trade at five other ports, and promised a large indemnity to be paid in silver dollars. Other treaties followed between China and the United States, France, and other European powers. They promised "most favored nation" treatment to each European power in turn, so that the treaty structure originally laid down between 1842 and 1844 came to be a general bundle of rights granted by China to the Western world as a whole. In some ways, the Chinese concessions were little more than the privileges Mediterranean nations had been granting to foreign trade communities for centuries. The Europeans could reside in the Chinese ports and could have their internal disputes settled by their own leaders – in this case, the consular representatives of the foreign power. But these treaties went much further: They also sheltered foreign merchants from the effects of Chinese law. In time, the treaty system

---

[13] John K. Fairbank et al., *East Asia: The Modern Transformation* (Boston, 1965), pp. 140–4; Daniel R. Headrick, *The Tools of Empire: Technology and European Imperialism in the Nineteenth Century* (Oxford, 1981), pp. 105–14. For more detail see Frederick Wakeman, Jr., "The Canton Trade and the Opium War," in Denis Twitchett and John K. Fairbank (eds.), *The Cambridge History of China*, vol. 10 (Cambridge, 1978).

gave similar legal protection even to the Chinese who happened to work for European firms.[14]

In effect, the Opium War imposed the Western commercial culture on China, at least on the part of China that traded with the West. Resident traders were followed by the full set of Western commercial institutions – banks, merchant houses, and insurance firms; in time, railways built by Western capital carried the entering wedge of Western economic order into the heart of the country. Hong Kong and the treaty ports were like Singapore in their superficial resemblance to nodes of a preindustrial trading-post empire, but the function was very different. Rather than serving the narrow interests of a particular nation or trading group, they were open to the full impact of international capitalism on the Western model. And the ecumenical trade on that model was not confined to Europeans. Indian merchants of many descriptions had been in the opium trade and went on to participate in the opening of China, just as Chinese and Arabs, Bugis, and Indians were involved in the fortunes of Singapore from the beginning. As of 1851, the "British" community in Canton included far more Indians than natives of Great Britain. Indeed, it counted more Parsees than Britons.

Consular representation

In the unequal treaties that followed the Opium War, officials with the title of Consul appear, exercising extraterritorial jurisdiction for European states. The office was another innovation of this transitional period, but its origins lay far back in the history of preindustrial trade diasporas. One common feature of these trade diasporas was the resident broker who had stayed long enough to act as intermediary between his original fellow-countrymen and members of the host society. We have seen it under the names *maigida, wakil al-tujjar,* one variant of the term *shabandar,* or simply as "chief," "governor," or "consul," who belonged to and spoke for a national segment of diaspora merchants in a trade center. In the Mediterranean basin during the European Middle Ages, consul was the term that caught on. But these early consuls were not different from the other kinds of community chief. They represented, not a government, but only the merchant community that chose them. Governments might ask for their services at times. It is possible that the occasional use of consuls as diplomatic agents was one origin of a kind of government-to-government representation associated with the office of am-

---

[14] Fairbank et al., *Modern Transformation,* pp. 96–9; John King Fairbank, *Trade and Diplomacy on the China Coast: The Opening of the Treaty Ports 1842–1854* (Cambridge, Mass., 1964); Yen-P'ing Hao, *The Comprador in Nineteenth-Century China: Bridge Between East and West* (Cambridge, Mass., 1970).

bassador toward the end of the Middle Ages. But, whereas ambassadors became regular government representatives by the early sixteenth century, consuls remained private until the eighteenth.[15]

Then, and in the early nineteenth century, consuls emerged from the diaspora communities to enter the government service. France was the first to recognize and appoint consuls to act for French commercial interests, and to consider them part of the state apparatus, whether paid or not. The practice was gradually taken up by other European states. Britain established a regular consular service in 1825, France in 1833. In time, the consular service was integrated into the older and more prestigious diplomatic service, though its prestige remained low far into the twentieth century. Many countries still filled out their network of consular representation by appointing honorary consuls, that is, a merchant of appropriate nationality who happened to live in a foreign city and would take over consular tasks on a part-time basis.

By the mid-nineteenth century, the consular corps formed a network that could act pervasively to create an internationally recognized body of commercial law and custom. In the non-Western world in particular, consuls were the cutting edge of commercial Westernization. And European attitudes about other cultures had changed by this time from the more tolerant views of the past, to an intense cultural arrogance. Where the HBC or the Compagnie des Indes might once have adapted its ways to local usage, even in bookkeeping, by the nineteenth century the goal of efficient exchange was universally understood to be achieved by making the "natives" do it in the European manner.

The consul's position sometimes went well beyond mere representation of national commerce. Consuls were prime agents of informal empire, with the military on call if necessary. The title of consul could sometimes be deceptive, however. It was often a euphemism to satisfy diplomatic niceties; for example, Britain governed Egypt through an official called British Agent and Consul General, whose actual powers were not far different from those of the viceroy of India. Other consuls held less real power, but nevertheless had great influence. In Africa before the European conquests of the 1880s and 1890s, consuls were important agents of informal empire. The British stationed a consul on the island of Fernando Po in the 1850s and 1860s as their principal agent for opposition to the continuing slave trade along the nearby African coastline. A British consul on Zanzibar in the 1870s and 1880s had a similar role.

---

[15] W. H. Moreland, "The Shabandar in the Eastern Seas," *Journal of the Royal Asiatic Society*, 28:517–33 (1920), pp. 520–1. Donald E. Queller, *The Office of Ambassador in the Middle Ages* (Princeton, N.J., 1967), pp. 66, 69.

Consular representation in the Ottoman Empire passed through another kind of transition. The Ottomans had dealt with foreign merchants
through their consuls as the standard and thoroughly Ottoman way of
doing things. And the early consuls had no rights against the Ottoman
state. They were simply there to keep the peace and settle disputes
among their own people. With the growth of European power in the
nineteenth century, however, the consuls of Continental European powers began to gain authority, especially in Egypt. The growth of extraterritorial jurisdiction was similar to the transition in China under the
unequal treaties. Where consuls once tried cases involving their own
nationals only, they began to try disputes between their own nationals
and Egyptian subjects – and finally, cases involving other foreigners and
Egyptians. From the 1850s on, consular jurisdiction so deeply penetrated
the Egyptian judicial system that most cases involving international business were tried by consuls.[16] Similar developments in Turkish territories,
including the Maghribi outliers of Tunisia and Libya, assured that Western commercial norms had already gained a strong foothold, even before
colonial rule began.

Fringe Westernization

Normally, communities of a trade diaspora learned about the culture of
the host society, not the other way round. But some people in the host
society had reason to learn from the visitors as well. On occasion, they
have assumed the role of cross-cultural brokerage in competition with
the "stayers" of the diaspora community, even replacing them altogether
in that role. This tendency was exceptionally strong along the coasts of
tropical Africa, where the death rate among European visitors kept them
from staying long enough to acquire a very deep knowledge of the local
culture.

The sequence of trade patterns at the mouth of the Gambia River is
indicative. At the beginning of maritime contact with Europe, the Portuguese traded from their ships, but they soon began to put men ashore
between voyages. Some took local wives, so that a community of Afro-
Portuguese, racially and culturally mixed, had come into existence by
the end of the sixteenth century. They and their children handled cross-
cultural brokerage very adequately until the late seventeenth century.
Increasing trade in slaves and gold, and increasing international competition among the Europeans, encouraged a shift to the fortified enclaves of competing trading-post empires, in this instance both French
and English. But to man the forts was expensive. European interlopers,

---

[16] David Landes, *Bankers and Pashas* (Cambridge, Mass., 1958), esp. pp. 82–102.

without the fixed expenses of the chartered trading companies that ran the forts and factories, were more competitive, especially when local Africans could offer brokerage services. By the 1760s, the African kingdom of Niumi at the river's mouth had established a regular system to control trade entering the river. It charged tolls, which the Europeans normally resented, but paid. It also provided services, at a price, including that of African interpreter-brokers who would travel upriver with the ships and conduct business on behalf of the captain with any shoreside sellers or caravan leaders the ship might meet. As a result, when the French captured and destroyed the English fort at James Island in 1779, it was not rebuilt. It had become cheaper to rely on African brokerage, until a new phase of growing trade brought the Europeans back in force after 1816.[17]

Elsewhere along the coast in the late eighteenth century, African trade communities also tended to adopt some elements of Western culture. In the Niger delta, for example, the Europeans had never built fortified factories, but had carried on trade from unfortified hulks anchored in the rivers. There, as on the Gambia, the Africans made it a point to learn the English ways of business – and, of course, the English language. It was not uncommon for an African slave trader to send a son or nephew to England for a few years of education so that he could become literate and learn commercial arithmetic. Here and there Africans sponsored schools in Africa itself to preserve and transmit what had been learned. In the 1780s, Antera Duke, an African slave trader at Calabar in present-day Nigeria, wrote a diary in English, which has been preserved and published in a critical edition.[18]

In the early nineteenth century, the British anti–slave-trade campaign become another source of fringe Westernization. The Royal Navy began to intercept slavers at sea. It used a new colony at Sierra Leone as a place to land the slave cargoes. Sierra Leone then became a center for Western missionary activity and public education for the ex-slaves. Fourah Bay College, later a university, began as a secondary school as early as the 1820s. Samuel Crowther, a recaptured slave and an early graduate of Fourah Bay, became the first African bishop of the Anglican church. Many others with a similar background went into trade, and many of those who had originally come from Yorubaland in present-day Nigeria returned to their homeland – if not precisely to their original hometowns, then often to Lagos, the new British-controlled seaport on the coast, where their cross-cultural skills were more valuable.[19]

---

[17] Philip D. Curtin, *Economic Change in Precolonial Africa: Senegambia in the Era of the Slave Trade*, 2 vols. (Madison, Wis., 1975), esp. 1:296–7.
[18] Daryll Forde (ed.), *Efik Traders of Old Calabar* (London, 1956).
[19] Jean Herskovits Kopytoff, *A Preface to Modern Nigeria: The "Sierra Leonians" in Yoruba, 1830–1890* (Madison, Wis., 1965).

Still others were able to make their way from American slavery back to Africa. Among them was Thomas Joiner, a Gambian who was sent as a slave to Virginia. He returned in the first decade of the nineteenth century. By the 1830s, he had become the most important shipowner in the trade of the Gambia River. In that capacity he was instrumental in choosing the site of Georgetown, the first upriver base of a new trading-post empire that grew into the British colony of the Gambia and later into the independent state.[20] But returnees from Brazil were far more common than those from North America. Many were Yoruba, like the "Sierra Leonians," and they also set out for Yorubaland and its vicinity. By the early colonial period, they had become the most important single commercial community in the French colony of Dahomey.[21]

An African's personal course toward Westernization could be highly various, but a number of Africans appeared on the Western side of the cultural line before the beginning of the colonial period – not merely Samuel Crowther, the Anglican bishop, but also an Anglican chaplain in a slave-trade post before the end of the eighteenth century, an acting governor of the Gold Coast, an important medical officer, and scores if not hundreds in lesser posts. Some of these Westernized Africans also remained in commerce, like the Brew family of Cape Coast in Ghana, which became a commercial dynasty of importance from the middle of the eighteenth century past the middle of the twentieth.[22]

Similar fringe Westernization was equally impressive elsewhere, especially in the Indian Ocean trade world, where a common culture of commerce already flourished before the end of the eighteenth century – and that culture became more and more Western through the nineteenth. The sons and grandsons of the banians who had served as cross-cultural brokers in the eighteenth century, came, by the early nineteenth, to be full partners in Western-style businesses in Calcutta, including banking, insurance, shipping, and the agency houses. In the second half of the century, their descendants tended to move out of the Bengali world of commerce – replaced to some degree by British capital generated in the industrial revolution, and in some degree by new men from other communities of Indian merchants. But important banian families, like the Tagores, continued to be a force in the intellectual and social life of British India, some of them culturally more Western than otherwise. A

[20] Curtin, *Senegambia*, 1:137–9.
[21] Pierre Verger, *Flux et reflux de la traite des negrès entre le golfe de Bénin et Bahia de todos os santos du dix-septième au dix-neuvième siècle* (Paris, 1968), esp. pp. 599–632.
[22] Robert W. July, *The Origins of Modern African Thought: Its Development in West Africa during the Nineteenth and Twentieth Centuries* (New York, 1967); Arthur T. Porter, *Creoledom: A Study of the Development of Freetown Society* (London, 1963); Margaret Priestley, *West African Trade and Coast Society: A Family Study* (London, 1969).

number of distinguished writers with this background, for example, published in English, not Bengali.[23]

Some of the Armenians who drifted into the orbit of Western trade made a similar transition. The transition of the Edward Raphael family from New Julfa to the British House of Commons is a spectacular example, (see Chapter 9, Communities of the Armenian diaspora). Similar shifts across cultural lines had taken place at all phases in the long history of trade diasporas. In the nineteenth century, drift toward the industrializing West was an obvious current. In earlier centuries, it might go the other way. Individual life stories often went unrecorded, but several people are known to have made the shift from Western to non-Western cultures and to have reached high office. One example on the West African coast is the Corker or Caulker family, founded by an English trader in the seventeenth century. After generations of intermarriage with the local African gentry, the Caulkers became rulers of a small chiefdom. In due course, the British annexed it to the colony of Sierra Leone, and several members of the family went on to become members of the Westernized intellectual elite in that colony and in the independent state that succeeded it.[24]

Similar movement also took place in China. The Polos are an obvious and early example of people who reached high office and returned to the West. In the nineteenth century, the drift was opposite, in spite of official resistance to Western influence. Pidgin or "business" English was already the lingua franca in Canton before the Opium War, using a Chinese word order, but with loanwords from Arabic and Portuguese as well as English. The Pidgin for money changer was *shroff*, from Arabic. The Pidgin for agent – that is, for a Chinese broker who did what the banians had done in Bengal – was *comprador*, from the Portuguese word for buyer.[25]

In the first half of the nineteenth century, Chinese, not Europeans, were the principal cross-cultural brokers on the Chinese coast, especially the compradors. This cultural interchange was especially complex because the original compradors first became associated with European firms in southern China. As the treaty ports opened up to the north in the 1840s and later, the European firms moved north with a whole raft of compradors, servants, and hangers-on – almost all Cantonese, if not Southeast Asian in origin. Since their language was unintelligible in the northern treaty ports, they found themselves acting between two cultures, both of which were alien. But they could often claim the same

---

[23] Dilip Basu, "The Banian and the British in Calcutta, 1800–1850," *Bengal Past and Present*, 92:157–70 (1973).
[24] Christopher Fyfe, *A History of Sierra Leone* (London, 1962), p. 10 and passim.
[25] Fairbank, *Trade and Diplomacy*, pp. 14 ff.; Hao, *The Comprador*, passim.

judicial and other privileges as the Europeans themselves, partly on account of their foreignness.

The abolition of the hong monopoly also made way for new institutions, and the existing compradors were able to take advantage of the opening. Many early compradors had been quite minor servants, but the class rose rapidly in importance. Some carried out the entire Chinese aspect of a foreign firm's business. An important comprador needed a whole staff of subordinate translators, shroffs, porters, and boatmen. It was the compradors who gained an intimate understanding of Western capitalism – not the heads of foreign firms who learned about China. Compradors also supervised the penetration of Western trade into the interior, while the Europeans remained in the ports.

As they accumulated capital, some of the compradors not only acted as agents of Western-style capitalism; they also became Western-style capitalists in their own right. Sometimes they worked alone, sometimes in partnership with Western firms. In 1862, one such enterprise with American leadership, but mostly Chinese capital, introduced the first commercial steamship service on the Yangtze, between Shanghai and Hangkow.

Some recent historical writing suggests that the compradors were guilty of a kind of economic treason in helping to introduce Western capitalist institutions into China. Many no doubt did take advantage of their position as honorary foreigners. Their knowledge of the Western world probably allowed them to take advantage of the foreigners as well. Praiseworthy or not, they were the principal carriers of the new, worldwide culture of commerce on the Chinese coast in the nineteenth century.[26]

The tools of European dominance

Many personal aspects of cross-cultural brokerage had been at work for centuries, building more ecumenical patterns of trade. From the mideighteenth century, institutional changes in the international economic order speeded the process in banking, finance, transportation, and communication. These changes rested, in turn, on the triumph of industrial technology, which made it virtually impossible for any non-Western society to resist Westernization, at least in the field of trade and exchange. Estimates of total world trade measure the weight of the change – from U.S. $700 million in 1700 to U.S. $38,150 million in 1914. The most rapid expansion was a ninefold increase between 1820 and 1880,

---

[26] Fairbank et al., *Modern Transformation*, pp. 154–5, 346–8, and 354–5; Fairbank, *Trade and Diplomacy*, passim.

generated by the spread of the industrial revolution to most of Western Europe and the United States.[27]

Among the most important of the technological changes for world trade were those in ocean shipping. Europeans had been world leaders in maritime technology since at least the middle of the sixteenth century. But their lead was not great enough to displace Asian shipping in Asian waters. In the mid-nineteenth century the shift to steam and steel began. By the outbreak of the First World War, the combination of iron hulls, high-pressure steam engines, and screw propellers guaranteed the preponderance of steam over sail on almost all long-distance ocean routes. Ocean freight rates dropped by 80 percent over the nineteenth century. But the new ships required, first of all, much more capital than most non-Western economies of the period could provide. They also required the special industrial know-how that, at that period, was narrowly located in the British Isles. As late as 1910, more than 60 percent of the tonnage passing through the Suez Canal was not merely European; it was British. Even the ships that were not British owned were often driven by British marine engines cared for by the ubiquitous Scottish marine engineer.[28] By 1900, anyone who wanted to ship goods competitively by sea had to do so in European ships, and this implied the acceptance of the whole international culture of Western shipping – from bills of lading to charges for demurrage.

The new technology hit even sooner in long-distance communication. Both the Dutch and the English East India Company were pretty much limited to the speed of sailing ships, and so were their Asian competitors. Up to the 1830s, a letter from Europe to India took five to eight months to round the Cape on a sailing ship. To receive an answer might take as long as two years. By the 1850s, the combination of train and steamer could bring a letter from London to Calcutta in thirty to forty-five days. By the 1870s, submarine cable had been laid and a message from Britain to India could be answered in the same day.[29] It was not just that Europeans had the tools; they also controlled access to them. Anyone who wanted to communicate at that speed had to follow the bureaucratic rules of the cable office. These were, needless to say, the rules of Western commerce.

For a non-Western country, the international postal service was open only to whose who conformed to the practices of the Universal Postal

---

[27] William Woodruff, "The Emergence of an International Economy 1700–1914," Carlo M. Cipolla (ed.), *The Emergence of Industrial Societies* (London, 1973), pp. 658–9.

[28] For a summary treatment of extremely complex changes see Headrick, *Tools of Empire*, pp. 129–49; A. J. H. Latham, *The International Economy and the Undeveloped World, 1865–1914* (London, 1978), pp. 26–32.

[29] Headrick, *Tools of Empire*, pp. 129–39.

Union, founded in 1874. Many non-Western countries had had reasonably efficient postal services – for the needs of a preindustrial society. China, for example, had had a good one, but in the nineteenth century, it no longer served the interests of foreign business efficiently, nor those of Chinese business as efficiently as Westernized Chinese businessmen wanted it to do. The result was a reconstruction of the postal service on the Western model, completed before the end of the century. Elsewhere, Europeans established their own post offices on foreign territory, when they thought the local service was inadequate, as several did in Tangier in Morocco and elsewhere.

One could pursue the theme of Western technological superiority and its impact on the world of commerce into the fields of banking, insurance, international monetary exchange, and much else. But, for trade diasporas, the conclusion is obvious. They could survive for a time in some places beyond the fringes of the international economy, but they had long since served their purpose in uniting an extremely diverse world. Their disappearance was itself a sign of their long-term success.

None of this should be taken as a sign that all human culture is to be homogenized under the impact of the West, that the "Cocacolanization" some people feared a few decades ago will inevitably take place. In some fields of human activity, to be sure, change is very hard to avoid. Where the West dominates world commerce, and in circumstances where competitive success or failure depends on using appropriate technology, the sweep of industrial technology is undeniable, and it has ended the era of the trade diaspora in cross-cultural trade.

Other aspects of the commercial culture, however, may well survive. This is especially the case *within* cultures. West African traders using trucks and telegrams may nevertheless keep important aspects of older kinship relations in the organization of the firm, just as Japanese industrial enterprise has retained its peculiarly Japanese way of going about things, even though it uses, and has even invented, some of the most up-to-date technology. Some of the old techniques are still competitive as well: The abacus and the electronic calculator are used side-by-side in Japanese retail shops. Religion is obviously much less affected by technological change than long-distance trade is; it may be worthwhile reflecting on the fact that the muezzin, who calls the faithful to prayer throughout the Muslim world as regularly now as ever in the past, normally does so through a public address system.

A final caveat should be added. In a study like this, which traces institutions through a long run of time and across many cultural boundaries, there are also costs. One price paid for following *cross-cultural* trade is an inability to deal adequately with anything else. A historian's implied omniscience was one of the less admirable aspects of an older tradition of historical writing. An unstated assumption that went with writing within a time-space unit like "England to the Norman Conquest" was that the author would tell about *all* the important events that fell within that framework. That was never possible, but for a comparative study like this one it is not even attempted. At best, this study presents one of several different ways of looking at the human experience, to be supplemented by others that abstract some other element from the total pattern of our known past.

Bibliography

This list of works consulted is arranged by chapter or pairs of chapters. This means that the division is sometimes geographical and sometimes temporal. Some works contributed to two or more chapters, but that happened seldom enough to repeat the listing. They are listed where the weight of their evidence seemed greatest. Cooperative works, such as conference reports and contributed volumes, are cited by individual author in the footnotes, but they are listed here only under the editor's name if a substantial number of articles from that volume is relevant to this study.

Chapter 1. Introductory and theoretical

Adams, Robert McC. "Anthropological Reflections on Ancient Trade." *Current Anthropology* 15:239–57 (1974).

Agnew, Jean-Christophe. "The Threshold of Exchange: Speculation on the Market." *Radical History Review*, 21:99–118 (1979).

Bratchel, M.E. "Italian Merchant Organization and Business Relationships in Early Tudor London." *Journal of European Economic History*, 7:5–32 (1978).

Braudel, Fernand. *Civilization and Capitalism: 15th–18th Century.* Vol. II, *The Wheels of Commerce.* New York, 1982.

Brown, Norman O. *Hermes the Thief: The Evolution of a Myth*, 2nd ed. New York, 1969.

Burghardt, A. T. "A Hypothesis about Gateway Cities." *Annals of the Association of American Geographers*, 61:269–85 (1971).

Christaller, Walter. *Central Places in Southern Germany.* Englewood Cliffs, N.J., 1966.

Cook, Scott. "The Obsolete 'Anti-Market' Mentality: A Critique of the Substantive Approach to Economic Anthropology." *American Anthropologist*, 68:323–45 (1966).

Dalton, George (ed.). *Economic Development and Social Change.* New York, 1974.
(ed.). *Primitive, Archaic and Modern Economies: Essays of Karl Polanyi.* New York, 1968.
"Primitive, Archaic and Modern Economies: Karl Polanyi's Contribution to Economic Anthropology and Comparative Economy." In *Essays in Economic Anthropology: Dedicated to the Memory of Karl Polanyi*, ed. by June Helm, Paul Bohannon, and Marshall D. Sahlins. Seattle, 1965. Pp. 1–24.

Dupré, Georges, and Pierre Philippe Rey. "Reflections on the Relevance of a Theory of the History of Exchange." In *Relations of Production: Marxist Approaches to Economic Anthropology*, ed. David Seddon. London, 1978. Pp. 171–208.

Fallers, Lloyd A. (ed.). *Immigrants and Associations*. The Hague, 1967.

Geertz, Clifford. "Ports of Trade in Nineteenth Century Bali." *Research in Economic Anthropology*, 3:109–22 (1980).

Glamann, Kristof. "European Trade, 1500–1750." In *The Fontana Economic History of Europe. Vol. 2, The Sixteenth and Seventeenth Centuries*, ed. by Carlo M. Cipolla. London, 1974. Pp. 427–562.

Herteig, A. E., H. E. Liden, and C. Blindheim. *Archaeological Contributions to the Early History of Urban Communities in Norway*. Oslo, 1975.

Hodges, Richard. "Ports of Trade in Medieval Europe." *Norwegian Archaeological Review*, 2:97–101 (1978).

Humphreys, S. C. "History, Economics, and Anthropology: The Work of Karl Polanyi." *History and Theory*, 8:165–212 (1969).

Kurmoto, Schinichiro. "Silent Trade in Japan." In George Dalton (ed.), *Research In Economic Anthropology*, 3:97–108 (1980).

Lampard, Eric. "Historical Aspects of Urbanization." In *The Study of Urbanization*, ed. by P.M. Hauser and Leo F. Schnore. New York, 1965. Pp. 519–54.

Le Clair, Edward E., Jr. "Economic Theory and Economic Anthropology." *American Anthropologist*, 64:1179–1203 (1962).

Leeds, A. "The Port of Trade as an Ecological and Evolutionary Type." In *Proceedings of the 1961 Annual Meeting of the American Ethnological Society Symposium: Patterns of Land Utilization and Other Papers*. Seattle, 1961. Pp. 26–48.

Lösch, August. *The Economics of Location*. New Haven, Conn., 1954.

McNeill, William H. *The Pursuit of Power: Technology, Armed Force, and Society since A.D. 1000*. Chicago, 1982.

North, Douglas C. "Markets and Other Allocation Systems in History: The Challenge of Karl Polanyi." *The Journal of European Economic History*, 6:703–16 (1977).

Polanyi, Karl. "Ports of Trade in Early Societies." *Journal of Economic History*, 23:30–45 (1963).

Polanyi, Karl, Conrad M. Arensberg, and Harry W. Pearson. *Trade and Markets in Early Empires*. New York, 1957.

Price, John A. "On Silent Trade." In George Dalton (ed.). *Research in Economic Anthropology*, 3:75–96 (1980).

Rodinson, Maxine. "Le Marchand meditérranéen à traverse les ages." In *Markets and Marketing as Factors of Development in the Mediterranean Basin*, ed. by C. A. O. Van Nieuwenhuijze. The Hague, 1963. Pp. 71–92.

Rotstein, Abraham. "Karl Polanyi's Concept of Non-Market Trade." *Journal of Economic History*, 30:117–126 (1970).

Rozman, Gilbert. *Urban Networks in Russia, 1750–1800 and Premodern Periodization*. Princeton, N.J., 1976.

Urban Networks in Ch'ing China and Tokugawa Japan. Princeton, N.J., 1973.

Sahlins, Marshall D. *Stone-Age Economics*. Chicago, 1972.

Salisbury, Richard F. "Trade and Markets." *International Encyclopedia of the Social Sciences*, 16:118–22 (New York, 1968).

Skinner, G. William (ed.). *The City in Late Imperial China*. Stanford, Calif., 1977.
"Marketing and Social Structure in Rural China." *Journal of Asian Studies*, 24:3–43 (1964).

Smelser, Neil J. "A Comparative View of Exchange Systems." *Economic Development and Cultural Change*, 7:173–82 (1959).

Smith, Carol A. (ed.). *Regional Analysis*. 2 vols. New York, 1976.

Smith, R. M. T. (ed.). *Market Place Trade: Periodic Markets, Hawkers, and Traders in Africa, Asia, and Latin America*. Vancouver, 1978.

Valensi, Lucette. "Anthropologie économique et histoire." *Annales: économies, sociétés, civilisations*, 29:1311–19 (1974).

Vance, James E., Jr. *The Merchant's World: The Geography of Wholesaling*. Englewood Cliffs, N.J., 1970.

Wallerstein, Immanuel. *The Modern World-System*, multivol. New York, 1974–.

Wilber, Charles K. (ed.). *The Political Economy of Development and Underdevelopment*, 2nd ed. New York, 1979.

Chapters 2 and 3. Africa

Abir, Mordechai. "Caravan Trade and History in the Northern Parts of East Africa." *Paideuma*, 14:103–20 (1968).
"Brokerage and Brokers in Ethiopia in the First Half of the Nineteenth Century." *Journal of Ethiopian Studies*, 3:1–5 (1965).
Ethiopia: The Era of the Princes. London, 1968.

Adams, C. C. "The Sanusis." *Muslim World*, 36:21–45 (1946).

Adams, William Y. *Nubia: Corridor to Africa*. Princeton, N.J., 1977.

Ajayi, J. F. Ade, and Michael Crowder (eds.). *History of West Africa*, 2nd ed. 2 vols. London, 1976.

Alagoa, E. J. "Long Distance Trade and States in the Niger Delta." *Journal of African History*, 3:319–29 (1970).

Alpers, Edward A. *Ivory and Slaves in East Central Africa: Changing Patterns of International Trade to the Later Nineteenth Century*. London, 1975.
"The Mzab." *Journal of the Royal Anthropological Institute*, 84:34–44 (1954).

Amat, Charles. "L'esclavage au M'zab, étude anthropologique des nègres." *Bulletin de la société d'anthropologie de Paris*, 7(3rd ser.):689–98 (1884).
"Anthropologie des M'zabites." *Bulletin de la société d'anthropologie de Paris*, 7(3rd ser.):587–600 (1884).

Amselle, Jean-Louis. *Les négociants de la savanne: histoire et organisation sociale des Kooroko (Mali)*. Paris, 1978.

Arhin, Kwame. *West African Traders in Ghana in the Nineteenth and Twentieth Centuries*. London, 1979.

Azarya, Victor. "Traders and the Center in Massina, Kong, and Samori's State." *International Journal of African Historical Studies*, 13:420–56 (1980).

Baier, Stephen. *An Economic History of Central Niger*. New York, 1980.
"Ecologically Based Trade and the State in Precolonial West Africa." *Cahiers d'études africaine*, 20:149–54 (1980).
"Trans-Sahara Trade and the Sahel: Damergu, 1870–1930." *Journal of African History*, 18:21–36 (1977).

Barbosa, Duarte. *The Book of Duarte Barbosa*. 2 vols. Edited from original composed about 1518 by Mansel Longworth Dames. London, 1908.

Binger, Louis. *Du Niger au Golfe de Guinée par le pays de Kong et le Mossi*. 2 vols. Paris, 1892.

Bohannan, Paul, and George Dalton (eds.). *Markets in Africa*. Evanston, Ill., 1961.

Bourdieu, Pierre. *The Algerians*. Boston, 1962.

Brett, Michael. "Ifriqiya as a Market for Saharan Trade from the Tenth to the Twelfth Century, A.D." *Journal of African History*, 10:347–64 (1969).

Bulliet, Richard W. *The Camel and the Wheel*. Cambridge, Mass., 1975.

Butzer, Karl W. "Rise and Fall of Axum, Ethiopia: A Geo-Archaeological Interpretation." *American Antiquity*, 46:471–95, (1981).

Chittick, Neville. "East Africa and the Orient: Ports and Trade Before the Arrival of the Portuguese." In UNESCO, *Historical Relations Across the Indian Ocean*. Paris, 1980. Pp. 13–22.

Chittick, H. N., and R. I. Rotberg (eds.). *East Africa and the Orient*. New York, 1975.

Cohen, Abner. *Custom and Politics in Urban Africa: A Study of Hausa Migrants in Yoruba Towns*. Berkeley, 1969.

Cordell, Dennis, D. "Eastern Libya, Wadai, and the Sanusiya: A Tariqa and a Trade Route." *Journal of African History*, 18:21–36 (1977).

Curtin, Philip D. *Africa Remembered: Narratives of West Africans from the Era of the Slave Trade*. Madison, Wis., 1967.

Economic Change in Precolonial Africa: Senegambia in the Era of the Slave Trade. 2 vols. Madison, Wis., 1975.

"Africa in the Wider Monetary World, 1250–1850." In *Silver and Gold Flows in the Medieval and Early Modern Worlds*, ed. by John F. Richards. Chapel Hill, N.C., 1983.

Curtin, Philip D., Steven Feierman, Leonard Thompson, and Jan Vansina. *African History*. Boston, 1978.

Dike, K. Onwuka. *Trade and Politics in the Niger Delta, 1830–1885*. Oxford, 1956.

Dunn, Ross E. "The Trade of Tafilalt: Commercial Change in Southeast Morocco on the Eve of the Protectorate." *International Journal of African Historical Studies*, 6:271–304 (1971).

Resistance in the Desert. Madison, Wis., 1977.

Dupré, Georges. "Le commerce entre sociétés lignagères: les Nzabi dans la traite à la fin du XIX_e siècle (Gabon-Congo)." *Cahiers d'études africaines*, 12:616–58 (1972).

Ekejiuba, F. Ifeoma. "The Aro Trade System in the Nineteenth Century." *Ikenga*, 1:11–26; 2:10–21 (1972).

Evans-Prichard, E. E. *The Sanusi of Cyrenaica*. Oxford, 1949.

Flint, John E. (ed.). *The Cambridge History of Africa*, vol. 5. Cambridge, 1976.

Forde, Daryll (ed.). *Efik Traders of Old Calabar*. London, 1956.

Fyfe, Christopher. *A History of Sierra Leone*. London, 1962.

Garrard, Timothy F. "Myth and Metrology: The Early Trans-Saharan Gold Trade." *Journal of African History*, 23:443–61 (1982).

Good, Charles M. "Periodic Markets and Traveling Traders in Uganda." *Geographical Review*, 65:49–72 (1975).

"Salt, Trade and Disease: Aspects of Development in Africa's Northern Great Lakes Region." *International Journal of African Historical Studies*, 5:543–86 (1972).

Gray, Richard (ed.). *The Cambridge History of Africa*. vol. 4. Cambridge, 1975.

A History of the Southern Sudan 1839–1889. Oxford, 1961.

Gray, Richard, and David Birmingham (eds.), *Pre-Colonial African Trade: Essays on Trade in Central and Eastern Africa before 1900.* London, 1970.

Hamdum, Said, and Noel King, *Ibn Battuta in Black Africa.* London, 1975.

Handwerker, W. Penn, "Market Places, Travelling Traders, and Shops: Commercial Structural Variation in the Liberian Interior prior to 1940," *African Economic History,* 9:3–26 (1980).

Harms, Robert W. *River of Wealth, River of Sorrow: The Central Zaire Basin in the Era of the Slave and Ivory Trade, 1500–1891.* New Haven, Conn., 1981.

Hartwig, Gerald W. "The Victorian Nyanza as a Trade Route in the Nineteenth Century." *Journal of African History,* 11:535–52 (1970).

The Art of Survival in East Africa: The Karebe and Long Distance Trade. New York, 1976.

Hill, Richard, *Egypt in the Sudan 1820–1881.* London, 1959.

Holsinger, Donald C. "Migration, Commerce and Community: The Mizābís in Eighteenth- and Nineteenth-Century Algeria." *Journal of African History,* 21:61–74 (1980).

Howard, Allen. "The Relevance of Spatial Analysis for African Economic History: The Sierra-Leone Guinea System." *Journal of African History,* 17:365–88 (1975).

Ibn Battuta, Muhammad. *Ibn Battuta in Black Africa,* trans. and annotated by Said Hamdun and Noel King. London, 1975.

Isaacman, Allen F. *Mozambique: The Africanization of a European Institution, The Zambezi Prazos, 1750–1902.* Madison, Wis., 1972.

Isichei, Elizabeth. "Historical Change in an Ibo Polity: Asaba to 1885." *Journal of African History,* 10:421–38 (1969).

Johnson, Marion. "Calico Caravans: The Tripoli-Kano Trade after 1880." *Journal of African History,* 17:95–117 (1976).

"The Ounce in Eighteenth-Century West African Trade." *Journal of African History,* 7:197–214 (1966).

Jones, Adam. "Who Were the Vai?" *Journal of African History,* 22:159–78 (1981).

Jones, G. I. *The Trading States of the Oil Rivers.* London, 1963.

Kobishanov, Y. M. "Aksum: Political System, Economics and Culture, First to Fourth Century." In UNESCO, *General History of Africa.* 8 vols. projected, 2:381–99. Paris, 1981.

Kopytoff, Igor. "Aghem Ethnogenesis and the Grassfields Ecumene." In *Contribution de la recherche ethnologique à l'historie des civilisations du Cameroun,* ed. by Claude Tardits. 2 vols., 2:371–81. Paris, 1981.

Lespès, René. "Quelques documents sur la corporation des Mozabites d'Alger dans les premiers temps de la conquêt." *Revue africaine,* 66:197–218 (1925).

Levtzion, Nehemia. *Muslims and Chiefs in West Africa: A Study of Islam in the Middle Volta Basin in the Pre-Colonial Period.* London, 1968.

Lewicki, Tadusz. "Traits d'historie du commerce transsaharien: marchands et missionaires ibadites au Soudan occidental et central au cours des VIIIe–XIIe siècles." *Ethnografia Polska,* 8:291–311 (1964).

Lovejoy, Paul E. "Polanyi's 'Ports of Trade'; Salaga and Kano in the Nineteenth Century." *Canadian Journal of African Studies,* 16:245–77 (1982).

Caravans of Kola: The Hausa Kola Trade, 1700–1900. Zaria, 1980.

"The Role of the Wangara in the Economic Transformation of the Central

Sudan in the Fifteenth and Sixteenth Centuries." *Journal of African History*, 19:341–68 (1978).

Lovejoy, Paul E., and Stephen Baier. "The Desert-Side Economy of the Central Sudan." *International Journal of African Historical Studies*, 8:551–81 (1975).

Maier, Donna. "Competition for Power and Profits in Kete-Krachi, West Africa, 1875–1900." *International Journal of African Historical Studies*, 13:33–50 (1980).

Manning, Patrick. *Slavery, Colonialism and Economic Growth in Dahomey, 1640–1960.* Cambridge, 1982.

Martin, Phyllis M. *The External Trade of the Loango Coast, 1576–1870: The Effects of Changing Commercial Relations on the Vili Kingdom of Loango.* Oxford, 1972.

McIntosh, Susan Keech. "A Reconstruction of Wangara/Palolus, Island of Gold." *Journal of African History*, 22:145–58 (1981).

Meillassoux, Claude (ed.). *The Development of Indigenous Trade and Markets in West Africa.* London, 1971.

Miracle, Marvin P. "Aboriginal Trade among the Senga and Nsenga of Northern Rhodesia." *Ethnology*, 1:212–22 (1962).

Newitt, M. D. D. *Portuguese Settlements on the Zambezi.* New York, 1973.

Northrup, David. *Trade Without Rulers: Pre-Colonial Economic Development in South-Eastern Nigeria.* Oxford, 1978.

Pankhurst, Richard. "The Trade of the Gulf of Aden Ports of Africa in the Nineteenth and Early Twentieth Centuries." *Journal of Ethiopian Studies*, 3:36–81 (1965).

Person, Yves. *Samori: une revolution dyula.* 3 vols. Dakar, 1968–75.

Peukert, Werner. *Der Atlantische Sklavenhandel von Dahomey 1740–1797: Wirtschaftsanthropologie und Socialgeschichte.* Wiesbaden, 1978.

Polyanyi, Karl, in collaboration with Abraham Rotstein. *Dahomey and the Slave Trade: An Analysis of an Archaic Economy.* Seattle, 1966.

Priestly, Margaret. *West African Trade and Coast Society: A Family Study.* London, 1969.

Roberts, Richard. "Long Distance Trade and Production: Sinsani in the Nineteenth Century." *Journal of African History*, 21:169–88 (1980).

Schildkraut, Enid. *People of the Zongo: The Transformation of Ethnic Identities in Ghana.* Cambridge, 1978.

Skinner, Elliott P. *The Mossi of the Upper Volta: The Political Development of a Sudanese People.* Stanford, Calif., 1964.

Stewart, Marjorie Helen. "The Role of the Manding in the Hinterland Trade of the Western Sudan: A Linguistic and Cultural Analysis." *Bulletin d l'IFAN*, 41:281–302 (1979).

Terray, Emmanuel. "Long-Distance Exchange and the Formation of the State: The Case of the Abron Kingdom of Gyaman." *Economy and Society*, 3:315–45 (1974).

Ukwu, Ukwu I. "The Development of Trade and Marketing in Iboland," *Journal of the Historical Society of Nigeria*, 3:647–62 (1967).

Vail, Leroy. "Suggestions Towards a Reinterpreted Tumbuka History." In *The Early History of Malawi*, ed. by B. Pachai. London, 1972. Pp. 148–67.

Vansina, Jan. *The Tio Kingdom of the Middle Congo 1880–1892.* London, 1973.
Kingdoms of the Savanna. Madison, Wis., 1969.
"Long-Distance Trade Routes in Central Africa." *Journal of African History*, 3:375–90 (1962).

Venture de Paradis. "Alger au xviiie siècle." *Revue africaine*, 39:266–314 (1895).
Verger, Pierre. *Flux et reflux de la traite des nègres entre le golfe de Bénin et Bahia de todos os santos du dix-septième au dix-neuvième siècle.* Paris, 1968.
Vigourous. L. "L'émigration mozabite dans les villes du Tell algerien." *Travaux de l'institut de recherches sahariennes*, 3:87–102 (1945).
Walz, Terrence. *Trade Between Egypt and Bilad-as-Sudan, 1700–1820.* Cairo, 1978.
Weiskel, Timothy C. "The Precolonial Baule: A Reconstruction." *Cahiers d'etudes africaines*, 18:503–60 (1978).
Wilhelm, H. "Le commerce précolonial de l'ouest (Plateau bamileka-grassfield, région bamoum et bafia)." In *Contribution de la recherche ethnologique à l'histoire des civilisations du Cameroun*, ed. by Claude Tardits. 2 vols., 2:485–501. Paris, 1981.
Wilks, Ivor. *Asante in the Nineteenth Century: The Structure and Evolution of a Political Order.* Cambridge, 1975.
"Wangara, Akan, and the Portuguese in the Fifteenth and Sixteenth Centuries." *Journal of African History*, 23:333–50, 463–502 (1982).
Wood, L. J., and Christopher Ehret. "The Origins and Diffusions of the Market Institution in East Africa." *Journal of African Studies*, 5:1–17 (1978).
Zarwan, John. "Indian Businessmen in Kenya during the Twentieth Century." Ph.D. diss., Yale University, 1977.

Chapter 4. Ancient Middle East

Adams, Robert McC. *The Evolution of Urban Society.* Chicago, 1965.
Heartland of Cities: Surveys of Ancient Settlement and Land Use on the Central Floodplain of the Euphrates. Chicago, 1981.
Austin, M. M. *Greece and Egypt in the Archaic Age.* Cambridge, 1970.
Austin, M. M., and P. Vidal-Naquet. *Economic and Social History of Ancient Greece.* Berkeley, 1977.
Beale, T. W. "Early Trade in Highland Iran: A View from the Source." *World Archaeology*, 5:133–48 (1973).
Bryson, Reid A., H. H. Lamb, and David L. Donley. "Drought and the Decline of Mycenae." *Antiquity*, 48:46–50 (1974).
Carpenter, Rhys. *Discontinuity in Greek Civilization.* Cambridge, 1966.
Casson, L. *The Ancient Mariners.* New York, 1959.
Charlesworth, Martin P. "Roman Trade with India: A Resurvey." *Studies in Roman Economic and Social History in Honor of Allan Chester Johnson*, ed. by P.R. Coleman Norton. Princeton, N.J., 1951. Pp. 131–43.
Trade-Routes and Commerce of the Roman Empire. Cambridge, 1926.
Colledge, Malcolm A. R. *The Parthians.* London, 1967.
Crawford, H.E.W. "Mesopotamia's Invisible Exports in the Third Millenium B.C." *World Anthropology*, 5:232–41 (1973).
Culican, William. *The First Merchant Ventures: The Ancient Levant in History and Commerce.* London, 1966.
Deimal, A. (ed.). "Sumerische Tempelwirtschaft zur Zeit Urukaginas und seiner Vorganger." *Analecta Orientalia*, 2. (n.s.): 71–113 (1931).
Earle, Timothy K., and Jonathan E. Ericsson (eds.), *Exchange Systems in Prehistory.* New York, 1977.
Finley, M. I. *The Ancient Economy.* Berkeley, 1973.

The World of Odysseus. New York, 1954.

Foster, Benjamin, "A New Look at the Sumerian Temple State," *Journal of Economic and Social History of the Orient*, 24:225–41 (1981).

"Commercial Activity in Sargonic Mesopotamia," *Iraq*, 39:31–44 (1977).

Gardin, G. C., and P. Garelli, "Études des établissements Assyriens en Cappadoce par ordinateur," *Annales: économies, sociétés, civilisations*, 16:837–76 (1961).

Garelli, Paul, *Les Assyriens en Cappadoce.* Paris, 1963.

Gelb, I. J. "On the Alleged Temple and State Economies in Ancient Mesopotamia," *Studi in Onore di Edouardo Volterra*, 6:137–54 (Rome, 1969).

Graham, A. J. "Patterns in Early Greek Colonisation." *Journal of Hellenic Studies*, 91:35–47 (1971).

Harden, Donald, *The Phoenicians.* London, 1962.

Hawks, Jacquetta, and Sir Leonard Wooley, *Prehistory and the Beginnings of Civilization.* Vol. I of the UNESCO *History of Mankind.* New York, 1963.

Heichelheim, Fritz M. *An Ancient Economic History: From the Palaeolithic Age to the Migrations of the Germanic, Slavic, and Arabic Nations.* 2 vols. Leiden, 1958–64.

Jones, Tom B. *Ancient Civilization.* Chicago, 1960.

Knorringa, Heiman. *Emporos. Data on Trade and Traders in Greek Literature from Homer to Aristotle.* Amsterdam, 1926.

Kohl, Philip L. "The Balance of Trade in Southwestern Asia in the Mid-Third Millennium B.C." *Current Anthropology*, 19:463–92 (1978).

Lamberg-Karlovsky, C.C. "Foreign Relations in the Third Millenium at Tepe Yahya." In *Le plateau iranien de l'asie centrale des origines à la conquête islamique.* Centre National de la Recherche Scientifique. Paris, 1977. Pp. 33–44.

"Trade Mechanisms in Indus-Mesopotamian Interrelations." *Journal of the American Oriental Society*, 2:222–9 (1972).

Larsen, M. T. *Old Assyrian Caravan Procedures.* Istanbul, 1967.

"Early Assur and International Trade." *Sumer*, 35:347–9 (1979).

Leemans, W. F. *Foreign Trade in the Old Babylonian Period.* Leiden, 1960.

The Old Babylonian Merchant: His Business and His Social Position. Leiden, 1950.

Mallowan, M. G. L. "The Mechanics of Ancient Trade in Western Asia." *Iran*, 3:1–9 (1965).

Moscati, Sabatino. *The World of the Phoenicians.* London, 1969.

Oppenheim, A.L. "The Seafaring Merchants of Ur." *Journal of the American Oriental Society*, 74:6–17 (1954).

Ozguc, Nimet. "Assyrian Trade Colonies in Anatolia." *Archaeology*, 22:250–5 (1969).

Peterson, David Andrew. "Ancient Commerce." Ph.D. diss., State University of New York, Binghamton, 1976.

Powell, M. A. "Sumerian Merchants and the Problem of Profit." *Iraq*, 39:23–29 (1977).

Renfrew, Colin. *Before Civilization: The Radiocarbon Revolution and Prehistoric Europe.* London, 1973.

The Emergence of Civilization: The Cyclades and the Aegean in the Third Millenium B.C. London, 1972.

"Trade and Culture Process in European Prehistory." *Current Anthropology*, 10:151–60 (1969).

Roebuck, Carl. "The Grain Trade between Greece and Egypt." *Classical Philology*, 45:236–47 (1950).

"The Organization of Naukratis." *Classical Philology*, 46:212–20 (1951).

Rougé, Jean. *Recherches sur l'organisation du commerce maritime en Méditerranée sous l'empire romain*. Paris, 1966.

Sabloff, Jeremy A., and C. C. Lamberg-Karlovsky (eds.). *Ancient Civilization and Trade*. Albuquerque, N. Mex., 1975.

Sams, Kenneth. "Patterns of Trade in First Millennium Gordion." *Archaeology News*, 8:45–53 (1979).

Sandars, N. K. *The Sea Peoples: Warriors of the Ancient Mediterranean, 1250–1150 B.C.*. New York, 1978.

Starr, Chester G. *The Economic and Social Growth of Early Greece, 800–500 B.C.* New York, 1977.

Van Seters, John. "What is Trade? The Nature of Egyptian Trade in the Eastern Mediterranean During the Second Millennium B.C." *Archaeology News*, 8:137–39 (1980).

Veenhoff, K.R. *Aspects of Old Assyrian Trade and its Terminology*. Leiden, 1972.

Wallace, M. B. "Early Greek Proxenoi." *Phoenix*, 24:189–208 (1970).

Warmington, E.H. *The Commerce Between the Roman Empire and India*. Cambridge, 1928.

Weiss, Harvey, and T. Cuyler Young, Jr. "The Merchants of Susa: Godin V and Plateau-Lowland Relations in the Late Fourth Millennium." *Iran*, 13:1–16 (1975).

Wright, Henry T. "A Consideration of Interregional Exchange in Greater Mesopotamia: 4000–3000 B.C." In *Social Exchange and Interaction*, ed. by E.N. Wilmsen. Ann Arbor, Mich., 1972.

Chapter 4. The Ancient Americas

Acosta Saignes, Miguel. "Los Pochteca." *Acta Antropologica*, 1:1–62 (1945).

Berdan, Frances F. "Distributive Mechanisms in the Aztec Economy." In *Peasant Livelihood*, ed. by R. Halperin and J. Dow. New York, 1977.

Bromley, Raymond J., and Richard Symanski. "Marketplace Trade in Latin America." *Latin American Research Review*, 9:3–38 (1974).

Brumfiel, Elizabeth M. "Specialization, Market Exchange, and the Aztec State: A View from Mexotla." *Current Anthropology*, 21:459–78 (1980).

Carasco, Pedro, and Johanna Broda (eds.). *Economía política e ideología en el Mexico prehispanico*. Mexico, D.F., 1978.

Chadwick, Robert E. L. "The 'Olmeca-Xicallanca' of Teotihuacán: A Preliminary Study." *Meso-American Notes*, 7–8:1–23 (1966).

Coe, Michael D. *The Jaguar's Children: Pre-Classic Central Mexico*. New York, 1965.

Dahlgren de Jordan, Barbro. *La Mixteca: Su Cultura e História Prehispanicas*. Mexico, D.F., 1954.

Diaz del Castillo, Bernal. *The Conquest of New Spain*. Harmondsworth, 1963.

Flannery, Kent V. "The Olmec and the Valley of Oaxaca." *Dunbarton Oaks Conference on the Olmec*. Washington, D.C., 1968. Pp. 79–110.

Gibson, Charles. *The Aztecs Under Spanish Rule*. Stanford, Calif., 1964.

Heizer, Robert F., and John A. Graham (eds.). *Observation on the Emergence of Civilization in Mesoamerica*. Berkeley, 1971.

Hirth, R.G. "Interregional Trade and the Formation of Gateway Communities." *American Antiquity*, 43:35–45 (1978).

Murra, John V. *The Economic Organization of the Inka State*. Greenwich, Conn., 1980.

Padden, R. C. *The Hummingbird and the Hawk: Conquest and Sovereignty in the Valley of Mexico, 1503–41*. Columbus, Ohio, 1967.

Peterson, Frederick A. *Ancient Mexico: An Introduction to the Pre-Hispanic Cultures*, 2nd ed. New York, 1962.

Rathje, William L. "The Origin and Development of Lowland Classic Maya Civilization." *American Antiquity*, 36:275–85 (1971).

Rathje, William L., and Jeremy A. Sabloff. "A Research Design for Cozumel, Mexico." *World Archaeology*, 5:221–31 (1973).

Renfrew, Colin. "Alternative Models for Exchange and Spatial Distribution." In *Exchange Systems in Prehistory*, ed. by Timothy E. Earle and Jonathan E. Ericson. New York, 1977. Pp.71–90.

Rougé, Jean. *Ships and Fleets of the Ancient Mediterranean*, trans. by Susan Frazer. Middletown, Conn., 1981.

Sabloff, Jeremy A., and William L. Rathje. *A Study of Changing PreColumbian Commercial Systems, the 1972–73 Seasons at Cozumel Mexico*. Cambridge, 1975.

Sahagun, Fr. Bernardino de. *Florentine Codex. Book 9 – The Merchants*, trans. by C. E. Dibble and A.J.O. Anderson. Salt Lake City, 1959.

Sanders, William T., Jeffrey R. Parsons, and R.S. Santley. *The Basin of Mexico: Ecological Processes in the Evolution of a Civilization*. New York, 1979.

Sidrys, Raymond (ed.). *Papers on the Economy and Architecture of the Ancient Maya*. Los Angeles, 1978.

"Supply and Demand among the Classic Maya." *Current Anthropology*, 20:594–7 (1979).

Smith, Michael E. "The Aztec Marketing System and Settlement Pattern in the Valley of Mexico: A Central-Place Analysis." *American Antiquity*, 44:110–25 (1979).

Tourtellot, Gair, and Jeremy A. Sabloff. "Exchange Systems among the Ancient Maya." *American Antiquity*, 37:126–35 (1972).

Wolf, Eric R. *Sons of the Shaking Earth*. Chicago, 1959.

Chapters 5 and 6. The trading world of the Indian Ocean
before 1500

Adhya, G. C. *Early Indian Economics: Studies in the Economic Life of Northern India and Western India c. 200 B.C.–A.D. 300*. Bombay, 1966.

Ahmad ibn Majid. *Arab Navigation in the Indian Ocean Before the Coming of the Portuguese*. London, 1971.

Ahmad Makubl. *Indo-Arab Relations. An Account of India's relations of the Arab World from Ancient up to Modern Times*. Bombay, 1969.

Anand, R. P. "Maritime Practice in South-East Asia until 1600 A.D. and the Modern Law of the Sea." *International Comparative Law Quarterly*, 30:440–54 (1981).

Appadorai, A. *Economic Conditions in Southern India, 1000–1500 A.D.* 2 vols. Madras, 1936–51.

Ashtor, Eliahu. *A Social and Economic History of the Near East in the Middle Ages.* Berkeley, 1976.

"The Karimi Merchants." *Journal of the Royal Asiatic Society,* 1956: 45–56 (1956).

"Banking Instruments between the Muslim East and the Christian West." *Journal of European Economic History,* 1:553–73 (1972).

Ayyar, K. R. Venkatarama. "Medieval Trade, Craft, and Merchant Guilds in South India." *Journal of Indian History,* 25:269–80 (1947).

Benjamin of Tudela. "The Perigrination of Benjamin the sonne of Jonas..." In *Samuel Purchas, Hakluytus Posthumous or Purchase His Pilgrimes,* 20 vols., 8:523–93. Glasgow, 1905.

Boulnois, Luce. *The Silk Road.* London, 1966.

Chakraborti, H. *Trade and Commerce of Ancient India.* Calcutta, 1966.

Chandra, Moti. *Trade and Trade Routes in Ancient India.* New Delhi, 1977.

Duby, Georges. *The Early Growth of the European Economy: Warriors and Peasants from the Seventh to the Twelfth Century.* Ithaca, N.Y., 1974.

Elvin, Mark. *The Pattern of the Chinese Past.* Stanford, Calif., 1973.

Fourquin, Guy. *Histoire économique de l'occidente mediévale,* 2nd ed. Paris, 1969.

Goitein, Solomon Dob Dritz. "From the Mediterranean to India: Documents on the Trade to India, South Arabia, and East Africa from the Eleventh to the Twelfth Century." *Speculum,* 29:181–97 (1954).

A Mediterranean Society. 3 vols. Berkeley, 1967–78.

Studies in Islamic History and Institutions. Leiden, 1976.

Haeger, John W. (ed.). *Crisis and Prosperity in Sung China.* Tucson, 1975.

Hartwell, Robert. "A Cycle of Economic Change in Imperial China: Coal and Iron in Northeast China, 750–1350." *Journal of Economic and Social History of the Orient,* 10:103–59 (1967).

Huan, Ma. *The Overall Survey of the Ocean's Shores,* trans. and edited by J. V. G. Mills. London, 1970.

Jhao, Ju-Kua. *Chau Ju-kua: His Work on the Chinese and Arab Trade in the 12th and 13th Centuries, Entitled Chu-fan-chi,* ed. and trans. by F. Hirth and W. W. Rockhill. First published 1911. Taipei, 1970.

Kuo, Tsung-fei. "A Brief History of the Trade Routes between Burma, Indochina, and Yunnan." *T'ien Hsia Monthly,* 12:9–32 (1941).

Kwanten, Luc. *Imperial Nomads: A History of Central Asia, 500–1500 A.D.* Philadelphia, 1978.

Labib, Subhi Y. *Handelsgeschichte Ägyptens im Spätmittelalter (1171–1517).* Wiesbaden, 1965.

"Egyptian Commercial Policy in the Middle Ages." In *Studies in the Economic History of the Middle East,* ed. by M. A. Cook. London, 1970. Pp. 64–77.

"Karimi." *Encyclopedia of Islam,* 4:640–3 (1979).

Lambton, Ann K. S. "The Merchant in Medieval Islam." In *A Locust's Leg: Studies in Honour of S. H. Taqizadeh.* London, 1962. Pp. 121–30.

Lane, Frederick C. "Fleets and Fairs: The Functions of the Venetian Muda." In *Studi in Onore di Armando Sapori.* Milano, 1957. Pp. 649–63.

Venice: A Maritime Republic. Baltimore, 1973.

Venice and History. Baltimore, 1966.

Lewis, Archibald. "Maritime Skills in the Indian Ocean, 1368–1500." *Journal of the Economic and Social History of the Orient*, 16:238–64 (1973).
Naval Power and Trade in the Mediterranean, 500–1100. Princeton, N.J., 1959.
Lo, Jung-pang. "Maritime Commerce and its Relation to the Sung Navy." *Journal of the Economic and Social History of the Orient*, 12:57–101 (1969).
Ma, Laurence J. C. *Commercial Development and Urban Change in Sung China (960–1279)*. Ann Arbor, Mich., 1971.
Majumdar, R. C. *Ancient Indian Colonization in South-East Asia*, 2nd ed. Baroda, 1963.
Hindu Colonies in the Far East, 2nd ed. Calcutta, 1963.
Mas Latrie, Louis comte de. *Traités de paix et de commerce et documents divers concernant les relations Chrétiens avec les Arabes de l'Afrique septentrionale au moyen age...*" Paris, 1866.
Miller, J. Innes. *The Spice Trade of the Roman Empire: 29 B.C. to A.D. 641*. Oxford, 1969.
Miskimin, Harry A, David Herlihy, and A. L. Udovitch (eds.). *The Medieval City*. New Haven, Conn., 1977.
Needham, Joseph. "Abstract of Material Presented to the International Maritime History Commission at Beirut." In *Sociétés et compagnies de commerce en orient de dans l'océan indien*, ed. by M. Mollat. Paris, 1971.
Science and Civilization in China, multivol. Cambridge, 1954–.
Nilakanta Sastri, K. A. *A History of South India*. Madras, 1948.
Foreign Notices of South India from Megasthenes to Ma Huan. Madras, 1939.
Parker, John (ed.). *Merchants and Scholars*. Minneapolis, 1965.
Polo, Marco. *Marco Polo: Description of the World*, ed. by Arthur Christopher Moule and Paul Pelliot. 2 vols. London, 1938.
Pulleybank, E.G. "Han China in Central Asia." *International Historical Review*, 3:278–86.
Rabinowitz, L. *Jewish Merchant Adventures: The Study of the Radanites*. London, 1948.
Raychaudhuri, Tapan, and Irfan Habib. *The Cambridge Economic History of India*. 2 vols. Cambridge, 1982.
Reischauer, Edwin O., and John K. Fairbank. *East Asia: The Great Tradition*. Boston, 1960.
Richard, Jean. "European Voyages in the Indian Ocean and Caspian Sea (12th–15th Centuries)." *Iran*, 6:45–52 (1968).
Richards, D. S. (ed.). *Islam and the Trade of Asia: A Colloquium*. Philadelphia, 1970.
Rossabi, Morris. "Ming China and Turfan 1406–1517." *Central Asiatic Journal*, 16:213–22 (1972).
Samarrai, A. "Medieval Commerce and Diplomacy, Islam and Europe A.D. 850–1300." *Canadian Journal of History*, 15:1–21 (1980).
Sheiba, Yoshinobu. *Commerce in Society in Sung China*. Ann Arbor, Mich. 1970.
Smith, D. Howard. "Zaitun's Five Centuries of Sino-Foreign Trade." *Journal of the Royal Asiatic Society*, 1958: 167–77 (1958).
Srivastava, B. *Trade and Commerce of Ancient India*. Varanasi, 1968.
Stillman, Norman A. "The Eleventh Century Merchant House of Ibn 'Awkal (A genize study)." *Journal of the Economic and Social History of the Orient*, 16:15–88 (1973).
Thapar, Romila. *A History of India*. vol. one. London, 1966.

Tibbetts, G. R. *Arab Navigation in the Indian Ocean before the Coming of the Portu-
guese.* London, 1971.
Toussaint, Auguste. *History of the Indian Ocean.* Chicago, 1966.
Unger, Richard W. *The Ship in the Medieval Economy, 600–1600.* London, 1980.
Vlekke, B. H. M. *Nusantara: A History of the East Indian Archipelago.* Cambridge,
1943.
Wake, C. H. H. "The Changing Patterns of Europe's Pepper and Spice Imports,
ca. 1400–1700." *Journal of European Economic History*, 8:361–403 (1979).
Wheatley, Paul. *The Golden Khersonese: Studies in the Historical Geography of the
Malay Peninsula before A. D. 1500.* Kuala Lumpur, 1971.
Whitehouse, David, and Andrew Williamson. "Sasanian Maritime Trade." *Iran*,
11:29–60 (1973).
Wolters, O. W. *Early Indonesian Commerce: A Study of the Origins of Srivijaya.*
Ithaca, N.Y., 1967.
Yamamoto, Tatsuro. "Chinese Activities in the Indian Ocean Before the Coming
of the Portuguese." *Diogenes*, 111:19–34 (1981).
Yu, Ying-shih, *Trade and Expansion in Han China.* Berkeley, 1967.

Chapters 7 and 8. The trading world of the Indian Ocean
after 1500

Andaya, Leonard Y. *The Heritage of Arung Palakka: A History of South Sulawesi
(Celebes) in the Seventeenth Century.* The Hague, 1981.
The Kingdom of Johor 1641–1728: Economic and Political Developments. Kuala Lum-
pur, 1975.
"An Outline of the Social and Economic Consequences of Dutch Presence in
South Sulawesi Society in the Late 17th and Early 18th Centuries." Paper
presented at the Symposium on the Western Presence in South-East Asia,
Manila, January 25–8, 1982.
Arasaratnam, Sinnappah. *Dutch Power in Ceylon 1658–1687.* Amsterdam, 1958.
"Some Notes on the Dutch Malacca and the Indo-Malayan Trade 1641–1670."
Journal of Southeast Asian History, 10:480–90 (1969).
Aubin, Jean (ed.). *Mare Luso-Indicum: Études et documents sur l'histoire de l' Océan
Indien et des pays riverains a l'époque de la domination portugaise.* 5 vols. Geneva,
1971–.
Basu, Dilip. "The Banian and the British in Calcutta, 1800–1850." *Bengal Past
and Present*, 92:157–70 (1973).
Blusse, Leonard, and Femme Gaastra (eds.). *Companies and Trade: Essays on
Overseas Trading Companies during the Ancient Regime.* The Hague, 1981.
Boxer, Charles R. *Fidalgos in the Far East, 1550–1770.* The Hague, 1948.
*Franciso Vieira de Figueiredo: A Portuguese Merchant-Adventurer in Southeast Asia,
1624–1667.* The Hague, 1967.
The Dutch Seaborne Empire, 1600–1800. New York, 1965.
The Portuguese Seaborne Empire, 1415–1825. New York, 1969.
Burns, Michael. "All Hail Ye Bugis Schooners." *Orientations*, 11:43–9 (1980).
Cady, John F. *Southeast Asia: Its Historical Development.* New York, 1964.
Chaudhuri, K. N. *The Trading World of Asia and the English East India Company
1660–1760.* Cambridge, 1978.

Chaudhuri, Susil. *Trade and Commercial Organization in Bengal, 1650–1720.* Calcutta, 1975.

Ch'en Ching-ho. *The Chinese Community in the Sixteenth Century Philippines.* Tokyo, 1969.

Dale, Stephen Frederick. *Islamic Society on the South Asian Frontier: The Mappilas of Malabar, 1498–1922.* New York, 1980.

Das, Dipakranjan. *Economic History of the Deccan From the First to the Sixth Century A.D.* Delhi, 1969.

Das Gupta, Ashin. *Malabar in Asian Trade 1740–1800.* Cambridge, 1967.

Dermigny, Louis. *La Chine et l'Occident: Le commerce à Canton au XVIIIe siècle, 1719–1833.* 3 vols. and album. Paris: 1964.

Diffie, Bailey W., and George D. Winius. *Foundations of the Portuguese Empire, 1415–1580.* Minneapolis, 1977.

Disney, Anthony R. *Twilight of the Pepper Empire: Portuguese Trade in Southwest India in the Early Seventeenth Century.* Cambridge, Mass., 1978.

Dobbin, Christine. *Urban Leadership in Western India: Politics and Communities in Bombay City, 1840–55.* Oxford, 1972.

Dulaurier, Edouard. "Institutions maritimes de l'archipel d'Asie." In *Collection de lois maritimes antérieures au xviiie siècle,* vol. 6, ed. by J. M. Pardessus. Paris, 1845.

Fairbank, John K. "Tributary Trade and China's Relations with the West." *The Far Eastern Quarterly,* 1:129–49 (1941).

(ed.). *The Chinese World Order: Traditional China's Foreign Relations.* Cambridge, 1968.

Fairbank, John K., and S. Y. Teng. "On the Ch'ing Tributary System." *Harvard Journal of Asiatic Studies,* 6:135–247 (1947).

Fairbank, John K., Edwin O. Reischauer, and Albert M. Craig. *East Asia: The Modern Transformation.* Boston, 1965.

Felix, Alonso, Jr. *The Chinese in the Philippines.* 2 vols. Manila, 1966.

Furber, Holden. *Rival Empires of Trade in the Orient, 1600–1800.* Minneapolis, 1976.

Glamann, Kristoff. *Dutch Asiatic Trade, 1620–1740.* The Hague, 1958.

Gopal, Surendra. *Commerce and Crafts in Gujarat, 16th and 17th Centuries: A Study of the Impact of European Expansion on a Precapitalist Economy.* New Delhi, 1975.

"Gujarati Shipping in the Seventeenth Century." *Indian Economic and Social History Review,* 8:31–40 (1971).

Grottanelli, Vinigi L. *Pescatori del Oceano Indiano.* Rome, 1955.

Habib, Irfan. *An Atlas of the Mughal Empire.* New York, 1980.

Hall, D. G. E. *A History of Southeast Asia.* London, 1955.

Hambly, G. "Introduction to the Economic Organization of Qajar Iran," *Iran,* 2:69–81 (1964).

Hawkins, Clifford W. *The Dhow.* Lymington, 1977.

Hazelhurst, Layton W. "Caste and Merchant Communities," In *Structure and Change in Indian Society,* ed. by Milton Singer and Bernard S. Cohn. Chicago, 1968.

Hodgson, Marshall G. S. *The Venture of Islam: Conscience and History of a World Civilization in Three Volumes,* 3 vols. Chicago, 1974.

Hourani, G. F. *Arab Seafaring in the Indian Ocean in Ancient and early Medieval Times*. Princeton, N.J., 1951.

Kling, Blair B., and M. N. Pearson (eds.), *The Age of Partnership: Europeans in Asia before Dominion*. Honolulu, 1979.

Kobata, A. "The Production and Uses of Gold and Silver in Sixteenth and Seventeenth Century Japan." *The Economic History Review*, 2nd ser., 18:245–65 (1965).

Koentjaraningrat, Raden Mas, *Introduction to the Peoples and Cultures of Indonesia and Malaysia*. Menlo Park, Calif., 1975.

Kuchhal, S. C. "The Managing Agency System," In *The Industrial Economy of India*, ed. by S.C. Kuchhal. Allahabad, 1963.

Lineton, Jacqueline. "'Pasompe' Ugu': Bugis Migrants and Wanderers." *Archipel*, 10:173–201 (1975).

Linschoten, John Huyhgen van. *The Voyage of John Huyhgen van Linschoten to the East Indies*. 2 vols. London, 1885.

MacKnight, C. C. "The Nature of Early Maritime Trade: Some Points of Analogy from the Eastern Part of the Indonesian Archipelago." *World Archaeology*, 5:198–210 (1973).

———. "The Rise of Agriculture in South Sulawesi before 1600." Unpublished paper, 1981.

———. "The Study of Praus in the Indonesian Archipelago." *The Great Circle*. 2:117–28 (1980).

Magalhães-Godinho, Vitorino. *L'économie de l'empire portugais aux xve et xvie siècles*. Paris, 1969.

———. *Os Descobrimentos e a Economía Mundial*. 2 vols. Lisbon, 1963.

Mahalingan, T.V. *Economic Life in the Vijayanagar Empire*. Madras, 1951.

Marques, António Henrique de Oliveria. *History of Portugal*. 2 vols. New York, 1971.

Meilink-Roelofsz, M. A. P. *Asian Trade and European Influence in the Indonesian Archipelago Between 1500 and about 1630*. The Hague, 1962.

Mollat, M. (ed.). *Sociétés et compagnies de commerce en orient et dans l'océan indien*. Paris, 1971.

Moreland, W. H. "The Shabandar in the Eastern Seas." *Journal of the Royal Asiatic Society*, 28:517–33 (1920).

Parkinson, C. Northcote. *Trade in the Eastern Seas 1793–1813*. Cambridge, 1937.

Pearson, M. N. *Merchants and Rulers in Gujarat: The Response to the Portuguese in the Sixteenth Century*. Berkeley, 1976.

Prins, A. H. J. *Sailing from Lamu: A Study of Maritime Culture in Islamic East Africa*. Van Gorcum, 1965.

Purcell, Victor. *The Chinese in South East Asia*. London, 1965.

Quaison, Serafin D. *English "Country Trade" with the Philippines, 1664–1765*. Quezon City, 1966.

Reading, Douglas K. *The Anglo-Russian Commercial Treaty of 1734*. New Haven, Conn., 1938.

Reid, Anthony. "A Great Seventeenth Century Indonesian Family: Matoaya and Pattingalloang of Makassar." *Majalah Ilmu-Ilmu Sosial Indonesia*, 8:1–28 (1981).

———. "The Rise of Makassar." In press.

Saguchi, Toru. "The Eastern Trade of the Kohkand Kmanate." *Memoirs of the Research Department of the Toyo Bunko*, 24:47–114 (1965).

Sakamaki, Shunzō. "Ryukyu and Southeast Asia." *Journal of Asian Studies*, 23:383–90 (1964).
Scammell, G.V. "England, Portugal, and the Estado da India, c. 1500–1635." *Modern Asian Studies*, 16:177–92 (1982).
Schurz, William Lytle. *The Manila Galleon*. New York, 1939.
Serjeant, Robert Bartram. *The Portuguese off the South Arabian Coast: Hadrami Chronicles*. Oxford, 1963.
Simkin, C. G. F. *The Traditional Trade of Asia*. London, 1968.
Sinha, Pradip. "Approaches to Urban History: Calcutta (1750–1850)." *Bengal Past and Present*, 87:106–19 (1968).
Skinner, G. William. *Chinese Society in Thailand: An Analytical History*. Ithaca, N.Y., 1957.
Sopher, David E. *The Sea Nomads: A Study Based on the Literature of the Maritime Boat People of Southeast Asia*. Singapore, 1965.
Steensgaard, Niels. *Carracks, Caravans and Companies: The Structural Crisis in the European-Asian Trade of the Early Seventeenth Century*. Copenhagen, 1973.
Steinberg, David Joel, David K. Wyatt, John R. W. Smail, Alexander Woodside, William R. Roff, and David P. Chandler. *In Search of Southeast Asia*. New York, 1971.
Tobing, Philip Oder Lumban. *Hukum Pelajaran dan Perdangangan Amanna Gappa: Pembahasan Philogis-Kulturil Dengan Edisi Jang Diperpendek Dalam Bahasa Inggris*. Makassar, 1961.
University of Western Australia. *The Indian Ocean in Focus: International Focus on Indian Ocean Studies*. Perth, 1979.
Verlinden, Charles. *The Beginnings of Modern Colonization*. Ithaca, N.Y., 1970.
Viraphol, Sarasin. *Tribute and Profit: Sino-Siamese Trade, 1652–1853*. Cambridge, Mass., 1977.
Warren, James Francis. *The Sulu Zone, 1768–1898: The Dynamics of External Trade, Slavery, and Ethnicity in the Transformation of a Southeast Asian Maritime State*. Singapore, 1981.
Yambert, Karl A. "Alien Traders and Ruling Elites: The Overseas Chinese in Southeast Asia and the Indians in East Africa." *Ethnic Groups*, 3:173–98 (1981).
Yule, Henry. *A Narrative of the Mission to the Court of Ava in 1855*. London, 1968.

Chapter 9. The overland trade of the Armenians

Ambrose, G. "English Traders at Aleppo (1658–1756)." *Economic History Review*, 3:246–67 (1931–2).
Anderson, Matthew Smith. *Britain's Discovery of Russia 1553–1815*. London, 1958.
Attman, Artur. *The Russian and Polish Markets in International Trade 1500–1650*. Goteborg, 1973.
Barbour, Violet. *Capitalism in Amsterdam in the Seventeenth Century*. Baltimore, 1950.
Berry, Lloyd E., and Robert O. Crummey (eds.). *Rude & Barbarous Kingdom: Russia in the Accounts of Sixteenth-Century English Voyagers*. Madison, Wis., 1968.
Carouthers, Douglas (ed.). *The Desert Route to India: the Journals of Four Travelers*

by the Great Desert Caravan Route Between Aleppo and Basra 1745–1751. London, 1929.

Carswell, John. *New Julfa: The American Churches and Other Buildings*. Oxford, 1968.

Chardin, John. *Sir John Chardin's Travels in Persia*. First published in 1686. London, 1927.

Davis, Ralph H. *Aleppo to Devonshire Square: English Traders in the Levant in the Eighteenth Century*. London, 1967.

Donzel, E. J. van. *Foreign Relations of Ethiopia, 1642–1700: Documents Relating to the Journeys of Khodja Murad*. Leiden, 1979,

Ferrier, R. W. "The Agreement of the East India Company with the Armenian Nation 22nd June 1688." *Revue des études arméniennes*, 7(n.s.): 427–43 (1970).

"The Armenians and the East India Company in Persia in the Seventeenth and Early Eighteenth Centuries." *Economic History Review*, 26:38–62 (1973).

Gulbenkian, Roberto. "Philippe de Zagly, marchand arménien de Julfa, et l'établissement du commerce persan en Courlande en 1696." *Revue des études arméniennes*, 7(n.s.):361–99 (1970).

Hanway, Jonas Walden. *An Historical Account of British Trade Over the Caspian Sea*. 2 vols. London, 1754.

Herbert, Sir Thomas. *Some Yeares Travells into Africa and Asia...* London, 1677.

Jeannin, Pierre. "The Sea-borne and the Overland Trade Routes of Northern Europe in the XVIth and XVIIth Centuries." *Journal of European Economic History*, 11:5–59 (1982).

Kevonian, Keram. "Marchands arméniens au XVIIe siècle." *Cahiers du monde russe et sovietique*, 16:199–244 (1975).

Khachikian, Lvon. "The Ledger of the Merchant Hovannes Joughayetsi." *Journal of the Asiatic Society* (Calcutta), 8:153–86 (1966).

"Le registre d'un marchand arménien en Perse, en Inde et en Tibet (1682–93)." *Annales: économies, sociétés, civilisations*, 22:231–78 (1967).

Lang, David Marshall. *Armenia: Cradle of Civilization*, 2nd ed. rev. London, 1978.

Lockhart, L. "Isfahan." *Journal of the Royal Central Asian Society*, 37:248–61 (1950).

Macler, Frederic. "Les Arméniens de Galicie." *Revue des études arméniennes* 6:7–17 (1926).

Morgan, E., and C. H. Cooke (eds.). *Early Voyages and Travels in Russia and Persia by Anthony Jenkinson and other Englishmen*. 2 vols. London, 1885.

Morgan, Jacques de. *The History of the American People*. Boston, 1965.

Morse, Richard M. *The Bandeirantes: The Historical Role of the Brazilian Pathfinders*. New York, 1965.

Olearius, Adam. *Rélations du voyage en Muscovie, Tartarie et Perse*. 2 vols. Paris, 1679.

Pankhurst, Richard. "The History of Ethiopian-Armenian Relations." *Revue des études arméniennes*, 12(n.s.):174–345 (1977).

Rooy, Silvio van. "Armenian Merchant Habits as Mirrored in the 17th–18th Century Amsterdam Documents." *Revue des études arméniennes*, 3(n.s.):347–558 (1966).

Savory, Roger. *Iran under the Safavids*. Cambridge, 1980.

Seth, M. H. *The Armenians in India*. Calcutta, 1937.

Spicer, Edward H. *Cycles of Conquest: The Impact of Spain, Mexico, and the United States on the Indians of the Southwest, 1553–1965*. Tucson, 1962.

Struys, Jan. *The Voyages of I. Struys through Moscovia, Tartary, India, and Most of the Eastern World*. London, 1684.
Taunay, Alfonso de Escragnolle. *Curso de bandeirologia*. Rio de Janeiro, 1946.
Tekekian, C. D. "Marseille, La Provence, et les arméniens." *Mémoires de l'Institut Historique de Provence*, 5:5–65 (1929).
Willan, T. S. *The Early History of the Russia Company 1553–1603*. Manchester, 1956.
The Muscovy Merchants of 1555. Manchester, 1953.

Chapter 10. The fur trade

Benningsen, Alexandre, and Chantal Lemercier-Quelquejay. "Les marchands de la cour ottomane et le commerce des fourrures moscovites dans la seconde moitie du XVIᵉ siècle." *Cahiers du monde russe et sovietique*, 9:363–90 (1970).
Berindei, Mihnoa. "Contribution a l'étude du commerce ottoman des fourrures moscovites: La route moldavo-polonaise 1453–1700." *Cahiers du monde russe et sovietique*, 12:393–409 (1971).
Bigger, H. P. (ed.). *The Works of Samuel de Champlain*. 6 vols. Toronto, 1922–36.
Bishop, C.A. *The Northern Ojibwa and the Fur Trade*. Toronto, 1974.
Carlos, Ann. "The Causes and Origins of the North American Fur Trade Rivalry: 1804–1810." *Journal of Economic History*, 41:777–94 (1981).
Crutchfield, James A., and Giulio Pontecorvo. *The Pacific Salmon Fisheries: A Study of Irrational Conservation*. Baltimore, 1969.
Davey, Richard. *Furs and Fur Garments*. Westminster, 1896.
Delort, Robert. *Le commerce des fourrures en Occident a la fin du moyen age (vers 1300–vers 1450)*. Rome, 1978.
Eccles, W. J. A. "A Belated Review of Harold Adams Innis, The Fur Trade of Canada." *Canadian Historical Review*, 40:420–41 (1979).
"A Response to Hugh M. Grant on Innis (and the Canadian Fur Trade)." *Canadian Historical Review*, 62:323–9 (1981).
Fisher, Raymond Henry. *The Russian Fur Trade, 1550–1700*. Berkeley, 1943.
Ford, Richard I. "Barter, Gift, or Violence: An Analysis of Tewa Intertribal Exchange." In *Social Exchange and Interaction*, ed. by Edwin N. Wilmsen. Ann Arbor, Mich., 1972.
Galbraith, John S. *The Hudson's Bay Company as an Imperial Factor, 1821–1869*. Berkeley, 1957.
Gibson, James R. *Feeding the Russian Fur Trade: Provisionment of the Okhotsk Seaboard and the Kamchatka Peninsula, 1639–1856*. Madison, Wis., 1969.
Gould, J. R. "Externalities, Factor Proportions, and the Level of Exploitation of Free Access Resources." *Economica*, 39:383–402 (1972).
Graburn, Nelson H. H., and B. Stephen Strong. *Circumpolar Peoples: An Anthropological Perspectus*. Pacific Palisades, Calif., 1973.
Grant, Hugh M. "One Step Forward, Two Steps Back: Innis, Eccles, and the Canadian Fur Trade." *Canadian Historical Review*, 62:304–22 (1981).
Heidenreich, Conrad E. *Huronia: A History and Geography of the Huron Indians*. Toronto, 1971.
Heidenreich, Conrad E., and A. H. Ray. *The Early Fur Trade: A Study in Cultural Interaction*. Toronto, 1976.
Hunt, George T. *The Wars of the Iroquois: A Study in Intertribal Trade Relations*. Madison, Wis., 1960.

Innis, Harold A. *The Fur Trade in Canada.* Toronto, 1956.

Jablow, Joseph. *The Cheyenne in Plains Indian Trade Relations, 1795–1840.* New York, 1951.

Jenness, Diamond. *Indians of Canada,* 7th ed. Ottawa, 1977.

Kerner, Robert J. *The Urge to the Sea: The Course of Russian History.* Berkeley, 1942.

Krech, Shepard III (ed.). *Indians, Animals, and the Fur Trade: A Critique of Keepers of the Game.* Athens, Ga., 1981.

Lantzeff, George V. *Siberia in the Seventeenth Century: A Study of the Colonial Administration.* Berkeley, 1943.

Lewis, Oscar. *The Effects of White Contact upon Blackfoot Culture, with Special Reference to the Role of the Fur Trade.* New York, 1942.

Martin, Calvin. *Keepers of the Game: Indian-Animal Relationships and the Fur Trade.* Berkeley, 1978.

Moodie, D. Wayne, and John C. Lehr. "Macro-Historical Geography and the Great Chartered Companies: The Case of the Hudson's Bay Company." *Canadian Geographer,* 25:277–83 (1981).

Ray, Arthur J., and Donald Freeman. *"Give Us Good Measure": An Economic Analysis of Relations between the Indians and the Hudson's Bay Company Before 1763.* Toronto, 1978.

Rich, Edwin E. *The Fur Trade and the Northwest to 1857.* Toronto, 1967.

Robson, Joseph. *An Account of Six Years Residence in Hudson's Bay: From 1733 to 1736 and 1744 to 1747.* Toronto, 1965.

Rotstein, Abraham. "Fur Trade and Empire: An Institutional Analysis." Ph.D. diss. University of Toronto, 1967.

Trigger, Bruce G. *The Children of Aataentsic: A History of the Huron Peoples to 1660.* 2 vols. Montreal, 1976.

"The French Presence in Huronia: The Structure of Franco-Huron Relations in the First Half of the Seventeenth Century." *Canadian Historical Review,* 49:107–41 (1968).

"Trade and Tribal Warfare on the St. Lawrence in the Sixteenth Century." *Ethnohistory,* 9:240–56 (1962).

Turner, Frederick Jackson. *The Character and Influence of the Indian Trade in Wisconsin: A Study of the Trading Post as an Institution,* new ed. Norman, Okla., 1977.

Wishart, David J. "The Fur Trade of the West, 1807–1840: A Geographical Synthesis. In *The Frontier in Comparative Studies,* ed. by David Henry Miller and Jerome O. Steffan. Norman, Okla., 1977.

Chapter 11. Postscript

Adas, Michael. *Prophets of Rebellion: Millenarian Protest Movements against the European Colonial Order.* Chapel Hill, N.C., 1979.

Emerson, Rupert. *Malaysia: A Study of Direct and Indirect Rule.* New York, 1937.

Fairbank, John King. *Trade and Diplomacy on the China Coast: The Opening of the Treaty Ports 1842–1854.* Cambridge, Mass., 1964.

Gallagher, John, and Ronald Robinson. "The Imperialism of Free Trade." *Economic History Review,* 6(n.s.):1–15 (1953).

Hao, Yen-P'ing. *The Comprador in Nineteenth-Century China: Bridge Between East and West.* Cambridge, Mass., 1970.

July, Robert W. *The Origins of Modern African Thought: Its Development in West Africa during the Nineteenth and Twentieth Centuries*. New York, 1967.
Landes, David. *Bankers and Pashas*. Cambridge, Mass., 1958.
Latham, A. J. H. *The International Economy and the Underdeveloped World, 1865–1914*. London, 1978.
LeFevour, Edward. *Western Enterprise in Late Ch'ing China*. Cambridge, 1968.
Porter, Arthur T. *Creoledom: A Study of the Development of Freetown Society*. London, 1963.
Priestly, Margaret. *West African Trade and Coast Society: A Family Study*. London, 1969.
Spaulding, Jay. "Slavery, Land Tenure and Social Class in the Northern Turkish Sudan." *International Journal of African Historical Studies*, 15:1–20 (1982).
Twitchett, Denis, and John K. Fairbank (eds.). *The Cambridge History of China*. Vol. 10, *The Ch'ing*. Cambridge, 1978.

Index

Abbas (the Prophet's uncle), 235
Abbas the Great, 149, 187
Abbasid caliphate: foundation and influence of, 104–5; Indian Ocean trade of, 106–9; trade to China from, 105; mentioned, 91, 121, 185
Aboh, 29
Acapulco, 144, 150
Aceh, 148, 160, 162, 170
Adams, Robert McC., 61, 63
Addis Ababa, 41
Aden: in fifteenth-century Asian trade, 128–9; mentioned, 19, 98, 114, 122, 132, 140, 148
Adrianople, 186
Adriatic Sea, 117
Adulis, 100
Aegean region, early trade of, 71, 73–81
Aegean Sea, Italian commerce in, 119
Afghanistan, 96, 105, 183, 187, 191
Africa: "ivory frontier" in, 209–11; secondary empire in, 234–40; trade diasporas in, 14–59; see also East Africa, North Africa, West Africa
Africa, northern, map, 22
Afro-Arabs, secondary empires of, 235
Afro-Eurasian landmass, culture and diseases of, 207–14
Afro-Portuguese, 247
Agalawa, 54
Agency houses, 176
Agra: Armenian merchants in, 194; mentioned, 187, 193
agricultural revolution, 60–1
Agung, 232–3
Akbar, 149
Akkad, 61, 66, 68
Akkadian (language), 68
Aksum, early trade of, 100
Al Mina, 78

Alaska: fur depletion in, 218; mentioned, 179
Albany, 216, 220
Alberta, 222
Aleppo: caravan trade of, 199; foreign traders in, 198; mentioned, 66, 182, 191, 193
Alexander the Great: conquests of, 80; mentioned, 7, 76, 88, 94, 104
Alexandretta, see Iskanderun
Alexandria: in fifteenth-century Asian trade, 128–9; trade practices in, 132; mentioned, 113, 114
Algeria: Mizabi of, 11, 49–51; mentioned, 14, 23
Algiers, 50
Algonkian (languages), 213
Algonquin, 214, 220–1
Alladian (people), 17
Almeida, Francisco de, 139
Amboina, see Ambon
Ambon, 154, 155
Americans: in China, 251; native, see Amerindians
Amerindians: culture and ecology of, 213–14; epidemiology of, 207–9; exchange practices of, 227–9; pre-Columbian trade of, 81–7; role of in fur-trade strategy, 117; and violence, 218–19
Amorite, 67–8
Amoy, see Xiamen
Amsterdam: Armenian trade manual from, 193; mentioned, 178, 196, 203
Amu Darya, see Oxus River
Anatolia: Akkadian fortresses in, 66; Assyrian trade to, 67–70; Hittites in, 73–4
Ancona, 193
Andean region: early trade in, 88; population decline in, 208
Anglican church, see Church of England